# THE MEDITERRANEAN WORLD IN LATE ANTIQUITY AD 395–700

This thoroughly revised and expanded edition of *The Mediterranean World in Late Antiquity*, now covering the period AD 395–700, provides both a detailed introduction to late antiquity and a direct challenge to conventional views of the end of the Roman empire. Leading scholar Averil Cameron focuses on the changes and continuities in Mediterranean society as a whole before the Arab conquests. Two new chapters survey the situation in the east after the death of Justinian and cover the Byzantine wars with Persia, religious developments in the eastern Mediterranean during the life of Muhammad, the reign of Heraclius, the Arab conquests and the establishment of the Umayyad caliphate.

Using the latest in-depth archaeological evidence, this all-round historical and thematic study of the west and the eastern empire has become the standard work on the period. The new edition takes account of recent research on topics such as the barbarian 'invasions', periodization, and questions of decline or continuity, as well as the current interest in church councils, orthodoxy and heresy and the separation of the miaphysite church in the sixth-century east. It contains a new introductory survey of recent scholarship on the fourth century AD, and has a full bibliography and extensive notes with suggestions for further reading.

*The Mediterranean World in Late Antiquity AD 395–700* continues to be the benchmark for publications on the history of late antiquity and is indispensable to anyone studying the period.

**Averil Cameron** was until recently Professor of Late Antique and Byzantine History at the University of Oxford and Warden of Keble College Oxford.

# ROUTLEDGE HISTORY OF THE ANCIENT WORLD
Series Editor: Fergus Millar

# THE MEDITERRANEAN WORLD IN LATE ANTIQUITY 395–700 AD

## Second Edition

*Averil Cameron*

Routledge
Taylor & Francis Group

LONDON AND NEW YORK

First published 1993.
This second edition published 2012
by Routledge
2 Park Square, Milton Park, Abingdon, Oxon OX14 4RN

Simultaneously published in the USA and Canada
by Routledge
711 Third Avenue, New York, NY 10017

*Routledge is an imprint of the Taylor & Francis Group, an informa business*

© 1993, 2012 Averil Cameron

*British Library Cataloguing in Publication Data*
A catalogue record for this book is available from the British Library

*Library of Congress Cataloging in Publication Data*
A catalog record for this book has been requested

ISBN: 978–0–415–57962–9 (hbk)
ISBN: 978–0–415–57961–2 (pbk)
ISBN: 978–0–203–80908–2 (ebk)

Typeset in Garamond by
Swales & Willis Ltd, Exeter, Devon

Printed and bound in Great Britain by the MPG Books Group

# CONTENTS

# LIST OF FIGURES

# LIST OF MAPS

# ACKNOWLEDGEMENTS

Unless otherwise stated, the images are the author's own. The following images have been reproduced with permission:

| | |
|---|---|
| Cover image | Saint Thecla with Wild Beasts and Angels, Egyptian, 5th century CE Limestone, 3¾ × 25½ inches (9.5 × 64.8 cm). By kind permissions of The Nelson-Atkins Museum of Art, Kansas City, Missouri. Purchase: William Rockhill Nelson Trust, 48–10. Photo: Jamison Miller |
| Figure 1.3 | Empress Ariadne, c. AD 500. Courtesy of Kunsthistorisches Museum, Vienna |
| Figure 2.1 | © The Trustees of the British Museum |
| Figure 2.2 | © The Trustees of the British Museum |
| Figure 2.3 | © The Trustees of the British Museum |
| Figure 3.1 | Nave. Rome, Basilica of Santa Maria Maggiore. © 2011. Photo Scala, Florence |
| Figure 3.4 | © The Trustees of the British Museum |
| Figure 5.1 | © RMN / Les frères Chuzeville |
| Figure 6.3 | Firenze, Biblioteca Medicea Laurenziana, Ms. Plut. 9.28, c. 95v. Courtesy of Ministero per i Beni e le Attività Culturali, Italy. Any further reproduction prohibited. |

# PREFACE TO THE FIRST EDITION

The shape and parameters of this book are explained by the fact that it was conceived as part of a series designed to replace the earlier Methuen History of the Ancient World, though of course the latter had no volume with the present scope, and the concept of 'late antiquity' still lay firmly in the future. As it happens, while the present volume (the last chronologically in the series) antedates the writing of that projected on the fourth century, it follows on from my own book in another series, the Fontana History of the Ancient World. Though entitled simply *The Later Roman Empire*, the latter effectively ends where the present book begins, with Augustine as the bridge. The effect therefore is that despite minor differences of format and scale between the two, the reader will find in them an introduction to the whole period of late antiquity from, roughly, the reign of Diocletian (AD 284–305) to the late sixth century AD, where A.H.M. Jones also ended his great work, *The Later Roman Empire* (Oxford, 1964).

As most people will be well aware, this period has been the focus of a great upsurge of interest in the generation that has passed since the publication of Jones's massive work; in the past twenty years it has found its way for the first time on to ancient history syllabuses in many universities, with corresponding effects on courses in medieval history and (where they exist) Byzantine studies. The addition of two extra volumes to the new edition of the Cambridge Ancient History (now in progress) is also symptomatic of this changed perspective; together, they will cover the period from the death of Constantine (AD 337) to the late sixth century. Peter Brown's small book, *The World of Late Antiquity* (London, 1971), still provides an exhilarating introduction from the perspective of cultural history. The influence of that book has been enormous, yet despite this tremendous growth of interest in the period, and despite a mass of more specialized publications, many of them excellent, it is still difficult to find a book or books in English which provide a general introduction for students to the many and varied aspects of the period about which they need to know. The present book adopts an approach that is part chronological and part thematic. No real attempt can be made in such a compass to provide a full narrative of events, and I have tried to do this only in those parts where it seemed particularly necessary or where the evidence was particularly difficult of access. Luckily, a useful brief narrative is provided in Roger Collins's recent *Early Medieval Europe 300–1000* (London, 1991). The present book has a different and wider scope. I devote particular attention to issues currently debated, such as urban change and patterns of settlement, where much of the evidence is archaeological, partly in order to point up the great change that has taken place in our approach to and understanding of the period since Jones, fundamental though his work remains in many other spheres. Cultural and social history occupy a large amount of space for similar reasons. Ideally, too, a book of this kind would be much more fully illustrated than has been possible here; however, there are fortunately many accessible guides to hand, which I have indicated as often as possible in the notes. The book's main emphasis is on the empire rather than the periphery or the emergent kingdoms of the west, and so it points towards the east, where the institutions of Roman government survived at least until the seventh century when a more 'Byzantine', that is 'medieval', state gradually emerged. There are many excellent introductory works on the medieval west, and other areas given less coverage here (Spain, Italy, the northern provinces, the Balkans) have been treated in specialist works mentioned in the notes. But there are as yet fewer recent books which do justice to the equally important history of the eastern provinces in the fifth and sixth centuries. We still need a detailed history even of the crucial reign of Justinian (AD 527–65). Finally, some parts of the book necessarily have a certain provisional or exploratory character, precisely because the necessary research is proceeding at very uneven rates, and many questions are still without answers. That is of course also one of the greatest attractions of the field.

I wish to thank several friends and colleagues for spotting errors and providing advice, among them Lawrence I. Conrad, Han Drijvers and Bryan Ward-Perkins, and especially Wolf Liebeschuetz. Ian Tompkins and Lucas Siorvanes generously read the whole typescript, and Fergus Millar, the series editor, was not merely encouraging but also patient. The book is meant as a starting-point, not a terminus. If readers are annoyed by it or frustrated at not finding what they want, I hope they will also be stimulated into pursuing it somewhere else and finding the right answers for themselves.

Averil Cameron
London, July, 1992

# PREFACE TO THE SECOND EDITION

The period of nearly eighteen years since the publication of *The Mediterra-nean World in Late Antiquity* has seen a veritable explosion in the amount of publications on the period. I am therefore very pleased to have been able to revise and expand its original contents, and in particular to extend the book's chronological coverage by adding two new chapters taking it up through the seventh century and including the emergence of Islam. The Byzantine–Persian wars of the late sixth and early seventh century, the Persian conquests and the subsequent victories of the Emperor Heraclius, followed quickly by the Arab invasions, have all received a great deal of recent attention, as have the continuing religious divisions in the seventh century and the wider cul-tural linguistic and religious landscape of the eastern provinces. The decline or disappearance of Byzantine urbanism in the seventh century has long been a topic for Byzantinists, and the question of the survival or decline of cities in the eastern empire continues to be a major topic for students of late antiquity, especially in the light of new archaeological and epigraphic work. The circum-stances in which Islam itself developed, and the reasons for the success of the Arab conquests are of course enormous subjects, and they too have acquired a new salience with the development of two competing views of late antiquity: on the one hand, a return to an emphasis on the fall of the western empire and the rise of 'barbarian' successor states in the west; and on the other, a more eastern-focused view of a 'long late antiquity' lasting well into the Umayyad period, or even as late as the mid-eighth century. On the latter view, the de-velopment of Islam belongs firmly within the world of late antiquity. Such is the approach of the influential *Late Antiquity. A Guide to the Postclassical World*, edited by G.W. Bowersock, Peter Brown and Oleg Grabar, and published by Harvard University Press in 1999. It is a view that is not without its critics, and these different perspectives are discussed in the Introduction and Conclusion. But it is hardly surprising if the peoples and cultures of the region where Islam first took shape should now attract such an amount of scholarly attention.

Many of the specific themes addressed in the previous publication have been revised and further developed in recent scholarship; both text and notes have been extensively revised, especially the notes, and new material added in many places, as well as substantial extra coverage to take the narrative well into the Islamic period. I am grateful to Geoffrey Greatrex and Shaun Tougher, the two readers, for their valuable suggestions for expansion and revision. It was not my intention in the early 1990s to provide an overall narrative account but rather an accessible analysis of the major areas of interest and importance in the period. A reliable account is now available in Stephen Mitchell's *History of the Later Roman Empire, AD 284–641* (Oxford: Blackwell, 2007), and there have been other helpful publications, including Philip Rousseau, ed., *A Companion to Late Antiquity* (Chichester: Wiley-Blackwell, 2009) and Scott Johnson, ed., *Handbook to Late Antiquity* (Oxford: Oxford University Press, 2011). The aim of the present book remains that of providing a critical synthesis of the many key themes which emerge during this extremely important and now much studied and much debated period.

I wish to thank Matthew Gibbons and Amy Davis-Poynter at Routledge for their enthusiastic help in making this revised edition possible, and again my thanks go to Fergus Millar, not only an inimitable series editor but also a constant inspiration and a very good friend, and to Robert Hoyland for invaluable help in the final chapters. Since shortly after the publication of the first edition I have been based in Oxford, and I should also place on record my debt to the very lively seminars, lectures and conferences on late antiquity and Byzantium which have been such a regular feature in these years. *Late Antique Archaeology*, the series of edited volumes published by Brill, Leiden, originated in conferences organized in Oxford by Luke Lavan and Bryan Ward-Perkins, and the Oxford Centre for Late Antiquity (OCLA) hosts an extraordinarily wide range of events and activity; it has now been joined by the Oxford Centre for Byzantine Research (OCBR). I must also mention the many Oxford graduate students, including those I have supervised since 1994, and my visiting graduate students from Budapest, Münster, Nizhny Novgorod and Princeton, who have acted as a constant stimulus and who with my senior colleagues in several different faculties make Oxford such a very rewarding place. I dedicate this revised edition to them and to all the colleagues and friends who, by themselves contributing so much to the study of late antiquity and being so generous with their time and expertise, have done so much to make my own work possible.

Averil Cameron
Oxford, February, 2011

# ABBREVIATIONS

BAR       British Archaeological Reports
*CTh*       *Codex Theodosianus*
*CJ*       *Codex Justinianus*
Migne, *PG*    J.P. Migne, *Patrologia Graeca*
PLRE      J.R. Martindale, ed., *The Prosopography of the Roman Empire*, vol.
            2, AD 395–527; vol. 3, parts 1–2, AD 527–641 (Cambridge:
            Cambridge University Press, 1980, 1992)

## Collections of sources in translation not included in the general bibliography

Coleman-Norton, P.R., ed., *Roman State and Christian Church* (London: SPCK, 1966)

Lee, A.D., ed., *Pagans and Christians in Late Antiquity: A Sourcebook* (London: Routledge, 2000)

Maas, Michael, ed., *Readings in Late Antiquity: A Sourcebook* (London: Routledge, 2000)

Wimbush, V., ed., *Ascetic Behavior in Greco-Roman Antiquity: A Sourcebook* (Minneapolis: Fortress Press, 1990)

# INTRODUCTION

PART I: APPROACHING THE PERIOD

## The division between east and west

In the year AD 395 the Emperor Theodosius I died, leaving two sons, both of whom already held the rank of Augustus. Arcadius became emperor in the east and Honorius in the west. From then on the Roman empire was effectively divided for administrative purposes into two halves, which, as pressure on the frontiers increased through the fifth century, began to respond in significantly different ways. AD 395 was therefore a real turning point in the eventual split between east and west.[1]

Until then, and since the time of Diocletian (284–305), the late Roman empire had been a unity, despite having at times a multiplicity of emperors, and embracing all the provinces bordering on the Mediterranean and much more besides (Map 0.1). While Constantine had made himself sole emperor by eliminating his rivals, and thus destroyed the tetrarchic system from which he had emerged himself, there were often multiple emperors in the fourth century, and the idea that emperors had their own territorial spheres and bases was not new. However, Theodosius himself (379–95) had not hesitated to move from Constantinople to the west when it was necessary to deal with potential challenges, and there had not been a formal division. In the west the empire stretched as far as Britain and included the whole of Gaul and Spain, while in the north the frontier extended from Germany and the Low Countries along the Danube to the Black Sea. Dacia, across the Danube, annexed by Trajan in the early second century, was given up at the end of the third after a series of Gothic invasions, but otherwise the empire of Diocletian was impressively similar in extent to that of its greatest days in the Antonine period. To the east, it stretched to eastern Turkey and the borders of the Sasanian empire in Persia, while its southern possessions extended from Egypt westwards to Morocco and the Straits of Gibraltar; Roman North Africa (modern Algeria and Tunisia) was one of the most prosperous parts of the empire during the fourth century.

In Diocletian's day, though Rome was still the seat of the senate, it was no longer the administrative capital of this large empire. Emperors moved from

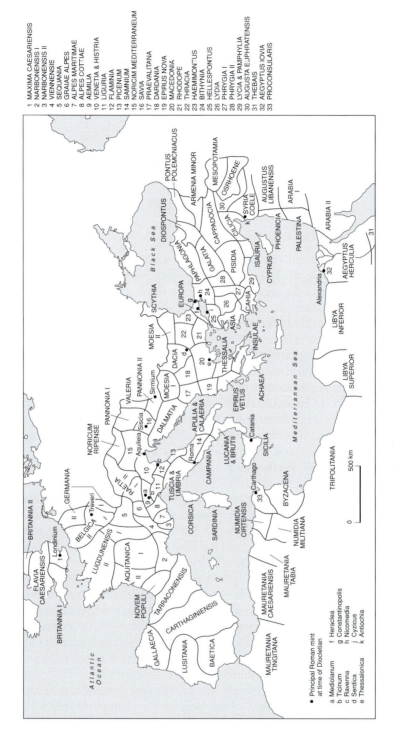

Map 0.1 The Diocletianic provinces of the late Roman empire

1 MAXIMA CAESARIENSIS
2 NARBONENSIS I
3 NARBONENSIS II
4 VIENNENSIS
5 SEQUANIA
6 GRAIAE ALPES
7 ALPES MARITIMAE
8 ALPES COTTIAE
9 AEMILIA
10 VENETIA & HISTRIA
11 LIGURIA
12 FLAMINIA
13 PICENUM
14 SAMNIUM
15 NORICIM MEDITERRANEUM
16 SAVIA
17 PRAEVALITANA
18 DARDANIA
19 EPIRUS NOVA
20 MACEDONIA
21 RHODOPE
22 THRACIA
23 HAEMIMONTUS
24 BITHYNIA
25 HELLESPONTUS
26 LYDIA
27 PHRYGIA I
28 PHRYGIA II
29 LYCIA & PAMPHYLIA
30 AUGUSTA EJPHRATENSIS
31 THEBAIS
32 AEGYPTUS IOVIA
33 PROOCONSULARIS

• Principal Roman mint
  at time of Diocletian

a Mediolanum    f Heraclea
b Ticinum       g Constantinopolis
c Ravenna       h Nicomedia
d Serdica       j Cyzicus
e Thessalonica  k Antiochia

one base, or 'capital', to another – Trier in Germany, Sirmium or Serdica in the Danube area or Nicomedia in Bithynia – taking their administrative apparatus with them. By the end of the fourth century, however, the main seats of government were at Milan in the west and Constantinople in the east. The empire was also divided linguistically, in that while the 'official' language of the army and the law remained Latin until the sixth century and even later, the principal language of the educated classes in the east was Greek.[2] But Latin and Greek coexisted with a number of local languages, including Aramaic and Syriac in Syria, Mesopotamia and Palestine, and Coptic in Egypt (demotic Egyptian written in an alphabet using mainly Greek characters) as well as the languages of the new groups which had settled within the empire during the third and especially the fourth century, in particular Gothic.[3] By the late sixth century, Arabic was also beginning to emerge (Chapter 9). Even in the early empire, laws had circulated in the east in Greek, and there had always been translation of imperial letters arid official documents, so that on the whole the imperial administration had managed to operate successfully despite such linguistic variety. But from the third century onwards local cultures began to develop more vigorously in several areas; the eventual divide between east and west also became a linguistic one (as has often been noted, Augustine's Greek was not perfect, and his own works, in Latin, were not read by Christians in the east), but especially in the east, language use was in practice highly complex.

The period covered by this book saw a progressive division between east and west, in the course of which the east fared better. Even though it had to face a formidable enemy in the Sasanians, its economic and social structure enabled it to resist extensive barbarian settlement far more successfully than the western empire could do; there was no 'fall of the eastern empire' in the fifth century, and the institutional and administrative structure remained more or less intact until the Persian and Arab invasions in the late sixth and seventh centuries. The east was also more densely urbanized and from the fourth century onwards the Near Eastern provinces achieved an economic prosperity and size of population unparalleled until modern times. Nevertheless many details remain debated, and the sheer volume of recent archaeological evidence makes this one of the fastest developing scholarly areas in the period. Though poorly documented, the Persian invasion and occupation in the early seventh century has been thought to have had a severely negative effect, especially on the cities of Asia Minor, but in Syria and Palestine its impact is hard to trace in the archaeological record, and Umayyad Syria remained prosperous; similarly, little if any archaeological damage can be securely attributed to the Arab conquests (Chapter 9). In the west, by contrast, the government was already weak by the late fourth century, and the power of the great landowning families correspondingly strong. Furthermore, the western provinces had been badly hit earlier by the invasions and civil wars of the third century. The defeat of the Roman army at Adrianople in AD 378 (see below) was a symbolic moment in the weakening of the west, and pressures grew steadily until in AD 476 the last Roman emperor ruling from Italy was deposed; this date therefore traditionally marks the 'fall of the western empire'. The eastern Emperor Justinian's much-vaunted 'reconquest' (Chapter 5), launched from Constantinople in the 530s, aimed at reversing the situation, but was only partially successful. North Africa remained under Byzantine rule until the late seventh century, and a Byzantine presence was maintained in Italy in the face of Lombard incursions, based round the exarchate of Ravenna, but the west remained divided in the late sixth century, the Merovingian Franks ruling in France and the Visigoths in Spain. In Italy itself, the eventual but very hard-won Byzantine victory hailed in the settlement known as the 'Pragmatic Sanction' of AD 554 and accompanied by concerted attempts to impose orthodox Christianity, not least in Theoderic's capital at Ravenna, met with a new challenge from the Lombards; the Fifth Ecumenical Council held by Justinian in Constantinople in 553 received a negative reception in Italy, and the papacy, especially under Gregory the Great (590–604), acquired considerable secular power in the context of increasing fragmentation. All the same, much that was recognizably Roman survived in the barbarian kingdoms, and the extent of real social and economic change is still debated.[4]

The debate about periodization (when did the ancient world come to an end?) is livelier than it ever was. On the one hand, we have the concept of a 'long' late antiquity, with continuity observable even as late as the Abbasid period,[5] on the other, a reassertion of the 'fall' of the Roman empire in the fifth-century west.[6] However, Christopher Wickham's magisterial book, *Framing the Early Middle Ages. Europe and the Mediterranean, 400–800* (2005),[7] avoids such choices, while also providing a comparative analysis of overall trends which affected both west and east. Peregrine Horden and Nicholas Purcell, *The Corrupting Sea. A Study of Mediterranean History* (2000), also avoid periodization, by concentrating on continuities over very long periods. For Peter Heather, the story of the first millenium is that of the transition from a Roman, Mediterranean hegemony to the beginnings of Europe.[8] Whether the notion of a Mediterranean world really does work for late antiquity, or whether this is an example of 'Mediterraneanism', rather like Orientalism,[9] is a topic to which we will return at the end of this book.

## Previous approaches

The transition from classical antiquity to the medieval world was the subject of Edward Gibbon's great work, *The Decline and Fall of the Roman Empire* (1787), and very few themes in history have been the subject of so much hotly debated controversy or so much partisan feeling. For Marx and for historians in the Marxist tradition, the end of Roman rule provided cardinal proof that states based on such extreme forms of inequality and exploitation as ancient slavery were doomed eventually to fall. On the other hand, many historians, including Gibbon himself, and the Russian historian M.I. Rostovtzeff, who left Russia in 1917, also saw the later empire as representing a sadly degenerate form of its earlier civilized and prosperous self, which (like Gibbon) they regarded as having reached its apogee under the Antonines in the second century AD. Rostovzeff applied to Rome the lessons he had taken from the Bolshevik revolution in Russia, and saw the later Roman empire as a repressive and uncouth system which had emerged through the destruction of the 'bourgeoisie' by the peasants and the army, an example of state control at its worst.[10]

In English scholarship the period covered in this book has been dominated by A.H.M. Jones's massive work, *The Later Roman Empire 284–602. A Social, Economic and Administrative Survey* (Oxford, 1964), also issued in shortened form as *The Decline of the Ancient World* (London, 1966). Jones was much influenced by the emphasis given by Rostovtzeff to social and economic factors, and his great work consists in the main of thematic chapters on individual aspects of late Roman society rather than political narrative. Jones had travelled extensively over the Roman empire, and taken part in archaeological work, but he wrote before the explosion of interest and activity in late Roman archaeology and made little use of archaeological evidence himself; instead, he demonstrates a incomparable mastery of the written material, and this means that his book remains a fundamental guide. Jones defined the period chronologically as reaching from the accession of Diocletian (AD 284) to the death of Maurice (AD 602), a choice of coverage which the first edition of this book essentially followed but which I believe now needs to be extended in order to take account of the trends in current scholarship.[11]

Jones's approach was pragmatic and concrete; he was not very interested in the questions of religious history which many now regard as primary and exciting factors in the study of late antiquity. For him, studying the development and influence of the Christian church in this period meant following its institutional and economic growth rather than the inner feelings of Christians themselves. He looked to Christian writing principally for social and economic data, and most famously, he included Christian monks, ascetics and clergy in the category of 'idle mouths' who now had to be supported by the dwindling class of agricultural producers, and who in Jones's view contributed to the difficulties to be faced by the late Roman government, and to its eventual decline. J.H.W.G. Liebeschuetz's book, *The Decline and Fall of the Roman City* (2001), is a modern treatment which returns to the theme of Christianity as a negative factor in the history of the Roman empire.

Jones's work opened up the period to a new generation of English-speaking students. They were soon to be stimulated by the very different approach of Peter Brown, vividly expressed in his brief survey *The World of Late Antiquity* (1971), published only a few years after Jones's *Later Roman Empire*. Brown is altogether more enthusiastic, not to say emotive, in emphasis. Instead of dry administrative history, 'late antiquity' now became an exotic territory, populated by wild monks and excitable virgins and dominated by the clash of religions, mentalities and lifestyles. In this scenario, Sasanian Persia in the east and the Germanic peoples in the north and west bounded a vast area within which several new battlelines were being drawn, not least between family members, as individuals wrestled with the conflicting claims of the church and their own social background. Great new buildings, churches and monasteries epitomized the rising centres of power and influence; the Egyptian and Syrian deserts became the home of several thousand monks of all sorts of backgrounds, and the eastern provinces a heady cultural mix, ripe for social change.

This very different perspective has attracted criticism for being based largely on the evidence of religious and cultural development and failing to do justice to economic and administrative factors.[12] But it has had immense value as a stimulus to further work and to the establishment of 'late antiquity' as a field of study in its own right. One of the most notable and important developments in this field in recent years has also been the amount of interest shown in the period by archaeologists, especially after pioneering work done since the 1970s on the dating sequences of late Roman pottery, which together with a more rigorous approach to excavation made possible an accurate chronology for late Roman sites. One should also mention the level of interest shown at present in urban history, which is especially relevant to this period, the latter part of which saw a basic transformation in urban life, and indeed the effective end of many, though certainly not all, classical cities in the eastern Mediterranean (Chapter 7). The synthesis of the new archaeological material often remains incomplete – some is badly published or still awaiting publication – and in many cases the interpretation is controversial, but no historian of the period can ignore it.[13]

One of the striking features of Brown's *World of Late Antiquity* was the use it made of illustrations and visual evidence, yet visual evidence has proved more difficult for historians to use than archaeological, perhaps because art history as a specialist field has been perceived to rest on different methodological principles. It has also been difficult to escape the deep-rooted assumption of a clear-cut distinction between Christian and non-Christian art, and the corresponding notion that late antique art represented a step towards a more spiritual, because more religious, style. The work of Jas Elsner and others offers an important corrective,[14] as have several exhibitions emphasizing objects from the secular sphere and 'daily life' over religious art. The concept of material culture, more neutral than 'Christian', or classical, seems to offer a promising way round this problem, but materialist approaches to this period find it difficult to accommodate the huge amount of evidence for religiosity and religious change. There needs to be a synthesis between these approaches and that of cultural history, which has its own problems in finding a satisfactory explanation of religious change.[15]

## 'Late antiquity'

The terminology used by scholars for historical periods, in this case terms such as 'late antiquity', 'medieval' or 'Byzantine', is on one level largely a matter of convenience. However, the question of where to draw a line between the later Roman empire, or late antiquity, and Byzantium has proved difficult. Many books on Byzantium choose the inauguration of Constantinople by Constantine (AD 330) as their starting point, since Constantinople remained the capital of the Byzantine empire until its fall in 1453, but others only begin with the sixth or seventh centuries. From a quite different perspective, western theologians tend to place a major break at 451, the date of the Council of Chalcedon; however, this is to exclude the large and growing amount of scholarship – historical as well as theological – that deals with the eastern church in the period that saw the rise of Islam. Readers of this book may therefore find that they will also be consulting modern works which at first sight seem to belong to other disciplines or specialisms, and should not be put off by a seemingly irrelevant title.

Terminology does matter, and whether we like it or not, it shapes our perceptions, especially of controversial issues. The title of this book, *The Mediterranean World in Late Antiquity*, invites consideration of the two concepts 'Mediterranean' and 'late antiquity'. The first will be discussed further in the Conclusion. As for 'late antiquity', this is a term which has come to denote not simply a historical period but also a way of interpreting it – 'the late antiquity model', or what I have called elsewhere for shorthand 'the Brownian model', since it has been so much associated with the work of Peter Brown. As suggested already, this has been an enormously fruitful way of looking at the period, and has the great advantage of avoiding the 'decline and fall' scenario, but it does not preclude critical approaches or changed emphases, as is clear from several of the contributions to Philip Rousseau's *Companion to Late Antiquity*. I hope that these will become clear in the chapters that follow.

## The sources

The source material for this period is exceptionally rich and varied, including both the works of writers great by any standards, and plentiful documentation of the lives of quite ordinary people. Changing circumstances also dictated changes in contemporary writing: St Augustine, for example, was a provincial from a moderately well-off family, who, having made his early career through the practice of rhetoric, became a bishop in the North African town of Hippo and spent much of his life not only wrestling with the major problems of Christian theology but also trying to make sense of the historical changes taking place around him. Instead of a great secular history like that of Ammianus Marcellinus in the late fourth century, Augustine's Spanish contemporary Orosius produced an abbreviated catalogue of disasters from the Roman past which was to become standard reading in the medieval Latin west, while numerous calendars and chronicles tried to combine in one schema the events of secular history and the Christian history of the world since creation. In the sixth century one man, the Roman senator Cassiodorus, composed *Variae*, the official correspondence of the Ostrogothic kings, a history of the Goths, and later, after the defeat of the Goths by the Byzantines in 554, his *Institutes*, a guide to Christian learning written at his Italian monastery of Vivarium in Caiabria. The history of the Goths was written in Latin in Constantinople by Jordanes, and has been the subject of important recent scholarship, though recent years have seen a corrective to the previously strong influence of Jordanes's account on modern views about the Goths (Chapter 2).[16] A century earlier Sidonius Apollinaris, as bishop at Clermont-Ferrand in Gaul, had deplored barbarian rusticity and continued to compose verses in classical style. A host of Gallic ecclesiastics in the fifth century, especially those connected with the important monastic centre of Lérins, wrote extensive letters as well as theological works, and this was also the age of the monastic rules of John Cassian and St Benedict. At the end of the sixth century, the voluminous writings of Pope Gregory the Great, the lively *History of the Franks* and hagiographical works by Gregory of Tours, another bishop of Roman senatorial extraction, and the poems of Venantius Fortunatus, combine with other works to provide a rich documentation for the west in that period. Two other great figures in the intellectual and theological history of the early medieval west were Isidore of Seville (*c.* 560–636) and Bede (672/3–735), author of the history of the English church. In 668 Theodore of Tarsus (602–690), an easterner who had studied in Constantinople, became Archbishop of Canterbury, and established a school and scriptorium there for the copying of manuscripts.

The Greek east was even more productive. Secular history continued to be written in the classical manner, and although the works of several fifth- and sixth-century writers survive only in fragments, we have all eight books of the *History of the Wars* in which Procopius of Caesarea recorded Justinian's wars of 'reconquest'. Procopius is undoubtedly a major historian; in addition, his *Buildings*, a panegyrical account of the building activities of Justinian, provides an important checklist for archaeologists, while his scabrous *Secret History*, immortalized by Gibbon's description of it, has provided material for nearly a score of novels about the variety artiste who became Justinian's wife, the pious Empress Theodora (Chapter 5). With its greater cultural continuity, the east was better able than the west to maintain a tradition of history-writing in the old style, and it continued until Theophylact Simocatta wrote under the Emperor Heraclius about the Emperor Maurice (AD 582–602).[17] Other writers, however, composed ecclesiastical history, including in the fifth century Socrates and Sozomen, both of whom continued Eusebius' *Ecclesiastical History* in Constantinople in the 440s, the Syrian Theodoret, bishop of Cyrrhus, and the Arian Philostorgius, whose work is only partially preserved. In the late sixth century the tradition was continued, again in Constantinople, by the Chalcedonian Evagrius Scholasticus, writing in Greek, and the Miaphysite John, bishop of Ephesus, writing in Syriac.[18] The Christian world-chronicle characteristic of the Byzantine period also begins now, with the sixth-century chronicle of the Antiochene John Malalas, ending in the year 563, and there are very many saints' lives in Greek and Latin, and sometimes in other languages such as Syriac, Georgian, Armenian or

Ethiopic; the frequency of translation to and from Greek and eastern languages, especially Syriac, is a very important aspect of eastern culture in this period.

An enormous number of saints' lives (the genre known as hagiography) survive from this period, after the example set by Athanasius' unforgettable *Life of Antony* (*c.* 357–62), and this material has provided the stimulus for some fine recent work. Saints' lives can provide historical information, but they are also invariably written with an apologetic purpose, and many are based on the rhetorical structure of encomium or panegyric. They therefore need to be used with caution by the historian, though they also provide very important ways into social and cultural questions. Indeed, the recognition of the great importance of rhetoric in all forms in the interpretation of late antique writing has been one of the major advances since 1993, as instanced in many contributions to the influential *Journal of Early Christian Studies*. Saints' lives are also well represented among the texts covered in the series Translated Texts for Historians, which at the time of writing has published more than sixty volumes. Designed to make important, but otherwise hard to find, texts available in reliable translations and with annotation, this wide-ranging series is one of the most important factors in making late antiquity so accessible a field. The impact of its recent publication of the entire Acts of the Council of Chalcedon (451), followed by those of the Second Council of Constantinople in 553,[19] a major departure for the series, is already evident.

In addition to the abundant written sources, there is a wealth of documentary material, ranging from the proceedings of the major church councils (Ephesus, 431, Chalcedon, 451, Constantinople, 553) to the law codes of Theodosius II and Justinian. The acts of the second council of Ephesus (449) are known from the proceedings of the Council of Chalcedon two years later, and partly survive in Syriac (Chapter 1). The official document known as the *Notitia Dignitatum*, drawn up some time after AD 395 and known from a western copy (see Jones, *Later Roman Empire*, Appendix II), constitutes a major source for our knowledge of the late Roman army and provincial administration. There is also a large and increasing number of dedicatory inscriptions from the Greek east in the fifth and sixth centuries, sometimes written in classicizing Greek verse, and while major public inscriptions are few in comparison with their number in the early empire, large numbers of simple Christian funerary epitaphs survive, often inscribed in mosaic on the floors of churches, which also frequently carry dedications by the builder or the local bishop. In churches of the Near East these are sometimes written in Aramaic or Syriac. The first inscriptions in Arabic script begin to appear in the sixth century. Important papyri also survive from the desert region of the Negev in modern Israel, from Petra in Jordan and from Ravenna in Italy, as well as from Egypt. Language change, especially as demonstrated in the epigraphic evidence, is a major concern of current scholarship.[20] Finally, the archaeological record is now huge, and increasing all the time, and while it is still necessary to consult individual excavation reports, more and more recent publications provide overall or regional surveys of archaeological evidence; these are noted at suitable points below, especially in Chapters 7 and 8.

## Main themes

A major issue in the period is that of unity and diversity. In what sense is it still possible to think of a 'Roman' world after the fifth century? Some would say that there was already a major downturn in prosperity, especially in the west, and with it the disappearance of the traditional Roman elite lifestyle. There is evidence to support such a view, especially from Britain, which Rome ceased to regard as a province in 410. Bryan Ward-Perkins has memorably described what happened as 'the disappearance of comfort'.[21] A major programme of building under Anastasius (491–518) and especially Justinian (527–65) partly explains the survival of sixth-century basilicas (and fortifications) at many sites in the Balkans, but by the end of the century new threats, combined with economic decline, were leading to a retreat in many places to more secure hilltop fortifications. The important city of Thessalonica suffered particularly badly from Slav attacks in the seventh century, and Constantinople was threatened by Huns in 559 and besieged by Avars and Persians in 626. Justinian's fortifications did not protect the Peloponnese, and a general economic downturn is posited by c. 700 by Michael McCormick (see also Conclusion).[22]

On the other hand, a wealth of evidence shows that the eastern provinces, and especially the Near East, continued to prosper. While the Persian wars of the sixth century and Persian invasion of the early seventh century brought major damage to some urban centres, such as Antioch and Sardis, other cities, such as Scythopolis (Bet Shean in Israel), show little sign of decline until the eighth century, while the Arab conquests hardly show in the archaeology of the Near East.[23] The state of these provinces on the eve of Islam and the degree of continuity and change that can be traced in the Umayyad period is one of the liveliest issues in current scholarship, and recent work suggests that there was considerable local variation; a micro approach is needed. The question of whether the development of Islam does indeed belong in the context of late antiquity, as argued by a growing number of late antique scholars, is also being challenged by some Islamicists;[24] it is also noticeable that important developments under the Umayyads in the east, in Iraq and the former Persian empire, are not usually central in the scholarship on late antiquity, though they too are part of the story of continuity and change. Perhaps the days of grand generalizations about the end of antiquity are over.

The title of this book also evokes a current debate: in what sense can or should we talk of a 'Mediterranean' society, and indeed, if this is permissible, how is that affected by this apparently increasing divergence between west and east? I will return to these questions in the Conclusion. Meanwhile it will be enough to refer to some of the responses to Horden and Purcell's first volume, *The Corrupting Sea*.[25]

Other major themes to be considered must include what has commonly been seen as the process of Christianization, although a better formulation in the light of current work would be religious change, encompassing the relations between a whole variety of religious groups, the degree of local variation, questions of religious identity and especially self-identity, the history of Judaism in the late Roman empire, and especially in Palestine on the eve of Islam, and the context and processes which gave rise to another major religion of the book. Far more has been written on all these subjects since the publication of the first edition of this book, not least perhaps under the stimulus of external events. But the discovery of rich new material, including for instance pre-Islamic monotheistic inscriptions from south Yemen, and the publication of studies of spectacular synagogues in Palestine, notably at Sepphoris, have also made new interpretations possible. A hugely increased scholarly interest has also developed in the divisions in the eastern church after the Council of Chalcedon, drawing especially on the very rich written evidence in Syriac sources (Chapters 5, 8 and 9).

Diversified, localized and fragmented, the Roman army, or rather armies, of the fifth and sixth centuries were far different in composition and equipment from those of earlier days. Whether the army could now effectively keep out the barbarians, and if not, why not, were questions as much debated by contemporaries as by modern historians; the nature of the late Roman army, and the context of defence and frontiers, together with the new revisionist approaches towards the barbarian invasions, need therefore to be discussed again (Chapters 2, 5 and 8).

Finally, the late Roman economy (Chapter 4). How much long-distance exchange continued and for how long, and if it did, in whose hands was it? Large estates and landowners are argued by some to be more important players than has recently been assumed, while the traditional problem of the status of 'coloni' has been subjected to radical new interpretations. In the Near East, the reasons for the prosperity of hundreds of 'dead villages' in Syria, some of whose remains can be clearly seen, with stone houses and public buildings still standing to their upper levels, are still not fully understood; yet the local population was clearly able to engage in fairly elaborate forms of exchange. Christopher Wickham has stressed the effects of the ending of the *annona* system in the early seventh century, and the impact of the seventh-century invasions included a massive loss to the eastern empire of basic tax revenue. In Umayyad Syria, the Muslims instituted a completely different tax system, and as their priorities crystallized, elements of the Roman provincial structure inevitably began to weaken. But many questions remain about economic life towards the end of our period, and this perhaps cautions more than anything else against the too easy absorption of the early Islamic world into that of late antiquity.

## PART II

## The fourth century

Although the overall period covered in this book begins only in 395, it will be useful to provide a short introduction to the fourth century.[26] Traditionally, and certainly in English-speaking scholarship since Jones's *Later Roman Empire*, the 'later Roman empire' has been thought of as beginning with the reign of Diocletian (284–305). A strong division was made between the mid-third century, seen as a time of civil strife, usurpation and financial crisis manifested in debasement of the coinage and spiralling prices, or even the virtual collapse of the monetary economy, and the era which followed, when policies associated with Diocletian led to greater bureaucratization, attempts to control prices by law, an attempted power-sharing between two Augusti and two Caesars, collectively known as the 'tetrarchs', and a new division of the provinces and separation of civil and military rule, together with a much increased pomp and ceremony surrounding the imperial court ('an Oriental despotism').[27] The extent of the so-called 'third-century crisis' remains debated, and some recent works also resist this sharp dividing line and lay emphasis on the connections between the later empire and what went before.[28] 'Late antiquity' as defined by Peter Brown in *The World of Late Antiquity* of 1971 (subtitled *From Marcus Aurelius to Muhammad*) is generously envisaged as inclusive at both ends of its chronological range.

Scholars are still divided on whether the reign of Constantine (306–37, sole reign 324–37) represented a 'revolution', or substantially continued trends already evident during the immediately preceding period.[29] Constantine's famous 'conversion' before his defeat of Maxentius at the Battle of the Milvian Bridge in AD 312 and his religious stance and policies are still at the centre of the debate, which shows no sign of abating, but the administrative, financial and military aspects of his reign are also important. Constantine himself was a product of the tetrarchic period. He was the son of Constantius Chlorus, who had risen through the army to be promoted by Diocletian to Caesar and subsequently became Augustus, and had successfully circumvented the hostility of his rivals to have himself declared Augustus by his father's troops when the latter died at York in 306; the years 306–312 were spent eliminating rival contenders in the west, and his final defeat of Licinius, emperor of the east, in AD 324, made him sole ruler of the empire. This spelled the end of the tetrarchic system introduced by Diocletian; instead, Constantine adopted a dynastic policy for the succession. He promoted his own sons to the rank of Caesar and at the end of his life he initiated a new settlement in the hope of guaranteeing the succession. These hopes were not realized, but after 324, Constantine had been able, as no other emperor had been able to do for many years, to preside over a more secure and settled empire.

Constantine's victory in 324, followed by the death of Licinius, was marked by the immediate issue of important legislation reinforcing the new security already offered to Christians.[30] But Constantine had not waited until 324 to introduce change; already in the winter of 312–13 he intervened in disputes between Christians in North Africa, calling a meeting in Rome to settle them, and then a council at Arles in 314. The issues were not new, especially in North Africa: the question was how the church should treat the *lapsi* (compromisers) in the aftermath of persecution. It was thus a very modern problem, with church property and careers at stake, and North Africa was not the only part of the empire where these divisions showed themselves. However, this early effort on Constantine's part at solving inter-Christian disagreements was unsuccessful, and in 315 we find him threatening the persistent hardline 'Donatists'. By 321, under pressure of other concerns and apparently realising the limits of practicality, he advised the mainstream catholic Christians in North Africa to be patient and wait for God to bring justice. But the great Council of 411, at which St Augustine was prominent, shows that the Donatist and catholic division in North Africa remained a major problem throughout the fourth century, and even the strong measures taken at that time failed to eliminate Donatism completely. By 324, Constantine had learned from his earlier mistakes. He now called a much bigger council of bishops, to meet at Nicaea and settle a further dispute identified with the views of an Alexandrian priest called Arius about the relation of the Son to the Father in Christian theology. This time the meeting resulted in a statement of faith, to which all had to subscribe, and which was eventually to become enshrined as the Nicene Creed; public resources were deployed, and the few who refused to sign the Council's statement were exiled. The Council of Nicaea took on an iconic status: the number of those attending was soon claimed to have reached 318, an improbably high figure, but the same as that of the servants of Abraham, and Theodoret of Cyrrhus, writing in the fifth century, told an affecting story of how some of those present had been mutilated in the persecutions. When Constantine invited the assembled bishops to dinner, it was claimed that he even kissed the eye sockets of some who had been blinded.[31]

These were powerful precedents for the subsequent position of the church, its bishops and Christians generally in the empire, but they did not make the empire officially Christian, as many still imagine. However, Constantine also set about building churches, at first on the sites of Roman martyr shrines and, in the case of the Lateran basilica, on the site of the demolished barracks of the imperial guard of his defeated enemy Maxentius. This huge basilica was to be the seat of the bishop, and was sited away from the main existing Christian areas but near an imperial palace. We know about Constantine's Roman churches and the donations he made to them mainly from a sixth-century history of the bishops of Rome, and some, including St Peter's on the Vatican hill, may have been built by his successors rather than Constantine himself. Yet while even in the time of persecution there were certainly some substantial church buildings, Constantine's imperially sponsored churches in Rome, Antioch, Jerusalem and elsewhere in the Holy Land instituted a new development in architecture and in Christian visibility. It is interesting therefore, that in his newly refounded city of Constantinople ('the city of Constantine'), begun after his victory over Licinius in 324, he seems to have concentrated on the secular buildings needed for an imperial centre rather than the panoply of churches we might have expected (Chapter 1). Constantine was a traditionalist as much as an innovator. He seems to have had a special sense of affiliation towards the sun god, and much of his legislation on matters affecting religion was ambiguous; after all, more than 90 per cent of the population was still pagan. Nor was religion his only or even perhaps most important concern; he also continued Diocletianic precedent, if with developments of his own, in military and administrative matters. He turned to members of elite Roman senatorial families in building his administration while also expanding the senatorial order and cutting its territorial connection to the city of Rome. If the empire's financial stability improved during his reign, this had much to do with increased security. A new gold coin, the solidus, was introduced under Constantine, allegedly made possible by the availability of gold confiscated from temples, but also by special taxes on the rich; it remained the highest value currency in the Byzantine empire for many centuries, but the problem of inflation of the base metal coinage used by most people was not so easily solved.

Constantine was controversial in his own day and is still an iconic figure, as demonstrated by several exhibitions held to commemorate the 1700th anniversary of his proclamation at York. For many, his support of Christianity will always be the most important thing about him. But he deserves a broader and more objective approach; in particular he invites comparison with Augustus, as an emperor who also came to power by eliminating his rivals in civil war, and found subtle ways of dealing with division and hostility within the upper class. Each succeeded in establishing a new elite, and each was a master of public relations. In each case too, religious change was a feature of their reign, but in both cases it was embedded in a broader context.

Constantine also resembled Augustus in that he failed to ensure a smooth succession. His death in 337 while en route to campaign against Persia was followed by an awkward period of uncertainty before his three surviving sons were all declared Augusti. In the process, the descendants of Constantine's half brothers, who included the future emperor Julian (361–63) were set aside or even eliminated. Constantine's sons promptly turned on each other in civil conflicts which continued until Constantius II (337–61) emerged as sole emperor in 353.[32] Constantius continued his father's policy of intervention in church affairs, but in a context of reaction against the decisions taken at the Council of Nicaea. Athanasius, bishop of Alexandria and a strong pro-Nicene supporter and propagandist, had already been exiled in the last years of Constantine and was condemned several times by church councils, and exiled twice more under Constantius. However, 'Arianism' is a term that strictly denotes a whole spectrum of theological understanding rather than a single position. The Council of Nicaea had resulted in a statement according to which the Son was of the same substance (*homoousios*) as the Father, but dissatisfaction with this formula was now represented by groups variously known as Anomoeans or Homoeans. Constantine himself had veered away from the Nicene position before his baptism and death in 337 and this continued under his son and successor Constantius II. The disputes continued until the Council of Constantinople called by Theodosius I in 381, the second 'ecumenical' council, which returned to the Nicene formula, and after which the 'Nicene' creed ceased to be questioned as the central statement of Christian belief.

Of the three sons of Constantine who gained power after their father's death in 337, Constantine II had been eliminated in 340 and Constans fell to the usurper Magnentius at Autun in 350. Gallus and Julian, the grandsons of Constantine's father Constantius II and Theodora, had been regarded up to then as threats to the succession, but Constantius now made Gallus Caesar while he himself moved to crush Magnentius; however, Gallus was killed at Constantius' orders in 354. As sole ruler, Constantius made a famous visit in 357 to Rome, no longer the seat of government in the west, which was memorably described by the historian Ammianus Marcellinus, whose surviving history is a main and very important source from the year 354.[33] The historian was struck by the emperor's pose of grandeur and impassivity ('as if he were an image of a man', *Hist.* 16.10.10), and this brought out in him all his considerable powers of virtuoso description. The years of Constantius' sole reign were also occupied in dealing with military threats in the west from the Alamanni and Sarmatians and in the east from the Sasanians, who took Amida (Diyarbakir in eastern Turkey) in 359. He brought back Gallus' half-brother Julian from his studies at Athens and the latter successfully campaigned as Caesar against the Alamanni, winning a major battle at Strasburg in 357. But in 360 Julian's troops proclaimed him Augustus in Paris,[34] news that Constantius heard while campaigning in the east. There was little likelihood that Constantius would accept Julian as co-emperor, and the latter marched east, entering Constantinople to general acclaim in December 361, a few weeks after Constantius had died in Cilicia.

Julian's short reign as sole emperor (he died from a spear wound in mysterious circumstances when on campaign against Persia) is one of the most controversial, partly because of his own considerable and self-conscious literary output. Brought up a Christian, at first under the care of Eusebius the bishop of Constantinople, he was later allowed contact with leading philosophers at Ephesus and Athens, and adopted an enthusiastic form of pagan Neoplatonism. Among his writings are a hymn to King Helios and a treatise against Christianity (*Against the Galilaeans*) and as emperor he attempted to ban Christians from teaching and to organize paganism along the institutional lines adopted by the Christian church. However, he lacked the persuasive and other skills necessary to carry this through, even in a city still full of intellectuals and many pagans such as Antioch, where he arrived from Constantinople in July 362 and where he stayed for some months before setting off on his eastern campaign.[35] Not only did Christians such as Gregory of Nazianzus, Ephraem the Syrian and John Chrysostom react violently against this threat;

Julian's eccentricities also managed to alienate the pagan population, who lampooned and jeered at the emperor. He further excited Jews and outraged Christians with an abortive plan to rebuild the Temple at Jerusalem.[36] Julian was not easy to assess: his rise inspired pagan philosophers and intellectuals such as Eunapius and Libanius, but the historian Ammianus Marcellinus, who had served as an officer in Gaul and on the Persian expedition in 363, and admired Julian greatly, was also clear-sighted about some of his faults. Julian was the only emperor after Constantine to try to promote paganism, but his personal unpredictability, his lack of tact and his proneness to grand gestures made it unlikely that he could have been successful in reversing the solid gains which Christians now enjoyed, even had his reign lasted longer.

Julian's death at Samarra, east of the Tigris, left the army dangerously exposed and his successor, Jovian, an obscure cavalry officer, proclaimed by soldiers on the field, immediately had to deal with a major Persian attack. The price of extricating the Romans from this difficult situation included the surrender of Nisibis and Singara on the frontier with Persia, and led to the removal of Ephraem the Syrian from Nisibis to Edessa.[37] Jovian survived for only one year and was succeeded by Valentinian I (364–75), a Christian officer originally from Pannonia, also chosen by the army, who within weeks co-opted his brother Valens (364–78) as co-emperor. Their accession marked a new dynastic departure, and they were able to fight off a challenge in Asia Minor from Procopius, another officer, who was related to the Emperor Julian and had been promoted by him; he had even been responsible for burying Julian's body in Tarsus.[38] In a clear dynastic move, Valentinian also made his seven-year old son Gratian consul in 366 and Augustus in 367, as the first of the 'boy-emperors'. Gratian survived on the throne until he was killed by his own soldiers at Lyons in 383, while attempting unsuccessfully to control the threat to Britain and Gaul mounted by the Spaniard Magnus Maximus; when Valentinian I died in 375 his generals had declared his four-year old son Valentinian II Augustus, and the Spaniard Theodosius I was recalled from exile in Spain and declared Augustus by Gratian in January 379, a few months after Valens was killed on the field in the disastrous defeat of the Roman army by the Goths at Adrianople (below and Chapter 2).

The advent of the Pannonian emperors marked a new and ominous turn. In the first place, as Ammianus' account made very clear, it brought profound issues about succession and legitimacy to the fore.[39] Valentinian was easily presented as uncouth, not least because he kept two she-bears as pets; Valens is compared to a beast of the arena.[40] Their reign was also marked by a notorious series of trials of members of the senatorial class on charges which included conspiracy and magic, and which gave Ammianus plenty of scope to underline the cruelty of Valentinian.[41] Julian had campaigned to secure the frontier along the Rhine and the Danube, and Valentinian and Valens at first sought to consolidate relations with the Alamanni and Goths by diplomacy. By 369 Valens had adopted a more aggressive stance and forced the Gothic leader Athanaric to sue for peace, ending the subsidies previously paid to them by Rome. But by 376 Gothic envoys had come to Valens in Antioch asking to be allowed to cross the Danube into Thrace; Valens, engaged in preparations for renewed warfare against the Persians, was in no position to refuse, and the Tervingi and Gruethingi crossed the Danube on a mass of boats, rafts and canoes. Ammianus' explanation is that they were being pushed by movement of the Huns into their own territories[42] but the attractions of sharing in Roman prosperity were also a major factor. Roman hopes of peaceful settlement by the Goths, if such existed, were quickly dashed; the Goths began to pillage Thrace and Valens hastily patched up peace with Persia and sent a too-small force to deal with the situation. A battle damaging to both sides was fought in 377, and in 378 Valens engaged the Goths at Adrianople without waiting for the arrival of Gratian and the western army. The result was a disaster for the Romans compared by Ammianus to the Roman defeat by Hannibal at Cannae, with the emperor himself among the dead.[43]

What used to be called the 'barbarian invasions' have been among the most debated issues in late antique scholarship since the publication of the first edition of this book.[44] Earlier scholarship was strongly marked by attempts to trace an unbroken Germanic identity, but this and the old idea of massive numbers of German invaders pressing on the frontiers of the empire has given way since the 1990s to the concept of ethnogenesis, referring to the processes whereby barbarian groups gradually acquired a self-conscious identity, largely through their contact with the Romans;[45] this has gone alongside a revisionist interpretations of material evidence by archaeologists.[46] In the case of the Ostrogoths a self-serving royal genealogy of the Amals was produced by Jordanes, a Gothic writer in sixth-century Constantinople, drawing on an earlier work, now lost, by Cassiodorus. One of the key issues in the current debates concerns the extent to which Jordanes's account should be used by modern historians.[47] The assumptions attached to the idea of ethnogenesis have also come under criticism, and this too centres on the problematic concept of ethnicity. In fact the categories 'Romans' and 'barbarians' are themselves derived from the tendentious accounts in our Roman sources and did not of themselves correspond to real differences; indeed, the 'barbarians' usually aspired to the advantages of being Roman. Using the common designation of 'Germanic' imports ethnic assumptions, and even the term 'barbarian' is perhaps now best used simply to denote 'non-Roman', without ethnic connotations. This sensitivity to issues of identity and self-definition also involves a rethinking of the concept of frontiers, as can be found in much of the scholarship since the early 1990s, for example in the series of conferences with the title *Shifting Frontiers*. These are difficult issues, and indeed ethnicity and identity remain major topics for both east and west in late antiquity.[48] The de-emphasizing of barbarian identities may have been taken too far, and the minimizing of invasion and conflict in the story of Roman-barbarian relations in the west in late fourth and fifth centuries has itself provoked a reaction, notably from Peter Heather and Bryan Ward-Perkins, who again stress the 'fall' of the western empire in the fifth century under the pressure of barbarian invasion.[49]

Both Heather and Ward-Perkins, especially the former, are mainly concerned with the western empire, but are also reacting against what they see as the excessively bland approach established by Brown, *The World of Late Antiquity*.

According to Ammianus, whose narrative stops at this chronological point, the Goths came dangerously close after their victory at Adrianople to threatening Constantinople itself, but while they had defeated and killed a Roman emperor, capturing the city was far beyond their capacities, and in 381 Roman forces drove them back from Macedonia and Thessaly into Thrace; Athanaric had died in Constantinople early in 381 and was given a ceremonial funeral, and a treaty was concluded in 382; it was accompanied by grants of land. Some contemporaries, including Ambrose, bishop of Milan, realized that these events were the beginning, not the end of Roman difficulties, but the orator Themistius depicts the treaty as an act of far-sighted Roman generosity inspired by the new emperor Theodosius.[50]

Theodosius I (379–95) spent much of his reign in Constantinople, apart from his move to crush Magnus Maximus in northern Italy in 388, and Eugenius, defeated at the river Frigidus between Aquileia and Emona in 394. Milan, the episcopal seat of Ambrose, was an imperial residence in this period, and Theodosius himself died there in 395, but from the early fifth century Ravenna became the main imperial centre in the west. Theodosius visited Rome in 389, where he was praised in an extant speech by the Gallic orator Pacatus. Valentinian II was expected to base himself in Trier, under the eye of the Frankish *magister militum* Arbogast, but met his end when Eugenius made common cause with Arbogast and took the title of Augustus. Though he was a Christian himself, his attempt was represented as a pagan challenge to the Christian Theodosius and his young sons Arcadius and Honorius, both now also Augusti, and caused some excitement among the Roman senatorial aristocrats; however, the view put forward by Herbert Bloch in 1963 and maintained by many others thereafter that there was a real 'pagan reaction' has now been shown to be fundamentally misconceived.[51]

The final decades of the fourth century marked a distinct intensification of the Christian offensive. The pro-Nicene Ambrose, bishop of Milan since 374, was a forceful advocate and politician who had to deal with several emperors, their families and their rivals.[52] He influenced first Gratian and then Valentinian II to resist the pleas of the senate, led by Symmachus, to restore the altar and statue of Victory to the senate house in Rome, he resisted imperial pressure to favour the Homoeans, and in the case of Theodosius he used his power to deny the emperor communion as a weapon and forced him to do humiliating public penance for the actions of imperial troops at Thessalonica. In Rome another forceful churchman, Damasus, had become pope (bishop of Rome) in 366 amid scenes of public tumult, and in the early 380s was the patron there of the controversial Jerome, while in the east John Chrysostom was preaching in Antioch and became an equally controversial bishop of Constantinople in 398.[53] Under the late fourth-century emperors a series of laws were brought in laying down increasingly severe penalties and exclusions, not only on pagans and Jews but also on heretics.[54] Penalties against Manichees, 'Eunomians', 'Phrygians', 'Priscillianists' and 'Donatists' were laid down in constitutions starting in 381, and similar civil disabilities were also applied to 'apostates' from Christianity, whether to paganism or Judaism. It would be a mistake to imagine that this legislation was everywhere enforced, or even that it represented laws applicable to the entire empire. It has come down to us in the Theodosian Code, a highly edited collection made under Theodosius II (408–50). But it had more than symbolic importance. It could be exploited by powerful bishops, who could claim imperial support even more confidently than before;[55] it also invited informers to lay charges against individuals, and even allowed the possibility of challenging inheritances from persons alleged to have been Manichees or 'apostates'. Sometimes it also led to public prosecutions of which detailed accounts remain, as in the case of Augustine's two public debates with Manichaeans in Hippo in 392 and 404, for which the surviving texts by Augustine are actually records made as part of the legal process.[56]

By 395 it was possible to feel that the organisational and military changes introduced under the tetrarchy and continued by Constantine had on balance been successful.[57] The empire had recovered economic stability and was largely able to maintain and defend its provincial organization; it was even able to conduct offensive wars. But the problem of ensuring a smooth succession to the imperial power had not been resolved, though much effort had been expended on it. The state was now taking, and was willing to take, a far more interventionist approach towards religious change, even if it still had to balance the competing claims of established practice. The Christian church, represented by leading bishops, and indeed also some influential ascetic figures, was far more visible than before. It was also developing systematic mechanisms for defining doctrine, notably through church councils, and this process would continue in the fifth century with the councils of Ephesus (431 and 449) and Chalcedon (451).[58] On the other hand, there were already at the end of the fourth century signs of the religious conflict that was to be one of the features of urban life in the fifth century (Chapter 7). Finally, the last decades of the fourth century presented some troubling precedents in relation to the rise to power of a class of military power-brokers, and the likely future problems in dealing with pressure from non-Romans, while in the east the Sasanian state remained a powerful danger to the security of the cities of the eastern provinces.

# 1

# CONSTANTINOPLE AND
# THE EASTERN EMPIRE

## The city of Constantinople

On the death of Theodosius I in AD 395, Constantinople had been an imperial
seat for over sixty years, since the refoundation of the classical city of Byzantium as Constantinople ('the city of Constantine') by Constantine.[1] Although
it is common to refer to it as the eastern capital, this is not strictly correct:
Constantine founded it along the lines of existing tetrarchic capitals such as
Nicomedia, Serdica and Trier, and although he resided there for most of the
time from its dedication in 330 to his death in 337, he seemed to envisage a
return after his death to an empire partitioned geographically between several
Augusti.[2] It was not a novelty in itself when on the death of Theodosius I the
empire was 'divided' between his two sons Honorius and Arcadius. What was
different now was the fact that the two halves of the empire began to grow
further and further apart.

Constantinople was the scene of some bitter disputes among Christians in
the late fourth century, but it was still not yet a fully Christian city. Eusebius,
writing of Constantine's foundation in sweepingly panegyrical terms, would
have us believe that all traces of paganism were eliminated. However, this
would have been impossible to achieve in practice, short of deporting the
existing population, and indeed, the later pagan historian Zosimus tells us that
Constantine founded two new pagan temples.[3] According to the fifth-century
ecclesiastical historian Sozomen, the new city was given a senate and senate
house, with classical statuary,[4] and it had a Basilica and a Capitol. Presumably
the latter was at first a temple like the Capitol in Rome, but teaching went on
there in the fifth century as the seat of the so-called 'University', and by then
it was surmounted by a cross.[5] Constantine adorned his city with many classical statues, taken, Eusebius assures us, from pagan temples and put there
as objects of derision, but more likely because they were expected as part of
the adornment of a grand and monumental late antique urban centre.[6] Many
were crowded onto the *spina* in the middle of Hippodrome, others placed in
the public squares.[7] It was Constantine's son Constantius II (337–61) rather
than Constantine himself who was mainly responsible for the first church
of St Sophia (burnt down in the Nika riot of 532 and replaced by Justinian
with the present building: Chapter 5), and also for the church of the Holy

Apostles adjoining Constantine's mausoleum.[8] Constantius was extremely pious himself, but the effects of the attempted restoration of paganism by his successor, Julian (361–63), were felt at Constantinople as elsewhere, and there were still pagans at court – indeed, Constantius' panegyrist, Themistius, was a pagan. At the end of the century, John Chrysostom, who became bishop of Constantinople in 398, directed many of his sermons against the dangers of paganism. The fourth century, after the death of Constantine, was a time of ferment and competition both between Christians and between pagans and Christians, when despite imperial support for Christianity, the final outcome was still by no means certain. It was also only in the fifth century that church building began to take off on a major scale. Again, while Constantinople had been referred to as 'New Rome' since the time of Constantine, it was only the council summoned by Theodosius I at Constantinople in 381 that gave its bishop a primacy of honour over all other patriarchates save Rome. In an earlier gesture intended to bolster the Christian claim of the new city and claim apostolic status for it, Constantius II deposited relics of Timothy and Andrew within the empty sarcophagi of Constantine's mausoleum.[9]

Constantinople had an advantage, as the seat of emperors, but it was not immune from religious and political pressures. After Theodosius I became emperor in 379 he quickly issued an edict together with Gratian condemning all heresies. This affected Constantinople, where the Christians were divided and there was a strong and vociferous Arian population. In 380 Theodosius

*Figure 1.1* The base of the obelisk in the Hippodrome, showing the emperor in the imperial box receiving gifts from barbarians

*Figure 1.2* Istanbul: Justinian's church of St Sophia

ordered Arians to be expelled from churches, and promoted the orthodox Gregory of Nazianzus as bishop against strong opposition. He then called what became known as the Council of Constantinople (381), or Constantinople I, a council of 150 eastern bishops who met in the church of St Irene; those present confirmed Gregory and (if not very wholeheartedly) the Nicene faith. However, the election was still contested, and, unhappy at the situation, Gregory stepped down and returned to Cappadocia; he left a record of his feelings in an autobiographical poem, and while it is true that he was already a bishop, and that transfer from one see to another had been forbidden at Nicaea, Sozomen at least thought that his election would have been acceptable.[10] But the affair illustrated the capacity of the patriarch of Alexandria to interfere in Constantinopolitan politics, and tensions were still high when Theodosius installed orthodox relics in a church which had previously belonged to the Arian party, following this by bringing the supposed head of John the Baptist to the city. Moreover the conversion of the Goths to 'Arian' rather than Nicene Christianity also added to the explosive mix in the city,[11] and John Chrysostom as patriarch allowed the Goths who lived there a church, though only for orthodox worship;[12] he successfully insisted on this even when under pressure from the emperor, nervous about the needs of the Gothic troops led by Gainas. The latter had successfully ousted the powerful eunuch minister Eutropius, but such was the hostility to the foreigners that a large number were massacred after taking refuge in the church, and the church was burnt down. The Goths were expelled from Constantinople in 400 and Gainas became the victim of inter-Gothic rivalries. A main, but difficult, source for Eutropius and the Goths in Constantinople is a speech by Synesius, who visited Constantinople sometime during these years as an envoy from Cyrene, and stayed for three years.[13] Thus religious issues were mixed in Constantinople, with politics surrounding the reliance on eunuchs in the administration, rivalry between the western and eastern courts and the danger of relying on German soldiery. This was a crisis time for Constantinople.

By the reign of Justinian in the sixth century, the population of Constantinople had reached its greatest extent, and may on a generous estimate have approached half a million. So large a number of inhabitants could only be supported by public intervention, and Constantine had instituted an elaborate system of food distribution based on that at Rome.[14] It was from the late fourth century onwards that much of the expansion took place – something of its scale can be imagined from the fact that the original number of recipients of the grain dole was set at only 80,000. The *Notitia urbis Constantinopolitanae* (*c.* 425–30) lists 14 churches, 52 colonnaded streets, 153 private bath complexes and several cisterns. The aqueduct constructed in 373 by the Emperor Valens provided further essential water supply, and water was carried to the city from multiple sources in the Thracian hinterland; new harbours were also necessary.[15] The walls built in the reign of Theodosius II in the early fifth century, and still standing in large part today, though heavily restored, enclosed a much larger area than that of the original Constantinian circuit, and though Constantinople did not equal Rome in population size, even at its height, it nevertheless provides a remarkable example of urban growth.

Pagan critics of Constantine, such as Zosimus, were highly critical of his foundation:

> the size of Constantinople was increased until it was by far the greatest city, with the result that many of the succeeding emperors chose to live there, and attracted an unnecessarily large population which came from all over the world – soldiers and officials, traders and other professions. Therefore, they have surrounded it with new walls much more extensive than those of Constantine and allowed the buildings to be so close to each other that the inhabitants, whether at home or in the streets are crowded for room and it is dangerous to walk about because of the great number of men and beasts. And a lot of the sea round about has been turned into land by sinking piles and building houses on them, which by themselves are enough to fill a large city.
>
> (*New History* II.35, trans. Ridley)

Of course the city failed to live up to modern standards of urban planning, but the description vividly brings out both the extent of public investment and the consequent hectic growth. The heart of the city had been planned by Constantine himself – it included the imperial palace (greatly extended by later emperors), the adjoining Hippodrome and the Augusteum, a great square leading to the church of St Sophia, a main processional street (the

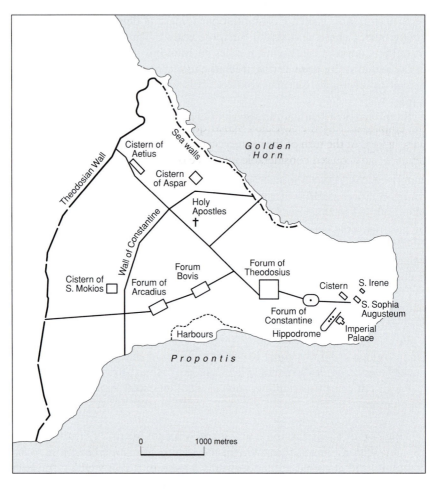

*Map 1.1* Constantinople

Mese) leading to Constantine's oval forum with its statue of himself wearing
a crown of rays like the sun god and placed on the top of a porphyry column,
and Constantine's own mausoleum, where he lay symbolically surrounded
by empty sarcophagi, one for each of the twelve apostles. Despite the later
proliferation of churches, this was originally less a new Christian city than a
complex of public buildings expressive of imperial rule.

Whatever Constantine's own intentions may have been, Constantinople
did gradually assume the role of eastern capital. Legislation under Constantius
regularized the position of the eastern senate (though it could not approach
the wealth and prestige of that of Rome), and there were both eastern and
western consuls; as the *Notitia Dignitatum* recognizes, by the end of the fourth
century the same basic framework of administration existed in both east
and west, and a division of the empire into two halves therefore posed no

administrative difficulties.[16] But in practice, during this period, the eastern government grew stronger while the western one weakened.

## The east *c.* 400

The turn of the century nevertheless found the east facing some severe problems, chief among them the threats posed by the pressure of barbarians on the empire, and by the so-called 'Arian question'. As we have seen, the two were linked. At the turn of the century, certain Gothic leaders and their military retinues had acquired considerable influence over the government at Constantinople, and when Synesius arrived there he found city and court deeply divided about how to deal with this potentially dangerous situation. This was not the only problem. Like his brother Honorius in the west, the eastern Emperor Arcadius was young and easily influenced by unscrupulous ministers. In this way the eastern and western governments became rivals; the western court poet Claudian, the panegyrist of the powerful Vandal general Stilicho, gives a luridly pro-western account of the situation, especially in his scabrous attacks on the eastern ministers, Rufinus, master of offices, consul and prefect of the east, and the eunuch Eutropius, head of the young emperor's 'Bedchamber'.[17] Though he cannot rival Claudian's level of invective, Zosimus' account is similar in tone:

> The empire now devolved upon Arcadius and Honorius, who, although apparently the rulers, were so in name only: complete control was exercised by Rufinus in the east and Stilicho in the west ... all senators were distressed at the present plight.
>
> (*New Hist.*, V.1.9)

Even allowing for distortion, matters looked unpromising. The weakness of the imperial government is shown by the fact that in 400 Gainas had only recently been given the job of suppressing the troops led by his kinsman Tribigild who were devastating Asia Minor, only to join them himself and march on the city. The choice for the eastern government was stark: either it could follow a pro-barbarian policy and continue to attempt to conciliate such leaders, or it must attempt to root them out altogether. Both eastern and western courts were hotbeds of suspicion and intrigue, and the divisions which resulted led to the murder of Rufinus in 395 and the fall of Eutropius in 399, and were subsequently to lead to the fall and death of Stilicho in 408.

Theodosius I's policy in relation to the Goths was to settle them on Roman land, but this did not remove the danger, and in 395 Constantinople employed the traditional policy of using subsidies to buy off Alaric, the leader of the Visigoths, who was plundering land dangerously close to the city.[18] This proved disastrous; in the following year Alaric devastated the Peloponnese and large parts of the Balkans, an area whose control was disputed between east and west. A major part of the problem lay also in the fact that Gothic soldiers formed a large part of the Roman army itself. Nevertheless, the east was in a better position to buy off the raiders than the west; furthermore, significant voices, including that of Synesius, were raised in favour of expelling the Goths. When Gainas attacked Constantinople in 400, his coup was put down (albeit by another Goth, Fravitta, subsequently made consul for 401), and with it the pro-German group within government circles was defeated. This result was extremely important for the future of the eastern empire, for though the danger of barbarian pressure was to recur, the influence of barbarian generals on the eastern government was checked, and the east was able to avoid having to make the massive barbarian settlements which so fragmented the western empire. The consequences for the west were also momentous, for Alaric and his followers moved from the Balkans to Italy, besieging Rome in 408–9, demanding enormous payments in return for food and taking the city itself in 410.[19] The sack of Rome was an almost unimaginable event which caused shivers to run down the spine of St Jerome in Bethlehem and sent rich Christians fleeing to the safety of North Africa and asking Augustine how God could have let this happen.

## Religious issues

The violence in Constantinople in 400 also had a religious side to it, and in the case of Rome the very fact that Alaric and his Visigoths were Christian made it doubly difficult for Christians such as St Augustine to explain why God had allowed the sack of Christian Rome to happen.[20] By the middle of the fifth century the west was still the target of repeated barbarian assaults and settlements (Chapter 2) and the east was threatened by the Huns; however, the east also had other concerns. Arcadius was succeeded by his son Theodosius II (408–50), only seven years old when his father died.[21] Theodosius II's long reign provided a stable period of consolidation during which the imperial court was characterized by an extremely pious atmosphere especially connected with the most strong-minded of his three sisters, Pulcheria, who became Augusta and regent in 414. Pulcheria chose Theodosius' bride – the intellectual Eudocia, formerly named Athenaïs and allegedly of pagan Athenian origin, selected by means of an imperial beauty-contest – and the relationship between the two women was predictably stormy. However, Eudocia too had a strong influence on the church in the east, notably through the patronage she exercised on her visits to the Holy Land.[22] To this period belong the First Council of Ephesus (431), at which the title Bearer of God (Greek *Theotokos*) was officially recognized for the Virgin Mary, the Second Council of Ephesus (449), and that of Chalcedon (451), when the orthodox doctrine of Christ's two natures, divine and human, was decreed (see below). The First Council of Ephesus and that of Chalcedon were landmarks in the history of the church, and together they represent an important stage in the working out of the complex implications of the creed agreed at the first ecumenical council at Nicaea (325). It is also to the reign of Theodosius II that we owe the Theodosian Code, a massive achievement, which aimed to collect all imperial constitutions since Constantine, and which is our major source, with the later Code of Justinian (Chapter 5) for late Roman law.

The extraordinary amount of documentation surrounding the ecclesiastical councils and the Theodosian Code itself marks a new stage in record-keeping. We know little about the actual process of producing the conciliar records (Acts), but the actual proceedings, and the original records, were largely in Greek, though they were often then translated into Latin, or survive in Syriac. This was true of the first ecumenical council held at Nicaea in 325 under Constantine, at which the Latin-speaking emperor's efforts to greet the assembled bishops in Greek made a favourable impression. It was partly because the attendance at these councils was overwhelmingly eastern (Chapter 3), but also because the dominant, and the official, language of the eastern empire was Greek. In contrast, Latin remained the language of legislation, and both the

*Figure 1.3* A Byzantine empress in her regalia, depicted on a leaf from an ivory diptych, late fifth or sixth century. Vienna, Kunsthistorisches Museum

*Codex Theodosianus*, as it was called, and its sixth-century successor, the *Codex Justinianus*, were compiled in Latin. Even if Greek was the basic language in use, as Fergus Millar insists, Latin naturally remained important in the upper levels of education and Theodosius II also established Latin teaching at public expense in Constantinople (Chapter 6). The production of the Theodosian Code, completed in 437 and promulgated in 438, was a massive effort of compilation and editing. All laws were issued in the names of both or all reigning emperors, irrespective of where they originated, and dated by the Roman calendar, and in fact took the form of imperial letters ('constitutions') addressed to officials, or sometimes the Senate.[23] The emperor described his motives in ordering the collection in a constitution of February, 438; he wished to replace the mass of law books, imperial letters and other material,

> which close off from human understanding a knowledge of themselves by a wall, as though they were swallowed up in a thick cloud of obscurity.
>
> (trans. Harries)

Darkness would give way to light, and laws would be brought together in the name of 'brevity'. However, interpreting this mass of material is far from simple, and at times one could wish that the compilers had done less editing rather than more. Theodosius himself may have been weak and easily influenced, as contemporaries suggest ('meek above all men which are upon the face of the earth', according to the church historian Socrates, *Historia Ecclesiastica* VII.42), but his reign was extremely important in the civilianization of the eastern government in the fifth and sixth centuries. Tellingly, Socrates and Sozomen, who composed continuations of Eusebius' *Ecclesiastical History* in Constantinople in the 440s, both seem to have been lawyers.

Not all went smoothly in the early fifth century. In 403 quarrels between John Chrysostom and the Empress Eudoxia, two hot-tempered and outspoken characters, had led to the bishop's deposition by the so-called Synod of the Oak, and, after his return and yet another perceived affront, to a second exile in the following year.[24] As with the events of AD 400, this was a dramatic story. On Easter Saturday, after John's condemnation, 3,000 new Christians were about to be baptized when the service was broken up by soldiers, and on the night when he left Constantinople, a mysterious fire broke out in the church of St Sophia which burned down the senate house and some of its many classical statues; pagans blamed John's supporters, many of whom refused to communicate with the bishop who replaced him. John had other powerful enemies, notably the Syrian Severian of Gabala and the forceful Theophilus of Alexandria, who objected to John's support of the Tall Brothers, a group of monks who had fled from Theophilus' anti-Origenist activities in Egypt; but it was especially remembered that he had referred to the Empress Eudoxia in a sermon as Herodias and Jezebel, and that she had been offended by another he had preached against the vices of women. Although John had wealthy and influential women among his own following, especially the deaconess Olympias, the jewels and display of rich ladies were also a frequent target of his preaching. The real forces at work behind his condemnation, which was judged illegal in the west by a synod called by Innocent I, were several and varied, but personalities and personal feelings certainly played a large part.

Similar passions aroused in a religious context were demonstrated at Alexandria, a stronghold of paganism and the seat of the major philosophical school after Athens.[25] Here the policies of Theodosius I had acted as an incitement to the burning of the great temple known as the Serapeum (after the Egyptian god Serapis) by monks in 391;[26] now the aggressive patriarch Cyril raised the emotional tension to such a pitch that Christians were attacked by Alexandrian Jews when they gathered together on hearing that the church was on fire. In 415 Christians in turn lynched the female Neoplatonist philosopher Hypatia, Synesius' teacher:

> they dragged her from her carriage, took her to the church called Caesareum, where they completely stripped her, and then murdered her with tiles. After tearing her body in pieces, they took her mangled limbs to a place called Cinaron, and there burnt them. This affair brought no small opprobrium, not only upon Cyril [bishop of Alexandria], but also upon the whole Alexandrian church. And surely nothing can be further from the spirit of Christians than massacres, fights, and such-like things.
>
> (Socrates, *HE* VII.15, trans. from Stevenson, *Creeds*)

It is certainly true that the sources, especially Christian sources, often make claims about violence between pagans and Christians that have to be treated with scepticism, but Alexandria was undoubtedly prone to such outbursts of violence, and trouble stirred up by excitable religious leaders or monks became common as the urban population in many cities of the east steadily grew during the fifth and sixth centuries (Chapter 7).[27]

### Fifth-century councils

The two great church councils of Ephesus and Chalcedon also have to be seen against this context; they aroused passions equal to those surrounding any political issue in the modern world, and were just as much influenced by personal, social and local rivalries. Unlike the Second Council of Ephesus in 449, both rank among seven recognized 'ecumenical' councils, starting with the Council of Nicaea in 325 and ending with the Second Council of Nicaea in 787. However, many other councils and synods were held as well, either local and limited in character, or, just as frequently, recognized as binding only by part of the church. As we have seen, attendance at the Council of Constantinople (381) was eastern; the pope was not present, but the council was recognized as ecumenical by Chalcedon. As the church became more and more influential, and more embedded in general society, division between the great sees and between individual bishops could and did lead to major splits with long-term repercussions. This was particularly the case after the Council of Chalcedon, for much of the east, especially in Syria and Egypt, refused to accept its decisions and went on to form its own ecclesiastical hierarchy during the reign of Justinian, a factor which had profound implications for the empire.[28] From the point of view of the state, imperial support for the church necessitated a clear understanding of what the church was as an institution, and was not compatible with quarrelling and division among the clergy. Whether the bishops themselves were as committed to church unity is less clear, but questions of church organization and the authority of episcopal sees were of pressing importance to them, and the many councils and church synods in this period dealt largely with these issues and other questions of church order. As for the doctrinal issues, despite the numbers of councils and the level of controversy, division continued unabated; if anything the councils actually increased the tension and inflamed division by polarizing the various groups and forcing them to define their positions ever more exactly. The eventual outcome of a long process was the growing split between the Byzantine empire in the east and the papacy in the west, especially after 800,[29] but the eastern empire was already internally divided in the fifth century over the relation between the divine and the human natures of Christ, a question which the Council of Chalcedon failed to settle for the longer term, just as the Council of Nicaea had failed to settle once and for all the question of the relation of Father and Son.

Christians had interpreted their faith in different ways since its beginning. However, the advent of imperial support, and the consequent public role assumed by the institutional church, gave an entirely new complexion to the process; what had been disagreement became not merely 'heresy', worthy of the strongest condemnation, but also a crime liable to punishment from the state. The Greek term 'heresy' originally meant simply 'choice'; but each Christian group in turn defined the choices of the rest as heresies, and in the late fourth century, before the legislation of Theodosius I, Epiphanius, bishop of Salamis in Cyprus, had composed a *Panarion*, literally a 'Medicine-Chest' or list of remedies, arguments directed against some eighty such objectionable 'heresies'; his work was to have a long life and was used by writers as different as Augustine and John of Damascus. The Councils of Ephesus and Chalcedon carried forward this attempt to arrive at a definition binding on the whole church, and both councils took place in a context of bitter rivalry. Again, personalities were much involved; one of the most striking, and some would say unscrupulous, both before and during the Council of Ephesus in 431, was Cyril, the nephew of Theophilus and bishop of Alexandria since 412, a formidable leader who dominated the proceedings through a mixture of cleverness, bribes and intimidation.

Nestorius, a monk from Antioch, made bishop of Constantinople by Theodosius II in 428, was also passionate, but he was no match for Cyril and in fact stayed away from the council proceedings. The issue was whether, and, if so, how, Christ had two natures. Cyril seemed to emphasize the divine, while Nestorius emphasized the human. Much later effort, especially in the sixth century, was to go into trying to reconcile the teachings of Cyril with the findings of the Council of Chalcedon. There was hot dispute at Ephesus I over the exact implications of the title *Theotokos* ('bearer of God'), which had been applied to Mary already but which now became a key issue; was she the mother of God, or only of Christ? This period also marked a distinct stage in the development of the cult of the Virgin, which was intensified by the debate over her title.[30] However, other issues were also in play including the rivalry between the more literal interpretation of Christianity associated with Antioch and the traditional position of Alexandria. The proceedings dragged on, with separate meetings held by Cyril's group and the Antiochenes, but after much argument and counter-argument, imperial manoeuvring, strong-arm tactics and intervention by Egyptian supporters of Cyril, the latter got the better of it and Nestorius was condemned and exiled.[31] Nestorius' own justificatory account survives in a sixth-century Syriac translation and is known as the *Bazaar*, or *Book, of Heraclides* (*c*. 450).[32] He went into prolonged exile, in 448 his books were ordered to be burned and his name became synonymous with heresy; it was later attached to the 'Nestorian' church (better, the Church of the East, for which see Chapter 9), laying stress on Christ's human rather than divine nature, which later established itself especially in the Sasanian empire, and spread eastwards from there as far as China.

The divisions continued, and the Antiochenes, especially Theodoret of Cyrrhus in northern Syria, did not easily accept Ephesus I; Cyril himself died in 444, and in 448 Eutyches, a monk in Constantinople and vociferous opponent of Nestorius, was condemned by the 'standing synod' of the city, the emperor called a new council and the proceedings against Eutyches were themselves challenged. The pope now intervened with a forceful document (the 'Tome of Leo', 449) asserting two natures, and a second council was held at Ephesus under the control of Cyril's successor Dioscorus. The Second Council of Ephesus in 449 ignored the Roman opposition, reinstated Eutyches and with the emperor's approval condemned Theodoret, Domnus of Antioch and Ibas (Hiba) of Edessa among others, including Flavian of Constantinople, who had gained the support of Pope Leo.[33] Such a reversal could not last, and Ephesus II became known as the 'Robber Council'. Theodosius died in 450, his sister Pulcheria chose and married Marcian, a suitable though elderly husband, and through him summoned a new council at Chalcedon in 451.

This was a very different affair.[34] The final definition of the Council of Chalcedon was signed by some 452 bishops, though the pope himself was not present; it condemned both Nestorius and Eutyches and drew on the arguments of both Cyril and Pope Leo. The Chalcedonian formula, asserting the two natures of Christ, became and remains fundamental to both the western and eastern churches. It developed and clarified the creed of Nicaea, according to which God was Father, Son and Holy Spirit, by further proclaiming that Christ was at all times after the Incarnation fully God and fully human: 'to be acknowledged in two natures, without confusion, without change, without division, without separation', thus rejecting both the Nestorian position and that of Eutyches. However, it was not uniformly accepted in the east, and led eventually to division between the eastern and western churches, and to further divisions in the east which persist to the present day. Recent scholarship, including the translation of the entire voluminous documentary record, has made it possible to appreciate the quite extraordinary amount of effort and procedural complexity that went into these proceedings, as well as the elaborate legal and documentary basis on which church business was now conducted.

The council also issued rulings (canons) on many practical issues of church order and discipline, including marriages contracted by dedicated virgins, and especially on the authority of bishops, also laying down that the bishops in each province should hold formal meetings twice a year. Importantly, it also continued the previous approach of the Council of Constantinople (381) in enhancing the status of the see of Constantinople, now affirming its equal privileges with Rome and giving it jurisdiction over the dioceses of Pontus, Asia and Thrace, a move which Pope Leo soon attempted to annul in a letter to the Empress Pulcheria.

The fifth-century west had been absorbed with its own doctrinal controversies, particularly in connection with the teachings of the British monk Pelagius on free will, against which Augustine fought a long battle. In North Africa another great set-piece council held at Carthage in 411, also leaving extensive documentary records, again condemned the local schism of Donatism and enforced catholic orthodoxy with strong coercive measures, of which Augustine approved as being necessary for the faith.[35] In the east the Emperors Leo, Zeno and Anastasius continued to wrestle with opposition to the Council of Chalcedon. Its opponents' cause was fought by a series of forceful leaders with exotic names – Timothy Aelurus ('the Cat') in Alexandria, Peter the Fuller in Antioch and Peter Mongus.[36] The so-called Henotikon ('Unifier') of 482, the name given to a letter from the Emperor Zeno to the rebellious church of Egypt, attempted to smooth over the disagreements about Chalcedon but instead antagonized Rome, which promptly excommunicated Zeno's advisers, Acacius, the patriarch of Constantinople, and Peter Mongus, the patriarch of Alexandria. There were also differences of view in Constantinople, and since Basiliscus, who had briefly usurped the throne during Zeno's reign (475–76), had supported the anti-Chalcedonians, Zeno's letter had political as well as religious aims. His successor Anastasius (491–518) at first tried to pursue a middle line, but later openly supported the anti-Chalcedonians, deposing a moderate, Flavian, from the see of Antioch and replacing him with Severus (512).[37] Religious disputes were frequently the starting-point or accompaniment of the violent riots which were a common feature of eastern city life from now on. In 493, statues of Anastasius and his wife were dragged through the streets of Constantinople, and also in Anastasius' reign there were serious disturbances after the emperor proposed a non-Chalcedonian addition to the words of the liturgy:

The population of the city crowded together and rioted violently on the grounds that something alien had been added to the Christian faith. There was uproar in the palace which caused the city prefect Plato to run in, flee and hide from the people's anger. The rioters set up a chant, 'A new emperor for the Roman state', and went off to the residence of the ex-prefect Marinus the Syrian, burned his house and plundered everything he had, since they could not find him. … They found an eastern monk in the house whom they seized and killed, and then, carrying his head on a pole, they chanted, 'Here is the enemy of the Trinity'. They went to the residence of Juliana, a patrician of the most illustrious rank, and chanted for her husband, Areobindus, to be emperor of the Roman state.

(John Malalas, *Chronicle,* trans. Jeffreys, 228)

## Emperor and city

The obscure army officer Marcian (450–57) succeeded Theodosius II in a political settlement ratified by his marriage to Pulcheria. He proved to be a careful and competent ruler, but he left no heir, and the succession was decided by the powerful head of the army, Aspar, in favour of Leo (457–74), who was on his staff.

The imperial succession always remained unstable, never having been completely formalized since the early empire. When, as on this occasion, there was no direct heir, it was left to the army (or those elements nearest to the centre of power) and the senate to settle the matter; the religious role of the patriarch, or bishop of Constantinople, only came to be formally recognized from the late fifth century on. However, popular assent, in practice that of the people of Constantinople, was also an important factor. In such a situation too much was left to chance, especially when the possibility of rioting was ever-present. It is probably no coincidence that we now begin to have records of something like a formal inauguration procedure, or that the main elements of this were taken from military custom.[38] Leo was invested with the torque, a military collar, in the imperial box in the Hippodrome in full view of the soldiers and people, and then raised on a shield in an improbably military ceremony, only then putting on an imperial diadem. The patriarch was also involved, but there was as yet no religious crowning as such, or anointing, or any of the trappings associated with medieval coronations, though by the seventh century the ceremony had moved to a church setting.

Imperial inaugurations and many other public occasions were accompanied by the shouting of acclamations by the crowd. These might be spontaneous, perhaps like the acclamations at Edessa in the context of Ephesus II (a mixture of the patriotic and the formulaic, and recorded as an official record) or very formal and even more repetitive, as with the acclamations of the senate at the reception of the Theodosian Code, which are faithfully recorded in the documentation; this was to become a feature of later Byzantine court ceremonial. They often took the form of simple cries of 'long live the emperor' and the like, but they might also be elaborate metrical chants or, at times, doctrinal assertions. Sometimes the emperor in his imperial box would engage in a virtual dialogue with the people; a striking example survives in the so-called *Acta Calapodii* of the sixth century, where such a dialogue is recorded in the context of the Nika revolt of 532 (Chapter 5).[39] As often, these were a chance to air political and other grievances or to appeal to the emperor. In 532, the Green faction

> chanted acclamations concerning Calapodius the cubicularius and spatharius: 'Long life, Justinian, may you be victorious; we are wronged, o sole good man, we cannot endure, God knows, we are on the brink of danger. It is Calapodius the spatharocubicularius who wrongs us.'
>
> (*Chronicon Paschale*, trans. Whitby and Whitby, 114)

A surprising licence was at times employed: a few days later during the same uprising the emperor went into his box at the Hippodrome carrying the Gospel, and swore an oath to the people in order to pacify them, 'and many of the people chanted, "Augustus Justinian, you are victorious." But others chanted, "You are forsworn, ass".'[40]

That the Hippodrome was now the setting for such confrontations followed a precedent from the early empire when emperors and people had also met each other at the games. In the urban topography of Constantinople the practice was formalized, the Hippodrome being linked to the palace by an internal passage, and it was here that the emperor was expected to make his formal appearances to the people as a whole. We can see evolving in the fifth century the ritualized yet turbulent relation of emperor and people characteristic of later Byzantium, in which the 'factions' of the Hippodrome, the Blue and Green sides in the chariot races, played a major role both as participants in state ceremonial and, at times, especially in the early period, as instigators and leaders of popular disturbance (Chapter 7). Emperors tended to support one faction or the other, and it has frequently been supposed that these Blues and Greens also represented the religious divisions of the day; however, though a group in a given city at a particular time (Blues and Greens were prominent in the rioting which took place in many eastern cities at the time of the fall of the Emperor Phocas in 609– 10; Chapter 9) might take on a particular cause, there is no evidence to show that either faction was identified with one particular group. However, the combination of sporting enthusiasms and political unrest was dangerous and could be explosive. They were also naturally a target for the disapproval of conservatives such as Procopius. The sculpted reliefs on the base of the obelisk set up by Theodosius II in the Hippodrome show the emperor in his imperial box, surrounded by his court, not only with barbarians bringing gifts (Figure 1.1), but also with the performers and musicians in front of him. The Blue and Green supporters themselves sat in special places in the Hippodrome (many graffiti with messages such as 'Victory to the Greens' also survive carved on the seats of other theatres and circuses, as at

Aphrodisias and Alexandria), and, like partisans of all periods, they dressed in a special way:

> the part of their tunic which came to their hands was gathered in very closely round the wrist, while the rest of the sleeve, as far as the shoulder, billowed out in great width. When they waved their hands about while they applauded at the theatre and at the Hippodrome, or while they urged on their favourites in the usual way, this part actually ballooned out, so that unsophisticated people thought that their physique was so fine and strong that they needed garments like these to cover them. ... Their cloaks and trousers and most of all their shoes were classed as 'Hunnic', both in name and style.[41]
>
> (Procopius, *Secret History* 7)

## East and west

Important changes were taking place in the east during this period. They included a burgeoning of urban life, in strong contrast to the west (Chapter 7), the impact of local cultures, especially in Syria and Mesopotamia, where the border area with Persia acted as a two-way channel for transmission of language, ideas and material culture, and the emergence of new identities. A real shift of emphasis took place within the empire towards the very provinces where the opposition to Chalcedon was strongest (though not universal), and where Islam was to make its first impact outside Arabia. But even as the western empire began to fragment, the east still attempted to maintain its relations with the west. We have seen that the developing papacy had to be taken into account in religious affairs, and the idea of an empire of both east and west was not lost. The conquest of North Africa by the Vandals, who had overrun it and ruled the former Roman province since 430, was a very serious blow to the empire. The eastern emperor Theodosius II also intervened to confront them, but the Roman army under Boniface and Aspar was defeated in 432 and retreated to Carthage; soon after, Valentinian III recognized Vandal possessions in Numidia. In 441 an expedition sent from Constantinople was recalled under pressure of a serious attack by the Huns;[42] peace was made and by 442 Geiseric had gained the important city of Carthage, as well as the rich provinces of Proconsularis and Byzacena in modern Tunisia.[43] In 468 the Emperor Leo launched a massive expedition to free North Africa from the Vandals. But despite its size (over 1,000 ships) and the fact that it represented a joint effort with the western government, the expedition proved an ignominious and catastrophic failure through incompetence and disunity among the command. The possibility of success slipped away, and the general in charge (the same Basiliscus who later staged a coup against Zeno) barely escaped the anger of the populace at Constantinople, while the financial consequences were disastrous. The expedition had allegedly cost 130,000 lb of gold (Procopius, *Wars* III.6), and it is a measure of the underlying prosperity of the east at this period that it was able to absorb such a loss virtually within a generation. It was perhaps characteristic that the eastern government chose to concentrate its military effort on the dramatic target presented by Vandal Africa, just as Justinian was to do, but the failure of the expedition ruled out any thought of similar intervention in Italy itself. The Vandals remained in control of North Africa until defeated by Belisarius in 533–4, and when the line of Roman emperors in the west came to an end in AD 476, the east was already resigned to the situation and proceeded to deal by a kind of de facto recognition with the barbarian leaders who succeeded them. It was easier to close one's eyes, and it was some time before Constantinople fully realized that the west was in practice divided into several barbarian kingdoms, particularly as the kings for their part tended to adopt a deferential tone towards the eastern emperor.[44]

A means of maintaining relations with the west was through dynastic marriage, though this too could mean military action. On the death of Honorius in 423, Theodosius II intervened to support the claims of the young Valentinian, grandson of Theodosius I, against the usurpation of a certain John; in order to do this he had to recognize the position of Valentinian's mother Galla Placidia, widow of Honorius' short-lived colleague Constantius III, whom he had refused to recognize as empress only two years before, and who had now fled to Constantinople.[45] A force was dispatched under the Alan Ardaburius and his son Aspar to install Galla Placidia and her son, and Valentinian was duly made Augustus, and married in Constantinople in 437 to Theodosius' daughter Licinia Eudoxia, to whom he had been betrothed as a child. For the first part of his reign Placidia acted as regent, and relations between east and west were good. But Valentinian proved a fragile reed, and the influence of the general Aetius accordingly grew. However, the western court was also making marriage alliances with the barbarians, and Valentinian himself agreed to betroth his tiny daughter Eudocia to the Vandal Huneric. Older imperial women sometimes took matters into their own hands: after Galla Placidia's death in 450, Valentinian's sister Justa Grata Honoria chose to get herself out of an awkward situation by offering herself to the Hun king Attila, a foolhardy action with dire consequences (Chapter 2), but one to which Theodosius II gave his support.[46] Luckily for Honoria, and certainly for the empire, Attila died first, having just taken a new wife, one Ildico, and his empire broke up:

> on the morrow, when most of the day had passed, the king's attendants, suspecting something was amiss, first shouted loudly and then broke open the doors. They found Attila unwounded but dead from a haemorrhage and the girl weeping with downcast face beneath her veil. Then, after the custom of their race, they cut off part of their hair and disfigured their already hideous faces with deep wounds to mourn the famous warrior not with womanly tears and wailings but with the blood of men.
>
> (Priscus, fr. 24, trans. R.C. Blockley)

On the death of Valentinian III in 455, the intervention of the eastern emperor was no longer sought, but the idea of an eastern intervention was not altogether lost, and in 467 Leo helped to elevate Anthemius, the son-in-law of Marcian. This involved an unequal contest with a rival candidate, Olybrius, who was married to Valentinian III's other daughter Placidia and was being promoted by the Vandal king. The combination of circumstances in Italy and the growing power of barbarian individuals and groups now made such interventions by the eastern emperor less and less relevant. Even so, certain aristocratic families in the west, especially in Italy, remained wealthy and important in the sixth century during Ostrogothic rule, and their voice continued to be heard in Constantinople. For this reason, too, the balance struck in Ostrogothic Italy between Goths and Romans had to be delicately maintained. We shall return to this issue below, and when considering Justinian's attempt to reconquer Italy in the sixth century (Chapter 5).

### The barbarian question in the east

The immediate danger to Constantinople and the east in 399–400 had been averted, but the barbarian danger to Constantinople was not yet solved. Leo I (457–74) came to the throne as a member of the staff of a powerful Alan, Aspar, the son of Ardaburius, and Aspar seems to have aspired to the same kind of influence exerted by comparable barbarian generals in the west. Determined that this should not happen, Leo tried to counteract the German influence by recruiting heavily for the army among the Isaurians, a mountain people living in Asia Minor. The future emperor Zeno (then called Tarasicodissa) was their chief and married Leo's daughter Ariadne. Though Leo had to make concessions to Aspar by marrying him to another of his daughters, the fact that Aspar was Arian probably helped Leo to take the next step, that of removing Aspar and his father by having them murdered (471). But the promotion of Isaurians also had problems. Contemporary writers are very hostile to them, and refer to Leo himself as 'the Butcher'.[47] Moreover, Zeno was deserted by some of the Isaurians, who supported Basiliscus, the brother of his mother-in-law, the Empress Verina, in a successful coup (475); he therefore fled back to the wild mountains. Luckily for Zeno, Basiliscus' Miaphysitism so alienated the people of Constantinople that Zeno was encouraged to stage a return and have him executed. But Zeno's problems continued, and Verina's supporters, especially her son-in-law Marcian and his brother, marched against him. This too was unsuccessful, but Zeno had to face yet another threat from his fellow-Isaurian, the powerful general Illus, which turned into a real war lasting several years, during which Illus proclaimed Marcian emperor and tried to get help from Odoacer in Italy (Chapter 2). Marcian not seeming to Verina to be the best candidate, Leontius was proclaimed in his stead, and crowned by the empress (484). In this context too Zeno was victorious, though the remnants of Illus' party held out in the mountains for another four years. One can imagine the ferment created by such a prolonged period of uncertainty, and the tendency of individuals to switch sides in the tangled network of alliances. Anyone with a grudge against the emperor was liable to see their salvation in opposing him, and indeed Illus' supporters included the pagan intellectual Pamprepius. Zeno also had to contend with other problems from barbarians: on the fall of Aspar in the previous reign, Theodoric Strabo, the Ostrogothic leader, had managed to make Leo buy the safety of the Balkans by extorting political and financial concessions which included his own recognition, and having inherited this situation Zeno's first years were spent in uneasy balancing acts between Strabo and another Gothic leader, confusingly also called Theodoric. The eastern government alternated between promises of payment and threats of war; meanwhile, Thrace and Illyricum were the prey of the second Theodoric, Ostrogoth and future ruler of Italy. This time the east was exposed to the type of barbarian pressure already familiar in the west, and eventually Zeno was compelled to make substantial concessions by giving Theodoric territory in Moesia and Dacia as well as making him Master of the Soldiers in 483 and consul in 484. Not surprisingly the policy failed, and Theodoric marched on Constantinople in 487. Fatefully for Italy, but fortunately for the east, an opportunity presented itself: Zeno was able to commission Theodoric, secretly of course, to replace Odoacer, the general who had deposed Romulus Augustulus in 476 and now ruled Italy, Sicily and Dalmatia. Theodoric defeated and killed Odoacer and far from ruling Italy on Zeno's behalf, as the latter had intended, gained control of Italy himself (Chapter 2).

The resilience of the east is remarkable. It was helped by its capacity to pay subsidies in gold, as it had done already to the Hun Rugila and his successor Attila under Theodosius II. Annual payments to Attila amounted to 700 lbs of gold and, after a defeat inflicted by him on the imperial troops in Thrace, increased to 2,100 lb, with a payment of 6,000 lb under the treaty of 443. The demands made by Attila drove the eastern government to despair, but the Hun king managed to foil an assassination plot made by the eunuch Chrysaphius. On Theodosius II's death, Marcian took the risky line of refusing to give in to this blackmail and ended the annual subsidy. Again the east was saved from danger, this time by a change of mind on the part of Attila, who now turned towards Italy, where as we have seen he soon met his premature death.

When Anastasius was elevated to the throne in Constantinople in 491, Theodoric the Ostrogoth was establishing himself in Italy. Both sides were cautious towards each other, but in 497 Anastasius recognized Theodoric, who still held the post of Master of the Soldiers, as ruler of Italy, though in some sense still within the protectorate of the empire. Theodoric's exact constitutional position was more a matter of tact and delicate manoeuvring than of hard and fast definition (Chapter 2), and there was still a considerable way to go before the shape of Ostrogothic rule became clearer. But even if in theory and in sentiment the ideal of a unified empire survived, by the end of the fifth century the barbarian kingdoms which were to be Rome's early medieval successors were coming into being. It was a situation to which Constantinople would have to adapt.[48]

# 2

# THE EMPIRE AND THE
# BARBARIANS

The questions dealt with in this chapter have been transformed by a deluge of publications in recent years. Attention has shifted from the problem of the late Roman army and its use of federate troops to the barbarians themselves, the impact on them of their contacts with Rome, the development of concepts of ethnicity as they came under Roman influence, Rome's usually unsuccessful, or at least short term, attempts to deal with the issue, and the gradual emergence of discrete groups and eventually of the early medieval kingdoms. Modern studies of migration and ethnic identity are also influential, and have been used as a corrective to the old stereotypes of barbarian invasion, based on prejudiced Roman sources, and sharp distinctions between civilized Romans and the barbarian 'other'.[1] These newer approaches also imply a critical reading of the very influential *Getica*, the mid-sixth century Latin work written in Constantinople by Jordanes, which employs the familiar technique of genealogy to claim for the Goths a mythic beginning in Scandinavia before their encounter with the Roman empire.[2] Equally, and in contrast with much earlier scholarship, it has now been suggested that the overall ethnic term 'Germanic' is better avoided. On the newer and sceptical model, the barbarian groups did not come with their ethnicity ready made but developed it under the influence of contacts with Rome.[3] A similar process is argued to have taken place in relation to the Arab federates in the east in the sixth century (Chapter 9). Rome had indeed long used and integrated barbarians, even while attempting to assert Roman identity over foreigners. Numbers, cultural transfer and identity formation are all key issues now, as are debates about the interpretation of material evidence. Another development has been a new understanding of frontiers and their functions, which has moved away from the old notion of a clear-cut fortified barrier.[4] The concept of hordes of barbarians pouring in and overwhelming the empire has been well and truly discarded. In the light of these developments, Roman policy towards the barbarians has also had to be rethought. But as we have seen, these changed approaches have also gone along with a re-assertion of what is often called 'the fall of the Roman empire in the west'. From the perspective of this book this needs to be placed in the context of greater continuity in the east in late antiquity, and these issues will recur in the following chapters.

*Figure 2.1* The artistic patronage of the late Roman aristocracy: a marriage casket adapted for a Christian couple, Proiecta and Secundus, from the Esquiline treasure, Rome, late fourth century. Trustees of the British Museum

## AD 476

The fifth century saw one of the most famous non-events in history – the so-called 'fall of the Roman empire in the west', which according to traditional views took place in 476, when the young Romulus Augustulus, the last Roman emperor in the west, was deposed and replaced by Odoacer, a Germanic military leader, who followed Ricimer (457–72) and Orestes (475–6) as power-broker. Odoacer differed from his barbarian predecessors in that he did not attempt to rule through a puppet emperor; he sent an embassy of Roman senators to the Emperor Zeno (474–91) in Constantinople asking to be given the prestigious title of *patricius*. Zeno had only recently secured his own throne from the serious threat mounted by Basiliscus, and the emperor's reply was equivocal; the deposed Julius Nepos, who was also now seeking his aid, had been placed on the western throne with eastern support in 473. However, Odoacer satisfied himself with the title *rex*, and henceforth the only emperor was the eastern emperor in Constantinople.[5] Zeno had other problems to contend with, including dealing with two powerful Gothic leaders, Theodoric the Amal and Theodoric Strabo (Chapter 1), but eventually used the former to put down Odoacer (493); Theodoric promptly succeeded him, founding the Ostrogothic kingdom and ruling Italy until 526. The date 476 has traditionally provided a convenient point at which to place the formal end of the Roman empire, and Procopius of Caesarea begins his history of Justinian's Gothic war (535–54) by recounting the history of Italy from that point. Gradually, though not immediately, the eastern empire came to terms with the fact that it was left alone as the upholder of Roman tradition, and invented its own myths of *translatio imperii* to justify its new role; this included the claim that the *palladium* of Rome had been buried under the great statue of Constantine in Constantinople.[6] But the year 476 has no significance in the context of the economic and social changes that were taking place in the period; it is doubtful whether even the population of Italy at first noticed much difference. The changes which were taking place were long term and multiple, part of a gradual process which ate away at Roman territory in the west through settlement and force of arms, and which made it increasingly difficult for the Roman government in the west to field an adequate army or prevent the erosion of its tax-raising powers;[7] the loss of the rich provinces of North Africa was very serious, and in Gaul and elsewhere the local elites often had no choice but to make their own accommodation with the settlers. Sidonius Apollinaris, bishop of Clermont-Ferrand in the 470s, and himself from the landowning class, exemplifies the dilemmas which now faced the old Roman elite, caught between trying to maintain a remembered lifestyle while coming to terms with their barbarian neighbours.[8] The *Life* of Severinus of Noricum (Austria) by Eugippius, set in the 470s, depicts a kind of no man's land where previous structures had broken down.[9] Eastern emperors tried on several occasions during the mid-fifth century to intervene in western affairs, but this became less and less feasible as time went on, so that the eventual invasion of Italy under Justinian seems extraordinary, if not even quixotic (Chapter 5). In political terms, the fall of the feeble Romulus Augustulus was entirely predictable. But identities were complex, especially after the death of Attila in 451.[10] Odoacer was the son of Edeco, a Hun or Thuringian, leader of the Sciri and one of Attila's close allies. But he was only one in a long line of generals who had held the real power in the western empire since the late fourth century. When one of the first and most powerful of these, Stilicho, the Vandal *magister militum* of Theodosius I and regent for his son Honorius, fell in 408, suspected of treason (above, Chapter 1), he was succeeded by Romans in the high positions of *magister utriusque militiae* and *patricius;* but real power still lay with barbarian generals, in particular Aetius (*c.* 433–54). After the murder of Valentinian III in 455, his successor Avitus, a Gallic senator, was defeated by the Sueve Ricimer and an uneasy period followed before Majorian was officially proclaimed emperor in 457, only to be killed by the same Ricimer four years later. Again Ricimer was kingmaker, but his undistinguished choice, Severus, who had not been ratified by the eastern emperor Leo, died in 465, again leaving the west without an official ruler. When Leo imposed Anthemius, his own choice, the rivalry between Anthemius and Ricimer became first a scandal and then the occasion for open hostilities, in the course of which Anthemius was killed (472). Ricimer's final choice for emperor was Olybrius, the Roman husband of Valentinian III's daughter Placidia (see Chapter 1); but both Olybrius and Ricimer died before the year was out. The nominee of the Burgundian Gundobad was deposed by Julius Nepos with the encouragement of the Emperor Leo, only to be deposed in his turn in favour of the ill-fated Romulus Augustulus. It is a dreary and confused story, in which the principal players vary between barbarian or Roman commanders and members of the civilian aristocracy, with the eastern emperor invoked at times for the sake of respectability and at times attempting to interpose his own choice. Only occasionally did these power struggles at the top have a direct impact on government; Majorian (457–61), for instance, issued reforming legislation, but soon fell at the hands of Ricimer. There was no western Leo or Zeno. No western emperor had succeeded in establishing strong government after the death of Theodosius I, and while the eastern government in the later fifth century under Marcian and Anastasius had become progressively more civilian in style, the exact opposite happened in the west. Nor could the western government be said to represent strong military rule; on the contrary, both the territories occupied by the western empire and the Roman army had itself by now suffered fragmentation on a major scale. These processes are closely interconnected, with roots reaching back to the fourth century, but they will be treated separately here for the sake of clarity.

### Romans and barbarians: the late fourth century onwards

We have inherited a dramatic view of the Roman empire in the west as being submerged by successive waves of northern barbarian invaders. In fact, interaction with peoples from beyond the Rhine and the Danube had been a fact of life since the Marcomannic wars of Marcus Aurelius in the late second century, and indeed earlier. Until the mid-fourth century, however, it had generally been possible to contain them by a judicious deployment of force and diplomacy. These were settled peoples with social hierarchies. The arrival on the scene in 376 of the Huns, a nomadic people perhaps originating in the steppe-lands of modern Khazakhstan,[11] was a decisive moment on any view; as we have seen, Ammianus believed that it forced the Tervingi and Greuthingi to cross the Danube into Roman territory and led to their settlement in the Balkans by the Emperor Valens.[12] The Greek and Roman sources depict the event in lurid colours, but the Goths were neither a terrified rabble nor part of a great wave of invaders sweeping over the Roman empire. Complex social and economic factors lay behind their appearance in later Roman history, and when they came, they came as an organized military force. Only two years later came the battle of Adrianople (378), a blow that Rome never forgot. The Roman defeat was the signal for other barbarian leaders to cross into Roman territory. Alaric and his Visigoths entered Italy in 401, were defeated by Stilicho in 402, but returned in 408 to sack Rome two years later (Chapter 1). In 405 a certain Radagaisus collected a large barbarian army from across the Rhine and Danube and invaded Italy; on his defeat by Stilicho, 12,000 of them were enrolled in the Roman army.[13] But from then on groups of Alans, Vandals and Sueves were on the move across Germany and Gaul and into Spain and almost at the same time the usurper Constantine moved from Britain into Gaul.[14] The numbers involved are hard to assess on the basis of the patchy sources. Heather estimates the size of Radagaisus' force alone at 20,000 fighting men, which implies 100,000 including the women, children and others who travelled with them.[15] The story is complex, and the course of events confused by rivalries between different groupings, not to mention the problems presented by the sources. By the late 420s, however, as we saw in Chapter 1, the Vandals under Gaiseric crossed the Straits of Gibraltar into North Africa, reached Augustine's see at Hippo by 430 and took Carthage in 439. They were able to sack Rome in 455 and take Sicily in 468. The situation in the northern provinces was less clear-cut, and unlike the Vandal occupation in North Africa, did not cut off the critical food supply to the city of Rome; nevertheless Roman government and defence were crucially eroded. In the difficult conditions of the first decade of the fifth century, Zosimus tells us that the defence of Britain was formally abandoned by Honorius: 'Honorius sent letters to the cities in Britain, urging them to fend for themselves.'[16] Some of the troops in Britain, who had apparently supported usurpers before 406, remained in the province, but there was no longer a central authority, and Saxon raids now exacerbated the already confused situation. The rapid disappearance of Roman towns in Britain after several centuries of Roman rule is only one of the many puzzling features of the period.[17] In mainland Europe, the fifth century saw a lengthy jostling for position as different groups competed against each other and with Rome for land and influence. The west suffered more than once from the greater ability of the east to avert the danger by financial and diplomatic means, most conspicuously in the case of Alaric and the Visigoths, who were allowed by the eastern government to build up their strength in the Balkans, only to use it against Italy, demand large amounts of gold and silver and eventually sack Rome.[18] The sack itself, while perhaps not as destructive as it might have been, came as an enormous psychological blow to Christians and pagans alike, and caused many leading members of the Roman aristocracy to flee. But the chance event of Alaric's own death shortly afterwards, like that of Attila in a similar situation later, saved Rome from the possibility of long-term occupation. The Visigoths moved north under Athaulf and eventually ended up in Aquitaine, after a series of confusing episodes during which Galla Placidia married successively Athaulf and Constantius, *magister militum* and co-emperor in 421, and gave birth to the future Valentinian III (425–55).[19] The aftermath depended on the changing configurations of barbarian groupings, and their respective success in dealing with the imperial government (and vice versa). Various means were used. Further settlements were made *c.* 440 by the *magister militum* Aetius, of Alans in Gaul and Burgundians north of Geneva. Meanwhile, a new threat was posed by the Hun king Attila, who, having already extracted large subsidies, crossed the Danube in the early 440s, defeated the Roman armies sent against him on two occasions and succeeded in obtaining even higher annual payments of gold. He eventually turned towards the west, accepted the advances of Valentinian III's sister Honoria and demanded half the empire. The battle between the forces of Attila and Aetius on the Catalaunian Fields which followed in 451

*Figure 2.2* Composite buckle, Ostrogothic style, inlaid with cloisonné garnets, green glass and shell in gold cellwork, late fifth–early sixth century. Found in a female grave near the gate of the church of St Severin, Cologne. Trustees of the British Museum

was a temporary check, but did not prevent the Huns from invading Italy.[20] Again, the western empire had a lucky escape, for Attila's death (Chapter 1) brought the break-up of the Hun empire and removed the danger.

From now on, as the western government became progressively weaker, and it became less and less possible to sustain any coherent policy in relation to barbarian settlement. Even in the vacuum left by the death of Theodosius I in 395, Rome still occupied the centre in the shifting game of barbarian movements; by the end of the century no Roman emperor was left in the west, and we can see the first stage in the development of the early medieval kingdoms.[21] The first to be established was, as we have seen, that of the Vandals in North Africa. However, it was untypical in that it was overthrown by the imperial armies under Belisarius in AD 534 and replaced by well-established Byzantine rule lasting at least in part until the late seventh century. North Africa, in fact, represents the success story of Justinian's policy of reconquest; the irony was, however, that in contrast with the long history of Roman Africa before the arrival of the Vandals, the restored imperial province was governed by easterners from Constantinople whose language of administration was Greek (Chapter 5). The longest lasting of the Germanic kingdoms was that of the Franks,

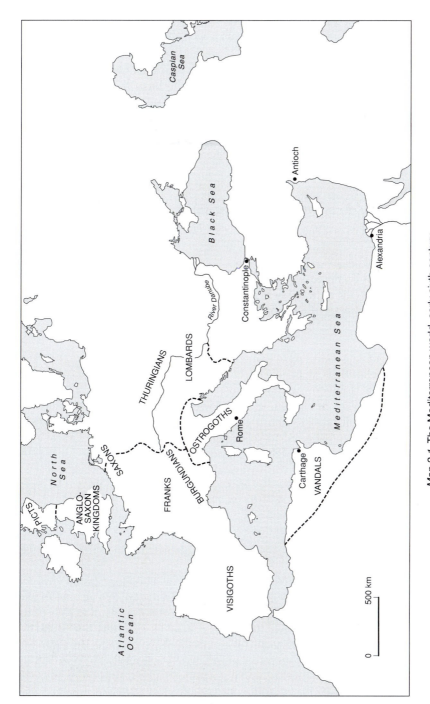

*Map 2.1* The Mediterranean world, early sixth century

established by their king Clovis (481–511) after their defeat of the Visigoths at Vouillé in 507 and lasting until 751. Although it was the Franks who gave their name to modern France. Clovis' descendants are usually known as the Merovingians.[22] They found a vivid chronicler in the late sixth-century bishop Gregory of Tours, whose *History of the Franks* is our main source, remarkable not least for its unrestrained cataloguing of the bloodthirsty doings of the Frankish royal family.[23]

Gregory provides a colourful account of the conversion and baptism of Clovis: the king's wife Clotild was already a Christian and tried unsuccessfully to convert her husband, but his reaction when her first son died after being baptized was one of anger:

> If he had been dedicated in the name of my gods, he would have lived without question; but now that he has been baptized in the name of your God he has not been able to live a single day!
>
> (*HF* II.29)

The king was finally converted after successfully praying to the Christian God for victory on the field of battle against the Alamanni, and was then baptized by bishop Remigius of Rheims, who, we are assured by Gregory, had raised a man from the dead.[24] The scene of the king's baptism was spectacular:

> The public squares were draped with coloured cloths, the churches were adorned with white hangings, the baptistry was prepared, sticks of incense gave off clouds of perfume, sweet-smelling candles gleamed bright and the holy place of baptism was filled with divine fragrance. God filled the hearts of all present with such grace that they imagined themselves to have been transported to some perfumed paradise. King Clovis asked that he might be baptized first by the Bishop. Like some new Constantine he stepped forward to the baptismal pool, ready to wash away the scars of his old leprosy and to be cleansed in flowing water from the sordid stains which he had borne so long.
>
> (*HF* II.31)

In this mass spectacle, more than 3,000 of his army were said to have been baptized at the same time.

In Italy, the Ostrogothic kingdom founded by Theodoric lasted until 554 when its last king, Teias, was finally defeated by Justinian's general Narses after nearly twenty years of warfare (Chapter 5). But the arrival in Italy of the Lombards in 568 meant that Byzantine control in Italy was not to last for long, except in a limited (though still important) form from the late sixth until the mid-eighth centuries under an exarch based at Ravenna.[25] After 568 the situation in Italy was confused and fragmented, and it was in this period that the popes, especially Gregory the Great (590–604), acquired much of their enormous secular influence and economic power.

Ostrogothic Italy retained many continuities with the Roman past,[26] among them the survival of many of the immensely rich and aristocratic Roman families who continued to hold office under the new regime. It is a remarkable fact that the Roman senate survived during the fifth century, through all the political changes, and its members continued to be appointed to traditional offices and to hold the western consulship even under the Ostrogoths; the consulship was in fact ended by Justinian himself in 541.[27] Many of these Roman families were extremely wealthy, and Procopius, who describes the Gothic wars in detail from the eastern point of view, particularly identifies with this class, most of whom lost their land and position, and many of whom were reduced to a pitiable state by the Justinianic war, unless they were able to flee to the east where they often also possessed estates.[28] Like many others of this class, Cassiodorus, whose highly rhetorical and bureaucratic Latin letters (*Variae*), many written as Theodoric's *quaestor*, are another of our main sources for the period, was one of the prominent Italians who left for Constantinople.[29] Before that, he had written a *Gothic History*, used by Jordanes in his *Getica*,[30] and after the wars ended and he had returned to Italy, the *Institutes*, a set of precepts on Christian learning, and other theological works. Cassiodorus founded the monastery of Vivarium on his family estate near Squillace, which was to become one of the most important medieval centres for the copying and preservation of classical texts. A traumatic event had taken place in relations between the Ostrogoths and the Roman upper class in Italy in AD 523–4, when Theodoric had unexpectedly turned on and eventually executed two of its most prominent members, Symmachus and Boethius, author of the Latin classic, the *Consolation of Philosophy*. The case was sensational – Symmachus held one of the most prestigious names among the late Roman aristocracy, while Boethius' two sons had both been given the consulship and he had been consul himself in 510 and was Theodoric's *magister officiorum*. Boethius' *Consolation* was written in prison as he mused on his fate; he imagines himself

*Figure 2.3* Coin of Theodoric the Ostrogoth (d. 526). Trustees of the British Museum

visited by the Lady Philosophy, and engages in extended discussion of fate, free will and the fickleness of fortune, and includes a number of long poems, which are of themselves of great interest.[31] But the deaths of Symmachus and Boethius were exceptional; Theodoric seems to have shared the general respect for Roman tradition, and the Ostrogothic regime was not in general oppressive.[32]

The defeat of the Visigoths by Clovis at Vouillé in AD 507 put an effective end to their kingdom in Gaul, which had had its capital at Toulouse since 418, and to the descent of the Balt dynasty which had ruled since Alaric I at the end of the fourth century.[33] In the troubled period which followed, Theodoric, whose daughter had married the son of the Visigothic Alaric II, intervened, and Visigothic rule passed temporarily into Ostrogothic hands. More important in the longer term, however, was the movement of the Visigoths into Spain, which had already happened before the end of the fifth century; there, especially from the time of the Ostrogothic Theudis (431–48), they were to establish a kingdom which, despite some Byzantine success in the context of Justinian's reconquest, lasted until the arrival of the Arabs in the early eighth century.[34]

## Barbarian settlement, the Roman state and the early medieval kingdoms

With the establishment of the barbarian kingdoms we pass into the traditional realm of early medieval history. But the continuities are such that it can also be argued that the period up to the later sixth century was still part of a surviving Mediterranean world of late antiquity. Despite the obvious changes in settlement patterns in the west, the available archaeological evidence seems to show that long-distance exchange and travel still went on, even if in reduced form.[35] The western kingdoms retained many Roman institutions, and even saw their relation with the emperor in Constantinople in terms of patronage. Their kings received Roman titles, and the former Roman upper classes survived in substantial numbers and adapted themselves in various ways to the new regimes. One who adapted, as we have seen, was Sidonius Apollinaris, of whom Gregory of Tours writes:

> He was a very saintly man, and as I have said, a member of one of the foremost senatorial families. Without saying anything to his wife he would remove silver vessels from his home and give them away to the poor. When she found out, she would grumble at him; then he would buy the silver vessels back from the poor folk and bring them home again.
>
> (*HF* II.22)

Both Gregory of Tours, the historian of the Franks, and Gregory's contemporary and friend Venantius Fortunatus, himself a Merovingian bishop and the author of Latin poems on political and contemporary subjects, came from this class, as did Pope Gregory the Great.[36] Germanic law existed in uneasy juxtaposition with Roman; the Ostrogothic kingdom had one law for the Goths and another for the Roman population, while successive Visigothic law codes, beginning with the Code of Euric (c. 476) and the Romanizing Lex Romana Visigothorum of Alaric II (506), followed by an extensive programme of lawmaking in the Visigothic kingdom of the sixth and seventh centuries, gradually brought about a unification of the German and the Roman traditions.[37] The eastern government pursued a pragmatic policy, knowing that it was in no position to impose a western emperor, but not admitting (or, no doubt, believing) that the current regimes were permanent. When the time came, it was ready to use one against another. The fact that the Goths in Italy, like the Vandals and, at this period, the Visigoths, were Arian was, perhaps paradoxically, a help to imperial diplomacy, for it made it possible to represent Justinian's invasion of Italy in 535 in religious terms. Seeking aid from the catholic Franks, the emperor wrote:

> The Goths have seized Italy, which is our possession, by force, and have not only refused to return it, but have committed wrongs against us which are past endurance. For this reason we have been forced to go to war against them, a war in which both our common hatred of the Goths and our orthodox faith dictates that you should join us, so as to dislodge the Arian heresy.
>
> (Proc., *Wars* IV.5.8–9)

The imperial rhetoric was backed by gold, and by the promise of more if the Franks agreed; not surprisingly, perhaps, they were not to prove very loyal allies.

In studying the process of barbarian settlement in the territory of the western empire, we must distinguish between formal grants made by successive emperors and governments and the longer process of informal settlement patterns. In practice, a continuous process of settlement reaching back at least to the fourth century had long ago undermined Roman control of the west and, through the use of non-Romans as troops, had eroded any sense in which there could still be a single Roman army. Control of the land, and therefore of tax revenues, was also seriously affected (see below).[38] Contemporary literary sources written from the Roman point of view are imbued with anti-barbarian stereotyping, and give only a very imperfect and one-sided picture of the process and extent of settlement, and consequently historians have turned to the evidence from archaeological finds, especially those from graves, as markers of different barbarian 'cultures'. However, this approach has also been challenged as too simplistic and as methodologically unsound; reading off ethnicity from grave goods can be as deceptive as taking the literary sources at face value.[39] The reasons for settlement might vary greatly, from invasion and imperial grants of land to resettlement through service in the Roman army, and it is often difficult to identify the reasons in individual cases. In the same way, it is often impossible to connect known historical events such as invasions, or even in some cases longer-term settlement mentioned in literary evidence, with available archaeological remains. The newcomers often tended to take over the customs of the existing provincial population, making traces of barbarian settlement even harder to detect. There are obvious resonances, even if also differences, with issues of migration and settlement in today's world. In the present case, despite the many difficulties and controversies surrounding the archaeological evidence, a steady process of small-scale cultural and demographic change had been taking place in the western provinces long before the formation of the barbarian kingdoms as we know them. The scale of this process, with the concomitant economic factors, was such that by the mid-fifth century the former Roman villas in the western provinces had in many cases been abandoned or gone into decline, and the role of the former Roman landowning class been transformed.[40] In the western provinces the Roman government was not so much faced with discrete incursions as with a slow but steady erosion of Roman culture from within. The process was not of course understood in these terms by contemporary writers, who paint a lurid picture of Romans versus 'barbarians'; for this reason contemporary interpretations of highly charged events such as the battle of Adrianople and the barbarian settlements which followed it are particularly liable to mislead.[41] The moral and political explanations given in the literary sources are not adequate to explain what was happening on a broader scale, and indeed, most of the long-term changes lay outside government control. Yet it was these changes, rather than any political events, which would in the long run detach these areas from effective imperial rule, and fatally so once that control passed from the hands of a weak western emperor to those of a government in far-away Constantinople.

The impact of this process on the late Roman economy was profound (see Chapter 4).[42] But wealth also played a direct role in the empire's dealings with barbarians in the fifth century in the form of the subsidies paid by the Roman government to various groups, either as reward for quiescence or as inducements to go elsewhere; again modern parallels are striking. Although the eastern government was better placed to make use of this device than the western (Chapter 1), and was still making large payments to some groups in the late sixth century (Chapter 8), the policy proved useful at different times to both.[43] When the new emperor Justin II cut off subsidies to the Avars in 566 this was highly provocative, but Justinian's use of subsidies was scathingly criticized by the conservative Procopius:

> On all his country's potential enemies he [sc. Justinian] lost no opportunity of lavishing vast sums of money – on those to East, West, North and South, as far as the inhabitants of Britain and the nations in every part of the known world.
>
> (*Secret History* 19)

The convenient practice of using barbarian troops as federates for the Roman army, a prominent feature of this period, was also expensive, and their maintenance could involve money as well as supplies.[44] But the amounts of gold that might be involved as subsidies or payments to barbarian leaders were large: in AD 408, for example, Alaric demanded 4,000 lb of gold for his recent operations on behalf of the imperial government in Epirus. The example of Alaric and his Goths also shows how easily clever barbarian leaders could play off east and west. The Visigoths are said to have invaded Italy in 401 because the eastern government had cut off their regular subsidies.[45] Why this should have happened is not clear, but Thrace was also threatened at the time by Goths under Gainas and other barbarians who are described as Huns; at any rate, Alaric saw more advantage in moving against Italy, where he was alternately fought and bought off by Stilicho. The latter's dangerous policy of attempting to buy the service of Alaric and his troops ended when he himself fell in AD 408; but when this happened and Alaric's demands for payment in return for retreating to Pannonia were rejected, and he besieged Rome (408–9), he fixed the price of movements of food into the city at 5,000 lb of gold and 30,000 lb of silver.[46] The cat-and-mouse game continued, and we find Alaric's successor Athaulf alternately plundering Italy and fighting on the Roman side in Gaul.

> When Athaulf became king, he returned again to Rome, and whatever had escaped the first sack his Goths stripped bare like locusts, not merely despoiling Italy of its private wealth but also of its public resources.
>
> (Jordanes, *Get.* 31)

His marriage to Galla Placidia was another kind of barbarian manipulation:

> Then Athaulf set out for Gaul, leaving Honorius Augustus stripped of his wealth, to be sure, yet pleased at heart because he was now a sort of kinsman of his.
>
> (ibid.)

In 418 what remained of the Gothic army of Alaric was settled on Roman land in Aquitaine: 'they received land in Aquitaine from Toulouse to the ocean'.[47] The twenty or more years of plundering, negotiating, bargaining and fighting before the Gothic settlement vividly demonstrate the ambiguities, the cost and the dangers with which the Romans were faced in their attempts to deal with the barbarians. Nor is it clear on what terms the land was granted, or later settlements were made; indeed, they must surely have varied from one case to another.[48] The traditional view is that the barbarians, beginning with the Visigoths, were to be entitled to a share of the land on which they were settled, in the surprisingly high proportion of two-thirds to one-third. Examples would be the settlements of Alans and Burgundians in 440 and 443 (*Chron. Min.* I.660) and Ostrogothic Italy, where, however, the share may have been one-third rather than two-thirds; the rent paid on the share thus received was itself known as 'thirds' (*tertiae*).[49] But there are many uncertainties, arising not least from discrepancies among the sources and a lack of hard evidence. A generation ago Walter Goffart proposed a quite different reading of the evidence from the later law codes, according to which it was not the land itself, but the tax revenues from the estates which were divided between barbarians and Romans,[50] and this has given rise (and still does) to intense discussion. Controversy surrounds the meanings of the Latin terms *hospitalitas* and *sors*, and the evidence is very incomplete; in practice, arrangements probably changed with changing conditions, and while land does seem to have been at issue in the settlement with the Visigoths in 418, it may not have been in the case of the Ostrogoths and does not accord with evidence from Cassiodorus.[51] By contrast, there is no evidence from northern Gaul, for example, to tell us about the arrangements which were made there. The reality was surely more varied than has usually been allowed in modern debate, and the fifth century in any case only marked the beginning of a much longer process.[52] But while the settlement of barbarians may not have represented an 'existential struggle',[53] it did spell the end of the Roman empire in the west. The question may indeed be asked why these groups, once settled, did not integrate fully and simply become absorbed. But they had by then begun to develop their own identity, and the answer may be that it was simply too late.

## Barbarians and the late Roman army

It has often seemed as though it was the Roman army that was spectacularly unable to defend the western provinces; one historian has called his chapter on the fifth century 'The disappearance of an army'.[54] What had happened to the Roman army, and why it does it seem to have been so unsuccessful? Older assumptions were that the recruitment of barbarians into the army was one of the factors that led to poorer performance. This is a factor mentioned in the contemporary sources, together with complaints about weakened frontiers. The latter is usually blamed on a particular emperor – thus the pagan historian Zosimus lays most of the blame on the Christian Constantine. Soldiers are regularly depicted in the sources from the fourth century onwards as debauched, 'soft' and undisciplined. The late Roman practice of billeting soldiers in towns often lies behind such criticisms, and indeed in the early empire, citizens of the more peaceful provinces had rarely seen soldiers at first hand, much less experienced their rough behaviour.[55] The anonymous author of the treatise *De Rebus Bellicis* (late 360s) already complains about the high cost of the army and the weakening of frontier defence (*De Rebus Bellicis* 5), and the soldiers settled on the frontiers known as *limitanei* are frequently blamed for alleged poor performance.[56]

The fact that these complaints come in so stereotyped a form indicates that their form has much to do with the prejudices of the contemporary sources. But the army of the late fourth and fifth centuries was certainly different from that of the early empire.[57] Many of the changes, such as the stationing of troops in or near cities rather than in large masses on the frontiers, stemmed from the fact that under the reforms of Diocletian and Constantine the late Roman army was paid in supplies as well as in cash: there was a simple need for troops to be near the sources of collection of the taxes in kind which were now among their chief sources of pay. Provisioning the army and paying the soldiers in kind involved enormous logistical efforts, and from the fourth century there was a gradual reintroduction of pay in cash, especially gold, and particularly in the west.[58] According to the sources, Diocletian had strengthened frontier defence installations throughout the empire, but studies of the fortress of Lejun in Jordan and elsewhere show that the size of late Roman frontier fortresses and of the legions which manned them was far smaller than in the early empire. The late Roman army was the product of gradual evolution rather than of sudden change, and this evolution arose from a combination of different reasons, though it is true that the effects were felt acutely in the late fourth- and fifth-century west where fragmentation and progressive settlement, with a consequently lower tax revenue, were serious factors. The loss of the North African provinces to the Vandals also had a major impact on the resources of the east. However, by the sixth century, interruptions in army pay were also a constant complaint in the eastern sources, and the government was finding it increasingly hard to keep up numbers; it was able to field only small forces even for its prestige endeavours in Italy. Roman and Persian military dealings in the sixth century were also hampered by the fact that troop numbers in the eastern frontier areas seem to have been reduced (see Chapter 5).[59] By this stage also, barbarian bands known as *bucellarii* had come very near to being the personal retainers of individual generals, and reliance on mounted archers increased, part of a trend towards cavalry which had been taking place gradually over a long period, partly in response to the threat posed by Sasanian heavy-armed cavalry; however, Belisarius in Africa and Narses in Italy in the sixth century both still had a majority of infantry under their command.[60]

By the fifth century the Roman army included a high proportion of barbarian troops (Elton estimates that one in four soldiers in field armies were non-Roman). The recruitment of barbarians was certainly not new, but from the late fourth century units of barbarian troops had constituted a crucial element in late Roman military organization, even though they are for the most part not listed in the *Notitia Dignitatum*. This in itself tells us that the *Notitia*, which gives a set of 'paper' figures, is an unreliable guide to the nature of the Roman army as it was in practice. Barbarians could appear in several different guises – as units, in relatively small groups or as individuals enlisted by commanders for individual campaigns. In any of these cases, they had to be paid, whether through the *annona*, the official distribution in kind to the troops via the tax system, or directly in money and supplies. In the past such barbarian troops had frequently been drawn from outside the empire, but with the process of barbarian settlement a fundamental change took place and they came more and more from within the confines of the empire itself. There is little direct evidence that such troops were any less effective than Romans.[61] Some contemporaries naturally thought otherwise, and there was much contemporary concern during the aftermath of the battle of Adrianople; the military treatise of Vegetius, probably of this period, also reflects this conservative view. But if rank-and-file barbarian soldiers were not usually a problem, it was otherwise with powerful individuals, and we have already seen the power gained by individual barbarian generals who rose to hold the highest office of *magister militum*: Stilicho, Ricimer and Odoacer are the most conspicuous examples, and they posed a rather different threat.[62] This too began in the fourth century, and barbarian officers are frequently mentioned in the military narrative of Ammianus covering the years 353 to 378. In the ranks, barbarians held a variety of statuses, including those of *laeti* and *gentiles*, both referring to groups of settlers with an obligation to military service, *foederati*, individually recruited barbarians or units enrolled through treaties,[63] and *dediticii*, prisoners of war from beyond the frontiers. In practice there were probably barbarian troops in all the many different units of the army. Rather than appealing to a general drop in manpower (which is hard to establish), the explanation for this change is probably simply that it was easy. Barbarians were available in large, if not massive, numbers, and utilizing them in the army was a convenient way of deciding what to do with them and, it was hoped, also of neutralizing any capacity they might have for disruption; moreover the process did not interfere with the interests of the landowners who were emerging as more and more powerful in this period.

## The late Roman army

Barbarian invasion is one of the classic explanations put forward for the fall of the empire. It further implies the ineffectiveness of the late Roman army to contain the situation.[64] One issue is that of size: how large an army was at the disposal of the late Roman state? While calculations based on the *Notitia Dignitatum* (which lists the eastern army establishment *c.* 394 and the western one of *c.* 420) are difficult to make, they seem to suggest a size well over 400,000 or even more, depending on one's interpretation.[65] The mid-sixth-century writer John the Lydian gives a figure of over 435,000 (*De mens.* I.27), and later in the sixth century Agathias gives a total of 645,000 (*Hist.*V.13). The latter must be much too high even as a paper calculation, and it is simply incredible that the empire could have sustained so vastly increased an army. As we have seen, the *Notitia* also fails to take into account the very large proportion of barbarian federate troops who actually did much of the fighting, and Agathias admits that by his own day the actual overall size had been reduced to 150,000: 'whereas there should have been a total effective fighting force of six hundred and forty-five thousand men, the number had dropped during this period to barely one hundred and fifty thousand' (*Hist.* V.13). From the fifth century at least, the western government was simply no longer in a position to control the empire by military means. We must therefore conclude that the high figures tell us little or nothing about actual troop deployment; it is more important to understand the fragmentation of the army into several field armies and border commands and the limits on its effective deployment than to rely on overall size.[66] Roman urbanism and the Roman presence in the Balkans had suffered a severe decline by the end of the sixth century, Slav invasions brought more insecurity, and towns in the east often preferred even in the Justinianic period to make their own terms with Persian armies; the same pattern was repeated after the failure of Roman troops against the Arabs at the River Yarmuk in 636 (Chapter 9). Similarly, the changes in, or, as Roman writers saw it, the progressive weakening of the frontier system, should also be seen in the contexts of the long-term transformation of local settlement-patterns and of economic and social change. For contemporaries the concept of the frontier was an emotive issue; a simple equation was made between failing to keep up the frontier defences and 'letting in the barbarians'. Diocletian was remembered for having strengthened the frontiers by the building and repair of forts, Constantine for having 'weakened' them by supposedly withdrawing troops into a mobile field army:

> Constantine destroyed this security [i.e., Diocletian's alleged strong frontier defence] by removing most of the troops from the frontiers and stationing them in cities which did not need assistance, thus both stripping of protection those being molested by the barbarians and subjecting the cities left alone by them to the outrages of the soldiers, so that henceforth most have become deserted.
>
> (Zos., *New Hist.* II.34)

The actual situation was much more complex. Although the literary sources are unsatisfactory and the archaeological evidence hard to assess overall, the latter shows clearly enough the steady development of installations such as watch-towers and fortified stores-bases whose functions included ensuring the supply-system to such forward troops as remained, as well as watching and if possible controlling barbarians within Roman territory. It was now impossible to maintain a defensive line which could really keep barbarians outside the empire, and a variety of local expedients recognized contemporary realities.[67] The expedients chosen differed very much from one part of the empire to another, depending on the terrain and the nature of the threat; in northern Gaul a series of coastal forts had gradually come into being over a very long period; in North Africa the so-called *fossatum Africae* to the south was no help against Vandals arriving from across the Straits of Gibraltar; in the east, where there had never been a fortified line as such, the desert zones on the one hand and the powerful military organization and aggressive policies of the Sasanians on the other, presented a totally different situation. The many defensive installations in the eastern frontier region in the later empire may in any case have been designed not only for defence against invaders from outside the empire but also for the maintenance of internal security.

The apparently successful defence system of the early empire had worked largely because in most areas there had been no serious threat; once, however, nearly all the erstwhile frontier was under pressure there was no serious chance of maintaining it in the same way, and recourse was made of necessity to whatever best fitted local conditions. The change is best seen in the case of the northern provinces, where the old concentrations of force on the Rhine and Danube can now be seen to have been replaced by a fragmented and complex mixture of ad hoc and often unsuccessful defences. In the confused conditions of the fifth century it must often have been difficult to know exactly not only who was defending and who was attacking but also what was being threatened. Political factors compounded the local ones. In the fifth century, when, as we have seen, real power was often held by Germanic military leaders, the official abandonment of Britain by Honorius had been preceded by the suppression of Constantine III, who had been proclaimed by the soldiers in Britain; it was followed by the proclamation of another counter-emperor, Jovinus, at Mainz, whose support seems to have lain among Burgundians, Alans and Franks. In the confused conditions which followed, the elevation in 421 of Constantius, who had defeated Constantine III and married Galla Placidia, marked merely another passing event in a situation in which it must for much of the time have been difficult simply to know who was who.

When for some periods in the west, at least, it is hard to see the Roman army as anything other than a variety of different units without unitary structure or control, it is hardly surprising that the organization, supply and command of the diverse units which made up the late Roman army in the empire as a whole should have proved so difficult. Even if we take a less robust view of the actual numbers of troops, the sheer maintenance of the army can be seen to have posed a variety of problems in the fifth century, of which cost was only one. Once barbarian settlement was allowed and encouraged, the old frontiers no longer even pretended to keep out barbarians in any meaningful sense, while the growing presence of barbarians within the empire, combined with the activities of leaders such as Alaric and Gainas, meant that the army itself was hardly any longer an army of 'Romans'. Difficulties of recruitment in the face of the mounting power of landowners and their unwillingness to release labour, supply problems and the weakening of government structures, especially in the west, all contributed to make the late Roman army (if one can still describe it in such unitary terms) difficult, and in the west impossible, to maintain and control. Most of the literary sources harked back to supposedly better days which had gone for ever, but the sources also had a rhetoric of their own. When Synesius in Cyrenaica, who had lived with the bitter realities of provincial life for himself, says with tired resignation 'Pentapolis is dead', that is one thing;[68] but when conservative historians such as Zosimus, or Procopius, who also tended to be the most vocal, fail to understand the depth of the structural change that had taken place, and prefer to lay the blame on moral factors or individuals, we need to be fully aware how far such judgements have been conditioned by the education and cultural background of the writers.

## The erosion of the west

Late antiquity was a time of profound change, and if the impact of the barbarians was at times a matter of military conflict, it was also characterized by a gradual movement and seepage of new peoples into the former imperial territories. Even if we give up the old-established model of enormous numbers of invaders swamping the existing population, the effects of these changes were fundamental. No state in history can survive unchanged for ever; all are dependent on external factors as well as internal ones and so it was with Rome.[69] Since the reasons for this continuous migration of northern peoples remain obscure, one might be tempted to conclude that the voluminous historical literature on 'decline and fall' has in fact failed in its attempt to explain the end of the Roman empire in the west. But simple explanations are always inadequate for complex historical change. The negative attitudes of the Romans themselves towards barbarians, and their own tendency to see the problem in very black and white terms contributed largely to the problems and made serious integration and acculturation of barbarians more difficult. At the same time the process of barbarian settlement in the western provinces, whether ad hoc or officially encouraged, and the recruitment of barbarian troops in the Roman army, brought profound changes to social, economic and military structures which were in many cases already precarious, the nature of which was not readily understood by contemporaries and which they had few means of controlling. It was not a matter simply of invasion or conflict, but of development and dynamic relations. But we must also remember that the east in the fifth century, even while undergoing similar processes to those in the west, and facing similar dangers, supported a strengthened civilian government and increasingly prosperous economy, and kept its administrative and military structures sufficiently in place to be able to launch offensive wars in the west on a large scale under Justinian; this fact alone should be enough to make us remember the critical importance of context and local differences in explaining historical change.

# 3

# CHRISTIANIZATION AND ITS CHALLENGES

In the eighty or so years that elapsed between the so-called Edict of Milan (AD 313) and the legislation of Theodosius I, culminating in 391–2 (Introduction), the Christian church and its bishops had gained a strong position within the Roman state. Most historians would also agree that Christianity itself was by now a powerful factor in society at large, even though it was still very far from universally embraced. An emphasis on religion, and on Christianization in all its forms – belief, practice, art and architecture, social organization – is a key part of the modern concept of 'late antiquity'. But the ways in which this development is viewed by modern historians differ widely. The range of views has included, on the one hand, endorsement of the hostile attitude of Gibbon and, on the other, a triumphalist Christian perspective still apparent in some contemporary works. Other scholars play down the degree of religious change and emphasize the longevity and vitality of polytheism.[1] In much current writing on late antiquity, a cultural studies approach prevails; this can be seen in many contributions to the important *Journal of Early Christian Studies*. This agenda has also led to attempts to downplay the stress on religion and look for the secular, and for signs of religious indifference.[2] Emphasis on the importance of discourse, and on a rhetorical analysis of Christian texts, are increasingly prominent elements in the secondary literature,[3] and it remains a major challenge to reconcile these approaches with theological ones, and do justice to the enormous amount of Christian writing from the period.[4] In an earlier generation A.H.M. Jones and many others also made the growth of the church an important factor in explaining the end of the Roman empire.[5] Appearing only one year after Jones's *Later Roman Empire*, E.R. Dodds's classic *Pagan and Christian in an Age of Anxiety*[6] set a different agenda, asking whether and why the period from the third century onwards was more 'spiritual' than what had gone before. Dodds himself approached the issues in rationalizing and psychological terms, but his simple question has lain behind much of the flood of writing in recent years about holy men and ascetics, as well as the assumptions of a generation of leading art historians.[7] Much current writing is concerned to show that such preconceptions fail to do justice to the complexities of religion or religious change in late antiquity; indeed, other scholars prefer to concentrate on material culture or quantitative evidence.

Even when the power of religious beliefs to exercise a dynamic force in history is recognized, the amount of surviving evidence is such, and the level of bias in many of the sources also so great that it is still extremely challenging to understand the real nature of late antique religious change or the real religious contours of late antiquity. High on the list of questions now being addressed are: the date when paganism finally ceased to be a real alternative; the relations between Christians and Jews and the nature of Judaism and Jewish communities in late antiquity; the struggle to define Christian orthodoxy and condemn and eradicate heresy; the separation of the Chalcedonian and non-Chalcedonian churches after the failure of imperial efforts to preserve church unity; and, at the end of our period, the emergence of Islam as a new monotheistic religion.

Several collective works have been published in recent years on Christianity in late antiquity. Volumes two and (particularly) three of the French *Histoire du christianisme des origines à nos jours* cover most of our period,[8] and volume two of the *Cambridge History of Christianity*, edited by A. Casiday and F.W. Norris,[9] deals with the post-Constantinian period to 600. It is true, however, as powerfully argued by J. Rüpke,[10] that most of the huge amount of scholarship on religion, and especially on Christianity, in late antiquity has yet to contextualize it fully in relation to the dynamic social, political and economic developments in the period. As Rüpke writes, 'intensive inter-action across ethnic and religious divides is evident everywhere. It is manifested in social contacts and elite formation, in philosophical thinking and in juridical procedure, in architectural style and in economic exchanges.'[11] Studies of conversion manifest similar problems.[12] The level of Christianization is extremely hard to judge, and is often over-estimated when the Christian sources are taken too much at face value,[13] and the continuance of paganism or polytheism is misunderstood for similar reasons. The present chapter does not aim to solve these problems of methodology but rather to provide an introduction to key factors in religious development, inevitably with a focus on Christianity and starting with some basics.

## The physical setting: church building

In the post-Constantinian period churches became progressively grander and more visible. Once persecution ended, the way was opened for the development of ecclesiastical architecture as such. Constantine ringed the city of Rome with new churches built at established sites of Christian worship connected with the martyrs,[14] and city churches included St Peter's, over the site traditionally associated with Peter's death and burial, and the Lateran basilica, which became the cathedral church. He and his mother Helena each built churches in the Holy Land, including the Anastasis in Jerusalem, over the site believed to be the tomb of Christ, and the Church of the Nativity at Bethlehem where Jesus was born, and Constantine began the octagonal church at Antioch. Later emperors followed his example. In Constantinople the earliest major churches were those of the Holy Apostles, the first church of St Sophia and that of St Irene, and during the fourth century other major churches were dedicated in important city centres such as Antioch, Nicomedia, Milan and Aquileia, some receiving imperial sponsorship and reflecting the new phenomenon of emperors as patrons of Christian buildings. The large numbers of bishops attested in the records of church councils are in themselves some guide to the spread of church building in the empire generally, for each bishop will have required his own. In some cases, existing buildings were turned into churches. Constantine made over a secular building for this purpose to the catholic Christians of Cirta in North Africa when theirs had been seized by the rival Donatist party. Christians used the secular architectural styles that already existed, especially the three-aisled basilica, with its long naves leading to an apse; this was to become one of the dominant forms of church architecture for many centuries. The larger and more prestigious of these churches rivalled earlier public buildings in size and splendour and were often commemorated in contemporary sermons or in rhetorical descriptions, known in Greek as *ekphraseis*.[15] This account of the building (under the patronage of the Empress Eudoxia) of the cathedral at Gaza which replaced the Marneion, the great pagan temple, conveys something of the excitement felt by contemporaries, and also the extravagance of their claims to have rooted out all polytheist remains:

> The holy bishop had engaged the architect Rufinus from Antioch, a dependable and expert man, and it was he who completed the entire construction. He took some chalk and marked the outline of the holy church according to the form of the plan that had been sent by the most pious Eudoxia. And as for the holy bishop, he made a prayer and a genuflexion, and commanded the people to dig. Straightaway all of them, in unison of spirit and zeal, began to dig, crying out, 'Christ has won!' … and so in a few days all the places of the foundations were dug out and cleared.
> (Mark the Deacon, *Life of Porphyry*, 78, trans. Mango, *Art*, 31).[16]

Not all church building was imperial or undertaken by bishops; by the middle of the fourth century for example, a Syrian monk called Julian Saba had built a Christian chapel on the summit of Jabal Musa (Mt Sinai), a feat that was lauded by Ephraem the Syrian:

> The circumcised boast of Mount Sinai
> but you humiliated them down to the ground.
> This proclamation is great
> For now the church of the Son is on the Father's mountain.[17]

The decoration of these new churches took time to evolve, and we have no surviving examples earlier than the turn of the fourth and fifth centuries of the striking figural mosaic decoration familiar from such churches as

S. Apollinare Nuovo (*c.* 490) and S. Apollinare in Classe (530s–540s) at Ravenna.[18] S. Maria Maggiore in Rome, built under the patronage of Pope Sixtus III (432–40), is a spectacular surviving fifth-century example of a consciously classical style of church building; the elaborate mosaics on the triumphal arch, including a representation of the Virgin Mary in the dress of a Roman empress, draw for their biblical scenes on the existing secular repertoire. Similarly, the earliest surviving Roman apse mosaic, from the church of S. Pudenziana (end of the fourth century), also uses imperial motifs, showing Christ surrounded by the apostles in the style of representations of the emperor and the Roman senate.[19] The other main architectural type followed by church architects was based on the martyrium and used especially (but not only) for baptisteries, such as the octagonal Orthodox Baptistery at Ravenna (early fifth century). Many such baptisteries were attached to basilical churches, but Constantine's 'Golden Church' at Antioch, for instance, which does not survive, was also octagonal.[20] By the sixth century a much less classicizing architectural form had developed, with many variations ranging from the domed basilica to the so-called double-shell octagon of Sts Sergius and Bacchus at Constantinople.[21]

*Figure 3.1* S. Maria Maggiore, Rome. A fifth-century basilica with typical apse, long nave, windows and coffered ceiling. Many churches were built in this style, derived from Roman public buildings.

Justinian's 'Great Church' of St Sophia still stands in Istanbul where it was dedicated in 535 to replace the earlier building on the site destroyed by fire in the Nika revolt of 532 (Chapter 5). The massive dome we now see was dedicated at Epiphany, 563, after the original had collapsed due to an earthquake in 558. St Sophia was justifiably regarded by contemporaries as a masterpiece of engineering and design, and praised in a prose description in Procopius's *Buildings* and a hexameter panegyric by the poet Paul the Silentiary. Justinian's St Sophia was paralleled on a smaller scale elsewhere, for instance at Edessa (Urfa in eastern Turkey), where the existing church was rebuilt in the sixth century and also dedicated to the Holy Wisdom.[22] The more classical basilical form gradually gave way to the cross-in-square pattern familiar from Byzantine churches, whose architecture developed in step with the development of orthodox liturgy. In the fifth and sixth centuries, the public nature of these buildings and the prestige they brought to their builders, emperors or bishops alike is very apparent; another huge church, dedicated to St Polyeuktos and recently excavated, was built at Constantinople very shortly before St Sophia by Anicia Juliana, a lady from one of the very highest aristocratic families, evidently in direct rivalry with Justinian. Gregory of Tours tells how the gold ceiling of St Polyeuktos was the result of Anicia Juliana's attempt to outwit the emperor's designs on her fortune by using it up first on church decoration.[23] Her church was sumptuously decorated, with a gold ceiling and elaborately inlaid marble columns, and adorned with a seventy-six-line verse inscription round the nave, in which she celebrated the magnificence of her donation. To judge from a later account of its construction, Justinian's St Sophia, built so soon afterwards, was designed to outdo this church.

However, these important urban churches were only part of the story: there were also many hundreds of other, less well-known churches, not so spectacular, but just as influential locally in illustrating the impact of Christianity. A typical small sixth-century urban centre might have several, and many towns had what now seems an extraordinary number. Their construction did not follow need in terms of population size; rather, building or restoring a church was often, as in the case of the Byzantine churches restored and altered during the Vandal and Byzantine period on North African sites such as Sbeitla in Tunisia, a measure of local prestige, and might commemorate a particular saint and attract large numbers for associated festivals or liturgies. Expenditure by local well-to-do families which had gone in classical times towards the building or restoration of baths, stoas and other public buildings, was now diverted into churches and their furnishings. This is evident, for example, as late as the seventh century in parts of Syria, where even small village churches possessed elaborate collections of silver plate for liturgical use; these would consist of liturgical vessels, sometimes elaborately decorated with biblical or other scenes such as the communion of the apostles, and frequently with inscriptions giving the names of the donors, in simple formulae such as this one from a silver lampstand in the Kaper Koraon treasure, from a village east of Chalcis:

† Having vowed, they fulfilled their vow to (the church of) Sts Sergios and Bacchos. † Sergios and Symeoni(o)s and Daniel and Thomas, sons of Maximinos, village of Kaper Korao(n).[24]

Such items were sometimes stamped with official silver marks, which provide an accurate means of dating them. Many of the earlier Syrian churches were extremely simple in style, but here too elaborate buildings soon grew up, for instance spectacularly at the great pilgrimage centres of St Sergius at Resafa near the Euphrates, where the sixth-century cathedral again replaced an earlier building, and Qalaat Semaan, the sanctuary of St Symeon the Stylite, where a great church composed of four basilicas in a cruciform arrangement, with adjoining large cenobitic monastery and other buildings amounting to a virtual 'pilgrim village', grew up around the column on top of which the saint had lived for more than thirty years. Local traders soon also ensured also that the pilgrims would approach the site along a road lined with shops. At Palmyra, which had generally been thought to have gone into a decline after the defeat of Zenobia in the late third century, eight churches have been identified, including a sixth-century basilica on a scale similar to that at Qalaat Semaan.[25]

*Figure 3.2* The great church complex at Qalaat Semaan, Syria, with the remains of the pillar of St Symeon the Elder

*Figure 3.3* The huge site of Palmyra, a distinctive Nabataean and Roman city built in an oasis of the Syrian desert between Damascus and the Euphates

## The rise of bishops

As Constantine had realized, the network of bishoprics gave the Christian church a huge advantage over its rivals. Many of the new churches were the preserve of local bishops, and provided the setting for the moral, social and religious teaching which was a central part of their role.[26] We know of many powerful bishops during this period. Their influence extended well beyond what in modern terms would be purely church matters: Constantine had set a precedent in giving them secular jurisdiction and guaranteeing the maintenance of bishops and clergy, as well as releasing them from tax obligations. This was an exciting development at the time for bishops such as Eusebius of Caesarea, but soon put them in a complex position vis-à-vis the emperor, in that only the orthodox (that is, those officially approved at any one time) benefited.[27] In many individual areas they took on a leadership role which increased in scope in proportion to the difficulties experienced in keeping up the civil administration. In Ambrose of Milan we see an ambitious churchman keen to consolidate his own position, and who was able at times to exercise great influence over the Emperor Theodosius I.[28] Another 'political' bishop was John Chrysostom at Constantinople (Chapter 1); however, Gregory of Nazianzus, his predecessor as bishop of Constantinople, chose to retire under pressure of complaints about his election, and John himself was forced into exile. The church historian Socrates comments on the number of enemies the latter made through his strict moral teaching and habit of excommunicating backsliders:

> What contributed greatly to gain credence for these complaints was the bishop's always eating alone and never accepting an invitation to a feast. His reasons for thus acting no one knew with any certainty, but some persons in justification of his conduct state that he had a very delicate stomach and weak digestion which obliged him to be careful in his diet, while others impute his refusal to eat in company with any one to his rigid and habitual abstinence.
>
> (Socrates, *HE* VI.4)

In contrast to Ambrose and John, Augustine, their greatest contemporary, who had been strongly influenced by Ambrose in his conversion, about which he wrote in his unforgettable *Confessions*, spent the whole of his bishopric in the obscure town of Hippo on the North African coast, writing, preaching and living under a quasi-monastic rule.[29] Christian bishops were highly aware of the importance of communication, and Augustine was a master of the art of preaching and teaching; he wrote treatises about the best techniques of reaching every individual in the congregation, from the educated to the ignorant. We cannot unfortunately assess the impact on his local congregation of his extraordinarily modern understanding of the psychology of audiences, and one might be tempted to conclude that his genius was wasted in such a setting. However, among certain ecclesiastical circles and their upper-class followers the level of travel and letter-writing was such that ideas and influences could spread very quickly, and Augustine was in communication not only with such figures as Ambrose and Jerome but also with Christian aristocrats in Rome, some of whom fled to his side when Rome was sacked in 410; new letters and sermons by Augustine identified in recent years have vividly demonstrated many of the pastoral concerns with which he grappled. A very different figure was Theodoret, bishop of Cyrrhus in northern Syria in the mid-fifth century, another voluminous writer, theologian and controversialist, who also led a busy life dealing with the practical problems of his see. Theodoret wrote in Greek, but his see included a majority of Syriac speakers and some exotic ascetics.[30] Theodoret's theology was condemned at the Second Council of Ephesus and by the Council of 553, and he became a highly controversial figure from Ephesus I onwards, banned by the emperor from travel beyond his own see in 448 for disturbing the peace. Yet energetic though Theodoret was in fighting for his doctrinal beliefs, his many surviving letters demonstrate the care and attention which he also gave to pastoral matters, and while he was a particularly voluminous writer, this broad-ranging view of his role was not untypical.

As time went on, bishops became more, not less, important. They were usually drawn from the educated upper classes and had often had a thorough training in the classical rhetoric that still formed the main content of higher education. In the confused conditions of the fifth-century west they often saw themselves as the upholders of civilized values; some bishops, such as Martin of Tours, became the objects of cult themselves soon after their deaths.[31] By the sixth century many were adapting successfully to the needs of the new rulers, such as Venantius Fortunatus, panegyrist of the Merovingian dynasty and friend of Queen (later St) Radegund, who had retired to a convent at Poitiers, and to whom Venantius wrote courtly poems, like this one on her return from a journey:

> Whence has this countenance returned to me with its radiant light? What delay held you, too long absent? You had taken away my happiness with you, with your return you restore it, and you make Easter doubly a day for celebration. Though the seed just now begins to rise in the furrows, I, in seeing you this day, already reap the harvest.
>
> (*Poem* 8.10, trans. George, *Venantius Fortunatus*, 197)[32]

Paulinus, bishop of Nola, is an early fifth-century example of someone from an upper-class background who renounced much of his wealth to settle down at Nola in Campania, where he adopted the role of religious patron and built an ecclesiastical complex celebrating his patron St Felix, just as his friend Sulpicius Severus did in honour of St Martin at Primuliacum in Gaul.[33]

The enhanced importance of the papacy, which is especially apparent under Gregory the Great (590–604), was another product not only of the contemporary fragmentation of Italy in the late sixth century but also of the kind of personal ability and energy which a good many other bishops also showed. Clearly the see of Rome was likely to occupy a special position, in terms of both secular authority and religious prestige; similarly, the patriarch of Constantinople, though not technically superior to the other eastern patriarchs (of Antioch, Alexandria and Jerusalem) despite being declared second in precedence to that of Rome in 381, was liable to be both more personally involved in state politics, and more closely connected with the emperor. Emperors indeed might often intervene in appointing or exiling the patriarch. In 553, when the existing patriarch died just as the Fifth Ecumenical Council was beginning, the Emperor Justinian took care to promote a monk called Eutychius, a candidate whom he rightly believed would help to get the imperial view accepted. Having changed his own doctrinal views in 565, however, he deposed the same man when this time he refused to go along with them. Eutychius spent years in exile but was restored when his successor died, late in the reign of Justinian's successor Justin II (565–78). However, the relation between church and state was not so black and white as this might suggest; high-handed actions such as these were not in practice the norm, and theories of so-called 'Caesaropapism', i.e., the supposed control of the church by the ruler, go much too far.[34]

## Conflicts between Christians

Religious affairs could frequently be turbulent. In 391 Theophilus, patriarch of Alexandria, took the opportunity offered by anti-pagan legislation by Theodosius I to encourage Christians to fight with pagans at the hill where the great temple of Serapis was located, and they were further encouraged by a letter from the emperor which, in resolving the situation, named as martyrs the Christians who had been killed; this led to an attack on the temple itself, as well as destruction of busts of Serapis throughout the city, and assaults on other temples at Canopus (Chapter 1).[35] The situation at Alexandria was particularly explosive. It was the home of a strong pagan intellectual tradition and also of very forceful Christian leaders and their followers; the lynching of Hypatia was an exception which arose from local conditions. Christians often claimed in building inscriptions to have abolished pagan cult and converted temples into churches, and while it is necessary to read their claims with a degree of scepticism, such conversions can indeed be seen during the next two centuries all over the empire as part of the changing urban topography in late antiquity.[36] There were also many incidents involving violence between rival groups of Christians; for instance, the clashes between Arians and orthodox in Constantinople in the early fifth century.[37] Monks could be a disruptive influence, like the so-called 'Sleepless Ones' from Antioch who caused such trouble in Constantinople that they were attacked in 426 by rival mobs and had to be expelled in order to preserve the peace. Both the Council of Ephesus in 431 and the Council of Chalcedon in 451 were preceded by violent scenes between partisans. So great was the furore surrounding the rivalry between Cyril of Alexandria and Nestorius of Constantinople in 431 that the bishops themselves nearly came to blows, and the Second Council of Ephesus in 449 also concluded amid scenes of violence.

As we have seen, two important church councils, later to be remembered as 'ecumenical', took place during the fifth century – Ephesus (431) and Chalcedon (451) – and they were followed under Justinian by a second council of Constantinople (also known as the Fifth Ecumenical Council, 553–4). The sense of a universal faith defined by general councils had grown gradually from the time of the first Council of Nicaea (325), and many different issues remained matters of contention – from the central questions about christology (the definition of the status of Christ) to that of the authority of the major churches and the rank of the see of Constantinople in relation to Rome. Besides the records of their proceedings ('acts'), councils also issued rulings ('canons') on matters of doctrine, ecclesiastical authority and countless details of Christian behaviour, especially in matters to do with the clergy, such as clerical continence and celibacy, on which the west insisted more strictly than the east. The disputes were passionately argued and often resulted in bitter struggles between individual bishops and their supporters. It was the emperor's role to call ecumenical councils, and he could exert strong influence on their outcome, as Constantine had done in 325 and as Justinian did in 553–4. In the latter case, the proceedings lasted for many months, for most of which Pope Vigilius, who had been earlier summoned to Constantinople and unceremoniously treated by the emperor, refused to attend. After much harassment, a decree of excommunication, and vacillation on his own part, he was prevailed upon to recant his position, but he still did not attend the council, and Justinian's railroading of the council's decisions failed to convince the western church or to satisfy the east (Chapter 5).[38] After the Council of Chalcedon in 451, the Emperor Marcian issued an edict in which he hoped to persuade people that the controversies were finally settled:

> At last that which he wished, with earnest prayer and desire, had come to pass. Controversy about the orthodox religion of Christians has been put away; remedies at length have been found for culpable error, and diversity of opinion among the peoples has issued in common consent and concord.
>
> (Stevenson, *Creeds*, 341)

Later emperors including Zeno (474–91) tried to quell disputes and bring reconciliation, or by the seventh century even legislated to stop further discussion; Marcian's words were a statement of hope for the future rather than a description of what had actually happened.

It would be a mistake to see these doctrinal conflicts as mere surrogates for underlying 'real' issues of power and individual or ecclesiastical authority. Not only was religion – pagan/polytheist, Jewish or Christian – at the centre of the stage, but the Christian church was increasingly claiming a leading role in political, economic and social life, and its organization and beliefs mattered.[39] Christian doctrines and the many permutations according to which Christians could disagree, aroused the passionate feelings of contemporaries. Some of the matters of disagreement were practical ones, as, for instance, when to celebrate Easter, a matter on which local traditions differed, but strictly theological issues, such as the question of the divine and human natures of Christ and the status of the Virgin Mary, were seen as being even more important. In the early part of the period, Arianism, focusing on the relation of the Son to the Father, was still a major issue, particularly in relation to the contemporary barbarian problems, since nearly all the barbarian groups who converted adopted an Arian form of Christianity. By the middle of the fifth century the key issues centred on the divine and human natures of Christ. Nestorius was condemned by the Council of Ephesus (431), but his teachings lived on after Chalcedon in the insistence on Christ's humanity, which characterized the church in east Syria and Sasanian Persia (the Church of the East).

The opposite extreme was Monophysitism, or as many prefer, Miaphysitism (referring to those who believed that Christ had one wholly divine *physis*, or 'nature'), and it was this belief which, though condemned at Chalcedon, was to constitute the main obstacle to Christian unity in the next century and a half. When Justinian tried to reconcile the eastern churches by proposing a modification of the decrees of Chalcedon, he succeeded only in offending the west. Some indication of the strength of opinion can be judged from the fact that before Chalcedon, Eutyches, a priest of Constantinople taken to be an extreme 'one-nature' advocate, had been condemned by a local synod (448) and immediately reinstated by a rival council (the Second Council of Ephesus or 'Robber Council', 449) (Chapter 1). The new emperor Marcian and his pious wife Pulcheria were instrumental in bringing it about that the full Council of Chalcedon issued on 25 October 451 a decree affirming the two natures of Christ.[40] Discussion of the so-called 'Tome' (letter) of Pope Leo I, which laid emphasis on two natures (*substantiae*) (Chapter 1), occupied a great deal of the council's time. The Tome was regarded with suspicion by the followers of Cyril of Alexandria, and many easterners regarded the outcome of Chalcedon as a betrayal of the latter's principles. The difference was finally to crystallize into outright schism when, under Justinian the Miaphysite, Jacob Bar'adai, was ordained bishop of Edessa and proceeded to ordain non-Chalcedonian clergy throughout Syria, thus paving the way for a separatist church (known as 'Jacobite', after Jacob, or as 'Syrian Orthodox') which was to survive the Arab conquest, and which still exists today (Chapters 5 and 8).[41]

Thus despite the enormous effort and intense feelings which went into the councils, religious divisions were not healed; both the church of Rome and the catholic church of North Africa, which survived persecution during the Vandal period to re-emerge as a strong force after the Byzantine reconquest in 534, were strongly Chalcedonian, whereas the council met with opposition by many in the east. The emperors of the late fifth and sixth centuries found it increasingly difficult to achieve the ecclesiastical unity which was politically so necessary. Zeno (474–91) attempted to calm down the reaction to Chalcedon with a letter known as the *Henotikon*, and this held for a while, with the Emperor Anastasius (491–518) leaning towards the Miaphysites, but Justinian's uncle and predecessor Justin I (518–27) turned instead to the persecution of non-Chalcedonians, thus ending a breach between Constantinople and the strongly Chalcedonian papacy known as the 'Acacian schism' (484–518). Justinian's attempted reconquest of the west, conducted in the name of the restoration of orthodoxy, made these problems even more acute. In the seventh century the papacy was again set on collision course with the new religious policies of mononergism ('one energy') and monotheletism ('one will') promoted under Heraclius (610–41) and opposed both in Rome and in the east (Chapter 9).

## Emperors and the church

The emperors who followed Constantine were all Christian except for Julian (361–3) and all followed Constantine's example of active participation in church affairs. However, the actual situation was much less clear-cut. Eusebius of Caesarea developed a political theory which saw Constantine as God's representative on earth, and this idea was to become the basis of Byzantine political theory.[42] Emperors could make and depose patriarchs and summon and influence ecumenical councils. They could also engage in theological discussion themselves, and publish works on doctrinal issues, as Justinian did, and emperors legislated throughout the period on matters concerning the church, attempting, for example, to control access to ordination (which carried tax privileges), and regulating the powers of bishops.[43] But while emperors might also receive relics in formal processions and take part in the increasingly elaborate rituals of the liturgy in St Sophia, where they were accorded special privileges and entrance to the sanctuary, they were not themselves yet crowned or anointed in a religious ceremony. Bishops could on occasion humble emperors, and the church often resisted the imperial will. Direct conflict between emperors and patriarchs was to become a regular feature of Byzantine life in later centuries. In practice, the emperor and the church, or churches, stood in an uneasy relationship towards each other, a balance rendered still more delicate once imperial rule in the west ended.

The religious involvement of members of the imperial house did not show itself only in the political sphere. Constantine's mother, Helena, had set a precedent by visiting the Holy Land and founding churches there.[44] This did much to establish the idea of Christian pilgrimage, and travellers of all kinds made their way to Jerusalem and the Holy Land during the later fourth century. Some rich Christian ladies founded religious houses there which they ran on the model of their own aristocratic households:[45] Paula, Fabiola, Marcella, Melania all made the pious journey to Jerusalem and Bethlehem. Later in the fifth century the pattern was continued by Eudocia, the Athenian wife of Theodosius II, who left for the Holy Land in 438 after Melania's encouragement, delivering an elegant speech at Antioch on the way, which she concluded with a quotation from Homer.[46] She had Cyril of Alexandria with her, and was received at Sidon by Melania herself, whom she described as her spiritual mother.[47] However, Eudocia was a disruptive figure, and her rivalry with her deeply religious sister-in-law Pulcheria showed itself on her return; she found herself again in the Holy Land in virtual exile a few years later, and, once there, her estranged husband forced her to reduce the magnificence of her household. All the same, Eudocia's patronage in the Holy Land in general was extensive and included churches, monasteries and hospices, some of which she recorded in her own epigrams.[48] A later empress, Theodora, the wife of Justinian (died 548), was remembered by eastern Miaphysites for her protection in Constantinople of their clergy and the monks driven to take refuge there by her husband's policies. We are even told that Justinian as well as Theodora would visit the non-Chalcedonians in the Palace of Hormisdas, talk with them and seek their blessing,[49] and this was continued by their imperial successors, Justin II and his wife Sophia, who is also said to have inclined towards Miaphysitism. Theodora is notorious for beginning adult life as a variety performer in shows of dubious morality; after her elevation to pious respectability as empress she included among her charitable acts the foundation of a convent for reformed prostitutes known as 'Repentance',[50] and she was revered in the eastern church as a symbol of repentance in her own life. In the seventh century, Heraclius was one of the most energetic emperors in attempting to resolve the divisions in the eastern church, even after the split in the sixth century (Chapter 9), but he outraged the church by marrying his niece Martina as his second wife.

## Private and public religion

Emperors involved themselves in religious matters for reasons of state, but they were as committed as anyone else to the issues involved, and often, of course, personal interest and political advantage went side by side. As we saw, an apparent general increase in religious sensibility has been seen as one of the salient features of the age. This assumption might be tested through an approach in terms of private versus public religiosity, or of practice rather than belief,[51] and indeed we have a great deal of the sort of evidence (saints' lives, monastic anecdotes, ascetic literature) which seems to allow us glimpses of the lives of ordinary people. In the 1960s E.R. Dodds turned to psychology in order to explain what he saw as a turn to religious faith in the third century. Others have seen the change in terms of a growing irrationality and belief in the miraculous. But while there was certainly a great deal of attention devoted to religion in late antiquity, and while Christians produced large amounts of writing about it, it is another matter to deduce that individuals themselves had drastically changed. Much of the surviving literature is normative, explicitly designed to promote certain ideals of Christian life, and suggests a much greater conformity to these Christian ideals than was probably the case, when compared with more casual remarks made in passing in the same and other sources. Moreover, saints' lives are of their nature apologetic, designed to praise the saint and emphasize his or her role in converting pagans, Jews and backsliders; they often have other agendas too – for instance, to do with promoting one particular version of Christianity, or providing a foundation story for a local cult or pilgrim site. It was in the interest of the church and of individual bishops to emphasize the process of Christianization, play down the evidence for continuing pagan cults and claim that pagan temples had been totally destroyed. When assessing matters of belief and individual feelings in this 'age of spirituality', therefore, we must try to remember that much of the evidence we now have is designed of its very nature to lead to one conclusion only. The sermons preached by John Chrysostom in the late fourth century suggest that many among his regular congregation continued happily with practices he regarded as immoral and unchristian. As late as 691–2, the Council in Trullo, held in Constantinople, was still condemning pagan practices and trying to regulate the lives of those who seemed to be only nominal Christians. So while some kinds of evidence – for instance, letters and the Christian funerary inscriptions which began to appear on the mosaic floors of basilicas – do seem to allow us to perceive the change in personal faith, even here individual belief is often hard to detect beneath standard formulae.

## Pagans and Christians

It is nevertheless obvious that Christianity became increasingly important during late antiquity, both in terms of practice and – especially through preaching, personal contact and the regulation of membership of Christian congregations – in the personal lives of many people. This was certainly more evident in the cities, where the church was, as we have seen, highly organized, and it seems likely that pagan practices continued in the countryside much longer than in the towns; if we are to believe his own account, John, bishop of Ephesus under Justinian, converted 70,000 pagans in Asia Minor in the mid-sixth century.[52] 'Conversion' is perhaps not quite the right word; a Greek inscription from Sardis, for instance, records the internment of 'unholy and abominable pagans' there by the *referendarius* Hyperechios.[53] The persistence of pagan cult antagonized aggressive Christians and worried the authorities sufficiently for them to resort at times to violent measures, such as orders for the forcible closure of certain temples. Much of the polytheism of intellectuals centred on the philosophical schools of Athens and Alexandria (Chapter 6), and it is extremely hard to judge the broader extent of pagan survival when so much of the evidence is highly biased; however, it seems clear that pagan cult continued in many places long after it was officially outlawed.[54] Many reasons, of course, combined to make people adopt Christianity, including personal advantage for those hoping for preferment from a Christian government, simple convenience and avoidance of the strong anti-pagan measures taken by successive emperors. Conversion was not always whole-hearted or exclusive, and many, as always, continued with habitual practices and held a variety of conflicting beliefs at the same time; they would probably have been surprised to have this pointed out to them, though Christian writers and bishops did their best. There were still pagans among well-to-do families in early sixth-century Aphrodisias, and the student body at Alexandria in the same period contained both pagans and Christians; the two groups sometimes clashed (Chapter 6). Trials of pagans were still being held in Constantinople in the late sixth century after a scandalous series of events at Heliopolis (see below);[55] Justinian also conducted purges of pagan intellectuals in high places at Constantinople which led to death and confiscation of property, as well as the effective closure of the Neoplatonic Academy at Athens (Chapter 5):

> This caused great fear. The emperor decreed that those who held Hellenic [i.e. pagan] beliefs should not hold any state office, whilst those who belonged to the other heresies were to disappear from the Roman state, after they had been given a period of three months in order to embrace the orthodox faith.
>
> (Malalas, *Chronicle*, trans. Jeffreys, 263)

In considering the secular literature (and indeed art) of the period it is hard to draw the line between what is classical and what is actually pagan; indeed, 'Hellene' itself became the regular Greek word for 'pagan'.[56] The distinction was also seen as a problem by Christians themselves, some of whom attacked Greek classical literature and 'Hellenes' in no uncertain terms. The modern controversy about the secular Latin literature and classicizing art produced in Rome in the late fourth and early fifth centuries is also in part about a matter of definition: the appearance of classical or mythological themes is not in itself evidence that its owners or patrons were not themselves Christian, and patrons were as often Christian themselves as pagan; there was in any case considerable similarity between Christian and secular luxury artefacts such as silver plate and ivories and the modern distinction between Christian and 'pagan' objects is misleading.[57] However, religious allegiances among the Roman aristocracy of the late fourth and early fifth centuries were complex; despite the apparent attitude of the state to pagan cult, members of the senatorial aristocracy in Rome went on holding multiple priesthoods, and this was no empty formality, while emperors themselves continued to exercised some pontifical functions even while legislating about Christianity.[58] Cyril Mango is right to emphasize that the Byzantine thought-world owed more to 'a construct of the Christian and Jewish apologists built up in the first five or six centuries A.D.' than to any real conception of classical culture,[59] but he probably underestimates the persistence of pagan habit and practice – not necessarily to be identified with 'classical' ideas.

As for the actual process of Christianization within late antique society, it took place slowly. It is hard to judge the reality of religious conviction in a society from sources which are often polemical or exaggerated. It was a regular feature in Christian literature to compile catalogues of pagan cults and heresies, each with its Christian counter-argument, and this has led to a general caricature of paganism in the Christian sources. The trend started at least as early as the second century, and was a major theme in Christian writing thereafter; the 'Medicine chest' of 'remedies' against heresy written by the bishop Epiphanius of Salamis in Cyprus in the 370s quickly became a classic and was a model for Augustine and for many Greek writers including John of Damascus in the eighth century. As we have seen, the state officially claimed to be imposing Christianity from the reign of Theodosius I onwards; Christians took advantage of imperial legislation to attack pagan temples and statues, and occasionally the violence was carried out by soldiers at imperial command. However, attempts to carry out the orders were often greeted with resistance by the local population, and clashes could also arise from personal grievances and rivalries, as they did among the students at Alexandria.[60] The main temple at Aphrodisias, for instance, was not converted into a church until the sixth century, and well over a century after Theodosius, Justinian was still legislating against pagans and issuing laws against dissidents including heretics, Manichaeans and homosexuals, particularly those who were teachers.[61] But while Justinian certainly pursued a strongly pro-Christian policy, this

legislation should also be seen in relation to the traditions of previous imperial legislation and the generally repressive attitude of the state in this period
towards all minority groups, including, for instance, Jews and Samaritans, and
it is difficult to know what the charges really meant. The number of attested
trials is rather few, and while the situation of those who thought of opposing
the government may perhaps be gauged from the fact that Procopius says
at the beginning of his violently critical *Secret History* that he could only have
published his work during Justinian's lifetime on pain of death, one must also
make allowances for the literary trope of secrecy. In the high-profile trials
which took place in the 580s no less a person than the patriarch Gregory of
Antioch was summoned to Constantinople and charged with paganism. His
close friend, Anatolius, the provincial governor, was suspected of involvement with pagan cult in Edessa, and the affair developed to include suicide,
murder and an icon concealing an image of Apollo. The trials eventually took
place in Constantinople to the accompaniment of popular rioting against the
leniency of the Emperor Tiberius and the patriarch Eutychius, after which
Anatolius, the former governor, was thrown to the beasts in the Hippodrome,
then impaled and finally his body was torn apart by wolves.[62] The reign of
Justinian had also seen a hardening of Byzantine attitudes towards Jews and
Samaritans, especially after major Samaritan revolts in 529 and 555; in the
latter the proconsul of Palestine was killed. Predictably, during the affair in
the late sixth century, the hunt was extended to include Jews, Samaritans and
Montanists.

How genuine these charges were is hard to establish. Paganism certainly
offered a convenient handle for a political or personal attack, but the sources
generally suggest that in the east until a late date many people of all ranks did
retain beliefs and practices of pagan origin alongside their Christianity. By no
means every temple had been converted into a church when John of Ephesus, the future church historian, was sent in 542 on his evangelizing mission
to western Asia Minor. It seems that in the west, with its different history,
paganism was less persistent except in the countryside; this underlines its connection in the east with the as yet unbroken tradition of classical education
and culture. But even in the countryside, the fact that western bishops such
as Caesarius of Arles in the early sixth century placed a very high priority on
evangelization, suggests that the battle was by no means won.[63] Towards the
end of our period, mission in the northern provinces also came from outside, especially with the rise of the Celtic church and travels of missionary
monks.[64]

In attempting to trace the extent of the continuation of paganism in our
period, the concern of preachers and government alike for the eradication of
pagan practice is a striking feature, from John Chrysostom in Constantinople
at the turn of the fourth and fifth centuries to the acts of the late seventh-
century Council in Trullo. On one level it was important for Christian writers
both symbolically and tactically to assert their superiority over paganism, but
this can also be taken together with evidence drawn from a wide variety of

sources to indicate that pagan practice still continued. This will have been more the case in rural or remote areas – such as the Negev, where despite the building of churches in the towns most inscriptions were still pagan until the sixth century[65] – but was by no means confined to them. As Alan Cameron argues,[66] there was no single and clearly identifiable 'paganism', and pagan practice and belief took many different forms. One persistent theme which recurs in many different kinds of Christian texts of the period is the tendency to believe in fate and especially in astrology, and the stories of cures by healing saints and the many surviving amulets from this period show a wide range of continuing beliefs, just as Christian healing shrines sometimes continued earlier pagan practices. While Robert Markus has suggested that by the sixth century Christianization in the west involved a 'closing in of horizons',[67] it would be a mistake to imagine that Christianization was ever total, either in the west or in the east.

## Jews and Christians in late antiquity

A key development in recent scholarship has been a greater emphasis on the role played by Jews and Judaism in late antiquity; this has gone alongside a renewed debate about when it can be said with confidence that Christianity and Judaism were truly separate religions and with a tendency to set this process much later than previously assumed.[68] A particularly striking piece of evidence is provided by inscriptional evidence from Aphrodisias in Asia Minor which commemorates a 'memorial' set up by sixty-eight Jews, three proselytes and fifty-four *theosebeis* ('godfearers', that is, persons who attended the synagogue but had not yet fully converted to Judaism). Previously thought to date from the early third century, the two inscriptions which together give the names of all these people are now dated to the fourth and fifth centuries, and indicate a large and thriving Jewish community, which has also left its trace in numerous Jewish graffiti.[69] Late antique synagogues and Jewish communities have also been identified elsewhere – for instance, at Sardis (sixth-century) and at Hierapolis in Phrygia, Gerasa (Jerash) in modern Jordan, and recently Saranda in modern Albania – and we know from Christian complaints, among which those of John Chrysostom are particularly shrill, that Christians were often attracted enough to Judaism to attend the synagogues; this seems to have continued until a late date. Late antique Judaism was fragmented, and varied greatly from place to place, but it is clear from recent research that diaspora Judaism flourished and was well integrated into Roman society. It was also late antiquity that saw the flourishing of the great rabbinic schools of Palestine and Babylonia which produced the Mishnah and the Talmud. But from the reign of Theodosius I imperial legislation was increasingly negative towards the Jews, and while Judaism was never declared illegal, imperial legislation often classed Jews together with heretics and pagans; the Jewish patriarchate came to an end *c.* 425 and during his reign Justinian suppressed two Samaritan revolts with great severity. A string of literary dialogues, supposedly between Christians and Jews, had as their dramatic aim the discomfiture of the latter and their conversion to Christianity. But in Palestine itself the Jewish population grew during late antiquity and was able to build impressive synagogues with elaborate mosaic decoration.[70] Such was their strength as an element in the population that they were popularly believed by Christians to have assisted both the Persian army and the Arabs in the seventh century (Chapter 9).

## Monks, ascetics and holy men

This was the age of the holy man and the ascetic. It was now that the monastic movement spread throughout the Mediterranean, first with those who, such as Antony and Pachomius in the late third and early fourth centuries, retired to the Egyptian desert, then with a multitude of formal and informal religious communities of all types. Some monasteries followed the eastern rule of St Basil or, in the west, that of John Cassian, on which Cassiodorus' monastery at Squillace was based.[71] The numbers of monks could be very large, allegedly amounting to many thousands in Egypt alone: to take a few examples from the literary sources, in the early fifth century Palladius tells us in his *Lausiac History* that there were 2,000 monks at Alexandria, 5,600 male ascetics and hermits at Nitria, and 1,200 monks and twelve women's convents at Antinoe, while at Tabennisi there were 7,000 monks, including 1,300 in the monastery of Pachomius alone, as well as a women's monastery of 400 nuns. The great fifth-century abbot Shenoute, one of the most important early writers in Coptic, presided over several thousand monks and nuns at the White Monastery in Upper Egypt. However, it is important to emphasize the actual variety of the religious life at this period, which did not by any means always involve living in communities like these. Many dedicated religious, especially women, still lived in small groups or even in their own homes, while in the desert many communities adopted the form of the laura, where individual monks lived in their own cells around the central church, to which they typically returned weekly for common worship.[72] By the fifth century many who did not adopt the religious life themselves were also deeply influenced both by the ideals of asceticism and by the example of individual ascetics, or that they had taken some of these ideals into their own lives and their own faith. Ascetic aims were not limited to organized religious communities, nor indeed to Christianity; they were preached with equal fervour by the Neoplatonic philosophers of the fourth and fifth centuries, who advocated abstinence from sex, rich food and luxury of all kinds (Chapter 6). There were many similarities between pagan and Christian asceticism, especially at more intellectual levels, and Neoplatonic teaching advocated a bodily regime based on prudent restraint (*askesis* – 'training'), including sexual continence, following the precepts of the early Greek philosopher Pythagoras, who had been revived as a model, for instance, by the early fourth-century philosopher Iamblichus in his treatise *On the Pythagorean Life*.[73] But some Christians went much further, following the pattern laid down in the narrative of the temptations of Antony, directing more of their attention to the avoidance of sexual lust and adopting exotic forms of self-mortification.[74]

Monasticism has been seen as a kind of 'protest' movement against the institutionalized church, but this ignores the fact that the ascetic ideal in general (renunciation of bodily comfort, including warm clothes, adequate diet, cleanliness and especially sexual relations) had become prominent in early Christianity from an extremely very early date. For our understanding of the particular ways in which it was taken up in late antiquity the late-fourth century *Life of Antony*, attributed to Athanasius, is extremely important. It set the pattern for the classic ascetic life, with its opposition between the world and true spirituality, its lurid scenario of temptation overcome and its desert setting, where lions are tamed by the spiritual power of the holy man. In addition, it became required reading for educated Christians. Augustine heard of the powerful effect it could exert shortly before his own conversion to the ascetic Christian life in Milan in 387: he and his friend Alypius were visited by a Christian called Ponticianus, who

> told the story of Antony, the Egyptian monk, a name held in high honour among your servants [Augustine is addressing God], though up to that time Alypius and I had never heard of him. When he [Ponticianus] discovered this, he dwelt on the story, instilling in us who were ignorant an awareness of the man's greatness, and expressing astonishment that we did not know of him. ... From there his conversation moved on to speak of the flocks in the monasteries and their manner of life well pleasing to you and the fertile deserts of the wilderness.
>
> (*Conf.* VIII.6.14, trans. Chadwick, 192)

Monks occasionally engaged in highly political activity, and there could be sharp tensions at times between them and the civil authorities. But it is a mistake to separate 'monasticism', still extremely fluid at this period, from the ascetic movement in general, and there is no doubt that ascetic ideas and practice percolated through society as a whole. By the fifth century, some ascetics, especially in Syria, were practising spectacular forms of renunciation, such as the stylites, who lived for many years at a time on platforms on the top of specially erected pillars. We have already encountered Symeon the Elder, who died in 459, having lived for decades on a pillar at Qalaat Semaan in Syria. Daniel (died 493), a disciple of Symeon, lived on a pillar near Constantinople for thirty-three years, and Symeon the Younger (d. 592) had his pillar near Antioch.

All became famous in their lifetimes and their influence, prayers and advice were ought by people of all levels of society. Then there were the 'grazers' who lived only off grass and shoots, and some who chained themselves up and lived in cowsheds. Others so vehemently renounced worldly pretensions that they pretended to be insane. These included both men and women; one

*Figure 3.4* Pottery pilgrim token (*eulogia*) depicting St Symeon Stylites the Younger (late sixth–seventh century) on his pillar at the Wondrous Mountain near Antioch. Together with bottles (*ampullae*) containing holy oil, water or earth, such tokens were regularly taken home as souvenirs from pilgrim shrines.

example is the sixth-century ascetic known as Symeon the Holy Fool, who according to his seventh-century *Life* defied conventions to such an extent that on one occasion at Emesa (Homs) he tried to take a bath in the women's baths, only to be roundly beaten and ejected by the indignant women bathers.[75] Other forms of asceticism involved practical charity, as with Euphemia and her daughter in Amida, and Euphemia's sister Mary in Tella, recorded by John of Ephesus, who spent their lives caring for the sick and needy, but who were not afraid when they felt the need to embark on a pilgrimage to Jerusalem.

As with most historical phenomena, there are several convergent reasons for the popularity and prevalence of such holy men and women in this period. The classic discussion by Peter Brown, dating from 1971, suggested that they should be seen, especially in Syria, in anthropological terms, as a type of rural patron, defusing the tensions and difficulties felt by the villagers.[76] Brown's article acted as an enormous stimulus, but it was quickly pointed out that holy men were often to be found in or near cities, where they might attract the attention of the wealthy elite, or even the emperors (the stylite Daniel is such an example), and that functional explanations do not make clear how the ascetics were seen by contemporaries or necessarily how they viewed themselves, nor do they give enough attention to the rhetorical dynamics of many of the narratives on which we depend. There were in fact many different sorts of holy men and women; they were by no means an exclusively rural phenomenon, even though the ascetic idea of retirement from the world might make a rural or desert environment seem particularly appropriate. Fleeing into the farther desert is a *topos* in the monastic literature. When most would-be ascetics fled to the desert, however, whether in Upper Egypt, Judaea or Syria, they tended not to go very far from the settled areas on which they depended for food and sustenance. Archaeology reveals that the Judaean desert was crossed by a network of paths linking the monasteries together, and we know that in many cases the monks retained close relations with the organized church and the patriarch in Jerusalem. The staple diet of the Judaean monks seems to have been bread, for which it was necessary to buy wheat, sometimes from far afield since it could not be grown in the desert environment. Other activities of the monks, such as basket-weaving, also involved them in market transactions with the outside world, while the actual building of the monasteries implied a major investment and had a considerable effect on the local economy. The monasteries of the fifth and sixth centuries in the Judaean desert north and south of Jerusalem were themselves part of the process of settlement of population on marginal land which is a striking feature of Palestine and Syria in that period (Chapter 7).

Hospitality was seen as a central part of monastic duty. The coenobitic monastery of Martyrius not far from Jerusalem had a large hospice for visitors, with its own church and stables. Some solitaries fled to remoter places in order to escape the numbers of visitors, but it was part of the holy man's role to interact with the rest of society, as indeed Antony had done; thus, like many others, Amoun, an early monk at Nitria in Egypt, received visitors and performed miracles. The monks needed other people on whom to practice their charity, and to demonstrate the ascetic ideal, and hospitality was an important part of their way of life. The *Lives of the Desert Fathers* record many such visits:

> We also put in at Nitria, where we saw many great anchorites. Some of them were natives of that region, others were foreigners. They excelled each other in the virtues and engaged in rivalry over their ascetic practices, struggling to surpass each other in their manner of life. Some applied themselves to contemplation, others to the active life. When a group of them saw us approaching from a distance through the desert, some came to meet us with water, others washed our feet, and others laundered our clothes. Some of them invited us to a meal, others to learn about the virtues, and others to contemplation and the knowledge of God. Whatever ability each one had, he hastened to use it for our benefit.
>
> (Russell, *Lives of the Desert Fathers*, 105)

It suited the monks to complain about the visitors who disturbed their prayer, while actually encouraging them to come. Similarly, though, as we saw, ascetics did often enough live in towns, it was debated whether one could in fact practise holiness while living in the city. But it is a mistake to pose the issue too much in terms of urban versus rural life, for in the monastic discourse the 'desert' and the 'city' stood for individual spirituality and external ties respectively rather than for actual locations. And while the holy man needed other people, every community, large or small, also needed its own holy man; he might not be called upon very often, but his presence and his holiness were essential. All sections of society came to take this for granted; even the sophisticated Procopius relates how when Hephthalite archers in the Persian army of Cavadh tried to shoot at the holy man James, their arrows would not leave their bows. Jacob had taken himself to a retreat two days' journey from Amida where he lived on seeds; the proud local people had built a rustic shelter around him, with gaps allowing him to see out and to converse. Cavadh asked him to restore the firepower of his archers. James complied, and the king offered him anything he asked for, at which the holy man asked for the safety of any who chose to take asylum with him from the present war.[77]

Like much of the evidence used in Peter Brown's article, this example relates to Syria, where asceticism took a particularly striking form, in part because the ascetic ideal had been well established at an early date, and was not confined solely to Christianity – Gnostics, Marcionites and Manichaeans all preached renunciation.[78]

There was as yet no formal process for the recognition of a holy person as a saint, but holy men and women were soon recognized as such, and it was a function of hagiography, the writing of saints' lives, to justify their claim to holiness. The recognition of such special figures went together with an importance attached to their relics and an increasing belief in their capacity to perform miracles.[79] The possession of relics of saints or martyrs gave prestige and power to Christian sites and their bishops, and ordinary Christians began to be buried in and near their shrines. In the late sixth century the *Life* of Eutychius the patriarch of Constantinople devotes the section about his exile in the Pontus to a listing of the miracles he performed there. The shrine of Thekla at Seleucia with its huge church and all necessary buildings to accommodate large numbers of pilgrims was enlarged on a grand scale in the fifth century by the Emperor Zeno. Thekla, a character from a very popular work of early apocryphal literature, was an untypical saint, and the fifth-century *Life and Miracles of Thekla* is a much more literary production than most of the collections of such miracle stories. Several of these survive from the sixth and seventh centuries, associated with major shrines including those of the martyrs Sts Cosmas and Damian in Constantinople, Sts Cyrus and John at Menuthis in Egypt (composed by Sophronius the later patriarch of Jerusalem, for whom see Chapter 9) and St Demetrius in Thessalonica, and listing the miraculous cures and answers provided to pilgrims.[80] Saints and their shrines specialized in particular diseases (for instance St Artemios, whose shrine was also in Constantinople, specialized in curing hernias and genital diseases), and Sts Cosmas and Damian and St Cyrus were all reputed to have practised medicine themselves. The activities of such shrines required management and were not without their tensions. In the *Miracles* of Sts Cyrus and John there is an evident attempt to promote the healing powers of the saints over the alternative of 'Hellenic medicine'. The various collections of miracle stories also engaged in sectarian disputes, and during the sixth century there was evidently a rationalizing challenge to this burgeoning resort to the powers of saints, with several works written in the late sixth century to defend the idea that souls, especially the souls of saints, continued to exercise power after death. One such work was written by Pope Gregory the Great, who had spent time in Constantinople before he became pope and engaged in the debates going on there.[81]

Pilgrims also took home souvenirs – lamps, tokens, bottles for water from the River Jordan or earth from the Holy Land. The many surviving examples of such items are often dated to around the sixth century, and are an indication of the extent of the pilgrim trade experienced in Palestine and elsewhere at that period, including the shrine of St Menas not far from Alexandria in Egypt.[82] Clay tokens from the shrine of St Symeon the Younger, south-west of Antioch, offer another sixth-century example. These tokens often carried images of the saint, and are one manifestation of what came to be a growing veneration of holy images alongside the relics that were essential to the pilgrim shrines (Chapter 9). The experience of pilgrims when they visited these centres was complex, and no doubt exciting.[83] A pilgrimage centre would typically have one or more churches, with other buildings for the reception and care of pilgrims; such sites were also often the location for the major market and fair held in the area. Monasteries, too, built all round the Mediterranean, were sometimes on a big scale and included facilities for visitors, and many other hospices for travellers (*xenodocheia*) and hospitals for caring for the sick were founded by wealthy Christians and imperial patrons.[84]

## The church and wealth

As the institutional profile of the Christian church became more and more pronounced, tensions arose between its increasing wealth and its ideals of poverty and charity. Almsgiving had been a principle of the early church, and widows and orphans had been maintained by individual congregations since the second and third centuries. This took concrete form in the foundation of buildings financed for the very purpose. Through almsgiving, and through the financing of such institutions, the church, bishops, or, as often, individual wealthy Christians were effective in redistributing wealth; at the same time, through church building and other forms of patronage, these agencies took a major part in changing the appearance and the economic basis of urban life (Chapter 4). But though there was a clear relation between classical benefactions (*euergetism*) and Christian patronage, the aims and motivation of the latter also drew on other roots, in particular the Scriptural injunction to renounce wealth and give to the poor (Matt. 19:21). Unlike classical benefactions, Christian charity was, at least in principle, aimed at the poor, of whom indeed the Roman elite had been barely aware. Now, ironically, the poor acquired visibility.[85] Naturally, not all rich Christians were inclined to give up their luxurious lifestyles, as we learn from the sermons condemning them for continued ostentation, and a considerable literature built up which attempted to soften the Gospel saying by arguing that a rich man could indeed still be saved. But we also hear of many cases of individual renunciation of wealth, such as that of Paulinus of Nola, or the even more famous example of the Younger Melania (died AD 438), who with her husband Pinianus sold up her vast estates in order to live a life of Christian renunciation. Some acts of renunciation may have been somewhat less dramatic than they seem, in that the donors took care of their own family first, and rather than giving their wealth directly to the poor, tended to give it to the church for further distribution, thereby increasing the latter's wealth.[86] It was no small thing after all for the rich to give away substantial amounts of their family wealth, and such actions often caused ill-feeling within aristocratic families. Perhaps understandably, the monasteries which many subsequently founded were often run on somewhat aristocratic and privileged lines. A close reading of the writings advocating renunciation of wealth, which often took the form of sermons presenting an elaborate exegesis of what might seem rather clear Scriptural exhortations on the subject, indicates that the issue was not as straightforward as might appear.[87] Asceticism of this kind required energetic promotion and defence.[88] All the same, there is no doubt that spectacular giving did occur. Yet in the late fourth and early fifth centuries, when there were still many pagan members of the aristocracy – sometimes even in the immediate family of the giver – the practice caused them serious concern about the maintenance of family property. The tension between the demands of Christian renunciation and celibacy and the need for procreation and, in a traditional society, for the retention of wealth within families for the maintenance of society, became a real issue.[89] We need not suppose that the average Christian undertook the drastic measures of renunciation of wealth, or sexual abstention, but it cannot be doubted that a large proportion of wealth did seep away from production and towards the church, not least in the form of church buildings and their endowments. The poor certainly benefited to some extent from the process, and some monasteries, for instance in Palestine, themselves contributed to the local economy; however, the main beneficiary was surely the church itself, which was now able to lay the foundations of the vast wealth which it enjoyed in the later Middle Ages. The extent of this wealth, which had flowed into the church in the form of gifts and legacies ever since Constantine gave the church the power to inherit and removed the Augustan prohibition on celibacy among the wealthy classes, can be judged from the later *Liber Pontificalis* (based on a sixth-century original), which lists the extraordinary riches endowed on the Roman churches, including estates whose revenues would provide for their upkeep.[90]

Although as we have seen there were still a number of dramatic 'purges' of pagans under Justinian, and as late as 579–80, it is clear that by the sixth century Christianity was very firmly established within the fabric of the state. The fragmentation of the western empire, combined with the conversion of all the various barbarian groups as they came into contact with the Roman empire also allowed the church to assume a leading role in the successor kingdoms.

In the east, the church, while itself profiting from the growing prosperity of the fifth century, also played an active role in the redistribution of wealth which was changing the late Roman empire into a Christian medieval society. This process was hastened by the fact that the emperors, even if not all the leading members of society, took an active lead. We are still left with the difficulty of judging the extent to which this institutional Christianization was internalized by the average citizen, and have noted that our largely Christian sources may give a misleading impression. But it was of the nature of early Christianity not just to provide a cultic framework but also to teach, discipline and regulate the lives of its members to an exceptionally high degree. Pagan practice and pagan beliefs might continue, but the post-Constantinian church was determined to win hearts as well as minds.

# 4

# LATE ROMAN SOCIETY
# AND ECONOMY

Understanding the late Roman economy presents a particular challenge. Certain topics, such as slavery, taxation and the so-called 'colonate', which used to occupy a special place in the secondary literature, have undergone re-evaluation, while the vast amount of new archaeological and other evidence that is becoming available means that the whole subject has been transformed. The 'cultural' model of late antiquity based on the work of Peter Brown and others in the past generation has been accused of ignoring or at least underplaying important issues in economic and administrative history.[1] At the same time the size and nature of the late Roman economy is still disputed; current questions include the impact of state taxation and the exaction of the grain from Egypt and North Africa, the role of the super-rich with their large estates, the level of integration, and the degree to which there was a market economy. In the later part of the period, geopolitical factors pose in acute form the question of whether and for how long this was still a Mediterranean world at all.

Consideration of the late Roman economy (which involves also the consideration of groups such as landowners, tenants and slaves) is closely tied to historiographical models of decline and collapse. While as we have seen (Chapter 2), current revisionist approaches emphasize violence as a main factor in bringing about the end of the Roman empire in the west, internal factors have also been adduced by many historians anxious to explain Rome's fall.[2] A dark view of the later Roman empire is to be found, for instance, in Ramsay MacMullen's *Corruption and the Decline of Rome*.[3] According to these approaches, which were foreshadowed in M.I. Rostovtzeff's *Social and Economic History of the Roman Empire*,[4] the ancient world came to an end because of its own internal problems, among which were over-taxation and a decline in the capacity and willingness of elites to maintain urban life. Though for very different reasons, this was also the classic Marxist view, for which see especially Perry Anderson's *Passages from Antiquity to Feudalism*[5] and G.E.M. de Ste Croix's *The Class Struggle in the Ancient Greek World: from the Archaic Age to the Arab Conquests*.[6]

This negative picture of the later Roman empire (sometimes referred to disparagingly as 'the dominate', in order to convey the idea of autocratic rule supported by an unwieldy bureaucracy) has been held by many in the past to apply to the period from Diocletian onwards. However, much of the evidence adduced is impressionistic. Complaints about tax collectors or soldiers billeted in towns are indeed common, but similar examples can be found in almost any society, and need to be read with caution. Whether things had really changed significantly for the worse is hard to establish, and plenty of evidence from the Principate suggests that the condition of the peasant then was hardly any better. Individual instances of peasants taking evasive action at the tax collector's approach do not necessarily add up to a general picture of flight and collapse. Also fundamental to this view is the legal evidence, especially the often repeated laws in the Theodosian Code, by which successive emperors legislated to keep decurions in place in their towns and *coloni* on the estates in which they are registered. The picture of oppression and authoritarianism which these laws seem to suggest was endorsed in the past by scholars who have represented the later Roman empire as virtually collapsing under its own weight, and described it in terms such as 'totalitarian' and 'repressive'.[7] But as A.H.M. Jones recognized, when laws are constantly repeated, they must be presumed to be ineffective; moreover, laws need enforcement. Where the necessary apparatus for the latter is lacking, as it largely was in the Roman empire, it may be comforting for those in authority to repeat the law itself, but it does not necessarily follow that it was actually carried out in practice. Jones also recognized that social mobility was possible in the later Roman empire – probably even more so than under the Principate. But a wholesale re-evaluation in the last generation of the nature of the legal evidence, in particular the construction and evolution of the Theodosian and Justinianic Codes, has now led to a very different understanding of the actual significance of this legislation and of the working of law in late antique society (Introduction). Similarly, recent work on the papyrological evidence from Egypt, especially that relating to great landowning families, lies behind a new and more commercial view of the economy in the sixth century.[8] Taking the literary sources at face value can lead to equally overstated conclusions. Many previous discussions have taken literally the apparent statement by the Christian Lactantius, a biased and hostile source,[9] that Diocletian quadrupled the size of the army, and since the maintenance of the army was the single largest call on the state revenues, have then used this as the basis for a highly negative view of the economy in general. Similarly, despite Diocletian's measures to ensure better collection of revenue and an elaborate system of taxation in kind, it is far from certain that the level of taxation itself increased.[10] The few general statements that we have in contemporary sources on such matters as taxation tend to come from writers as biased and unsubtle as the pagan Zosimus or the fifth-century Christian moralist Salvian, and must be treated with considerable caution. Finally, in considering these methodological issues, it is also necessary to balance contrasts between east and west; if the structure of the state in the late fourth and fifth centuries was really as top-heavy and as liable to collapse from its own internal contradictions, why did the eastern empire resist fragmentation and maintain prosperity for a significantly longer period?[11]

It is the contribution of archaeology above all which has led historians to question the older view, and it is worth noting that A.H.M. Jones published his great work, *The Later Roman Empire*, in 1964, well before the current interest in late Roman and early medieval archaeology. Although Jones himself was very aware of the importance of archaeology and had travelled very widely round the provinces of the Roman empire, his work relies mainly on documentary evidence, and such a book would look very different today. The change is also a matter of new ways of looking at the subject. While the older assumptions of decline are still very much with us, many historians have been influenced by different approaches, especially comparative ones. Perhaps most interestingly, the debate about the ancient economy which has been going on since the publication of M.I. Finley's classic book, *The Ancient Economy*, in 1973,[12] has extended to the later empire, thus to some extent bypassing the supposed great divide that came with the third century and the reforms of Diocletian. The older model depends on a clear periodization based on the assumption of a massive tightening up of government control and consequent increase of government expenditure, generally attributed to Diocletian. Most books still make 'late antiquity' begin with the reign of Diocletian, and that is understandable, given the instability of the preceding period and the administrative innovations brought in from 284 onwards.[13] But if many, even if not all, of Diocletian's reforms were revisionist rather than fundamentally new, this in turn should cause us to pay more attention to the underlying economic structures and questions which hold good throughout the long history of the empire. Current research on the Roman economy focuses on such issues as technology and production, quantification, movement of goods and indicators of economic growth or decline rather than on competing overall models of economic primitivism or economic rationalism.[14] Intense efforts are currently being made to quantify the Roman economy.[15] But tracing the actual nature and level of market exchange remains difficult at all periods in the Roman empire, including late antiquity, not least because of the unevenness of the available source material.[16]

### East and west

There are nevertheless certain obvious issues which affect the later period specifically, including that of the increasing divide between east and west. The basic administrative, economic and military structures of the Roman state established in the early fourth century were still in place in the eastern empire at least up to the reign of Justinian, and often beyond. We must therefore look for special factors, such as those described in Chapter 2, to explain why the west should have been different.

The late Roman tax system was designed to cope with a situation in which continual debasement of the coinage had led to near collapse, and revenues had to be collected and payments made to the troops in kind; a regular census and the five-year indiction aimed at ensuring reliable collection of tax revenue for the state, and the scheme also involved elaborate matching of need and supply. The main item of expenditure as before was on the army, who were now paid in kind as well as money. Certain obvious consequences followed: army units (themselves far more varied in type and organization than previously) now tended, for instance, to be stationed near to the sources of supply, and thus in or near towns, instead of on the frontiers. While by the end of the fourth century more payments were made in cash, the central role of the state in collecting and distributing the *annona* (the army supplies) remained an important feature of the economy, in terms of both organization and stimulus to production; accordingly the eventual cessation of this state function was a major factor leading to economic fragmentation, as was the end of the grain requisitions for the cities of Rome and Constantinople. Basically the same system was in force in the east as in the west, but apparently with more success. A number of factors contributed to this. The east, for instance, had been urbanized earlier and more successfully than the west and, despite the ceaseless complaints of municipal councils and their spokesmen, most of these cities continued in existence or even flourished into the later sixth century and indeed beyond (Chapter 7). We hear a great deal about their problems, not least because our written sources tend to come from just this kind of milieu; thus Ammianus Marcellinus, Libanius, Julian and later Procopius all took up the cause of the cities versus the central government. But many of their complaints had an ideological basis; in practice, the fifth and early sixth centuries seem to have been a time of prosperity for many eastern regions, especially parts of Syria and Palestine (Chapters 7). Another obvious difference between east and west in economic terms relates to the constant and in the end more serious military action in the west in the fifth century; not only was the economic base itself weaker than in the east, but the demands on it were greater. As we have seen, the western government had great difficulty in maintaining military forces adequate for their task. A deeper and more structural difference also lay in the growth of an immensely rich and powerful class of senatorial landowners in the west during the fourth century, whereas wealth in the east was by comparison more evenly spread, at least until the growth of the large estates of which we know in Egypt in the sixth century (owned by families such as the Apiones with property in Constantinople and land elsewhere as well).[17] The combination of a weak government and wealthy and powerful landowners was crucial in determining the shape of the western economy from the late fourth century onwards.

Thus east and west were both similar and dissimilar in this period, and local factors are increasingly important from AD 395 onwards; yet many shared features remain and some similar trends can be observed, even though the rate of change may differ. The standard accounts of decline and collapse obscure these real differences. In contrast, the present lively state of archaeological investigation invites us to compare one site or area with another, and encourages the broader view; it also invites the question of how the traditional textual evidence and the increasing amount of material evidence relate to each other. This approach is inherent in Wickham's magisterial work. By the end of the sixth century, while it is still possible in some ways to speak of a Mediterranean world (see Conclusion), the west has largely fragmented. The eastern government and its provincial and defensive structures were tested both in the Balkans and in the east in major wars against the Sasanians, and Justinian's wars of reconquest may have overstretched the capacity of the eastern empire; while it is hard to quantify the impact of the plague which first hit the empire in 541, contemporaries viewed it as a catastrophe of major dimensions (Chapter 5). There were also structural factors which we can see reflected in the gradual metamorphosis of many cities in the eastern empire from late antique towns with public buildings and grand houses into smaller, more defensive and village-like formations, a process which had begun before the end of the sixth century (see below and Chapter 7). The Persian invasions of the early seventh century dealt another severe blow to parts of the east, and seriously challenged the ability of the state to maintain a military response. Eventual victory over the Persians was followed by the first Arab incursions into Syria in the 630s, which the eastern empire was unable to repel (see Chapter 9). Taking a long view, it is possible to argue that the east and west underwent similar processes, but at different times, the speed of change being regulated by the operation of local factors. Yet the resilience of Constantinople in maintaining its political existence is a remarkable feature of the seventh and eighth centuries, and there is ample evidence of cultural and local economic continuity through the Umayyad period.

## The organization of labour

Large-scale slavery declined in the Roman empire but the sources make it very clear that slaves continued to exist,[18] sometimes in very large numbers – for example, on the estates of senatorial landowners – and this continued in the east into the Byzantine period. As we saw in Chapter 3, when late Roman landowners became Christian, they sometimes sold their property in order to use the wealth for Christian purposes, in which case the slaves were sold too; this was the case with estates which belonged to Melania the Younger in the early fifth century. Slaves also often resulted from war, in which Romans as well as barbarians might be captured and enslaved. Slaves could also be bought, and were easily come by along the frontiers, and their existence is taken for granted in the barbarian law codes;[19] the example of Caesarius of Arles in the early sixth century shows that ransoming such slaves came to be seen as one of the duties of a Christian bishop.[20] Legal sources demonstrate the continued existence of slaves on the land and elsewhere, and the church also soon became a major owner of slaves. We can assume that part of the labour force on the land and in many forms of production will still have been servile. However, it is less clear what this meant in practice, or how slaves related to *coloni* – technically free tenants who were, in many areas, theoretically tied to their particular estates by imperial legislation, and over whom the landlords had rights which can look very like the rights of owner over slave. It was for instance possible to be described as *servus et colonus* (both a slave and a *colonus*), and slaves could also be tenants.

Recent historiography, under the influence of the reinterpretation of late Roman legislation on the subject, has radically questioned the traditional view of the *coloni*, which seemed to suggest a move towards a tied peasantry in the later Roman empire and thus underpinned ideas of immobility and decline; such a view was fundamental to Marxian ideological approaches to the period.[21] In contrast, according to a recent discussion, 'the 'colonate' was not a generalized condition of rural dependency', but rather arose in the context of the late Roman tax system and the desire by the authorities to track not only the ownership of the land itself but also the labour force. The state was interested in maximizing tax revenue and restricting any reduction in the agricultural labour force.[22] *Coloni* were registered by their landlords for tax purposes and the state had an interest in ensuring that tax liabilities were met. Hence, as we can see from the fifth-century Theodosian Code and the Justinianic Code a century later, late Roman emperors passed a mass of legislation which on the face of it sought to restrict the freedom of movement of *coloni* and tie them to the land; they also tended to use the familiar language of slavery. If these laws are taken at face value and were successful, we would have to conclude that the late empire was a time of real repression, in which the population was reduced to virtual serfdom.[23] Indeed, the concept of being 'free' became difficult to define, and the difference between slave and free may often have been slight or non-existent in practical terms: by the time of Justinian, for instance, tenants known as *adscripticii* (bound to the soil) were treated in the legal texts more or less as if they were slaves.[24] Yet the impression we get of these classes from other sources is far from being one of total repression and alienation,[25] and social mobility was surprisingly common at higher levels. There was thus evidently a large gap between theory and practice.

It is important to realize that late Roman law often followed, rather than led, social practice. The frequently repeated and often contradictory pronouncements of emperors do not signify authoritarian intrusions on the lives of individuals so much as vain attempts to regulate a situation which might in practice be beyond their control. Complexities and inconsistencies abound, not to mention those caused by the very processes of recording and codification. The legislation on *coloni* grew out of the difficulties experienced in collecting tax, and the state legislated essentially to control and trace the labour force on which the tax was due. Not surprisingly, given the ways of late Roman government, this legislation developed only gradually, and piecemeal, during the fourth century, and uncertainty as to the relation of slave and *colonus* in individual areas, and inconsistency between geographical regions, were among the results of the untidy process that was adopted. Legislation dealing with the status of *coloni* was also introduced at differing rates in different geographical areas, in Illyricum and Palestine not until the end of the fourth century. Furthermore, as the evidence of the Egyptian papyri suggests, there were many possible variations at the level of actual arrangements between landlord and tenant; loans, effectively mortgages, from large landowners to small were common, and defaulting borrowers were subjected to coercive measures from the lenders which were of more immediate concern than any imperial legislation. In general, it seems questionable whether conditions for the lower classes had in practice significantly deteriorated since the early empire. The condition of the poor, whether urban or rural, remained hard at all times. There had indeed been over the imperial period a progressive intensification of penalties applied to those convicted under the law, with an ever-widening division between the treatment of the rich and powerful and the cruel treatment (torture, chains, mutilation) meted out to the poor.[26] But the same process coincided during our period with a new consciousness of 'the poor' as a class, no doubt inspired by Christian teaching, which found expression, as far as the urban poor were concerned, in various forms of Christian charity,[27] while saints' lives attest to the role of the local bishop in alleviating economic distress in the country areas, and especially in providing food in times of famine.

The economic changes which took place in the late empire were not of a revolutionary nature. This was still a basically agrarian society, and much of the land was owned by large landowners and worked by tenants, whether slave or free. Again, though comparisons with medieval feudalism have been tempting, and important for Marxist historians, there was no simple chronological transition from late Roman *coloni* to serfdom.[28] It would also be a mistake to suppose that peasants in earlier centuries had had much possibility or inclination de facto to move away from their area, or that they had not also been dependent. As for the lower classes in the towns, it is equally difficult to get a fair picture of their lot when so much evidence is anecdotal and when so many of the literary sources are liable to exaggerate for their own purposes. Naturally it is easy, as in most periods, to find evidence in the sources of both urban and rural poverty, especially in relation to tax debts, but again one should be cautious about generalizing too much on the basis of this evidence. On the whole, change was slow: local and unforeseen factors such as famine, pestilence or the like constantly threatened an agrarian economy with few obvious technological advances, but were also part of the expected range of possibilities and could therefore be contained; external factors such as warfare were of course another matter.

We hear many complaints in this period from the town councillors, the *curiales*, about their difficulties in continuing to finance urban life, and a process of increased imperial intervention in the affairs of cities, especially their financial affairs, has generally been seen; this went along with corresponding changes in the traditional ways of urban government (further, Chapter 7).[29] This was another example of how in trying to deal with a situation, imperial legislation actually made it worse; emperors attempted to prevent the curials from leaving their duties while giving them the opportunities to do just that. The 'flight of the curials' was an indicator that the old style of urban administration was giving way. It is less clear when or exactly how this change occurred, though it seems to have happened later in the west. Under Anastasius (491–518) it was decreed that the governing body for cities should be drawn from 'the bishop, the clergy, the *honorati* (office-holders), the *possessores* (landowners) and the *curiales*'.[30]

It was from the curial class that office-holders were drawn, and for whom imperial office-holding was highly attractive. Imperial service was now the lucrative way to advancement: councillors themselves were by now often men of modest means who could not shoulder their former burdens, and when public monuments or statues were erected in eastern cities such as Aphrodisias it was usually by men who held imperial ranks and offices. Naturally this produced some statements of nostalgia, as well as serious tensions for individuals, and in the mid-sixth century John the Lydian reminisced about the time, now in the past, when councils still ruled the cities.[31] It was often the local bishop who stepped into the breach, and who became not merely an authoritative leader in the town but in many cases the apex of a much reduced municipal organization; see below, Chapter 7. Jones rightly emphasizes the very large number of posts (*dignitates*) that had to be filled on a regular basis, and the law codes assume that *curiales* frequently endeavoured to escape their lot and better themselves in the administration, the church or the army. This class as a whole was the subject of what Jones calls 'a vast and tangled mass of legislation', whereby the state attempted ineffectually to prevent the seepage and maintain the councils on whom the cities depended. This legislation did not attempt to address the overall problem, but was issued piecemeal and in response to local conditions, and with no likelihood of general enforcement.[32] Earlier attempts to return *curiales* to their cities if they had managed to secure a post in the administration failed, and in principle after 423 individuals could no longer escape their obligations in this way. Similarly, the fifth-century emperors were still attempting to stop the loophole opened by Constantine when he freed clergy from curial obligations, as was Justinian, when in 531 he allowed ordination of *curiales* only if they had spent fifteen years in a monastery first, and were willing to surrender a substantial part of their estate (*CJ* I.3.52). But despite the complaints with which the sources abound, with the exception of the not inconsiderable part now played by Christian charity one may suspect that the condition of the people remained much the same.

But if there was no economic revolution, certain new factors did become operative, including, on the one hand, settlement on a large scale and, on the other, the growth of the church as a major economic institution in its own right, with profound implications ranging from the role of bishops as urban and rural patrons and the diversion of resources into church building to the growth of monasteries and their potential impact on the local economy. It was factors such as these, combined with the centralizing tendency of the late Roman state and the severe damage caused in some areas and to some towns by invasion and war, which disturbed the balance of landholding and wealth and which inevitably brought profound change.

## The classes of late antique society

The senatorial class of the west had been a major beneficiary of the disturbances which took place in the third century, and was, moreover, at least in
part itself a product of the patronage of Constantine and his successors. Constantine extended the size of the senatorial class, and by severing its necessary
connection with the city of Rome, opened it up to new membership in the
east, making possible the development of a new senate centred on Constantinople.[33] However, the traditional aristocracy in the west retained its wealth
and its prestige, and one of the main features of the late fourth- and early
fifth-century west is the enormous wealth, by which we mean the enormous
landholdings, of the western senatorial class.[34] Perhaps because of unsettled
conditions in many areas, it had become possible to acquire vast estates – the
size of towns, we are told. A landowner would also expect to have at least one
town house in which he lived in extreme luxury, as we learn from Ammianus'
famous (and scathing) description of the fish ponds and table delicacies of
the Roman nobility of the late fourth century.[35] Owning estates on this scale
was a business in itself, even if the landlord was an absentee. According to
Ammianus,

> A journey of fair length to visit their estates or to be present at a hunt
> where all the work is done by others seems to some of them the equiva-
> lent of a march by Alexander the Great or Caesar.
>
> (*Hist.* 28.6)

Late Roman aristocrats commissioned luxury items for their grand houses, including manuscripts, silverware and ivory, and kept alive the tradition of artistic production in the classical manner. These were members of the aristocracy
and holders of the highest official honours, depicted on elaborately carved
ivory panels in all their panoply of office. They owned grand houses and could
afford to commission the best artists and craftsmen. In the sixth century great
Roman families such as the Anicii had large estates and lands in Egypt and
the east, and remained patrons of luxury items; they also intermarried both
with the new Germanic rulers and within imperial circles in Constantinople.
The upkeep of the estates of such families required armies of retainers and an
elaborate system of production and supply of goods. Owners were interested
in profits, and had perforce to devote a good deal of time simply to keeping
things going. Some of it was occupied in dealings for mutual benefit with
others in a similar position, transactions which reinforced the gift element
and the importance attached to display which were typical features of the late
Roman economy. Sulpicius Severus and Paulinus of Nola provide evidence
in their writings of typical gifts from one landowner to another of such commodities as oil and fowl, a practice also known from Sidonius in fifth-century
Gaul, and from bishops and kings in the Merovingian period; Pope Gregory
the Great was no different in this respect from a secular landowner of earlier

times. Landlords were certainly involved in production, and engaged in long-distance transport; it has been argued that both might take place within an exchange system involving either simply his own estates, or those of himself and his friends. If so, this was less an economic activity than a patronal relationship. Even the widespread appearance overseas of African pottery during our period may be partly a product of this mutual exchange rather than the result of new commercial market or production systems. However, recent studies have argued forcefully for the commercial activity of such families, and there has been greater emphasis on trade and profit as motivation for the long-distance movement of goods; the interpretation of the huge amount of evidence from late Roman pottery is critical here.[36] It seems obvious, as Wickham argues, that elite demand provided the stimulus for such activity. If it is true that the amount of land in the hands of great proprietors (the *potentes*) increased, and if we accept more recent views about the nature of their economic activity,[37] a very different picture emerges of economic and political factors in the late empire than the traditional one.

The enlargement and transformation of the senatorial class, greatly increased in numbers from the time of Constantine on, rendered the old equestrian class otiose; the latter eventually disappeared as its former offices were progressively renamed and redefined as senatorial. Nor was it enough to be called simply *vir clarissimus* (the standard senatorial rank in the early empire). Valentinian I in AD 372 laid down a senatorial hierarchy ranging from *clarissimi* to *spectabiles* and (at the top) *illustres*; these grades were attached to the holding of particular offices, and other privileges of rank, such as seats allotted at the Coliseum in Rome, also followed. The senate of Constantinople, on the other hand, differed from that of Rome since it was an artificial creation; while the Roman senate comprised families of vast wealth and pretensions to aristocratic lineage (even if in many cases they did not go further back than the third century), its counterpart in Constantinople was filled with new men. This feature in the long run helped its future continuance; being based on Constantinople itself, and before the late fifth and sixth centuries generally lacking the enormous estates of its counterparts in Rome, the eastern senate was better able to avoid tensions which developed between the Roman senate and the imperial government. But eastern senators also enjoyed substantial privileges, and their role as members of the traditional landowning class, allegedly preyed upon by the rapacious emperor, is emphasized in the *Secret History* of Procopius, who identified with their interests. Like their western counterparts, eastern senators were no doubt in a good position to evade the special tax (*collatio glebalis* or *follis*) which had belatedly been imposed on the senatorial class by Constantine. In the example of the senatorial class, we can in fact see the combination of tradition and innovation which is typical of the late empire; for while, on the one hand, the late Roman senate was essentially a service aristocracy which differed considerably from the senate of the early empire, it did not occur to anyone not to maintain existing social patterns, so that many of the outward signs of senatorial status and privilege were retained or even enhanced. In such circumstances, the Christianization, and in particular the conversion to asceticism, of members of leading senatorial families, which began to occur in Rome in the late fourth century, seemed to present a threat to status, wealth and tradition, and therefore met with considerable opposition.[38]

The later Roman empire was characterized by a high degree of competition for status and access to wealth and privilege, which we can see operative also in the centralized bureaucracy. Since posts in the imperial service could be highly lucrative, and released the holder from burdensome existing obligations, the bureaucracy drew off talent from the ranks of the *curiales* in the cities even as imperial legislation, conscious of economic and administrative needs, sought to keep them in their places. One of the most persistent of modern myths about the late empire is that of a top-heavy and rigid bureaucracy which wielded the hand of repression yet whose size made it unsustainable in relation to the existing resources of the empire. In fact the empire was engaged in a constant balancing act between what was perceived to be necessary and what was possible. There was in practice a high degree of social mobility, and the court and the office-holders had a natural tendency to proliferate. The nomenclature and emoluments of the imperial service paralleled those of the army; office-holders held titles of military equivalence and received military stipends. This had little to do with modern concepts of efficiency, though the government had at least an interest in filling the administration with people it deemed suitable; at the same time it also needed to maintain the numbers of *curiales* in each city (who were also the obvious candidates for openings in the imperial service), since on them fell financial responsibility and tax obligations at local level. The double bind in which the government found itself was further complicated by the willingness of individuals effectively to buy their way into the administration, and that of the government to sell offices within it – the attraction for the purchaser being the emoluments that went with the position, and often the possibilities for favour and extortion that it carried in addition. To a modern observer this suggests corruption,[39] and it was easy for contemporaries to abuse the system and for others to complain about them. We should remember, however, that for all its impressive state apparatus, the late Roman empire was still a very traditional society. Many official posts were sinecures, or unimportant in themselves, and John the Lydian, just such an official, has left a vivid account of what it felt like to serve in one of the great offices of the state in the sixth century.[40] In practice the combination of patronage, aristocratic prestige, the need to fill the ranks of the bureaucracy and at the same time its tendency to swell because of the advantages it offered to those lucky enough to secure a position implied a constant balancing act only partly evident at the time.

The practice of selling offices in the imperial administration provides a particularly delicate example: on the one hand, the late Roman and later the Byzantine governments were concerned to stop the abuse of the practice, while at another level each used it as a financial tool and mechanism for selection of officials. In 439 an oath was exacted from all those appointed to provincial governorships that they had not paid to secure office:

> we ordain that men appointed to provincial governorships should not be promoted by bribe or payment but by their own proven worth and your [i.e., the prefect's] recommendation; let them testify on oath that in gaining their responsibilities they have neither made any payment nor will they make any subsequently.
>
> (*CJ* IX.27.6 pr.)

Yet later emperors actually sold offices: Zeno, for instance, raised the price for the governorship of Egypt from 50 lb of gold to nearly 500 (Malchus, fr. 16, Blockley). Justinian again tried to stop the practice, repeating the earlier demand for an oath from those appointed. *Novel* 8 (535) forbade the practice of *suffragium*, i.e. the buying of office, for provincial governors (though there were fixed costs that governors were expected to take on), and the secular officials were required to take an oath that was strongly Christian and orthodox in character.[41] Bishops and clergy also commonly made payments for office; again, Justinian legislated against this, but later took the alternative course of regulating such payments.[42] The whole constituted a finely balanced ecosystem with both economic and political implications for the emperors, and they were reluctant as well as unable to upset it too drastically. As in most complex societies, they also had to balance the tension between two needs: to manage the expectations of the elite and to keep the machinery of government working. Justinian promoted a 'reform' agenda in his self-presentation, but whether efficiency was even a possible aim in practice, as distinct from official and legal pronouncements, is a fundamental question. 'Efficiency' is a modernizing concept, and it is unclear that the system of payment made the administration any less efficient than it would otherwise have been. Procopius claims that Justinian himself was selling offices again within a year of his edict of 535, and his successor, Justin II (565–78) legislated again in 569 to stop governors from buying their office.[43] The corollary, and the underpinning of the sale of offices, was, of course, the desire of the office-holders themselves to recoup the moneys paid while they held office, the prospect of which had been a powerful attraction to purchase in the first place. Regulation was therefore probably the best option for the government, and we can also see the close connection between their attempts at regulation and the changing processes by which officials, especially provincial governors, were appointed.

One of the main hallmarks of the late Roman administrative system was patronage and the use of influence. Recent work has increasingly emphasized the importance of patronage in understanding ancient society as a whole, especially in the context of the Roman empire, and the patronage system of the later Roman empire could involve not just networks of obligation, but also coercion and even violence.[44] Patronage has existed and does exist in many – perhaps even all – societies, but is present typically where the protection offered by the state is weak, where the social bonds are loose or where there is change and competition for place in the new scheme of things. In late antiquity, 'traditional patrons found themselves supplanted as patrons, but also impeded as landlords – and as tax collectors – by men with local authority, secular or religious. Their protests were echoed with legislation representing the fiscal interests of the central government.'[45] For when new actors – bishops, state officials – entered a stage on which patronage already operated on every level, and when the interests of the poor, the landlords and the state diverged, any existing equilibrium was broken. In such conditions the poor and the helpless looked where they could for protection. The state for its part made repeated attempts to declare this form of protection (*patrocinium*) illegal, on the grounds that it represented an evasion of the responsibilities of those who were its subjects, and an illicit appropriation of authority by those who took it on, not to mention the extra tips which they doubtless imposed. A law of 415 allowed the churches of Constantinople and Alexandria to retain villages which had come under their protection, provided that all taxes were paid and other obligations fulfilled,[46] but later emperors such as Marcian and Leo continued to try to end the practice, and Leo attempted to forbid all patronage contracts from 437 in Thrace and from 441 in the east.[47] Again, the practice itself and the government's inability to deal with it demonstrate not so much endemic corruption as the huge challenge presented to the bureaucratic system in relation to the vast and fragmented areas which it was attempting to control.

## Financing the state

Behind many of the problems which the state experienced, and which gave rise to these social difficulties, lay the need for tax revenue and the difficulties of collection. Many scholars have believed that the level of taxation was higher in late antiquity – so high in fact as to contribute substantially to increased extortion and consequent decline. However, while we have in the sources a number of figures for tax revenue and budgetary expenses, it is far from clear whether they are reliable or not, or how far they may have changed over the period we are considering. At least in the late empire there was now a regular tax period ('indiction') for which levels were fixed, and the system had been changed to take into account both labour force and quality of land. Constantine had imposed special taxes on senatorial wealth and on commerce, and had thus at last brought these sectors into the tax net. But taxation still fell mainly on the land and on agricultural production, and the government had little recourse in response to loss of land and shortage of manpower except to try to close loopholes and harangue the population through often repeated legislation such as that seeking to restrict movement of *coloni* and help landlords to keep their tenants and maintain the tax revenue:

> Whereas in other provinces which are subject to the rule of our serenity
> a law instituted by our ancestors holds tenants down by a kind of eternal

right, so that they are not allowed to leave the places by whose crops they are nurtured or desert the fields which they have once undertaken to cultivate, but the landlords of Palestine do not enjoy this advantage: we ordain that in Palestine also no tenant whatever be free to wander at his own choice, but as in other provinces he be tied to the owner of the farm.

*(CJ* XI.51.1)

The tax collector looms large in contemporary literature as a hated and dreaded figure, and the danger to those who could not pay was very real. Paphnutius, a hermit near Heracleopolis in the Thebaid, met a former brigand who told him how he had once come upon a woman who had suffered in this way, and asked her why she was crying; she replied:

'Do not ask me, master; do not question me in my misery but take me anywhere you wish as your handmaid. For my husband has often been flogged during the last two years because of arrears of taxes amounting to three hundred gold coins. He has been put in prison and my beloved three children have been sold as slaves. As for me, I have become a fugitive and move from place to place. I now wander in the desert but I am frequently found and flogged. I have been in the desert now for three days without eating anything.'
'I felt sorry for her,' said the brigand, 'and took her to my cave. I gave her the three hundred gold coins and brought her to the city, where I secured her release together with that of her husband and children.'

(Russell, *Lives of the Desert Fathers*, 95)

The repeated laws show, however, how little the government could actually do to enforce collection of revenue. The taxes were highly regressive: small peasant proprietors paid the same as great landlords for the same amount of land. And despite Constantine's reforms, the traditional emphasis on the land still led to a failure to tap major sources of wealth, whether from trade or, importantly, from senatorial incomes. In the latter case, especially, it was in part the nature of the tax laws themselves which enabled senators to amass colossal fortunes while the government went short. Emperors themselves shared the traditional view that exemption from taxation was a privilege to which rank and favour allowed one rightfully to aspire, and thus their grants of exemption were not simply a way of gaining popularity but an expression of this traditional attitude. Cancelling arrears was another common device, in the face of real inability to enforce the law, for political reasons or in response to these traditional attitudes, and there was little conception of budgeting for the future. On the other hand, as Jones points out, the eastern government at any rate seems to have been able to collect very substantial sums on a continuous basis;[48] this was despite the outflow of large sums of gold to buy peace with Persia, or for 'subsidy' payments to barbarian groups.[49] The sums expended for both purposes could be very high, and the practice continued over the whole period – from 434 annual payments of gold agreed by Rome to the Huns stood at 700 lbs, and rose to 2,100 lbs in 447, with a payment of 6,000 lbs to cover arrears; according to Priscus this required a much higher tax burden on the senatorial class in the east which some could hardly pay. Surviving hoards of gold solidi from across the Danube are testimony to these payments. As for commerce, the *chrysargyron* (gold and silver tax, so-called because it had to be paid in gold and silver, usually, in practice, gold) was consistently unpopular and was abolished in AD 499 by the Emperor Anastasius as the *collatio glebalis* (*follis*), levied on senators, had been by the Emperor Marcian.[50] Taxation was an ideologically charged issue, and emperors who raised taxes, even if like Justinian they did so for military purposes, are uniformly criticized in contemporary sources.

The late Roman taxation system was a complicated and unwieldy affair, full of inequities and far from perfectly administered. Apart from the cost of the imperial court or courts and the administration, the state's major item of expenditure went towards the maintenance of the army, and this was also the most difficult to organize. If it were true that Diocletian had really doubled, let alone quadrupled, the size of the army, as well as increasing the bureaucracy the economic problems of the later empire would indeed have been insuperable. Jones put the problem neatly in his famous statement that the late empire had too many 'idle mouths', i.e., non-producers, who had to be paid for from the diminishing resources of the empire.[51] But few historians today would be as confident as Jones was in 1964. As we have seen already (Chapter 2), Diocletian is more likely to have regularized the status quo than actually doubled the army in size, and it must be regarded as doubtful whether even that figure could be maintained after the late fourth century. Even at 400,000 plus (other recent estimates would put it higher, as noted earlier), the late Roman army was still an extremely large force, and such an army must certainly have represented a great drain on resources. An elaborate system of requisitioning and supply had to be in place to get the items needed to the troops who needed them. Since the later third century and under the Diocletianic system, much of the army's pay had been collected in kind, by means of a cumbersome set of arrangements which one is surprised to find working at all; in fact, while the method of calculation varied from province to province, it was possible from time to time to reduce the demand on a particular province, as with Achaea, Macedonia, Sicily, Numidia and Mauretania Sitifensis in the fifth century. However, the regular censuses necessary to keep the registers of land and population accurate tended not to be held, and great discrepancies could thereby arise. Once collected, the goods had to be transmitted to the necessary unit – a further process requiring complicated organization.

Other forms of taxation were also of great importance throughout the imperial period, especially the grain and oil requisitions for the food supply of Rome, a system Constantine also extended to his new foundation of Constantinople (Chapter 1). Since the Republic, the Roman government had considered it a priority to ensure the food supply for the capital, and had maintained free corn and bread doles for the purpose.[52] The grain came largely though not only, from North Africa and Sicily, where in each case its provision had a major impact on the local economies.[53] In the case of Rome, the loss of North Africa to the Vandals caused severe disruption, but the distributions went on and were eventually taken over by the church. In the east, the grain and oil *annona*, as it was called, accounted for a high proportion of long-distance transportation between Alexandria and Constantinople, and can be traced in the pottery evidence.[54] Egypt continued to supply Constantinople, but the link was abruptly broken by the Persian invasion of Egypt in the early seventh century.[55] There were other problems: the tickets on which the actual distributions were made had come to be passed on by sale or inheritance; the government tried at times to regulate these practices too, but as time went on, as with other late Roman taxes, the match between those theoretically qualified and those actually receiving the dole had already become less and less close. Nevertheless the movement of goods in connection with tax requirements was a central factor in the continuance of long-distance exchange across the Mediterranean and an important contributor to the maintenance of Mediterranean unity.

The army was also a powerful factor affecting the circulation of coin and could act as an economic stimulus as well as a drain for the state. By the beginning of our period, payment in kind was beginning to be commuted into gold, especially in the west, at varying rates of commutation which at times had to be regulated by the government, and in the sixth century payment in gold (pounds or *solidi*) was the norm. Gold raised in taxes from the central provinces made its way to where army units were located, and soldiers spent their pay locally. State spending also followed the development of imperial residences and provincial centres such as Milan and Ravenna in the west and Antioch in the east. Maintenance of the *cursus publicus* was another example where state spending acted as a local stimulus.[56] However, the development of Constantinople as the eastern capital and its own massive needs deprived the west of eastern resources; it was no longer possible to maintain a paid army along the Rhine and upper Danube in the fifth century or the lower Danube in the sixth. Britain too was left to its own devices and the army withdrawn in 410. The establishment of rule from Constantinople in North Africa after Belisarius's victory over the Vandals in 534 required major investment, as did the Justinianic wars in Italy and against the Persians. The presence of the army in a particular area, with all that it required for its maintenance – not just the pay and supplies of the troops, but also a good road system and transport and local support systems – could be a powerful economic stimulus and was no doubt one of the factors behind the undoubted prosperity and density of settlement in the fifth century in the south-eastern frontier areas, even in barren and difficult places such as the Hauran and the Negev, where there were many small military settlements in addition to the major fortresses. But by the sixth century much of the defence of the south-eastern part of the frontier area from Transjordan to Arabia had been left to Arab allies (Chapter 8), and barbarians were frequently used in the regular armies.

The gold *solidus* introduced in the early fourth century remained standard for centuries henceforth, but later emperors were unsuccessful in their attempts to reintroduce silver coinage on a stable basis. Inflation also continued, as can be seen from prices given in papyri, probably because the government minted too much of the small base-metal coinage. By the fifth century, however, there was effectively nothing between the gold *solidus* and the tiny copper denominations, whose rate, valued against the *solidus*, was constantly changing. The later fifth-century emperors, in particular Anastasius (491–518), who introduced a new large *follis* (498), were more successful in introducing some stability; here it is interesting to find that Anastasius' reform of the coinage continued trends already to be seen in the Vandalic and Ostrogothic coinages of the west.[57] The circulation and issuing of coinage was highly regionalized, with a system of local mints, and the gold and bronze currencies operated separately; nevertheless the economy was still highly monetized, and money changers became common, with banking also a significant element. The sixth-century church of San Vitale in Ravenna was built by a rich banker, Julius Argentarius, at a cost of 26,000 *solidi*.

Thus, as we have seen, the late Roman taxation system was highly complex and had many problems. Its most important part, the supplies for the army, was also the most difficult to organize. The regular censuses necessary to keep the registers of land and population accurate tended not to be held, and great discrepancies could arise. Once collected, finally, the goods had to be transmitted to the necessary unit – a further process requiring complicated organization. Commutation of tax in kind into gold, especially in the west, at varying rates of commutation which at times had to be regulated by the government, was a further factor, and in the sixth century payment in gold (pounds or *solidi*) was the norm. It is extremely difficult to assess the economic consequences of this state of affairs. On a priori grounds alone, the collection and distribution of taxes in kind, which continued in part well into the fifth century, and the constant fluctuation of value against the *solidus* of the base-metal/copper coinage (*pecunia*) would seem likely to have had a depressive effect on the existence of a market economy.

### The economics of urban change

There was, however, urban change at varying rates in different parts of the empire, and the degree of continuity or decline in urban contexts is one of the most contentious issues in current scholarship. This will be discussed further in Chapter 7; for now, it is enough to say that while there was great variety between east and west and within individual provinces, evidence from sites all over the empire suggests that the typical late Roman urban life, with peristyle houses and open public spaces, was by some time in the sixth century (the exact date postulated varies and is often a matter of controversy – the change came much earlier in the western provinces) giving way to an urban fabric which suited a different kind of social and economic life. Public buildings were not repaired, or fell out of use, their stone being used as *spolia* for purposes including fortification. Houses were subdivided; shops or workshops encroached on colonnaded streets. In the Balkans, urban sites began to give way to fortified hill settlements, while on the eastern frontier sites described by Procopius in his *Buildings*, such as Resafa/Sergiopolis near the Euphrates, were characterized by their military provision and fortifications and their large churches and episcopal buildings rather than by public streets or grand houses.[58] But it is difficult to generalize: the large urban site of Scythopolis in Palestine for example continued to flourish into the Umayyad period until it was hit by a major earthquake in 749, and the large number of 'dead cities' of northern Syria were able to maintain a prosperous lifestyle not based on state investment or the presence of large landowning magnates. Similar changes can be detected in different parts of the empire, as continues to be shown by a huge mass of recent and current work, but at very different rates and for different local reasons. They cannot be explained in simple or universally applicable economic terms, but rest on much deeper changes in society, and especially on the changing role of elites and degree of maintenance of the late Roman administrative structure.

### Long-distance trade and exchange

Over the last few decades the study of the vast amount of pottery evidence, and in particular the diffusion of amphorae, the containers of the late Roman world, has transformed our understanding of specialized production and exchange. The pioneering work of John Hayes in the early 1970s provided a typology of late Roman pottery which enabled archaeologists to date excavated material far more securely and to log stratigraphic evidence; these findings were also extended into the study of late Roman amphorae, particularly by Italian archaeologists. The evidence from ancient shipwrecks sometimes provides valuable dating material of this kind.[59] With the growth of Constantinople and the diversion of Egyptian grain to the eastern capital, an eastern axis, Carthage/Constantinople, became important, and long-distance exchange continued into the fifth century, without serious break after the Vandal conquest of North Africa in 439;[60] this eastern axis continued in existence throughout the period, as the importance of Constantinople reached its peak, until the Persian and then the Arab invasions cut the connections between Constantinople and Egypt.

Many questions suggest themselves as a result of these conclusions, of which the following are only the most obvious. For example, whether these findings actually represent trading links (the evidence of pottery will not tell us the why of transmarine exchange, only the how). What if anything can they tell us about the impact of the post-Roman kingdoms in the west on the Mediterranean economy? Finally, to what extent does this evidence tally with that of urban change to suggest that a significant weakening of the Mediterranean system can be located in the later sixth to early seventh centuries, i.e., after the Justinianic attempt at reconquest and before the Arab invasions?

All these issues are the subject of ongoing debate and considerable disagreement, not least because they raise ideological issues about trade and the nature of the ancient economy. Carandini, Panella and their colleagues see the evidence as reflecting trading patterns in a market economy. Among the questions still to be settled is that of the overall economic impact of the Vandal conquest, including that of the effect on North Africa (and the other conquered areas) of the cessation of Roman taxation. Wickham rightly underlines the importance for North Africa of the grain requisitions for Rome, which would have had the effect of requiring a highly developed navigation and export system from which other products could also benefit, and whose cessation was therefore likely to have serious effects. According to this argument, the enforced grain exactions for Rome and Constantinople called forth a considerable level of production that was itself non-commercial, but which served to underpin commercial networks.[61] According to Wickham, the eastern Mediterranean saw an agrarian boom in the fifth-sixth centuries and an 'active commercial exchange network which linked Egypt, the Levant, and the Aegean in overlapping ways'; this system collapsed in three generations after 600, in the face of political change, but was 'pretty stable' until then.[62]

## The fall of the Roman empire

There is no simple way to characterize the late Roman economy, or the actual effect on society of the government's attempts to control it. Certain trends are evident, not simply the profound impact of barbarian invasion and settlement during this period, but also more general developments such as the tendency towards the amassing of vast amounts of land by individuals, the return to taxation in coin (gold) instead of in kind, the growing gulf between east and west and the difficulty experienced by the government in ensuring the collection of revenues and staffing its own administration. The establishment of the post-Roman kingdoms in the west and the effects of the wars of reconquest had major economic repercussions; these will be discussed in Chapter 5. In the east, by contrast, there is evidence of population increase and of intensified agriculture and cultivation in areas such as the limestone massif of northern Syria and even in such unpromising areas as the Hauran and the Negev; this evidence will be discussed further in Chapter 7. On the other hand, by the late sixth century, following the effects of war and perhaps also plague, the Roman military presence in the east was clearly becoming harder and harder to maintain. Clearly it is misleading if not impossible to generalize over so wide an area and so eventful a chronological span. As we saw, older historiography connected a highly negative view of the supposed rigidity, corruption, and over-taxation of the later Roman empire with the reasons for the fall of the Roman empire, and modern historiography also abounds in confident value-judgements about decline and the end of antiquity, many of which rest on unacknowledged assumptions about the late Roman system. The current vogue for comparing the end of empires which has arisen since the collapse of the Soviet Union and more recently in relation to America, routinely draws on the 'end of the Roman empire' for comparisons, and has served to entrench these older views.[63] Much of the literature on the fall of Rome poses the question 'Why?' in terms of radical alternatives: either barbarian invasions or internal collapse; interestingly, for all his generally gloomy view of the late Roman system, A.H.M. Jones, opted for the former.

The late Roman administrative and economic system was certainly cumbersome and had many defects. Lacking modern communications, the state could neither operate efficiently nor respond easily to change. The government resorted all too easily to empty and hectoring legislation; officials did what they could, and often enriched themselves; the people learnt how to cheat the system. There is nothing surprising in that, and the power of inertia was also great. What is impressive, and remarkable in such a context, is rather that this highly traditional and very complex society did manage to survive so well for so long.

# 5

# JUSTINIAN AND
# RECONQUEST

The reign of Justinian (527–65) deserves treatment in its own right, as one of the most important and also the best-documented periods in late antiquity. It is also a key period for any consideration of the Mediterranean world and of the later Roman empire. Justinian's codification of the law, achieved within a few years of his accession (*Institutes*, 533; *Digest*, 533; *Codex Justinianus*, 534) gave him a place in Catholic European history as a great Christian legislator, and his reign also saw a dramatic intervention in the west – an attempt by the east, at first spectacularly successful, to recover the lost territories of the western empire. This was the so-called 'reconquest', which began with the dispatch of a triumphantly successful expedition against Vandal Africa in 533 under the general Belisarius, and continued for over twenty years of military action and many vicissitudes until the settlement known as the 'Pragmatic Sanction' of 554 signalled the hoped-for return of Ostrogothic Italy to Roman rule. But unlike the North African campaign, the war in Italy proved to be costly and difficult, while the security of the Balkans had to be addressed at the same time; moreover, the recovery of North Africa from the Vandals brought with it a need for military, administrative and building investment. While Justinian's armies were engaged in the west, war was waged simultaneously in the east against the Sasanians. Again, this was at first successful, but then, under the new king Chosroes I, it became far more difficult, and the peace treaty signed in 561 was very costly to Constantinople.

Justinian is also renowned for the building of the present church of St Sophia in Istanbul, and for scores of other churches and fortifications around the empire (even if, as seems to be the case, some attributed to him in contemporary panegyric had been achieved or were already under way under his predecessor Anastasius). His wife Theodora was one of the most famous and notorious of Byzantine empresses; together they had built the church of Sts Sergius and Bacchus in Constantinople and they directed policy together. They are both depicted in the mosaics of San Vitale in Ravenna (547, the year before Theodora's death) and their names appear on the apse of the church of the monastery on Mt Sinai (later named after St Catherine), built by Justinian and originally dedicated to the Transfiguration. Justinian survived a very serious insurrection (the 'Nika' revolt, 532) and a dangerous visitation of plague

(541–2). His reign saw a last flowering of Greek and Latin literary composition, within an administrative system that was still that of the late Roman empire. He followed the example of his predecessors in continuing to struggle to achieve church unity, actively intervening in theological debate and summoning the Fifth Ecumenical Council in Constantinople in 553. However, he was not successful in his attempts to unify the church, and his reign saw the formation of a separatist church in the east, while as we saw the council was also a failure in the west. Justinian's later years saw a succession of plots, disillusion and dangerous attacks from new enemies, Huns, Slavs and Avars. Edward Gibbon was not sure whether to count Justinian as the last great Roman emperor or the first of the 'Greeks' (by which he meant the Byzantines), and like Constantine Justinian has provoked very different assessments in modern historiography.[1]

### The early years: Justinian's codification of the law

Within only a few months after becoming emperor, Justinian announced to the senate his plan of initiating the vast enterprise of collecting, editing and codifying the whole of previous Roman civil law, a task which was completed within five years, and which resulted in the three works already mentioned, all in Latin: the *Codex Justinianus*, the *Digest* and the *Institutes*, which together made up the *Corpus iuris civilis*.[2] For this purpose he set up a commission led by the praetorian prefect John the Cappadocian to collect and edit all imperial constitutions from the reign of Diocletian onwards and including the *Codex Theodosianus*, as well as all subsequent new laws (*Novellae*). The new *Codex* was promulgated with amazing speed in April 529, and reissued in revised form in 534 by a new commission led by the *quaestor* Tribonian, who was also in charge of producing the *Digest*, a vast compendium of non-imperial civil law.[3] The *Institutes*, promulgated late in 533, were aimed at law students in Constantinople, Rome and Berytus (Beirut), and also regulated the five years required for legal study. The whole was nothing less than a complete statement of all Roman law, edited and brought up to date for the sixth century – nothing that was not included in these compilations could be cited or had the force of law. Some contemporary sources give an idea of how these books were actually used by students and lawyers in Justinian's reign, and of the difference their publication had made when compared to the confused body of material that had previously existed.[4] After their publication, Justinian continued to legislate, issuing new laws, known as *Novellae*; these were binding on the whole empire, and if addressed to Illyria or Africa they were issued in Latin, whereas those meant for the eastern provinces were in Greek. These were not collected, and soon led to the sort of contradictions and confusion that had existed before the publication of the *Corpus*.

Justinian's *Corpus* was not a Christian compilation as such, but the emperor appealed in it to God and the Trinity, and the legislation was proclaimed in the name of Christ as well as that of Justinian. Some of Justinian's own legislation did, however, deal with church matters, or show Christian influence, especially in matters of marriage and family. *Novel* 131 (545) also gave to ecclesiastical canons the force of civil law, which Justinian expected bishops to promulgate, ordering also that copies of the Gospels should be placed in secular courtrooms. He was also concerned that the new compilations should be widely known in the provinces, through the offices of the respective praetorian prefects.

Taken together, Justinian's codification of the law and his legislative activity were an extraordinary achievement. It was not surprising that he claimed divine aid, or that he used the rhetorical prefaces introducing the new law books and the later *Novellae* to present the work within the framework of Roman tradition or to justify what he was doing.[5] It went together with the emperor's energetic reforms in other spheres – for example, in the administration – and Justinian's law codes remained, albeit with modifications, the basis of both Byzantine law and much European civil law, so much so that the discovery of Procopius's scandalous and hitherto unknown *Secret History* (see below) in the early seventeenth century seemed to shake Justinian's reputation so severely that it was assumed to be a forgery.

## Procopius of Caesarea and Justinian's wars

Most of Justinian's reign is fully and dramatically reported by a major writer, Procopius of Caesarea, who has provided not only a nearly complete military narrative in his eight-book *History of the Wars*, but also a sensational deconstruction of the same events in his *Secret History*. The same author's panegyrical *Buildings*, in six books, listing and praising the building activity of Justinian, brings a further level of complexity to those attempting to understand Procopius as an author and evaluate his evidence as a historian.[6] In Procopius' works we have a body of historical writing in Greek as important and interesting in itself as that of any historian in antiquity and a wealth of detailed information on military matters, topography, finance, buildings, and much else. Procopius was a participant in and eyewitness of some of the campaigns which he describes, and although that certainly does not guarantee his accuracy as a reporter, it does give his writing an immediacy and an authority which strike anyone who reads it. Procopius began as the aide of the general Belisarius, and his accounts of the early campaigns against the Persians in the east reveal an enthusiasm which was to sour later when things went less well. His descriptions of Belisarius' invasion and reconquest of Vandal Africa, and of his early successes in Italy, are based on his own experience on those campaigns, including missions undertaken together with Belisarius' wife Antonina. However, after 540 Procopius seems to have stayed in Constantinople, and he became increasingly disappointed with Belisarius and with Justinian. The *Secret History* fills in the narrative of the early part of the *Wars* by giving the 'secret' and more personal side of what happened in those years, including notoriously salacious and scathing accounts of the two women, Theodora and Antonina. The literary techniques of Procopius' writings, including the *Buildings*,

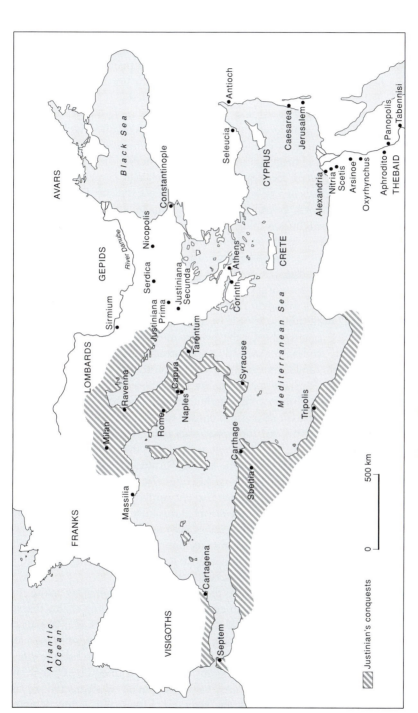

*Map 5.1* The 'reconquest' of Justinian

have still to be fully unpacked, and not surprisingly his versions have dominated much of the historiography.[7] Procopius was a major writer, if not one
of the first rank; it has recently been argued that he was at heart a pagan or a
Neoplatonist,[8] and there were indeed currents of Neoplatonism in sixth-century Constantinople, as can be seen in the work of John the Lydian and the
author of the anonymous treatise on political knowledge (Chapter 6).[9] However, it is not an easy matter to deduce Procopius' own religious position from
passages in his writings and there are many indications that he largely accepted
the Christian assumptions of his day.

Justinian's wars pose many questions, not least whether the emperor himself
had any clear intention of 'reconquering the west' when he launched the expedition against the Vandals in 533; it is more likely that the spectacular success over
the Vandals, after which Belisarius celebrated a magnificent triumph in Constantinople, suggested the possibility of a similar success against the Ostrogoths
in Italy. The outcome was in some ways ironic: it led in North Africa after 534
to the establishment of a Greek administration, imposed from Constantinople
in the name of Roman restoration, and set up in a province which was traditionally a bastion of Latin-speaking Christianity. Nevertheless, although the Arabs
established themselves in North Africa in the mid-seventh century, Carthage
itself did not fall until the late 690s.[10] In Italy an equally poignant effect of the
long years of war against the Goths by Byzantine armies was the effective
destruction of the Roman senate and the departure of many of the remaining
Roman aristocratic families to the east, where some of them formed a Latin-
speaking colony in Constantinople. Byzantine rule was established in Italy, but
a new challenge came almost immediately from the Lombards, and Justinian's
conquests came too late for the eastern empire to do more than maintain a partial presence in southern Gaul and Spain; although there was still a Byzantine
presence in Italy until the eleventh century, most of the west was already out
of the reach of Constantinople.[11] The lack of fortifications in Spain, in sharp
contrast to those in Byzantine North Africa, might be attributed to the financial
and military difficulties which Justinian had encountered by the 550s. Finally, it
might be argued that the cost and the effort of this huge and prolonged military
initiative, coinciding as it did with a major plague, continuing and expensive
wars against Sasanian Persia and new threats in the Balkans (Chapter 7), actually
weakened the eastern government and made it less able to deal with the military
challenges of the late sixth and early seventh centuries.

Justinian's wars are as susceptible to contradictory judgements as the rest
of his policies. The emperor himself enunciated high-sounding claims that he
was restoring the Roman past while issuing such severe laws against pagans
and all other dissidents that they have led one writer to compare him with
Stalin.[12] It was Justinian whose laws forbidding pagans to teach had the effect
of closing the thousand-year-old Academy at Athens, founded by Plato in the
fourth century BC, and who from time to time rounded up suspected pagans
among the elite. In contradiction, the same emperor is also often depicted
as a patron of letters and has been seen as one who inspired a classicizing

artistic renaissance.[13] These judgements need to be treated with caution. Yet the reign did see a notable amount of literary activity in classical genres and much spectacular imperial art, even if little has survived. Descriptions of the lost decoration of the ceiling in the Chalke entrance to the imperial palace by Procopius, and of Justinian's funeral vestment and the gold plate used in the palace in a Latin panegyric on the succession of Justin II by the North African writer Corippus, give an idea of this imperial iconography.[14] The last 'Roman'-style triumph was celebrated in Constantinople in 534 after Belisarius' victory of the Vandals, when the general led the captive Vandal royal family into the Hippodrome to prostrate themselves before the emperor; Procopius likens the spectacle to the famous earlier triumphs of Titus and Trajan.[15] But Justinian was also an avid theologian who enjoyed debating, even with clerics exiled by his own policies, and who wrote his own highly technical theological treatises.[16] Perhaps because of these contradictions, and like most other strong rulers in history, he aroused violent reactions among contemporaries. For the Chalcedonian church historian Evagrius, writing in Constantinople in the 590s and drawing on Procopius, Justinian 'fell among thistles and thorns' when at the end of his life he adopted a Julianist doctrinal position.[17] In his *Secret History* Procopius condemned him for greed, for 'bloodlust', and for overreaching himself, and the fiscal demands of his policies placed a heavy burden on the empire, especially on the wealthy classes. His reign marked the final reassertion of Roman military and imperial traditions aimed at the unification of east and west before the end of classical antiquity, and his legal codification the means whereby Roman law was transmitted and adopted in the European tradition. Yet the idea of reuniting the Mediterranean world under the rule of Constantinople could not succeed in the long term. Many motives were at work in the programme of western reconquest, taken as a whole, but those most commonly expressed and emphasized by contemporaries were the twin aims of imperial restoration and the championing of Christian orthodoxy in the territories now ruled by barbarians. These objectives run through the politics of Justinian's reign as a whole. In the same way the emperor seemed to be at one and the same time a conservative and an innovator – something which contemporaries found hard to understand or, often, to tolerate.[18]

There had been unsuccessful attempts by the eastern empire to dislodge the Vandals in the fifth century (Chapter 1). Their rule seemed well established and was extolled in the Latin poems by local poets collected in what is known as the Latin Anthology, and indeed North Africa remained the home of a vigorous literary culture in Latin.[19] However, the sometimes harsh pressure exerted by the Arian Vandals on the Catholic church and its leaders, combined with the natural desire of the emperor to succeed where others had failed, made them a tempting target. Justinian's expedition against them in 533 was despatched with a great sense of style. On board the ships was a force of 10,000 infantry and 5,000 cavalry, with the general Belisarius and his wife Antonina and the historian Procopius, Belisarius' right-hand man; they were seen off from Constantinople by the emperor and empress and the patriarch, who said prayers for

*Figure 5.1* The Barberini ivory. An emperor (probably Justinian) is shown in traditionally classicizing style and in triumphant pose with conquered peoples below, but with a bust of Christ above. Paris: Musée du Louvre

the expedition's success. Remembering the ignominious failure of the expedition sent by the Emperor Leo (Chapter 1), nobody had been in favour of the emperor's idea, says Procopius, and the only one who dared to speak against it to the emperor was his minister John the Cappadocian, whose long speech the historian records. However, a mysterious 'bishop from the east' conveniently reported a dream in which God had promised his help, and thus confirmed the emperor's enthusiasm to proceed.[20] Within months, Belisarius was back in Constantinople celebrating a triumph, and Justinian was thinking of Italy, where Belisarius was soon dispatched via Sicily, reaching Italy in the summer of 536.

The emperor had a pretext for war in the murder of his protégée Amalasuntha, the daughter of the Ostrogothic king Theodoric and mother of the dead Athalaric, who had misguidedly offered the throne to Theodatus.[21] Justinian also had good political reasons at home for mounting such an attempt, even against the prudent opinions of his advisers, for he had only recently weathered with extreme difficulty the great riot in Constantinople known as the 'Nika revolt' (from the cries of 'nika' ('victory') by the rioters). During the uprising, the emperor had allegedly only been prevented from fleeing altogether by the resolve of the Empress Theodora, who rallied the imperial party by declaring in ringing tones that she would never flee – 'empire is a fine shroud'.[22] The circus factions ('Blues' and 'Greens') were prominent in the rioting, and in Procopius' account of it, and participants in urban violence were all too likely to take up particular grievances; the factions reappear as players in the fall of the Emperor Maurice and the unrest in eastern cities which led to the overthrow of Phocas in the early seventh century (Chapter 9, and for urban violence, see Chapter 7). The hippodrome in Constantinople was the epicentre of the 'Nika' revolt, and it was here where imperial troops went in, led by Belisarius, and killed many of the crowd. The rioters voiced their demands in the form of shouting and acclamations addressed to the imperial box, and the flavour of this chanting is vividly conveyed in the seventh-century *Chronicon Paschale*.[23]

The immediate danger to the regime was averted, though only at the price of much destruction and great loss of life. Serious damage had been done to the official areas in the centre of Constantinople, including the church of St Sophia, and this was now rebuilt on a grand scale; the church as we see it today was rededicated in 535. Procopius claims that it was also felt that since the situation on the eastern front against Persia was satisfactory after the treaty of 533, a successful expedition might restore the emperor's reputation. This impression is reinforced by Procopius' emphasis on the opposition to Justinian's scheme, which he shared, and the role played in his narrative at this point by prophetic dreams – he even claims to have had a dream himself of Belisarius' future success. Belisarius' fleet landed at Ras Kapoudia on the east coast of Tunisia, and learned that Gelimer, who had deposed the relatively pro-Roman Hilderic in 530, was absent from Carthage. By September Belisarius had defeated the Vandal army outside Carthage and in a sensational move, entered the city, where, according to Procopius, who was there, he feasted in the palace and seated himself on Gelimer's throne.[24] A further victory in December resulted in Gelimer's surrender; in traditional Roman style, Justinian had already taken the victory titles of Vandalicus and Africanus.[25] This extraordinarily easy success, combined with the murder of Amalasuntha, made similar action against the Goths in Italy seem equally feasible. The reforming laws of this period have an optimistic and energetic tone which fits Justinian's confident expectations of imperial success.[26] He was not to know that the Italian campaigns would drag on for nearly twenty years, or that the price of the final settlement in AD 554 would be a devastated Italy.

## The eastern provinces and peace with Persia

Whatever the original intention may have been, ideas and policies changed with changing circumstances, and the hopeful beginning soon met with problems. In the east the Sasanians still presented a major military problem, and this lasted throughout the period of the western campaigns and beyond, passing in turn to Justinian's successors (Chapter 9). The story of Justinian's wars with Persia dramatically illustrates the actual lack of the necessary resources to pursue major campaigns in the eastern frontier area, or even to resist Persian raids, while simultaneously campaigning elsewhere, as well as the enormous cost to the eastern empire of securing temporary peace.

The two powers had remained in competition over the border territory and its population since the Sasanians first came to power in the third century.[27] Now, a series of not-so-glorious campaigns on the Mesopotamian frontier in the first years of Justinian's reign, as a result of which the future historian Procopius first became the intimate of Belisarius, came to a temporary end in 531 with the death of the Persian king Cavadh and the accession of Chosroes I. This is the point at which, if we believe Agathias, seven philosophers from the Academy at Athens, who had left after Justinian's law of 529, made their way to Ctesiphon in the hope that Chosroes would prove a Platonic philosopher-king. They found that 'those in authority were overbearing and vainglorious' and that the young king's much-vaunted acquaintance with philosophy was 'utterly superficial', and soon left Persia.[28] Procopius' version of these early campaigns in the east is biased towards Belisarius, as can be seen from the parallel account in the *Chronicle* of John Malalas.[29] A major treaty between the two powers was concluded in 533; the terms included a payment by Byzantium of 11,000 lb of gold, but apart from forcing a certain degree of retreat on both sides, left things essentially unchanged. It was not likely that a strong ruler such as Chosroes I, who was fully a match for Justinian, would rest content with this. Moreover, his timing was fatal for the Byzantines; after making hostile noises for some time, he invaded Roman territory again in 540, the very year when Belisarius was recalled from Italy. The second Persian war, in the 540s, was a very different affair from the first. The lack of an adequate Roman defence system is painfully obvious in the ease with which the Persian armies could approach towns such as Edessa and Apamea in Mesopotamia and Syria, and extort large payments of silver. The local bishops were the unfortunate middle-men in these transactions; the Persians took and burnt Beroea (Aleppo) while its bishop, Megas, was away appealing to the Roman command at Antioch for assistance, only to find that Justinian had given orders for no payments to be made for the safety of eastern cities, and that Ephraem, patriarch of Antioch, was under suspicion of being willing to hand over his city to the Persians. Returning to Beroea, the hapless Megas expostulated with Chosroes, but let out that he had received no funds for the safety of Antioch, whereupon the Persian king at once made for Antioch.[30] Those citizens who could, immediately left, and Chosroes besieged and sacked Antioch, second city of the eastern empire, a catastrophe which provoked Procopius to exclaim:

> I shudder when I describe so great a disaster, and pass it on to be Remembered by future generations, and I do not know what God's will could be in raising up the affairs of a man or a place, and then casting them down and wiping them out for no apparent reason.
>
> (*Wars* II.10.4)

We have a telling glimpse of the real situation at Antioch before the Persian siege when we see the patriarch, local bishops and Byzantine envoys from Constantinople all in urgent conference about what best to do. Since the Persians demanded payments in silver, the local population did its best to rid itself of as much silver as possible before they arrived. When the Persians did start the siege, the population was unwise enough to indulge in taunting the enemy from the walls, only to be subjected to a massacre when the Persians entered the city.[31] After this example, Chosroes was naturally able to ask an even higher price in silver for the safety of other cities such as Apamea, Chalcis and Edessa.

The early 540s also saw one of the greatest plagues in history. The disease, usually thought to be a form of bubonic plague, struck Constantinople and the eastern provinces in AD 542, having first struck in Egypt the year before, and is vividly described by Procopius, who was an eyewitness;[32] the emperor himself fell ill but recovered. Even allowing for exaggeration in the literary sources (the plague is also described by the Syriac church historian John of Ephesus), the level of casualties was clearly extremely high, perhaps approaching that of the Black Death. The church historian Evagrius, who was a child at the time, movingly describes its effects at Antioch, which fell heavily on his own family. The plague, he says, fell upon the east two years after the sack of Antioch, thus in 542, and was in some respects, though not all, similar to the Athenian plague of 430 BC described by Thucydides:

> I too, the writer of this history ... was afflicted in the early stages of the plague with the so-called buboes, while I was still just a schoolboy. In the various attacks of the plague many of my children died, as well as my wife and other members of my family, servants and country people, for the attacks returned up to my own day, as it were in cyclic progression. I lost my daughter, as well as the earlier ones, and her child, two years before the time of writing, when I was in my fifty-eighth year, the plague having returned four times to Antioch and this being the fourth attack in the cycle.
>
> (Evagrius, *HE* IV.29)

The sixth-century plague poses considerable problems for historians, in that despite the detailed accounts in literary sources, it is very hard to demonstrate directly from archaeological evidence (see Chapter 7). However, it cannot but have had a serious effect; the death toll had an immediate effect on imperial tax revenues and military manpower clearly apparent in subsequent legislation to recover taxes from the estates of those who had died intestate,[33] and in the great difficulties now experienced in sustaining the war on two fronts simultaneously.[34] The plague spread widely and struck in successive waves in both parts of the empire. However, historians differ greatly as to its probable effects or mortality rate, and the identification with bubonic plague, largely a retrojection from the Black Death, has been challenged; faced with the problems surrounding its interpretation, Peregrine Horden aptly describes the problem as 'a [historiographical] black hole at the centre of the Age of Justinian'.[35]

Despite the plague, a large Byzantine army gathered to defend Armenia in 543, but thanks to confusion and mismanagement on the Byzantine side a small force of Persians was able to kill the general Narses and inflict a heavy defeat at the fortress of Anglon near Dvin.[36] Eventually a five-year treaty was concluded in 545 at a cost to the empire of 2,000 lbs of gold. Even during this period, operations continued between the Arab allies of Byzantium and Persia, the Ghassanids and the Lakhmids, and a substantial Byzantine force, having previously laid siege to Petra in Lazica, which was held by the Persians, was able to destroy the Persian forces in Lazica twice in the course of the year 549. A further five-year treaty was concluded in 551 in Constantinople, the empire paying on this occasion 2,600 lbs of gold; but hostilities dragged on in Lazica, where a complex local situation exacerbated the difficulties caused by the rival powers. By 561, however, both sides had reasons for concluding a more solid peace, and the end of that year saw a fifty-years' peace agreed at Dara between Justinian's Master of Offices, Peter the Patrician, and the Persian ambassador Yesdegusnaph, with the Persians renouncing their claims to Lazica, but exacting from the empire the large annual sum of 30,000 gold *nomismata*, of which ten years' instalments would be paid in advance in two instalments. Existing frontiers were confirmed and trade across the borders was limited to those cities where there were customs facilities. A long and detailed account of the negotiations, which provides interesting information about contemporary diplomacy, and a complete text of the treaty itself, is given by the historian Menander Protector, who also records the letters sent by both rulers to ratify what had been agreed by their envoys. The letter of ratification from the Roman Emperor, bearing the usual superscription, is well known to us. The letter from the Persian king was written in Persian, and Menander provides a Greek translation:

> 'The divine, good, father of peace, ancient Khosro, king of kings, fortunate, pious and beneficent, to whom the gods have given great fortune and a great kingdom, giant of giants, formed in the image of the gods, to Justinian Caesar, our brother.' Such was the superscription, while the meaning of the text was as follows (I use a word-for-word translation, a

procedure I felt absolutely necessary lest, if I changed the phraseology, I be suspected of distorting something of the truth).

(fr. 6.1 Blockley, *Menander the Guardsman*, lines 175–87)

Among the clauses agreed was one relating to the movements of the Arab groups allied to each side, who were now a more and more important factor in the politics and settlement patterns in the east (Chapter 8), and another that guaranteed the status of the many Christians in Persia.[37]

## The war in Italy

The continuous drain of resources, manpower and indeed gold on such a large scale to the east helps to put the 'reconquest' of the west into a more realistic perspective. One of the striking features about the conduct of the campaigns is the small number of troops dispatched from Constantinople, which in turn evoked constant complaints from the generals that they were being starved of resources. Belisarius, for instance, found himself defending Rome with 5,000 men against a Gothic force of possibly 20,000. It is true that the Byzantine cavalry, as mounted archers, were more mobile and thus had an advantage over the Goths, who were armed with spears and swords; but their small numbers constituted a major problem, especially in the early 540s after Belisarius' recall to Constantinople, and Totila's accession as king of the Goths in 541. Sieges played a major role in Ostrogothic success in these years, and the Gothic superiority in numbers gave them the capacity to starve out the inhabitants of the towns, the resulting loss of Byzantine control leading to Belisarius' second Italian expedition in 544.[38] Even then he was consistently left without enough troops to give battle effectively, as Procopius bitterly reports:

> When he arrived in Italy, there was not a single day when things went right for him, because the hand of God was unmistakably against him … in spite of five years' effort he never once succeeded in disembarking on any part of the coast, unless there was a fortress handy: the whole of that time he sailed about, trying one landing-place after another.
>
> (*Secret History* 4.42; 5.1)

There were other factors that delayed a final victory, including, it would seem, the emperor's own suspicions of his generals, especially Belisarius. Though in fact he remained entirely loyal to Justinian, Belisarius was often recalled, and, if we believe the disappointed Procopius, even after the inopportune death in 550 of Germanus, the newly appointed general for the Italian campaign, he was kept in Constantinople doing nothing.[39] After his return in 549, and the fall and occupation of Rome for the second time by Totila, it had taken the latter's attack on Sicily and lobbying by prominent Italians now living in Constantinople to persuade Justinian to pursue the war with real force.[40] That the eunuch Narses was able to win the final battles, beginning with a naval battle in 551, owed much to his having insisted on being given enough resources to raise sufficient troops and pay the soldiers' arrears. In the encounter at Busta Gallorum (552), the Byzantines for once outnumbered the Goths, whose weakness in archery again told against them. The Gothic king Totila was fatally wounded in this battle, before which he performed a dramatic war-dance,

> wearing armour plentifully covered with gold, and the decoration on his cheek-plates as well as on his helmet and spear was of purple – indeed a wonderful display of regal splendour.
>
> (Proc., *Wars* VIII.31.18)

A few months later his successor Teias was also defeated in battle at Mons Lactarius. But even before this, Procopius' account had become more and more disillusioned about Justinian and imperial policy generally, and he left the closing stages of the war to be told by his successor Agathias in the early 570s.[41]

In taking on the task of reconquering Italy, Justinian clearly underestimated the power of the Ostrogoths to mount a long-term and serious resistance, as well as the consequent costs to the empire of keeping up the military effort year after year. He may have thought in terms of an offensive as short term as Belisarius' spectacular campaign against the Vandals. No one could have foreseen the plague of 541 or its drastic impact on the capital, and the relative quiet of the situation on the eastern frontier at the start of the Italian campaign was to prove illusory. Once conquered, North Africa, and eventually Italy, each required a new administrative organization – also costly. There was investment in religious structures, as with the large pilgrimage complex at Bir Ftouha in Carthage, dated to the 540s,[42] and in the case of Africa, this also meant a massive investment of men and resources for the province's defence, which added to the difficulty of carrying on the wars elsewhere. But in addition to all these factors, Justinian himself turned out to be an uncertain commander, suspicious of his subordinates and jealous of allowing them even the forces they needed for the task in hand.

Moreover, the military problems went hand in hand with those of maintaining religious unity. The closing stages of the Gothic war in the 540s and early 550s coincided with a tense period in ecclesiastical politics which led up to the Fifth Ecumenical Council held in Constantinople in 553–54, by which Justinian hoped to find a formula acceptable both to the anti-Chalcedonians in the east and to the church of Rome. Passions ran very high on all sides. The Latin-speaking North African bishops, who were strongly on the side of Rome and against the emperor, went to Constantinople en masse, while Pope Vigilius, still in the capital, spent months under virtual house arrest, and for a long time refused to attend the council altogether, only recanting in its final stages.[43] The crisis followed Justinian's own religious initiative in 543, known as the affair of the Three Chapters, because of his decree ordering the condemnation of the works of three earlier dyophysite theologians (Theodore of Mopsuestia,

Theodoret of Cyrrhus and Ibas of Edessa), and was raging throughout the later 540s, just when the war in the east and in Italy was going badly.[44] The emperor was again attempting to find a formula acceptable to the easterners,[45] but his decree roused strong opposition from the North Africans (see below) and in Italy. Pope Vigilius was summoned to Constantinople, but made slow progress and arrived only in the winter of 546–47; under pressure, he condemned the Three Chapters in 548 but then withdrew his condemnation and agreed to a new council in Constantinople. These upheavals coincided with the general political difficulties which Justinian was experiencing, and which are graphically recorded in book VII of Procopius's *Wars*. Finally the attitudes of the Roman population in Italy to Justinian's military intervention were by no means straightforward. Members of the senatorial class found their lands devastated by the war and their personal safety threatened, especially by the repeated sieges of Rome. After 540 a number of them, including Cassiodorus, found their way to Constantinople, where their presence constituted an important lobby and added to the number of Latin-speakers in the capital. The eastern government represented the Italian war as a war of liberation, but it was not obvious that it was regarded in the same way by the Romans in Italy themselves. When the war finally ended, the formerly prosperous Italy was left in a dire condition.[46]

Given all these problems and adverse factors, it is less surprising that the military campaigns ran into difficulties than that they could actually be sustained for so long; this can only be explained in terms of the generally prosperous and healthy condition of the eastern empire when Justinian came to the throne in the early sixth century. On the other hand, as we shall see, indicators of urban change begin to become apparent from the end of Justinian's reign (Chapters 7 and 8); if his ambitious programme of military reconquest and imperial reconstruction was not actually a contributory factor in that process, it certainly added to these difficulties.

## The cost of reconquest: North Africa

The speedy capture of North Africa from the Vandals provides a striking example of the continuing cost of conquest after the initial fighting was over. Already in April 534, before Belisarius' return, Justinian had confidently legislated for the future civil and military government of the newly reconquered territory.[47] Africa was placed under a praetorian prefect with seven provinces and soon had its own *magister militum*. The law looked back to the days of Roman rule in Africa, and showed no realization of the current importance of the local tribal groups, who were relegated to the role of enemies.[48] In Constantinople much was made of the victory. In a grandiose imitation of earlier Roman triumphs, Gelimer, the last Vandal king, was taken to Constantinople to walk in chains in Belisarius' procession, while Belisarius himself walked to the Hippodrome and prostrated himself before Justinian, who sat in the imperial box wearing the special triumphal garment known as the *loros*, to underline the lesson that victory belonged to the emperor, albeit a civilian one. But the next two decades were to prove much more difficult than had been anticipated. A new and more recalcitrant military threat immediately presented itself from the Berber tribes (*Mauri*), unforeseen by the easterners and conspicuously lacking in Procopius' narrative of the early stages of the reconquest, as well as from a mutiny in the Byzantine army; and while the eunuch general Solomon, and then John Troglita, fought successful, if hard, campaigns, the problem of dealing with hostile Berbers did not go away.[49] John of Biclar, a well-informed chronicler who lived in Constantinople, records what was evidently a dangerous situation in the 560s and early 570s, and there was more fighting in the 580s and 590s.[50] The condition of Africa is painted in gloomy terms in the 560s by the African poet Corippus who had come to Constantinople and composed a Latin panegyric on the accession of Justinian's successor, Justin II (565–78); on the whole, however, the province seems to have attained a reasonable degree of peace and prosperity by the later sixth century, and the expedition which was to overthrow Phocas in 609–10 and put Heraclius on the throne in Constantinople was dispatched from Carthage.

Africa was rich and fertile; the reconquest made its grain available for Constantinople, and its oil production reached a height in the seventh century, when according to later Arabic sources it was immensely rich. Justinian's regulatory law laid down provisions for a civil administration of 750 persons (staffed from the east), whose salaries amounted to over 17,500 *solidi* per year. In addition there was the cost of the military hierarchy, perhaps 500 strong, and the army itself.[51] Added to this regular expenditure was the special cost of defensive and other building works; these were necessary after a century of Vandal rule and in order to secure the reconquest. The imposition of immediate taxation was obviously a priority, as Procopius also recognized.[52] Thus having got rid of the Vandals, with whom many will have made a reasonable accommodation, the 'Roman' inhabitants, still Latin-speaking and with their religious loyalties centred on Rome, found themselves faced not only with heavy taxes and military rule, but with a situation in which the army billeted in their towns was by no means always able to defend them against an increasing threat of Berber raids. If Procopius' picture of Africa in the *Wars* is somewhat mixed, that in the *Secret History* is one of unrelieved gloom:

> Libya, for instance, in spite of its enormous size, has been laid so utterly waste that however far one went it would be a remarkable achievement to find a single person there.
>
> (*Secret History* 18)

In addition to their military and economic impositions, the newcomers used Greek instead of Latin, as the many surviving official seals make clear. By the mid-seventh century a formal debate in Carthage between the Monothelite patriarch Pyrrhus of Constantinople and Maximus Confessor was held in Greek (Chapter 9). Justinian had embarked on the war against the Vandals under the banner of restoring orthodoxy, yet very soon after the conquest the emperor in Constantinople began imposing a religious policy which the African church, traditionally linked with the church of Rome, found totally unacceptable. Among the leading African bishops who protested personally and in writing against Justinian's condemnation of the Three Chapters were Facundus of Hermiane and Primasius of Hadrumetum. After holding their own council at Carthage in 550, they were summoned to Constantinople, where they carried on their opposition and became the targets of imperial sanctions. Reparatus of Carthage was eventually deposed along with many others, and the chronicler Victor of Tunnuna, himself imprisoned for opposition to Justinianic policy, later recorded the imprisonment and poor treatment of African bishops in Constantinople. Thus the price of reconquest was high on all sides, and both the conquering power and the local populations got more than they had bargained for.[53] Africa was atypical, however, in that in the late sixth century, despite all this, and despite the hard fighting which ensued between the Byzantine army and the Berbers, it eventually did well, thanks to local factors – its own bountiful natural resources, the speed of the original conquest, which spared it from the lengthy war and frequent sieges which so devastated Italy, and perhaps also the situation under Vandal rule, which seems to have been better than was once thought and to have profited in turn from the prosperous condition of the late Roman province of North Africa. The real puzzle of Byzantine Africa lies in the lack of literary or documentary source material for the more peaceful second half of the sixth century, and certainly in the seventh, which makes a closer assessment of the economic and social effect of Byzantine reconquest extremely difficult. Yet the newly conquered province was not subject to the kind of invasion and consequent fragmentation experienced by Italy, or for example Greece, where Justinian's defence system failed to halt the Slav incursions of the late sixth century. Eastern cults arrived and many new Christian sanctuaries were built and others modified.[54] In the seventh century, Africa had remained safe from Persian conquest, and Maximus Confessor and other monks made their base near Carthage. Efforts were also made to convert Berber tribes, even in the sub-Sahara.[55] Arab armies arrived in Africa in the mid-seventh century and a new Islamic settlement was founded as Kairouan, but North Africa remained in the main a Byzantine province for much longer than Egypt.[56] Coin hoards indicate that the government in Constantinople was still able to invest in North Africa in the second half of the seventh century, and the eventual fall of Carthage to the Arabs came only in the 690s.

## Fortifications and other buildings

Even if some of the countless fortifications claimed for Justinian belong more probably to the reign of Anastasius, Justinian was a great builder. To judge from Procopius' account, much of the emperor's extensive building programme in the provinces was dedicated to defence. However, its overall scope and impact are hard to assess for a variety of reasons. The first has to do with the fact that our main literary source is Procopius' *Buildings*, written explicitly to praise Justinian, which makes extravagant claims for the emperor's achievements.[57] Since the work is also incomplete as a record (it omits Italy entirely and only gives lists of fortifications for the Balkans in book IV), and since individual statements often cannot be checked, this is a difficult text on which to base a fair assessment, especially as in those places where checking is possible from archaeological or other evidence Procopius is quite often found wanting (Chapter 7).[58] In addition, especially in the case of the forts and fortified sites in the northern provinces, many sites remain unexcavated, or, if they have been excavated, there is nothing in the material remains (for example, inscriptions or coins) by which they can be securely dated. It may well be that substantial parts of the programme which Procopius ascribes to Justinian were actually begun by Anastasius, and indeed it is entirely in the nature of panegyric to seem to claim the credit for building anew when in fact the work in question is a work of restoration. But even if Justinian was the restorer rather than the initiator, the sheer amount of building suggested by Procopius was enormous, implying capital investment in military installations on a massive scale.

How strategic or effective it was in terms of defence is another matter. Extensive fortifications were built in North Africa, but many served the purpose of housing troops for supply purposes rather than actual defence, and they were quite often modest in size. The building works in North Africa are described in some detail by Procopius in book VI of the *Buildings* and have been thoroughly studied.[59] However Procopius's narrative puts them in a wider context of building, and also emphasizes the importance of church building for Justinian's policy. His account of the building work in Carthage[60] is useful but incomplete, and one must remember that he himself left Africa at the same time as Belisarius, and so far as we know never returned. His sources for many of the building works he describes are indeed still unclear. When writing of Palestine in book V, he is, not surprisingly, a good guide, as a native of Caesarea, and his accuracy was spectacularly confirmed by the discovery of the Nea church in Jerusalem, dedicated to the Virgin.[61] As for the position of the walled monastery which still stands at the foot of Mt Sinai, where Moses saw God, it was built over the traditional site of the burning bush and in a location already inhabited by monks and hermits. Its location clearly shows a diplomatic and religious function, though Procopius claims that it was built to keep Saracen invaders from entering the province of Palestine.[62] This it could hardly do, positioned as it is in a cleft between two mountainous peaks; on the other hand, the Justinianic walls which surrounded the monastery remain one of its most striking features.[63] Justinian's motives in his buildings were religious as well as military; the site of the burning bush was enclosed within its walls, and the apse of the monastic church, built by a local architect from Aila and with an inscription on its roof beams which commemorates the death of Theodora in 548, is decorated with an impressive mosaic on the theme of the

*Figure 5.2* The walls of the monastery of St Catherine at the foot of Mt Sinai, built by Justinian and described by Procopius. The fine mosaic in the apse of its church depicts the Transfiguration; the dedication to St Catherine dates from considerably later.

Transfiguration.[64] But defence was certainly vitally important in Justinian's overall programme and in some areas his building work took the form of long walls, as at Thermopylae and the Isthmus of Greece.[65] Elsewhere it was a question of fortified refuges or, less often, actual fortresses.

Ambitious as it was, the scheme was unable to keep out the Huns from threatening Greece and even Constantinople in 558–9, when the aged Belisarius was recalled to confront them. Yet even allowing for exaggeration, Justinian's building programme represents an extraordinary outlay of resources, even during the years of maximum military effort. Procopius makes it clear time and time again that in the building programme, defensive and religious aims went hand in hand. There were also works of social welfare such as hospitals and hospices, and churches were built as often as forts, especially in newly reconquered territory, where they could serve as demonstrations of Roman power. Together with Justinian's military policy went a determined missionary activity. This can be seen in several areas; for instance, in Nubia and in the case of King Tzath of Lazica, whose conversion was the price of clientship; as Garth Fowden has shown, the eastern Mediterranean became a network of Christian client states.[66] Justinian was even willing to entrust the conversion of pagans in Asia Minor to a Syriac-speaking non-Chalcedonian, John of Ephesus. Even in the case of the provinces which were subject to military offensives, the wars were given the appearance of crusades undertaken to restore orthodoxy, although the reality of the situation often looked different when the local Roman population was faced with the choice between the local Arian rulers to whom they had become accustomed and the harsh actuality of the Byzantine intervention.

## The impact of war

For the eastern empire the drain in gold, men and other resources as a result of Justinian's wars was immense, especially when combined with the similar demands made on imperial funds by the war against Persia and the expensive treaties it entailed. There was a cost in public opinion too: the early euphoria could hardly be maintained, and as things became difficult, whatever the reason, the emperor lost popularity. Two works in particular reflect the doubts and criticisms:[67] Procopius' *Secret History*, with its violent tirades against Justinian and Theodora (who died in 548) and its catalogue of complaints and accusations against the abuses which Procopius claims had taken place; and John the Lydian's *De Magistratibus*, where an attempt is made to save the emperor's reputation by blaming everything on his ministers, especially the praetorian prefect, John the Cappadocian:

> Our emperor, gentlest of men, knew nothing of these affairs because everyone, though abused by the Cappadocian's unrestricted exercise of power, spoke in defence of that wicked man. ... Only the emperor's wife and helpmeet, who was most vigilant in her sympathy towards those suffering injustice, found it intolerable to ignore the destruction of the state. ... Naturally, then, the emperor, being a good man though slow to requite evil, was in the grip of a baffling situation.
>
> (*De Mag.* III.69, from Maas, *John Lydus*, 95)

Blame was also attached to Justinian's ministers by Procopius, but his account of the eventual fall of John the Cappadocian spares neither Justinian nor Theodora, who emerges as both vindictive and manipulative.[68] The social structures of sixth-century cities were also conducive to disturbances.[69] Justinian was indeed hesitant, especially in his handling of his ministers and generals, but it is only with hindsight that we see so clearly that the changes already taking place in the Mediterranean world would combine with the sheer size of the endeavour to prevent his military successes from lasting. Peace with Persia in 561 was bought at a high price, and new invaders in the shape of Lombards, Huns, Avars and Slavs soon reached Italy (568) and the Balkans. Justinian's new flagship city of Justiniana Prima (usually identified with Čaričin Grad, south of Niš) was merely one out of many sites in the Balkans that soon sank into obscurity (Chapter 7). Much of Italy was soon lost to the kingdom of the Lombards, and Byzantine control reduced to the exarchate of Ravenna and the duchy of Rome, which facilitated the development of a territorially based papacy.[70] On the other hand, the coastal territories gained by the expedition sent to Spain in 552 under the aged patrician Liberius, to help the pretender

Athanagild, were in the main kept by Byzantium until 624 and their defence put under a *magister militum* appointed by Constantinople.[71]

Leaving aside North Africa, the overall result of the 'reconquest' of the western provinces was that the eastern empire regained and retained a small portion of Italy and a much smaller portion of Spain during the ensuing period when the early medieval western kingdoms were taking shape. In itself this was a significant achievement. But in Italy the effects of the Gothic wars were destructive in the extreme. A law known as the 'Pragmatic Sanction' imposed a settlement on the model of that given to North Africa twenty years before. Pope Pelagius I (556–61), already alienated by Justinian's religious policies, complained in his letters that agriculture was devastated; in addition, the senatorial aristocracy had had its fortunes undermined if not destroyed, and many members had left for the east, while the senate itself collapsed as an institution and many towns, including Rome, suffered greatly during the hostilities.[72] Even if Italy's capacity for recovery is often underestimated, Ravenna especially showing evidence of growth and vitality,[73] profound underlying changes in urban structure, municipal organization and settlement patterns were already under way. The future Pope Gregory I spent some years in Constantinople in the 580s, where he established excellent relations with the family of the Emperor Maurice and the Italian senatorial exiles in the eastern capital, which, as his letters show, survived into his tenure of the papacy. But, as T.S. Brown points out, this group suffered severely from the attack made on the supporters of Maurice by Phocas (602–10), and with it, valuable connections between Constantinople and Italy were broken. Another factor which had made for difficulty in relations with Constantinople was the opposition of the Roman church to the Three Chapters decree and the Fifth Ecumenical Council of 553–4.[74] This was to continue. In the seventh century, too, despite the appointment of easterners to the papacy, Rome was the centre of opposition to the imperial policy of Monotheletism, and attracted African as well as eastern participants to the Lateran Synod held there which condemned the policy in 649 (Chapter 9). The African church, equally opposed to Constantinople, looked to Rome throughout this period as its natural ally. The church in Italy also gained economically and in other ways from the political changes in the later sixth century, in effect stepping into the shoes of the old senatorial aristocracy and acquiring both wealth and political influence. In this way, Justinian's own ecclesiastical policies, though aimed at the near-impossible task of achieving unity between the eastern and western churches, in practice proved a major difficulty in Byzantine relations with Rome and contributed to the growth in power of the Roman church and eventually the papacy.

In considering the effects of the reconquest policy on the provinces and on the empire generally, three factors need to be remembered: first, the immediate effects of war and of the subsequent administrative, economic and military settlements; second, Justinian's own energetic interventions in religious policy, which so far as the western provinces were concerned cut across the process of reunification; and third, the backdrop of urban and rural change which can be perceived in all areas throughout the period (Chapter 7). As for the eastern provinces, here too, Justinian failed to conciliate eastern religious feeling – indeed, it was his unsuccessful attempts to do so which led to the alienation in the western church and part of the east after the Fifth Council. In the 540s, even as non-Chalcedonian exiles were housed in the palace at Constantinople, Jacob Bar'adai was made bishop of Edessa and began ordaining Miaphysite clergy in the east, a fateful step which thus created a dual hierarchy in the east, especially Syria and Mesopotamia, and allowed the development of the Syrian orthodox or Jacobite church, so named after Jacob himself (Chapter 8).

## Justinian as emperor

Justinian's reign was extraordinary. Not only did it last for thirty-eight years (527–65), but it was also commonly agreed that he had been the effective ruler during the reign of his uncle Justin I (518– 27).[75] Justinian's own reign opened with a grand imperial gesture, the idea of codifying the whole of previous Roman law; amazingly, the work was completed in record time; the situation on the eastern frontier looked hopeful and the trauma of the Nika revolt seemed to have been overcome by the building of St Sophia and Belisarius' astonishingly successful expedition against the Vandals. Italy followed as the next imperialist objective, and a high point was reached with Belisarius' entry into Rome in AD 540. Whatever the mortality rate of the plague of 541–2, which even struck the emperor, the epidemic came as a severe blow. The population of Constantinople certainly suffered a sudden drop, and the losses among the rural population in the eastern provinces must have been serious, with adverse short-term consequences for the imperial tax revenues. Procopius says of the effects that when pestilence swept through the whole known world and notably the Roman empire, wiping out most of the agricultural community and of necessity leaving a trail of desolation in its wake, Justinian showed no mercy towards the ruined free-holders. Even then, according to Procopius, he did not refrain from demanding the annual payment of tax, not only the amount at which he assessed each individual, but also the amount for which his deceased neighbours were liable.[76]

The ensuing phases of both the Italian and the Persian campaigns were difficult, and command problems were added to those of supply and manpower. However, it is necessary to correct for the fact that Procopius, with his traditional mentality, tends to ascribe all difficulties to personal or class motives. Such criticisms show themselves most sharply in the *Secret History*, but they also permeate the *Wars*.[77] The fall of John the Cappadocian came in 541, but Procopius also accuses Peter Barsymes, who became praetorian prefect early in 543 and thus had major financial responsibility for provincial taxation and army supply and maintenance. At a deeper level lies the question of Justinian's own responsibility for the policies adopted during his reign. In this case while Procopius and other contemporary sources certainly personalize the reign in

*Figure 5.3* The fortress at Zenobia (Halabiye) on the Euphrates

a dramatic way, it does seem that one can recognize in the real Justinian the untiring and sleepless emperor portrayed in the *Secret History*.

As the reign drew on, with the death of the Empress Theodora in 548, the spectacular imperial initiatives of the early years gave way to other concerns, such as religious unity and the building of a longer-lasting peace with Persia. The 540s were dominated in Constantinople by the emperor's religious policies, but, as we have seen, the Fifth Council, which met in Constantinople and spent much time and effort in trying to get the support of the unfortunate Vigilius, was received negatively in both east and west. Justinian's later years were gloomy by comparison with the early part of the reign, with new barbarian threats and the emperor himself turning more and more to theological speculation. In his last years he made yet another unsuccessful attempt at conciliation by adopting the Julianist formula according to which Christ's body (being divine) was incorruptible, an old subject of controversy relating to the deeper question of the relation of God to matter in the Incarnation which was to go on to be a central issue throughout the seventh century (Chapter 9). Justinian's edict on the subject (564) resulted in the deposition of the patriarch of Antioch, who stood up to the emperor, and the exile of Eutychius, the patriarch of Constantinople, whose appointment the emperor had himself contrived in order to have an amenable patriarch in place at the Fifth Ecumenical Council. Eutychius was replaced by the ultra-orthodox John Scholasticus, a great supporter of Justinian's orthodox nephew and successor, Justin II, but Justinian's action and Eutychius' deposition left many loose ends, and the latter was briefly reinstated after the death of John Scholasticus in 575.[78]

Events and policies during the reign, and their effects, were thus deeply contradictory, as were the verdicts of contemporaries; we have unusually abundant literary sources, which portray Justinian both as a great and strong emperor and as a dangerous reformer. As we have seen, Procopius does both, and so, in milder tones, does John the Lydian, who had been an official in the praetorian prefecture and knew what he was talking about. The deacon Agapetus' eulogizing *Advice to the Emperor*, Paul the Silentiary's equally fulsome *Description of Hagia Sophia* and the anonymous and ambivalent *Dialogue on Political Science* represent the range of contemporary responses.[79] Justinian has featured in modern works as a Christian humanist, as the giver of Roman law to Christian Europe, as an intolerant and authoritarian persecutor of pagans and heretics and (anachronistically) as a prototype of totalitarian rule. All these judgements suffer from the tendency to confuse the man himself with the events of his reign, which is reinforced by the temptation to read off the personalities of Justinian and Theodora from two very striking surviving works: the *Secret History* of Procopius and the well-known mosaics of Justinian and Theodora in the church of San Vitale at Ravenna – especially as the rather podgy appearance of Justinian and the distant look of Theodora in the mosaics both seem to fit Procopius' descriptions of the emperor and empress:

> [Justinian] showed himself approachable and affable to those with whom he came into contact; not a single person found himself denied access to the Emperor, and even those who broke the rules by the way they stood or spoke in his presence never incurred his wrath … with a friendly expression on his face and without raising an eyebrow, in a gentle voice he would order tens of thousands of quite innocent persons to be put to death, cities to be razed to the ground, and all their possessions to be confiscated for the Treasury.
>
> (*Secret History* 13.1–2)

> To her bodily needs she [Theodora] devoted quite unnecessary attention, though never enough to satisfy herself. She was in a great hurry to get into her bath, and very unwilling to get out again. When she had finished her ablutions she would go down to breakfast, and after a light breakfast she would take a rest. But at lunch and supper she indulged her taste for every kind of food and drink. Again and again she would sleep for hours on end, by day until nightfall and by night till sunrise.
>
> (*ibid.*, 15.6–8)

We also have seem to have utterances from Justinian himself, who was a great legislator and author of theological treatises. But even if the contribution of Justinian himself can be assumed, works like these are inevitably written in a rhetorical mode that masks the personality of the author. It is similarly difficult to assess the emperor's contribution as patron of the culture of his age, especially in relation to visual art, for despite the mass of public works to which Procopius' *Buildings* testifies very little imperial art has actually survived. What little there is, such as the Barberini ivory (Figure 5.1), which is probably, though not certainly, Justinianic, shows what we would naturally have expected – a mixture of classicizing and traditional motifs; the same goes for the ivory diptych showing the Archangel Michael in the British Museum, one of the masterpieces of the period. But these are not known to have been imperially sponsored; nor are the famous mosaics of Justinian and Theodora at Ravenna, or indeed, even though the monastery itself was a Justinianic foundation, the great Sinai icons of Christ, the Virgin with angels and St Peter which are usually – though not by all – held to be Justinianic. The church of St Sophia in Constantinople (Figure 1.2), described in detail by Procopius in book I of the *Buildings* and by Paul the Silentiary in his hexameter poem on the rededication of the dome in January AD 563 after it had been damaged by earthquake, is a masterpiece, but it is not classical at all.[80]

Similar problems arise with the literary texts. In one sense, the reign is rich in classicizing literature, from Procopius' own works to the clever classical epigrams by Paul the Silentiary (a palace official) and several other office-holders such as Macedonius the consul and Julian the prefect, which were collected by Agathias and eventually passed into the Greek Anthology.[81] Both the technical expertise and the reading public were evidently still present. Literary production in the sixth century depended not only on the level of education and the circulation of books but also on patronage, and Procopius claims that the *Buildings* was an imperial commission, while Paul the Silentiary's poem on the restored St Sophia, written in formal hexameters, is a formal panegyric composed for an imperial occasion.[82] On the other hand, imperial themes were also addressed in the elaborate rhythmical *kontakia* (liturgical hymns) by the deacon Romanos, performed as part of the liturgy in a church of the Theotokos in Constantinople to which he was attached, and influenced by Syriac poetry and homiletic, and Justinian's reign saw the composition of the first important Byzantine chronicle, that of John Malalas.[83] All these writers used Greek, but Latin literature was also still being composed in Constantinople, including the *Chronicle* of Marcellinus, an early Illyrian protégé of Justinian, a short treatise by Junillus the *quaestor* and Jordanes' Gothic and Roman histories (Chapter 2). The number of educated Latin-speakers was augmented by the arrival of the exiles from Gothic Italy after 540, who included Cassiodorus, whose work on the Psalms was written in Constantinople. The monastery Cassiodorus founded at Squillace on his return to Italy became one of the most important medieval centres for copying manuscripts, while Cassiodorus's own *Institutes* was one of the most influential texts in the transmission of classical learning to the Middle Ages.[84]

Justinian was a strong emperor who initiated a series of extraordinarily ambitious policies, and carried most of them through in the face of great obstacles. But it is doubtful whether even without these obstacles the eastern empire would have been sufficiently strong in economic and administrative terms to sustain the extra burdens it was taking on.[85] And at the same time processes of social change were taking place throughout the Mediterranean world of which contemporaries were barely aware, yet which were conditioning the outcome of the very policies which they adopted.

# 6

# LATE ANTIQUE CULTURE
# AND PRIVATE LIFE

The title of this chapter in the original edition of this book was 'Culture and mentality'. 'Mentality' is a concept associated with the French historians and sociologists who together comprised the 'Annales School' in the twentieth century, whose aim was to look for deep-seated structures in history over long periods of time, including structures of thought and ideas in particular societies ('mentalities'). However, this concept, which could be broadly sociological or broadly psychological, has given way to considerations of discourse and power under the influence of Michel Foucault, and of symbols under that of Pierre Bourdieu,[1] and given the enormously wide variety of attitudes, beliefs and ideas highlighted by the last generation of writing about late antiquity it cannot be applied in any simple form. Peter Brown's *The World of Late Antiquity*, published in 1971, is a book whose approach has often been described as impressionistic or kaleidoscopic, and which presented a world of great variety. In later works Brown himself has turned more to cultural issues and to questions involving discourse and power,[2] and many others have taken this emphasis considerably further. Late antiquity used to be seen unproblematically as a time of increased spirituality.[3] This too needs to be challenged.

Peter Brown, who would probably best be termed a social historian, has defined the starting point of late antiquity as lying in a 'model of parity' which existed among the (male) urban elites of the high empire, with their civic paganism; what emerged from the upheaval of the third century was, on this view, 'Late Antique man'.[4] At the same time he has also suggested that late antiquity saw a distinct shift away from traditional public values towards the private sphere, and, with it, a significant step towards the growth of individual identity. He has also engaged with the suggestion made by the Italian historian Santo Mazzarino that late antiquity saw a 'democratisation of culture', a move away from the elite high culture of classical antiquity. Whether this was really the case, and if so how far it may have been connected with the process of Christianization, is a matter of considerable discussion,[5] and Brown has also argued against the common tendency to divide late antique culture into elite and popular. If values were changing, how far was this under the influence of Christianity? As we have seen, late antiquity has often been regarded on the one hand as an age of increased spirituality, but on the other of descent into superstition and irrationality. However, after the appearance of Peter Brown's *World of Late Antiquity* it would be difficult to find a single 'mentality' in this complex, dynamic and extremely varied world.

The period covered in this book was a time of change and variety. The change was at times violent and sudden but more often uneven and gradual, and sometimes hardly perceived by those living through it. The challenge for the historian is to find ways of doing justice to these processes without distorting the enormous mass of surviving evidence. The success of the series of conferences and publications under the title 'Shifting Frontiers' is precisely due to its recognition of the problems presented in capturing these multiple processes of change.[6] This is all the more the case given the resistance shown in recent scholarship to a one-dimensional emphasis on Christianization in late antiquity, even while recognizing that the Roman empire 'became Christian' between the fourth and sixth centuries. If in particular we take a longer chronological view, the religious changes that took place in late antiquity can better be characterized in the words of a recent discussion by Noel Lenski as the process whereby

> the kaleidoscopic plurality of religious cults once scattered across the ancient landscape gave way to a homogenization of religious power around the three interrelated Abrahamic traditions of Judaism, Christianity and Islam. These squeezed out competing religious traditions by successfully redefining religious truth along monotheistic and theologizing lines, and – in the instance of Christianity and later Islam – by deploying the coercive force of the state as a way to valorize and enforce the truths they purveyed.[7]

This formulation points to several trends in recent historiography: first, a tendency to place Christianity and the process of Christianization within a broader religious context; second, a recognition of the role played in religious and social change by writing, debate and theological issues, including the enormous weight placed by late antique Christian and Jewish writers (and by Muslim writers, even if considerably later) on exegesis, the interpretation and appropriation of classic texts; and third, an awareness of the place of coercion, whether used by the state or by other agents. It encapsulates the linguistic turn of the 1990s and its move towards a socio-historical paradigm of power and dominance. Lenski's discussion recognizes the importance of post-colonial approaches in recent scholarship on late antiquity, with a corresponding attempt to get behind the dominant narrative in order to investigate power relations, the dynamics of contemporary discourse, and subjects such as gender history and non-elite groups. The Marxist, structuralist and anthropological approaches familiar in previous decades of historiography on the later Roman empire have been joined by methodologies influenced by Foucault and Bourdieu, and notwithstanding a traditionalist and 'common-sense' reactions by some scholars, by a considerably heightened awareness of the literary analysis of textual evidence.[8] We have already emphasised the importance of archaeological evidence for any study of late antiquity, but we can also see in some scholars of the period, prominent among them Jas Elsner, an attempt to break down the gulf between textual and visual evidence. Given the wealth of visual evidence for late antiquity and the important developments that can be discerned, this needs to be taken much further.[9]

## The survival of traditional structures

It remains methodologically difficult to integrate these different approaches to late antique culture, and to accommodate both the religious and the secular; a further problem, less often acknowledged, is how far the huge quantity of religious evidence, or the processes of religious change in the period, can actually be reduced to matters of social or cultural history. First, however, we must ask to what extent the traditional high culture was still maintained, a question which is very much connected with urban civic culture.

Late antique secular education was maintained in cities all over the empire, and at the higher level in important centres such as Athens, Antioch, Alexandria, Constantinople and Berytus, the latter a particular centre of legal studies. Well-to-do parents sent their sons to leading teachers and to particular centres: Augustine was first taught in his home town of Thagaste, then sent with the help of a rich neighbour to Madaura, and then to Carthage. Much of his education was in the Latin classical authors, though he also learned Greek, and he went on to teaching posts in Thagaste, Carthage and Rome, from where he was appointed as a teacher of rhetoric in Milan in 384, to be joined there by his Christian mother Monica and several North African friends who were teachers or lawyers. His education included study of philosophy, and he was personally drawn to questions of natural philosophy, astrology and religion. For nearly ten years he was a Manichaean, and before his dramatic conversion back to Christianity under the influence of Ambrose in Milan he was also drawn to Platonism and belonged to an intellectual circle in which serious discussion of both Platonism and Christianity was the norm. The story of his early years story, vividly told in his *Confessions*, gives us an idea of education and intellectual life in the late fourth century.[10] The pattern did not change very much during the fifth century for people like him who came from the better-off classes in urban centres,[11] and was reinforced by the founding of the 'University' of Constantinople in 425 at the Capitol (not a university in a modern sense, but rather the establishment of teachers in both Latin and Greek in the main fields of grammar, rhetoric, philosophy and law).[12] In the sixth century east, Gaza was a major centre of teaching in addition to Constantinople, Athens (see below) and Alexandria; and Berytus remained the main centre of legal studies until hit by a major earthquake in 551.[13] Teachers attracted their own followings, and students whose families could afford it chose their centre of higher education according to its teachers.

Student life could be rowdy, and at times there was trouble between Christian and pagan students, as in late fifth-century Alexandria, where the

Alexandrian teacher Hypatia had been killed in Christian–pagan conflicts earlier in the century (Chapter 1); Zachariah, from Maiuma in Gaza and later
bishop of Mytilene, studied grammar and rhetoric in Alexandria and went on
to study law at Berytus; he wrote in his *Life* of the future patriarch Severus
about their student days in Alexandria and their adventures with pagan students including Paralius from Aphrodisias in Caria, a small and remote city
from which we happen to have good evidence for the persistence of paganism and the educational opportunities open to young men from the better-off
families. The interplay of religious affiliation with education is vividly illustrated by the fact that one of Paralius' brothers was a Christian and lived at
the time in a monastic complex near Alexandria, and the fact that while pagan
and Christian students studied together, religious rivalry sometimes erupted
into violence.[14] The extent and organization of higher education in Alexandria
has been spectacularly revealed by the excavation of an extensive late antique
urban complex in the city, in the area known as Komm el-Dikka, where a
large number of classrooms are preserved, where the pupils declaimed or performed their exercises in front of their teacher and fellow students.[15]

Teachers were needed to perpetuate the system, while in turn training in classical rhetoric was regarded as an essential qualification for the imperial bureaucracy and indeed for any secular office. We can see the process clearly in the
mid-fourth century, when Constantine's new governing class was very much

*Figure 6.1* One of the classrooms uncovered at Komm el-Dikka, Alexandria

in need of a brief tutorial in Roman history, and again a generation or so later, when the provincial rhetor Ausonius shot to prominence as praetorian prefect and consul, and the Egyptian poet Claudian became chief panegyrist of Stilicho and Honorius. Literary figures who became prominent in the fifth century included the historian Olympiodorus from Egyptian Thebes, who described himself as 'a poet by profession', and who was a pagan, well educated in the classical tradition and much-travelled, distinctly more enterprising than most of his peers. Priscus, another fifth-century Greek historian and more of a classical stylist than Olympiodorus, based his history on both Herodotus and Thucydides. He went on a mission to the Hun king Attila in 449 and expressed his admiration for him in his history, while criticizing Theodosius II for his policy of trying to buy off Attila. Yet another colourful character was Cyrus of Panopolis, also in Egypt, a poet who rose to the positions of prefect of the city, praetorian prefect and consul under Theodosius II, only to be accused of paganism in court intrigues and sent into exile as bishop of the small town of Cotiaeum in Phrygia.[16] Such a system perpetuated traditional attitudes, as indeed it was intended to do; not least, it imposed fixed categories of thought, and in particular impeded realistic perceptions of relations with barbarian peoples who were by definition seen as lacking in culture. In general the continuity of late antique elite education, based on rhetoric and philosophy, and directed to the classical authors, powerfully maintained and reinforced social attitudes. This was the *paideia* which was also essential for Christians ambitious to rise and have influence in the wider society. The only Christian alternative lay in the monastic and ascetic formation, and the tension between religion and secular education led to profound dilemmas for many, Augustine being perhaps the most conspicuous example.[17] It was a type of education that depended on access to an urban environment. For Procopius, as for Justinian, the idea of civilization also went hand in hand with that of cities; new cities were founded in the reconquered territory, while others were restored, and as long as the cities survived, the apparatus of traditional elite culture – baths, education, municipal institutions – had a chance of surviving as well. Even in Ostrogothic Italy, Amalasuntha, the daughter and only child of Theodoric, and learned herself, wanted a Roman education for her son,[18] and defended her choice of Theodahad for her husband (which was to prove unfortunate) to the Roman senate in terms of his education:

> To these good qualities is added enviable literary learning, which confers splendour on a nature deserving praise. There the wise man finds what will make him wiser; the warrior discovers what will strengthen him with courage; the prince learns how to administer his people with equity; and there can be no station in life which is not improved by the glorious knowledge of letters.
>
> (Cassiodorus, *Var.* X.3, trans. Barnish)

Many bishops had also received a high-level education in the classics, such as Augustine, Severus and Zachariah; others, such as Theodoret of Cyrrhus in northern Syria, chose to emphasize their religious upbringing and monastic connections, but clearly acquired an extensive knowledge of classical literature. Synesius in Cyrene and Sidonius Apollinaris in Gaul were both fifth-century bishops who were also accomplished authors in the classical manner. Sidonius, author of Latin panegyrics, poems and letters, came from a family with two generations of praetorian prefects and was himself city prefect of Rome in 468; other former office-holders who became bishops in the fifth and early sixth centuries were Germanus of Auxerre, and in the east Irenaeus of Tyre, Isaiah of Rhodes and Ephraem of Antioch.[19] Caesarius of Arles, Avitus of Vienne, Ennodius of Pavia and later Venantius Fortunatus were others who all drew on a rhetorical training in the classics.

Acquiring such a training was a matter of social background: it was necessary to be comparatively well-to-do and, usually, male. Only a few particularly favoured women gained access to these skills, such as Eudocia, the wife of Theodosius II, who was the daughter of a sophist in Athens and herself composed both secular and Christian poetry.[20] Greek verse composition was highly valued; many poets flourished in Egypt in the fifth century and were able to sell their services as panegyrists. Nonnus of Panopolis is the most important of the fifth-century poets: author both of an immensely long and elaborate hexameter poem known as the *Dionysiaca* and of a poetic paraphrase of St John's Gospel, he set a pattern of poetic style and diction which others followed extremely closely, while his mythological themes provide the literary context for the mythologizing mosaics of late antique sites in Syria, Jordan and Cyprus.[21]

In the late sixth century, Dioscorus from Aphrodito in Upper Egypt was still writing Greek verse on traditional subjects,[22] and at the court of Heraclius in the early seventh century, George of Pisidia was the author of panegyrical poems which combined classical metres and techniques with Old Testament imagery, while Sophronius, monk and patriarch of Jerusalem from 634–38, composed anacreontic verses on the capture of Jerusalem in 614 by the Persians.[23] A Christian school of Greek rhetoricians and poets flourished in sixth-century Gaza, which was also home to important monastic figures and the site of a spectacular synagogue mosaic.[24] A series of historians wrote classicizing histories in Greek in the fifth and sixth centuries,[25] and though the approach of the ecclesiastical histories of such writers as Socrates and Sozomen in the fifth century or Evagrius Scholasticus at the end of the sixth may have been somewhat different, these too were works written from the basis of a thorough training in rhetoric. A similar training continued to be available in Latin in the west. Servius' commentary on Virgil, Macrobius' *Saturnalia* and Martianus Capella's *De nuptiis Philologiae et Mercurii*, in nine books, belong to the first half of the fifth century,[26] while the North African poet Dracontius composed lengthy hexameter poems in the Vandal period, from which we also have the collection of short Latin poems known as the *Latin Anthology* and the epigrams of Luxorius.[27] The African Latin poet Corippus composed an eight-book hexameter poem on the Byzantine campaigns there in the 540s and later delivered a Latin panegyric in Constantinople on the

*Figure 6.2* Mosaic of the first bath of Achilles, from the House of Theseus, Paphos, western Cyprus, late fourth century

accession of Justin II in 565 (Chapter 5); it seems that Virgil went on being taught in North Africa after the reconquest in traditional school contexts, at least for a while. Everyone learning to write Latin seriously learned it from Virgil: papyrus finds from the small town of Nessana in a remote spot on the present Egyptian border show that this continued in the seventh century, long after the Arab conquest.

The literary production of late antiquity has been judged inferior to that of earlier more 'classical' periods. But it can also be seen as reflecting an age of fragmentation, when traditional literary accomplishment was fraught with uncertainty, defended with displays of virtuosity or applied to unfamiliar Christian uses. In some fields this presented itself as a new kind of poetics, observable from the fourth century onwards, with an emphasis on display and surface glitter, a style as eclectic in its way as that of contemporary architecture with its juxtapositions and its unashamed incorporation of earlier elements,[28] less a late antique mentality than a late antique aesthetic, and one that can all too easily mislead.[29]

## High culture – philosophy

Philosophy was vigorously practised in the fifth and sixth centuries, particularly at Athens and Alexandria, and the influence of philosophical ideas was clearly profound.[30] Many elements of the Platonic philosophical tradition had been absorbed into Christian teaching and had thereby become available to a wider public in a different guise. Neoplatonist teaching in the fifth and sixth centuries, however, was also often identified with paganism. As taught in the major centres, it took a highly elitist form, and among certain sections of the upper class it still enjoyed considerable prestige; as we saw, the family of Paralius in Aphrodisias sent its sons to Alexandria, and a number of important mosaics from Paphos in Cyprus and Apamea in Syria, home of a flourishing school especially notable for the early fourth-century philosopher Iamblichus, may suggest the diffusion of Neoplatonic ideas in the fourth century.[31] Athens was the particular home of Neoplatonism, the late antique version of Platonism associated in the first place with Plotinus, active in the third century, and in our period especially with Proclus, who arrived in Athens in 430 and became head of the school there at the early age of 25 or 26 in 437. He remained head of the school until his death in 485, when his *Life* was written by his successor Marinus.[32]

The Neoplatonists evolved their own system of philosophical education, in which the teachings of Aristotle and of the Stoics were harmonized with those of Plato to form an elaborately organized syllabus. The 'Aristotelian' philosophers of late antique Alexandria were as much Neoplatonists as the Athenians, and Simplicius, one of the last and greatest of the Athenian philosophers of this period, wrote a series of important commentaries on the works of Aristotle. But Neoplatonism was also deeply religious; indeed, it almost amounted to a religious system in itself. Neoplatonists sought to understand the nature of the divine and to evolve a scientific theology, practised asceticism (Chapter 3), contemplation and prayer, revered the gods and adopted special ways of invoking them ('theurgy'). They believed in the possibility of divine revelation, especially through the so-called 'Chaldaean Oracles' (second century), which claimed to be revelations obtained by interrogation of Plato's soul. For Proclus and his followers, Plato himself and his writings acquired the status of scripture. Naturally such teachings came to be identified with paganism, but many of the greatest Christian thinkers, such as Gregory of Nyssa and Augustine, were also deeply influenced by Neoplatonism. Certain of Plato's works, especially the *Timaeus* and the *Phaedrus*, were influential on many Christian writers, including Augustine, and there was much common ground between Neoplatonism and Christianity.[33] In Athens, Proclus headed a 'school' not so much in the sense of buildings or an institution (the teaching of the Academy seems still to have been conducted in a very informal way by modern standards) as in the fact that he had a group of pupils, on whom he exercised a charismatic influence and with whom he celebrated a variety of forms of pagan cult which included prayer, meditation and hymns, and even extended to healing miracles. When the father of a little girl, appropriately called Asclepigeneia, who was desperately ill, asked for Proclus' prayers:

> Taking with him the great Pericles from Lydia, a man who was himself
> no mean philosopher, Proclus visited the shrine of Asclepius to pray to

the god on behalf of the invalid. For at that time the city still enjoyed the use of this and retained intact the temple of the Saviour [i.e., Asclepius]. And while he was praying there in the ancient manner, a sudden change was seen in the maiden and a sudden recovery occurred, for the Saviour, being a god, healed her easily.

(Life of Proclus 29, trans. Edwards)

When in 529 Justinian forbade the teaching of philosophy in Athens,[34] seven Neoplatonist philosophers then active there, led by Damascius, the current head of the school, are said to have made a voyage in search of Plato's philosopher-king to Persia, where, they had heard, the new king, Chosroes I, was interested in Greek philosophy to the point of commissioning translations of Plato (Chapter 5). When they reached the Persian court, they soon became disappointed and returned, though not before securing a safe conduct for themselves under the terms of the peace treaty of 533. The story is told by Agathias in the context of a denunciation of Chosroes and a certain Uranius who had, according to Agathias, absurdly encouraged the king's philosophical pretensions.[35] It has given rise to much discussion, both as to the fate of the Athenian Academy itself and as to that of the philosophers, in particular Simplicius, who went on to conduct a vigorous polemic against his rival, the Alexandrian John Philoponus. One theory suggests that he spent the rest of his active life and founded a Platonic school at Harran (Carrhae) in Mesopotamia, known as a home of paganism until a late date. If correct (apart from possible local references in Simplicius' commentaries, it depends largely on a single statement in a tenth-century Arabic writer which may suggest the presence of Platonists there), this would have important consequences for the transmission of Greek philosophy into the Islamic world.[36] Priscian, another of the seven, wrote a treatise setting out the answers he had given to the questions of the Persian king. Agathias tells the whole story from the point of view of Hellenic superiority, but Chosroes was indeed known in eastern sources for his erudition and curiosity, and himself composed a history of his achievements.[37]

It was not least the intensity of philosophical debate even in the mid-sixth century that is so notable. Nor was it confined only to philosophers themselves. Philosophical thought also extended to monastic and theological circles,[38] and John Philoponus, the leading philosopher at Alexandria at that time, was himself a Christian. He wrote a long series of works in the course of which he argued against the view of Proclus that the world had had no beginning, though his own views were not fundamentalist enough for some Christians. Philoponus also espoused a particular form of Monophysitism known as Tritheism,[39] but there seems to have been room for a considerable range of approaches within the philosophical circles of Alexandria. Unlike Athens, which succumbed to the Slav invasions of 582 onwards, and where, if any philosophical teaching continued, it had no chance of doing so on a scale remotely comparable with its long past tradition, Alexandria was able to preserve its philosophical tradition until the Arab conquest.

## A changing world

If anything, the literary culture of late antiquity was even more class-based than previously. It required a specialized training, not only from writers but also from their audiences, and by the sixth century at any rate the spoken language in Greek was diverging markedly from this high literary language.[40] The traditional literary culture was still available in Constantinople under Heraclius (610–41), but as urbanism declined or cities were lost to Roman rule, a sharp decline set in; this also affected the availability of books and the knowledge of classical authors, and did not begin to be restored in the Byzantine empire until the ninth and tenth centuries. The social and cultural system which had produced and sustained this very elitist literature was in fact changing fast. One of the main changes was brought by Christianization, but Christian writers were themselves often both highly educated and extraordinarily prolific.[41] Many Christian writings are extremely rhetorical in character, and use all the panoply provided by a classical education. Augustine, perhaps the greatest Christian writer of the period, had been a teacher of rhetoric himself, and did not hesitate to use his skill to the utmost when he later came to write religious works. Bishops (including Augustine) and other Christian writers combined secular learning with Christian expression, not least in the form of letters,

*Figure 6.3* The shape of the world as imagined in the *Christian Topography* of Cosmas Indicopleustes. Florence, Biblioteca Medicea Laurentiana, MS Plut. IX.28, f. 95 v

which constituted a particularly flourishing genre among educated Christians in the early fifth century; a large number survive, testifying to a close network of shared culture and common interests stretching between Gaul, Italy, North Africa and elsewhere. But unlike most classical writers, Augustine was also supremely conscious of the techniques necessary in addressing himself to an uneducated audience, and kept returning again and again to the problems of reconciling intellectual and rhetorical aims with religious faith. His great work, the *City of God*, written in the aftermath of the sack of Rome by Alaric in AD 410, is less an extended meditation on the reasons for that event than an discussion of the place of the classical world and classical culture in the scheme of Christian providence.

## Christianity and popular culture

Hagiography – the lives of saints and holy men – was a major form of writing in late antiquity, and while its literary range varied greatly, many saints' lives were permeated with literary tropes from secular literature;[42] similarly, while Christian world chronicles, running from Adam to the writer's own day, have often been regarded as 'credulous', the genre began with the great Christian scholar Eusebius and the surviving examples have much in common with classicizing historiography.[43] But the impact of Christianization changed reading practices, especially through the availability of the Bible. A specifically Christian learning developed, with the early monastic communities in the west, as on the island of Lérins, setting a precedent in the late fifth century for the great medieval monastic centres of learning. A large body of sayings and lives of the 'desert fathers' (and a few 'mothers') in Egypt also developed, and Palladius' *Lausiac History* and Theodoret's *Historia Religiosa* collected stories of holy men and women.[44] A vigorous culture of translation had developed in the eastern Mediterranean by the sixth century for the circulation of saints' lives and Christian apocryphal texts dealing with Christ's descent into Hades and Mary's assumption into heaven; many such texts, originally composed in Greek, survive only in translations into Syriac, Georgian, Latin or later Arabic.[45] Unlike classical culture, Christianity did indeed consciously direct its appeal to all classes of society, explicitly including slaves and women. While it is true that St Paul's famous declaration that 'there is neither Jew nor Greek, there is neither bond nor free, there is neither male nor female; for ye are all one in Christ Jesus' (Gal. 3:28) did not, and was probably never meant to, lead to the abolition of social differences, nevertheless, along with such sayings as that about the difficulty of the rich man in entering the kingdom of heaven, Christianization did bring with it something of a change of attitude towards those groups who had been barely considered at all in the pagan Roman world.

The meeting of the old classical cultural and educational system with Christian ideas has often been associated with the idea of a 'new, popular culture', more universal in character and based less on the written word and more on the visual and the oral.[46] The increase in attention to Christian religious images in the later part of our period (Chapter 9) has also been ascribed to the influence of popular culture, and indeed one does at times find references to sacred pictures as a way of educating the illiterate. Thus Nilus of Sinai (fifth century), recommended decorating a new church with pictures from the Old and New Testaments:

> So that the illiterate who are unable to read the Holy Scriptures may, by gazing at the pictures, become mindful of the manly deeds of those who have genuinely served the true God and may be roused to emulate those glorious and celebrated feats.[47]

But Christian art and Christian writing alike were often as complex as secular, and in practice, members of the educated upper class were just as enthusiastic about icons, saints and holy men as ordinary people.[48] Even secular historians from the late fifth and sixth centuries, such as Zosimus (who was actually pagan) and Procopius (certainly not a 'popular' writer), seem to show a greater receptiveness to miracle and other religious factors as part of historical explanation.[49]

### Family and personal life

Christianization brought with it the rise of monasticism and the ascetic lifestyle (Chapter 3). Even if we take the figures given in contemporary monastic sources for monks and ascetics in Egypt with a degree of scepticism, the number of men and women in the empire as a whole who had dedicated themselves to the Christian religious life must have amounted to thousands by the fifth century, and some monasteries were very large, with refectories and accommodation for over 200 monks. The general principles of ascetic life were also shared in some pagan circles, notably among Neoplatonists, but they had no such monasteries, and belonged on the whole to elite groups in society; their numbers were therefore in comparison very limited.[50] It is difficult to know how widely the ideals of monastic and ascetic life were shared in society generally, but many saints' lives tell of families dedicating their children to the ascetic life at an early age. Even if idealized and presented within the framework of literary and religious cliché, saints' lives also seem to signal an increase in the attention given to individuals, and early Christianity has been seen as indicative of a new emphasis in this direction. The advance of Christianization also brought changes in attitudes to the dead, though in many cases there was still little difference between Christian and pagan burials,[51] and many monasteries, like that of Euthymius in the Judaean desert, incorporated the tomb of their founder and a charnel house for the monks themselves.

Social and religious change also had implications for family life: under Constantine the Augustan legislation which laid down penalties for members of the upper class who did not marry was lifted and from then on celibacy became a serious option even for the rich. Jerome's successful efforts to promote an extreme ascetic ethos among the daughters of the Roman aristocracy in the late fourth century are well known, and caused resentment in the parts of their circle that were still pagan. The promotion of ascetic lifestyles, including the dedication of daughters to lives of virginity, destabilized existing family structures and divided loyalties.[52] A common form of renunciation for this class occurred when a married couple who had produced one or two children to ensure the family inheritance, decided subsequently to abstain from sexual relations and sell their property for the benefit of the church. For Paulinus, who became bishop of Nola in Campania, and who took this step with his wife in the early fifth century, we have a good deal of detailed evidence in his own letters and other contemporary sources; but the most sensational case was undoubtedly that of the Younger Melania (so-called to distinguish her from her equally pious grandmother of the same name) and her husband Pinianus, chosen for her by her parents in an arranged marriage when she was 13. Melania and Pinianus sold their colossal estates c. AD 410, against the wishes of her father, Valerius Publicola, when she was only 20 and he 24. Melania and Pinianus had properties literally all over the Roman world; when they acquired several islands, they gave them to holy men. Likewise, they purchased monasteries of monks and virgins and gave them as a gift to those who lived there, furnishing each place with a sufficient amount of gold. They presented their numerous and expensive silk clothes at the altars of churches and monasteries. They broke up their silver, of which they had a great deal, and made altars and ecclesiastical treasures from it, and many other offerings to God.[53] According to her biographer, Melania made it clear that she did not wish to marry or have sexual relations, but had been forced to give way and had given birth to two children; when both died in infancy, her ascetic wishes finally prevailed. She owned estates in Spain, Africa, Mauretania, Britain, Numidia, Aquitaine and Gaul, several of them having hundreds of slaves, and her estate near Thagaste in North Africa is said to have been bigger than the town itself. Clearly the literal adoption of asceticism at the top ranks of society caused a sharp break with existing social practice, and a considerable disruption of family and inheritance. How far individual renunciation really redistributed wealth towards the poorer classes is less easy to judge (Chapter 3). Yet the development of Christian almsgiving and social welfare is also one of the major features of the period, and it took the form not merely of alms distribution, but also of the building and maintenance of charitable establishments such as hospitals and old people's homes. Christian charity, which in some senses replaced classical euergetism (civic endowments) – though the latter still continued in some cases – had very different objects and mechanisms.

Changes in family life and sexual practice are among the hardest things to judge with any accuracy. In the ancient world, from which we mostly lack personal sources such as private letters or diaries,[54] quite apart from any kind of statistics, the problem is doubly difficult. The goings-on in Merovingian royal circles, recorded, for example, by Gregory of Tours, make it clear that

Christianity made little difference to the morals of that court at least, except perhaps when a bold bishop dared to intervene. As for society in general, it is hard to know how much difference the general approval given to asceticism made in the sexual lives of the majority. While many sermons exhorted Christians to sexual continence, it would be natural to assume that there was in practice a gap between what was claimed by the preacher and the real situation. It would be equally dangerous, however, to conclude that they had no effect at all, and the large number of surviving saints' lives makes plain the extent to which such attitudes were presented as an ideal.[55] This does not mean of course that existing sexual practice changed dramatically in all, or even in many, cases. Only inscriptions can give much statistical information about family size in the ancient world (and even these are deceptive, for we rarely have a large enough statistical sample). On this basis a recent study concludes that there was no real difference between pagan and Christian families. It is interesting to find that among the better-off classes, which were able to afford funerary monuments, a family size comparable with the modern nuclear family seems to have been the norm. The church condemned contraception with a vehemence that suggests that it was seen as widely practised, but there were other means of limitation of family size, including the sale of infants and infanticide by exposure, a long-established practice in the ancient world.[56]

It would be a mistake to romanticize marriage or family life in the late empire – for most people, it remained both brutal and fundamentally asymmetrical, as can be seen from Augustine's discussion of the role of the father in the *City of God*, where what is emphasized above all is the power relation in which he stood towards the rest of the household, starting with his wife;[57] he also wrote a treatise 'On the good of marriage' and had had a longstanding concubine himself and the prospect of a marriage arranged by his mother.[58] In some Latin works of the fifth and sixth centuries, we do find more attention, even if somewhat equivocal, being paid to the role of Christian wives and mothers.[59] But life expectancy remained short, especially for women of child-bearing age, and infant mortality was high, while the methods available for limitation of families (not necessarily with the consent of the mother) were crude and painful. As for children, they are often the forgotten people in ancient sources, and it is not much easier to find evidence about their lives than it is in earlier periods.[60] This does not mean that individuals did not care about the children, but it does mean that children themselves were still given a low priority in the written record, a fact significant in itself. The Gospel sayings about children (see Matt. 19:14) lagged far behind those about rich and poor in their actual social effect.

Yet even on a minimalist view, the drain of individuals and resources from family control to the church in its various forms clearly did have a profound effect on society. Even if in an individual case a family did not send one of its members to the monastic life or change its sexual habits sufficiently sharply to reduce the level of procreation, it probably did, if it was rich enough, make gifts to the local church, and these themselves could be on a lavish scale. Perhaps more important than the practical results of these ideas in individual cases was the degree of moral and social control which the church now claimed over individual lives, and which can be seen, for example, in restrictions on marriage within permitted degrees.[61] Justinian legislated on matters such as divorce and the legal position of women in ways that offered a greater degree of protection (see below), but while Christianization may not have changed the hearts of individuals as much as has often been thought, there were important ways in which it did claim to control the outward pattern of their lives.

### Women and men

Christianity did, however, have the effect of bringing women into the public sphere.[62] Rich women, at any rate, could now travel to the Holy Land, found monasteries, learn Hebrew, choose not to marry or to become celibate, dedicate themselves to the religious life and form friendships with men outside their own family circle, all things which would scarcely have been possible before. In contrast, we might remember, nearly all Christian slaves and *coloni* remain among the great mass of unknown ancient people, whom nobody wrote about. When the alternative was probably a life of drudgery or boredom, asceticism offered at least the illusion of personal choice. Women were also seen in Christian writing as the repository of sexual temptation, and much of the theological literature of the period has a distinctly misogynistic tone, but at least no attempt was made to deny women's equal access to holiness, and, in some circles, close male–female friendships became possible in ways only paralleled in a few recherché Neoplatonist circles.[63] It is a notable feature of late antique Christian literature that it began to give attention to women in a way that would have been hard to imagine in the classical past. Like the poor, women became a subject of attention. Inevitably, we know most about upper-class Christian ladies such as Melania the Younger, Jerome's friend Paula and her daughters, or the deaconess Olympias, the friend of John Chrysostom. In view of Jerome's awkward temperament, it is touching to see that Paula, Fabiola and Eustochium were buried alongside him at Bethlehem, for it had been foretold that

> the lady Paula, who looks after him, will die first and be set free at last from his meanness. [For] because of him no holy person will live in those parts. His bad temper would drive out even his own brother.[64]

Women such as these were of course not typical; for most, it was not a matter of real change in lifestyle, and the range of possibilities was still defined in an extremely narrow way. Against the apparent broadening of opportunities ran the fact that precisely during this period the Virgin Mary emerged as a major figure of cult and worship. Much of the direct reason may have been christological, connected with the doctrinal issues debated at the councils of

Ephesus and Chalcedon (Chapters 1 and 3), though attention to Mary had been building up since the late fourth century, but the emergence of her cult also carried powerful symbolic messages for women: whereas Eve represented woman's sinfulness and potential to corrupt, Mary stood for her purity, demonstrated by virginity and total obedience.[65] This development in the cult of the Virgin, especially around the time of the Council of Ephesus (431),[66] was preceded by an increasingly strident advocacy of virginity by many of the late fourth-century Fathers; this, too, while not confined to women, tended to be presented in terms of the woman's traditional image as seductress. Since, as in most societies before and since, men still represented rationality, while women were defined in terms of their sexual identity, it is hardly surprising if the price of a degree of freedom for women was the denial of their sexuality. The highly popular fictional accounts of female saints such as Mary of Egypt, often former prostitutes, who concealed their sex altogether and dressed as men, usually to be revealed as female only on their deathbeds, demonstrate in extreme form the complexities and contradictions of Christian gender attitudes.[67]

Close study of the large amount of legislation on marriage and other matters affecting women from Constantine to Justin II (565–78) reveals both continuities and changes. Women are still seen as essentially dependent and in need of protection, their status is strictly subordinate to that of their husbands and their legal access is limited. The great bulk of Roman law affecting individuals was little changed by Christianization, and indeed much of it was re-enacted by the Christian emperors. But new legislation also concerned itself with the protection of public morality, and especially with the protection of chastity; it became much more difficult for a woman to initiate divorce, and obstacles were put in the way of remarriage; from Constantine onwards a succession of laws penalized women far more strictly than men for initiating unjustified divorce proceedings, until in 548 Justinian equalized the penalties. Even under the Christian emperors, however, marriage itself remained a civil and not a religious affair. On the other hand, the rights and obligations of mothers over their children were considerably strengthened, especially by Justinian, to whom the largest body of relevant legislation belongs, and all of whose innovations were actually in the direction of improving the legal position of women.[68] The real role of Christianization in bringing about such change is, however, far from clear; the law was changing during this period, certainly, but the motivation for those changes is another matter. Perhaps the most striking feature remains simply the amount of attention given in imperial legislation to matters concerning women; this is important enough in itself.

Thus the ways in which women could enter the public sphere, though they existed for a few, were still limited. The pagan intellectuals Hypatia and Athenaïs, the latter the daughter of an Athenian philosopher who became empress (as Eudocia) after she had been taken up by the Emperor Theodosius' pious sister Pulcheria (Chapter 1), were equally or even more exceptional. On the other hand, within the religious sphere, on a family basis or in the religious life, some women may have gained more status than they had had before. At least we can say that Christianization brought with it distinct changes in conscious-ness and new possibilities for individual and group identity. In some ways the constraints on women, which were great, actually intensified, but even within the constraints of contemporary moral and religious teaching, the inner self was not exclusively defined as male. But it was not only women whose lives and consciousness was affected by Christianization. Men too faced adjust-ments and were presented with dilemmas and opportunities. As we have seen, many adapted enthusiastically, but others, especially elite men of the Roman senatorial class, found more difficulty.[69] Late antiquity was also a time when eunuchs became established at court and in the higher administration, a fea-ture began early and persisted into the Byzantine period. There were eunuch generals, such as Narses and Solomon in the sixth century, and later even eunuch patriarchs. They were found useful by emperors as a 'third sex', and some families saw prospects of advancement in castrating their sons. Some rose high and became very powerful, as in the early fifth century, but they were also suspected and at times feared, and gave rise to a persistent strain of disapproval and distaste.[70]

## Material culture

Culture is not of course solely about mentalities and intellectual life. Material objects and material culture are part of what we mean by the overall term, and the incorporation of the study of material culture (including, but not limited to, art history) is a feature of the recent historiography on late antiquity.[71] Weights, lamps, textiles, pottery are all types of object that appear alongside luxury items in exhibitions, museum displays and illustrated books, and which feature in discussions of 'daily' or 'everyday' life. Wanting to avoid the asso-ciations of an emphasis on spirituality or on theological issues, some art his-torians also cast their subject in terms of material culture.[72] In this regard several issues present themselves during our period. They include the ques-tion already mentioned of how far ethnicity can be deduced from assemblages of archaeological material, and the related issue of what material culture can tell us about religious sensibility. In our period, material culture also changed alongside social changes, and as Christianity developed the cults of relics and religious images. Material culture also became highly contentious as these prac-tices were questioned, both by Christians themselves and under the impact of Islam (Chapter 9). What the impact was on individuals of the material culture which they experienced is a question that is being addressed for other periods but which still needs to be asked about late antiquity and Byzantium.[73]

In many ways this was a tumultuous period, when many existing social bar-riers were weakened, if not actually broken, and others formed. One of the most marked features of the period is clearly the progress of Christianization, which involved social change and the development of an authoritarian ideol-ogy.[74] But the fragmentation of Roman society in the west, the advent of barbarian settlement and the subsequent development of barbarian kingdoms also disturbed existing norms, though whether they brought any greater freedom is a different matter. In the eastern empire the sixth century, and especially the reign of Justinian, marked an apogee in the history of early Byzantium, with a strong emperor, powerful ministers and centralized government. At the same time, however, urban violence reached unprecedented levels (see Chapter 7), and there was much questioning of the relations of centre and periphery. The ambitious policies of Justinian brought the empire, and Justinian's successors, into difficulties which are clearly perceptible in their relations with the strong neighbouring power of Sasanian Persia in the late sixth century. Justinian was a codifier of the law and a legislator of unparalleled energy. But he did not succeed in achieving long-term security or internal harmony for the empire. The end of the sixth century brought the Persian occupation of the Byzantine Near East and renewed war with Persia on a major scale, followed immediately by the Arab conquests which seriously threatened Constantinople itself and led to the loss of huge amounts of territory. The urban structures of late antiquity, on which its educational system depended, underwent fundamental change. This is the subject of the next chapter, while Chapters 8 and 9 focus on the east, its prosperity in the sixth century and later, its religious ferment and the momentous events it experienced during the seventh century.

# 7

# URBAN CHANGE AND THE LATE ANTIQUE COUNTRYSIDE

An enormous amount has been written in recent years about towns in late antiquity. There are several reasons for this. In the first place, the development of late antique archaeology, which we have noted in many contexts already, is important. The effects are cumulative: there is not only more material available, but also more highly developed techniques for assessing it. This in turn has generated more good evidence, since the more sites that are well excavated and well recorded, the more possible it becomes to arrive at plausible interpretations of the data in an individual case. Unlike the medieval world, the civilization and high culture of classical antiquity, and thus also of the Roman empire, rested on a network of cities. The end of classical antiquity thus seems to imply the end of classical cities, and vice versa. There is also a special factor so far as the eastern empire is concerned, in that historians of Byzantium have been engaged in a controversy of their own about the disappearance or survival of cities during the seventh century, and thus whether or not there was a more or less complete break or discontinuity between medieval Byzantium and its classical roots; many cities did disappear in this period but some cities in the Near East seem to have carried on a vigorous urban life well into the Islamic period.[1] So little excavation has taken place in Anatolia which focuses on the later Byzantine period that the same may in fact be true there. But the outpouring of work on late antique urbanism remains extraordinary. It is not perhaps surprising if there is now something of a turn towards emphasizing villages and small settlements (below), but more excavation of sites from the later Byzantine period might indeed case us to modify the prevailing picture.

## Town and countryside

Though on the whole in the Roman empire the maintenance of culture, government and administration depended on cities, the proportion of the population working on the land was extremely high, and the proportion of overall revenues that derived from the land was even higher. Only a very few ancient cities – Rome, Constantinople, Antioch and Alexandria – were large by modern standards, and most were extremely small. The population of Constantinople at its height in the sixth century may on a very generous estimate have approached half a million; that of Rome, perhaps more than a million under Augustus, had declined considerably by the later Roman period and was further reduced during the Gothic wars of Justinian;[2] in the east, only Antioch and Alexandria came anywhere near these two. The countryside accounted for by far the greatest mass of the population, and, through agricultural production, contributed the basis of most of the empire's wealth; this remained broadly the case despite the great expansion in urban settlements starting in the fourth century, and despite an increased emphasis in modern scholarship on commercial exchange. Even if trade, or rather, production, was more important in the global economic equation than has sometimes been thought (Chapter 4), the land continued to provide the economic base; and cities on the whole, rather than being primary centres of production themselves, continued to depend on their rural hinterland.[3] In recent archaeological and economic studies increasing attention has been given to country as well as city, and a growing amount of attention is being given to villages and the village economy.[4] The change has also come about under the influence of survey archaeology, in which excavation is not undertaken but all surface finds are picked up and recorded over a given geographical area; more modern techniques such as GIS are also now becoming common.[5] Major surveys have been conducted in widely separated regions, which focus on a given area and include all surface remains, thus taking a broad chronological sweep which can allow insights into diachronic change not possible on the basis of other evidence. The evidence thus produced may of course be much more informative for one period than for another, and there are some basic methodological problems inherent in all such surveys;[6] nevertheless, some have produced important evidence for late antiquity. Starting in the 1950s, pioneering surveys have covered sites in Italy (the South Etruria surveys),[7] Spain (Guadalcuivir), North Africa (Libyan valleys and Caesarea and its hinterland in modern Algeria),[8] Cyprus and Greece (Boeotia, Melos and Methana). Differences in settlement density in the later part of the period soon revealed themselves between west (South Etruria) and east (Boeotia), but the dangers inherent in such generalization have also been pointed out.[9] In northern Syria the pioneering work of G. Tchalenko long dominated the field, with his attribution of the prosperity observable in the substantial architecture of the 800 or so villages on the limestone massif to an olive monoculture; subsequent work points to greater diversification and the level of prosperity is still clearly visible in the dense network of remains including standing structures.[10] In Cyprus surveys indicate increased density of settlement in late antiquity through to the mid-seventh century. Modern Jordan and Israel have also been well studied, and it is clear that in the now arid Negev, settlement reached a dramatic peak in the late antique period. Studies of this kind focusing on Palestine and Syria are particularly important in assessing population movement and for judging the state of these areas on the eve of the Arab conquests; they will be discussed in more detail in Chapter 8.

The deluge of information from these areas and elsewhere (much more such work is currently going on or is still unpublished) opens up many exciting possibilities, but at the same time presents some major difficulties. It is tempting to use it at once in order to draw general pictures of what was happening in a wider province or area. But survey work can yield misleading results, for a variety of reasons including such simple matters as the actual difficulty of identification of some kinds of sherds and the possible intervention of pure chance in accounting for certain 'assemblages' (the technical term for the range of materials found). Recognition of these dangers is an important issue for archaeologists, and adds to the difficulties which historians experience in using survey publications. It is obviously extremely difficult in any case to keep up with the latest situation in such a fast-moving field, and anything written on this basis runs the risk of running out of date very quickly. It is also difficult to gain access to all the publications, which tend to be very scattered and often in obscure journals or archaeological reports. But the impact of this work is very great, particularly in certain geographical areas, and the very fact that so much has been done and is still going on means that a history of the later Roman empire in the old style is simply inadequate for today. One of the major disadvantages of studying ancient history has always been the paucity of the available evidence, and especially the lack of documentary sources. 'Total' history in the sense in which the term was used by the French Annales school, i.e., history which takes in all the long-term and underlying structures and considers every kind of evidence, material as well as textual, will never be possible for the ancient world by comparison with the early modern and modern periods; but the prospect has come much nearer than anyone would have expected.

### Using archaeological evidence

Studies of individual towns in conjunction with their rural hinterland mark a valuable first step, but the sites for which an integrated treatment of texts and material evidence is possible remain relatively few. One important site where this kind of work is being undertaken is Sagalassos in south-west Anatolia.[11] But in general where urban sites are concerned, all sorts of practical constraints dictate the course of archaeological work, especially the extent of subsequent settlement. Many major late antique cities will never be excavated, simply because they have been the site of continuous settlement ever since the ancient period; on such a site, the traces of the late antique and medieval city may now be barely visible. For similar reasons, in many other cases only small areas can be excavated. This is largely the case with the city of Constantinople.[12] Excavations took place in the Great Palace area as early as the 1930s, but the layout of the palace in its different phases still has to be largely reconstructed from difficult textual evidence; however, a fresh look at the records of the earlier excavations has led to modification of the conclusions drawn by the earlier excavators, and has contributed to the debate about the dating of the Great Palace mosaics.[13] Further excavation has taken place in and near the Hippodrome and on the site of the great church of St Polyeuktos built by Anicia Juliana in the early years of Justinian's reign (Chapter 3); the city walls have received attention and recent publications focus on specific neighbourhoods. The spectacular excavation at Yenikapi of the late antique harbour attributed to Theodosius, in the course of rescue archaeology connected with building a new metro system for Istanbul, has so far revealed the well-preserved remains of some forty Byzantine boats from the seventh century and later, and added an extraordinary amount of evidence, some of which is already on display in the Istanbul Archaeological Museum. An important study of the elaborate installations which secured the water supply of Constantinople, using the evidence of physical remains, literary sources, later historical and geographical accounts and the study of Byzantine masons' marks, has also added greatly to our understanding of how the city could sustain such a large population in the late antique and early Byzantine period.[14] Nevertheless, the fact that so much work in the city has concentrated on individual churches indicates another important factor operative in determining the nature of archaeological research; namely, the motivation for selection of sites. This has often been dictated by an intense interest shown in churches, their architecture and their mosaic decoration. But like the recent work on the city's water supply, an important study of the dating evidence provided by brickstamps allows a different view of its urbanism to emerge.[15] Carthage, on the other hand, provides an example of an important late antique city where major excavation was prompted in the 1970s by the threat of development and undertaken on an international scale with the support of UNESCO. During the Islamic period, the centre of settlement moved to nearby Tunis, and ancient Carthage became part of a residential suburb. Systematic excavation over a large area was therefore impossible, but teams from several different countries were assigned specific areas within the ancient urban complex. Their interests and priorities differed, and some of the sites chosen also yielded material rich in one particular period and less so in others. But taken together, it would be hard to overestimate the importance of these results (Chapter 4), not least in providing a systematic and large body of well-recorded evidence which would act as a benchmark for methodology and interpretation in other parts of the late antique Mediterranean.

Since the development of late antique archaeology as a serious study, effectively only from the 1970s, archaeological and epigraphic evidence has been a fundamental aspect of all assessments of the period. A spectacular example of what can be shown by such evidence is provided by the case of Aphrodisias in Caria (south-west Turkey), a city only sparsely attested in literary sources, which has yielded an astonishing amount of evidence from its abundant inscriptions and its excavated remains about urban development and city life in late antiquity.[16] Since it was a major centre of sculpture production, drawing on famous marble quarries, it has also turned up a mass of splendid finished and half-finished late antique sculpture which is extremely important not only in the context of Aphrodisias itself but also for wider issues of iconography and style. Some of this evidence, like the literary evidence for the families of Paralius and Asclepiodotus already noted (Chapter 6), tells us much about the survival of pagan and classical culture in a provincial town; this is especially true of the striking series of sculptured heads of late antique philosophers.[17] Finally, many Greek inscriptions also survive from Aphrodisias, through which we can trace the efflorescence of Greek verse inscriptions and thus the availability of training for this specialized literary accomplishment in the fifth-century east. These are only some of the results of the excavations conducted at Aphrodisias over a thirty-year period to date. In particular, the Aphrodisias inscriptions give us a virtually unbroken record of urban history from the city's acquisition of free and federate status during the Triumviral period to its change of name in the early seventh century from Aphrodisias (city of Aphrodite) to Stauropolis (city of the Cross) and its survival as a shadow of its former self through the eighth and ninth centuries, when sources are almost absent, only to undergo some rebuilding like other Byzantine sites in the tenth and eleventh centuries. As we have seen, Aphrodisias is an important centre for our knowledge of late paganism, but here too the prominent temple of Aphrodite was converted into a church, probably in the late fifth century.[18]

Aphrodisias provides an example of a site with an extraordinarily rich and spectacular amount of archaeological remains, including sculptural and epigraphic material of breathtaking quality and importance. A good many of the later inscriptions are undatable, because their conventional language and style remained so constant over the period, but it is possible here, as it rarely is elsewhere, to piece together a real, if incomplete, view of changing patterns in city life in the late antique period. Some other sites offer this possibility too, each in its own way, among them Ephesus in Asia Minor and Apamea in Syria.[19] But even apparently clear archaeological evidence, coins or inscriptions, and or pottery dating may be unreliable. Archaeological evidence can only tell us what happened, not why it happened, and it is only as good as the methodology adopted by the archaeologists in question permits.[20] It is of course tempting, in the absence of specific indications, to link certain sorts of archaeological evidence to historical factors or events known from other sources. Procopius's *Buildings,* a detailed account of the building activity of the Emperor Justinian, provides a particularly good example of a text frequently used in this way. However, it omits Italy altogether, for reasons on which we can only speculate, and the ample and literary treatment given to Constantinople in book I is not carried through in the rest of the work, which in places consists only of lists of names of fortifications.[21] Previous emperors, such as Theodosius II and Anastasius, had engaged in the building of major urban fortifications, with famous surviving examples at Constantinople, Thessalonica and Dyrrachium. However, city walls were commonly repaired and rebuilt over long periods and many of the late Roman fortifications in the Balkans and elsewhere cannot be dated from the material evidence alone. It is therefore always tempting to suppose a given site or fortification to be Justinianic work; yet closer study of the *Buildings* reveals that Procopius often exaggerates or misrepresents the nature and extent of Justinian's building programme, and recent studies have suggested that some of these structures may in fact, like the great walls of Amida (Diyarbakir), have been earlier constructions, subsequently much rebuilt, or merely refurbished under Justinian. On the other hand, many of Procopius' statements are confirmed by other evidence, so that we cannot be uniformly sceptical. A case in point is his account of Carthage and North Africa, where omissions and exaggerations make his evidence infuriating to use, but which is nevertheless clearly based on firsthand experience.[22] A final illustration of the range of problems encountered is provided by the evidence (both archaeological and literary) for earthquakes and plague in the late antique and early Byzantine period. Non-specific damage to material remains is frequently attributed to a convenient earthquake; however, this may fail to take into account the fact that unless the literary sources give precise details, there is usually no way of knowing its scale – it may well have been a mere tremor. Sometimes indeed the cause of the damage is very clear, as at Scythopolis,[23] but even when major earthquakes are known to have taken place, they have in most historical periods proved a stimulus to rebuilding, often on a large scale, as can be seen in the case of Antioch in our period. As for plague, despite what seem like detailed and authentic literary accounts and references to plague in the sixth century (and later, especially in the Near East), it has proved notoriously difficult to trace its effect on the ground, and this remains a serious puzzle for historians.[24]

### The decline of cities and the end of classical antiquity?

With this growth in archaeological investigation, the question whether late antique cities were in decline has typically been rephrased in terms of urban change or transformation. If we put together the evidence from archaeological investigation of sites very widely scattered round the Mediterranean, a general picture seems to emerge of contraction, and of shifts in urban topography, and there is evidence from widely different regions to suggest that significant urban change was already taking place before the end of the sixth century.[25] A contrast has been drawn between the west, where urban life seems to have been in decline already by the late fifth century, and the east, where many, if not all, scholars hold that late antique urbanism continued to flourish well into the Islamic period.[26] However, the picture is not uniform, and new evidence and new interpretations are emerging all the time. There is unlikely to be a single or simple cause for these changes, even if in individual cases particular local factors may be plausibly adduced. But by the end of the period now covered, deep-seated social and economic change seems to have been taking place all round the Mediterranean, if at varying pace and for local as well as macro reasons. The rest of this chapter will investigate the process in more detail and we will have cause to return to it in the case of the eastern provinces in Chapters 8 and 9.

## The late antique town

What do we mean by the late antique city? The model of the typical provincial city of the Roman empire, with its monumental architecture, its public buildings, baths, theatre, temples, forum, broad colonnaded streets and perhaps also its circus or amphitheatre, continued into late antiquity – Aphrodisias in its heyday provides a good example. Such cities were planned for public life and well equipped for the leisure of their well-to-do citizens, the members of the curial class, who were also the city's benefactors; here and at Ephesus their statues and inscriptions proudly display their generosity and civic pride.[27] With the coming of the fourth century, the upkeep of the cities had become more difficult and building had slowed down, but the arrangement of public space remained much as it had been. Such cities seemed to contemporaries to be the embodiment of culture. Procopius describes in panegyrical terms the founding of a new city at the spot where Belisarius' expedition landed in North Africa, and where, he claims, a miraculous spring had gushed forth to give them water just when they needed it; with the building of a town wall and all the accoutrements of a city, the rural population of the headland henceforth adopted civilized manners and lived like men of culture:

> The rural people have cast aside their ploughshares and live like city-dwellers, exchanging their rural lifestyle for civilization.
>
> (*Buildings* VI.6.15, cf. *Vandal Wars* I.15.31ff.)

Elsewhere Procopius lists among the standard attributes of a city, stoas, a bath, an aqueduct and lodgings for magistrates.[28] This model was already coming under strain when Procopius wrote. It was an urban style which had required public and private investment, both to build and to maintain its public buildings. It also implied a life of cultured leisure, or at least civic involvement, if only for the richer citizens, with a range of public activity, in the forum, at the baths, at the circus, while in the Roman period its temples characteristically looking out over the forum implied the survival of paganism.

## The changing city

Just such a city, named Justiniana Prima, and generally identified with Čaričin Grad (45 km south of Niš), is attributed to the initiative of the Emperor Justinian and commemorated his own birthplace in Illyricum – or so Procopius claims, for his account of this new foundation is even vaguer than it is for the new city on the African coast, simply listing some of the standard elements noted above.[29] Yet generalizations are dangerous, and close examination of every site and literary reference is needed. 'Classical' cities were far from being the norm everywhere, if they ever were. The large sixth-century site of Androna in Syria, for instance, is identified as a *kome*, a large village, like others in the east in this period, though it had such urban features as two sets of circuit walls, large extra-mural reservoirs, a *kastron*, a Byzantine bath, and nearly a

*Figure 7.1* Serjilla, one of the 'dead' cities in north-west Syria (Photo: James Pettifer)

dozen churches. The 'dead cities' of the limestone massif were also in fact large villages, though with urban features.

At Aïn Djelloula, north west of Kairouan in modern Tunisia, a Latin verse inscription records building work of the prefect Solomon (534–56 and 539–44), which included *censura, status, cives, ius, moenia, fastus* ('[fiscal and municipal] authority, [civic] order, citizens, law, public buildings and *fasti* [a legal calendar and list of magistrates])'; the city added the name of the Empress Theodora to its own name and became Cululis Theodoriana; yet of this town Procopius says merely that it was given 'very strong walls' by Justinian. Building and fortification continued in North Africa, and an inscription from Henchir Sguidan to the north east reveals fortifications carried out by the prefect Thomas in the reign of the Emperor Tiberius (578–82) and the naming of the fort as Anastasiana, after Tiberius' wife; the same Thomas had also carried out fortifications in the reign of Justin II and Sophia (565–78), when Iunci seems to have been renamed Sofiana Iunci, and is known from the Latin epic of Corippus.[30] North Africa is a special case; having been recovered from Vandal rule, the province needed organization, investment and defence from Berber attack. The same defences were, however, of little avail against the later Arab expeditions, and this prompts a re-examination of their nature and purpose, including their geographical locations.[31]

In the Balkans, urban life had been sharply interrupted by the Hunnic and Ostrogothic invasions, and Anastasius' and Justinian's programmes of restoration and fortification were mainly palliative. Despite Procopius' claims, it seems that there was little secular urban life in these settlements by the sixth century, and building and signs of culture begin to dry up together. This is the picture at late antique Nicopolis and Philippopolis in Bulgaria.[32] Military needs and provision for an increased local role for bishops now took precedence over the spacious civic structures of earlier times.[33] Circumstances were also difficult in Greece, where late sources suggest that in the late sixth century some cities, including ancient Sparta, Argos and Corinth, were abandoned by their inhabitants in favour of safer places. Archaeological and other evidence does not always confirm this oversimplified picture, but it does seem that the pattern of urban settlement was changing significantly during the later sixth and seventh centuries. At Corinth, the remaining population retreated to the fortified height of Acrocorinth, and this became typical of Byzantine settlements in Greece. This impression of a search for places of refuge is reinforced in many sites in the Balkans, where inhabited centres contracted and regrouped around a defensible acropolis, or were abandoned in favour of such positions elsewhere. The early Byzantine walls at Sparta enclosed only the ancient acropolis and not the civic centre; it was presumably hoped that they would provide a place of refuge for the population in time of attack.[34] The late *Chronicle of Monemvasia* connects the move of population in Greece explicitly with the Slav invasions of the 580s, but the extent of Slav movement and settlement is a contentious subject, and both the chronology and the archaeological record are hard to trace.[35] According to the same source, the population of Lakedaimon, ancient Sparta, settled at Monemvasia, a rocky crag on the east coast of the Peloponnese, very hard of access; however, the actual date of the foundation of Monemvasia is extremely obscure, and Sparta remained inhabited in the Byzantine period. The general phenomenon of population movement, if it happened in this way, was probably more gradual, and a number of different factors may have been operative in bringing it about, including possibly a shift in economic activity. Whatever the reasons for the new pressures from Avars and Slavs (Sclaveni) in the late sixth century, the empire found the threat difficult to deal with, and resorted to a mixture of diplomacy, subsidies and warfare to try to control it. Athens itself was not occupied, but both Athens and Corinth suffered attack in the 580s, which shows clearly in the coin evidence, and which caused considerable destruction by fire, and Thessalonica was besieged; the Long Walls of Constantinople were attacked more than once by Sclaveni and Avars in the same decade. These Slavs were described by the Emperor Maurice in his *Strategikon*:

> [The Slavs and the Antes] are both independent, absolutely refusing to be enslaved or governed, least of all in their own land. They are populous and hardy, bearing readily heat, cold, rain, nakedness and scarcity of provisions ... Owing to their lack of government and their ill feeling toward one another, they are not acquainted with an order of battle.
>
> (Maurice, *Strategikon*, 11.4, trans. Dennis)

Although Athens was used as a base against the Slavs nearly a century later by the Emperor Constans II (662–3), new building, if any, involved subdivision into smaller rooms and the use of former fine buildings as sites for olive-presses. Similar phenomena are also encountered frequently in North Africa, and at the village of Olympos in Attica, for instance, such re-use involved a former baptistery.[36]

The last two features, subdivision and 'encroachment' on the sites of former grand buildings in urban centres, can be seen in different forms in many other regions. Typically, the large houses, maintained in many areas into the sixth century or even later, are divided into smaller rooms for multiple dwelling, often with mudbrick floors over or instead of the splendid mosaics which are so characteristic of the fine houses. This can be vividly seen at Carthage, where a large peristyle house (built round a courtyard in classical style) in the 'Michigan sector' was subdivided into much poorer accommodation by the seventh century, and where the same smaller divisions appear elsewhere in the city. At Apamea, peristyle houses were restored after the capture of the city by the Persians in 573, and apparently maintained until the Arab conquest. But elsewhere 'encroachment', either by poorer dwellings or, commonly, by small traders and artisans, frequently occurs over existing public spaces, such as the forum or, as at Anemurium in southern Turkey, on the site of the *palaestra*. In the latter case this change of use had started early, after the disruption to the city caused by Persian invasion in the third century, and the artisanal activity in the area apparently flourished; but by the late sixth and seventh centuries the other civic amenities such as baths and aqueducts were no longer functioning. A particularly striking example is found at Sbeitla in modern Tunisia, where an olive-press, perhaps seventh-century, sits right on top of the former main street.

*Figure 7.2* An olive-press astride a former main street, Sbeitla, Tunisia, probably seventh century

Burials within churches, which are common in the great basilicas of the period, indicate changed religious attitudes rather than economic pressures (Chapter 6); however, the presence of burials within central areas of the town, and even on the sites of earlier fine housing or public buildings is another common feature, seen vividly at Carthage and other North African sites in this period and indicating a major shift in the use of urban space. It has been tempting in the past to think in terms of economic necessity, 'squatting', and, where there is some textual evidence to support the idea, as at Carthage, of an influx of refugees from invasion in other areas. Local factors will also have been important; for instance, at Luni near La Spezia on the west coast of Italy, where the decline of the marble trade from nearby Carrara must have affected the town, and where, though it survived into the seventh century, a clear decline in material wealth can be seen from at least the sixth century. Local conditions differed: some of the major cities of Asia Minor, Ephesus and Sardis, for example, which had enjoyed a period of prosperity and expansion in late antiquity, seem to have maintained late antique civic life until the Persian invasions of the early seventh century.[37] Very little serious archaeological work has taken place on the Byzantine period in any of these sites, and generalizations carry certain dangers, but the phenomena are so widespread, even if the pace varies in different places, that it seems clear that a general process of urban change was going on, and that this must be connected not simply with causes such as plague or invasion, but with overall administrative and economic factors, including the relation of provincial cities to the central administrative organization.

Recent and ongoing archaeological work at sites in the western Mediterranean including Classe, the port of Ravenna, the islands, and North Africa, indicates a changing economy in these urban environments, with centres of production (kilns, olive-presses and metal workshops, for instance) now established within the former public areas, but also with new developments such as warehouses, indicating new patterns in sea-borne trade. By the seventh century new developments can be seen in coastal sites; for instance at Naples.[38] A coastal city such as Marselles remained dynamic in the seventh century, and benefited from the trade of Frankish Gaul as well as the Mediterranean. Western shipwrecks suggest that while trade was on a reduced scale and differently configured than previously, it was still lively. Mediterranean trade certainly continued, and eastern amphorae continue to be found at western sites in the seventh century, if not in the same numbers, while new types start to appear. Although interpreting such evidence is heavily dependent on the limited number of excavated sites, such excavations are increasing in number and some of this work, still in its early stages, seems to be pointing in the direction of a break in the eighth, not the seventh century; it thus serves as a corrective to the previously dominant resort to explanations of change in terms of 'decline'. It is important also to stress that seventh-century Byzantium had not lost its western role, as can be seen in the 660s in the intervention of the Emperor Constans II (641–68) in Italy against the Lombards, launched from Syracuse in Sicily, and his visits to Rome, Calabria and Sardinia. Evidence from the reign of the same emperor and later also shows that Byzantium continued to hope for continued control of parts of North Africa. But there are signs that a new western Mediterranean system was beginning to emerge.

In the east, the picture inevitably looked somewhat different. Antioch, the second city of the eastern empire, was hard hit in the mid-sixth century by fire (525), plague, earthquake (526 and 528) and sack by the Persians (540), followed by the deportation of many of its citizens to Persia; however, Procopius describes a substantial urban rebuilding, imperially financed, after the 540 disaster.[39] But the rebuilt city was on a smaller scale, and the city's cathedral, finally destroyed in the earthquake of 588, was not restored.[40] According to John of Ephesus, the patriarchate of Antioch was the scene of lurid campaigns against alleged paganism, which reached as far as two bishops, Rufinus and Gregory. The case was referred to the emperor, but the colourful patriarch Gregory returned from his acquittal in Constantinople with permission to build a new circus;[41] however, the Persian attack in 611 followed by the Arab invasions curbed urban renewal in Antioch. In other eastern cities, such as Laodicea and Damascus, earlier views about the encroachment over the colonnaded streets of late antiquity by little shops or artisanal buildings as characteristic of a transition to the medieval souks of the medieval period have been questioned.[42] There were more complex changes going on than straightforward economic impoverishment, and indeed the government tried to control the subdivision of public buildings and ensure their maintenance. Invasions and natural disasters were certainly factors which caused damage to cities in late antiquity, but they were not the only reasons for change, nor have they always left much trace in the archaeological record.[43]

## Interpreting urban change

As argued above, archaeological evidence is often difficult to interpret and, in particular, difficult to link directly with historical events. But in some cases, as in that of street building at Caesarea in Palestine, there was still considerable activity going on in the later sixth century, and Justinian's building programme included some spectacular achievements, such as the great Nea church at Jerusalem, which is shown on the sixth-century mosaic map of the city from Madaba in Jordan. In this case, excavation dramatically and unexpectedly confirmed the accuracy of Procopius' description.[44] Major building work also took place in a number of Near Eastern cities after the middle of the sixth century, among them Gerasa (Jerash) in Transjordan, and some magnificent floor mosaics from churches in the area date from the seventh and even the eighth centuries.[45] Striking and lavish mosaics continue to be revealed from synagogues in the Near East, most recently and spectacularly from Sepphoris. Many of these synagogue mosaics contain motifs and iconography clearly recognizable from pagan contexts and drew without self-consciousness on a common artistic repertoire; while various explanations have been put forward for Jewish use of pagan imagery, the sheer magnificence and lavishness of these mosaics cannot fail to impress.[46]

Arguments about prosperity versus decline are not easy to balance. It is partly a question of what indicators one uses. Whittow, for instance, argues for the prosperity of Edessa (Urfa, south-east Turkey) in the sixth century from the large sums of gold paid to Chosroes I in 540 and 544, and the quantities of silver in the city when it was captured by the Persians in 609.[47] In contrast it has been deduced from a study of settlement patterns in the region that while settlement density reached an unprecedented peak from the fourth to the sixth centuries, from the seventh century there was a dramatic fall in occupation.[48] Edessa continued as an urban centre through the Islamic period until the Byzantine recovery in the tenth century, but the silver it possessed in the sixth century does not tell us very much about the general distribution of wealth or about urbanism as such. Complex readjustments seem to have been taking place in many areas, which involved both rural and urban sites and their mutual relationships. There are, moreover, serious gaps in our knowledge due to the uneven degree of excavation and the lack of certain sorts of evidence. For reasons of local settlement, little may survive now of a place known to have been a prosperous city, while casual information from textual sources such as the *Life of Symeon the Fool* (for Emesa/Homs, seventh century, but referring to the sixth century), the *Miracles of St Demetrius* (early seventh century, Thessalonica) or the *Life* of Theodore of Sykeon (for late sixth-century Anatolia),[49] sometimes belies any general theory of urban decline. Even more important to remember is the fact that the picture is literally changing all the time as new evidence comes to light and existing theories are revisited. Many excavations on major sites are still continuing, and one season's work can and does frequently modify previous results – the important site of Pella, one of the Decapolis cities in Jordan, a city extensively studied in the late antique and early Islamic periods since the 1980s by Alan Walmsley, is a case in point. Finally, a reliable ceramic typology for the Near East is only now beginning to be agreed, and it also seems likely that there was much more regional variation than previously supposed.

How far it is possible to generalize, even within these limitations, let alone across the Mediterranean, is obviously very questionable. It is worth rehearsing again some of the main factors that have been adduced by historians as agents of urban change, starting with the plague which hit Constantinople and Asia Minor in the mid-sixth century and continued to strike Syria in successive waves throughout the seventh century. Though the effects may be hard to quantify (see Chapter 5), it is hard not to think that plague must have been a factor in undermining the generally thriving state of cities in the Near East in the early part of the sixth century. But since neither epigraphic nor papyrological sources offer clear evidence of the scale of mortality, and one can make only a general connection between urban and settlement decline and the factor of plague, it is dangerous to use the plague of 541 as a dating reference in the absence of other evidence. On the other hand, arguments which seek to downplay its effects in relation to individual sites must logically be equally suspect.[50] One can find extreme variation among historians in the amount of weight that they are willing to attach to the sixth- and seventh-century plague. Yet this seems to have been the first appearance of bubonic plague in Europe and its impact should have been far greater than that of the regular diseases which ravaged ancient cities as a matter of course. To take just one example from the literary sources outside the three main descriptions of the epidemic by Procopius, John of Ephesus and Evagrius, when the plague struck their monastery, the monks of the Judaean monastery of Chariton went en masse to the ancient holy man Cyriacus, who was living as a hermit at Sousakim, to ask for his help against the disease, and brought him to live in a cave nearby.[51] At present it does not seem possible to do more than leave the matter open. Second, according to the literary sources, the sixth century also experienced a high incidence of earthquakes, which in some cases can, as we have seen, be plausibly connected with the material record. But some of the literary evidence for earthquakes in the period may be attributable to increased recording of earthquakes by Christian chroniclers interested in pointing out the signs of God's wrath rather than to a quantitative rise in their actual incidence. Third, other external factors can also be adduced for reduced prosperity in certain areas, such as a possible withdrawal of military resources, which would imply a lower level of economic demand in the region in the future, and poorer roads and communications.[52]

How far did Christianization play a role in the move away from the civic life of classical antiquity, with its baths, temples and public entertainments? Liebeschuetz has argued that the process contributed to a decline in the old civic values, but Michael Whitby points to the role of bishops and the new Christian framework in the continuing success of many cities.[53] The munificence of public benefactors did not give way in any simple sense to Christian charity; the two more frequently existed side by side. Bishops fulminated against the games and the theatre, and some objected to public baths on moral grounds, but often to little effect. The great temples slowly and gradually went out of use and were often converted into churches – though not everywhere, not always without protest and sometimes only at a late date; as we saw, Christians themselves tended to make grandiose claims which were not always justified.[54] But church building on a large scale certainly changed the appearance and feel of towns, and even average-sized towns in the sixth century might contain far more and far larger churches than their population would seem to warrant; furthermore, they often went on being extended and altered after other forms of public building seem to have stopped, a feature which is strikingly exemplified by the large churches of Sbeitla in North Africa. The church and individual bishops gradually assumed more and more responsibility not only for civic leadership but also for social welfare in their communities, in the distribution of alms and maintenance of hospices and by storing food and distributing it in the times of famine which were a regular feature of ancient urban life.[55]

Eutychius, the sixth-century patriarch of Constantinople, performed this service for the people of Amasea during his years of exile beginning in 565, and the early seventh-century patriarch of Alexandria known as John the Almsgiver acquired his epithet from his reputation for urban philanthropy. Other holy men and monks also performed similar roles: a story told about St Nicholas of Sion, near Myra in Lycia, tells how when the plague struck the metropolis of Myra in the sixth century, Nicholas was suspected of warning neighbouring farmers not to go to the city to sell their provisions for fear of infection. The governor and the city magistrates sent for the saint from his monastery, and Nicholas visited several settlements, where he slaughtered oxen and brought wine and bread with him to feed the people.[56] Bishops and clergy had long been involved in the affairs of cities and countryside and in negotiations with the provincial governor, as is clearly apparent in the letters of Theodoret of Cyrrhus in Euphratensis (northern Syria) in the fifth century, where villages rather than towns seem to have been the norm, while in early seventh-century Alexandria the patriarch John the Almsgiver was dealing with matters of trade and taxation alike. The presence of holy men and, in the east, of stylites, such as Symeon the Elder at Qalaat Semaan in the fifth century and Symeon the Younger near Antioch in the sixth, around both of whom substantial monasteries grew up, impacted on the rural economy (Chapter 3). Pilgrims required services, and bought local goods including pilgrim *eulogiai*, essentially religious souvenirs, and any important shrine or location of a notable holy man was soon surrounded by substantial and varied buildings which required technical building skills. To some extent these, and other large monastic complexes contributed to a ruralization of the economy.

While the fabric of life in both town and country had thus changed significantly with Christianization, Christianity did not itself directly bring about urban change. Rather, by stimulating church building, by diverting wealth from secular causes and by influencing social practices, it was one among a range of other factors which together converged to change and undermine the urban topography and economic organization inherited from the high empire. The shifting economic relation between the civic authorities and the church, which came to represent, let us say by the later sixth century, an actual shift of resources in favour of the latter, was an important feature of the period.[57] As a result, the church's agents, especially bishops, took on the role of providers and distributors of wealth which formerly lay with the civil authorities. Since the role of cities within the empire had always been closely identified with finance – exchange, monetary circulation, collection of taxes – this shift inevitably had profound consequences.[58]

## Economy and administration of late antique and early Byzantine cities

As we saw, since the fourth century, the *curiales*, the better-off citizens on whom the government depended for the running of cities, had been

complaining loudly about their increased burdens (Chapter 4). Both the cho-
rus of complaint and the theme itself were of long standing, and those who,
such as the Emperor Julian, the rhetor Libanius or the historians Ammianus
Marcellinus and, later, Procopius, saw themselves as champions of traditional
values invariably also took up the cause of the cities whose future they perceived to be under threat.[59] There were some grounds for their fears: government pressure on the curial class, who provided a convenient target for
ways of increasing revenue or at least trying to ensure its collection, certainly
increased as time went on. The city councils themselves faced financial difficulties, especially those with splendid buildings to keep up. Many found it
difficult to keep their councils up to strength with enough *curiales* of adequate
income. The wealth of curials also varied greatly; many of them were village
landowners of quite modest means while richer ones might hold widely dis-
persed estates. Cities showed an obstinate tendency to survive, and two hundred years after Constantine most were still in a reasonable state, while some
were more densely populated and more prosperous than they had ever been,
but we now also hear of leading citizens under different terms – *honorati* (ex-
officials), or 'notables' or 'grandees'.[60] The urban elites of 'late late antiquity'
were not identical with the old curial class, though there was no doubt over-
lap. They now included churchmen, and especially in the Balkans, defence
needs now loomed large on their horizon. They also included some of the
successful landowners whose influence was clearly felt in the economy of the
sixth century.[61] The 'notables' were recognized in imperial legislation under
Anastasius (491–518), and co-existed awkwardly with councils; by the fifth
century the governor and other civic officials (*defensor, curator, pater*) gained
increasing importance and councils gradually dropped out of participation
in appointments to the latter posts in favour of the notables. Both John the
Lydian and Evagrius, in the middle and late sixth century respectively, suggest
that councils no longer functioned. As for ordinary people, they had no official role, but they could and often did demonstrate and express their views,
as we shall see below.

The style of life which these cities had supported for so long had already
begun to change in many places, and urban life was certainly drastically cur-
tailed in the seventh century (and long before that in most places in the west).
The pressures of invasion, insecurity and increased military expenditure by
the central government were felt in differing degrees in the west and east
and the effects of the Persian and Arab invasions in the east will be discussed
later. A.H.M. Jones famously saw the increased numbers of monks, bishops
and clergy as a component in the excessive number of 'idle mouths' who constituted a drain on the late Roman state, and it is true that these men might
otherwise have been producers, or indeed soldiers, or even, as Arnaldo Momigliano thought, have lent their abilities to running the cities and the empire
better. Yet such a formulation ignores the structural change that was taking
place in the balance of town and country. The number and size of gifts and
legacies made to churches, strikingly demonstrated in the rich silver treasures

161

owned by small eastern churches, are not so much a sign of the prosperity of the region as of an economic situation in which local donors chose to direct their wealth towards otherwise obscure village churches;[62] this silverware contrasts with the impressive late Roman silver found in late fourth-century Britain, which demonstrate the still surviving but soon-to-end wealth of rich Christian households.[63] John of Ephesus' *Lives of the Eastern Saints* gives a vivid picture with much circumstantial detail of village life around Amida (Dyarbakir) in Mesopotamia.[64] Rural monasteries were also a very important element affecting the relation between town and country; they attracted donations, attracted recruits, sometimes in very large numbers, and were themselves economic units impacting on their surroundings.

We should not therefore be surprised if the rich epigraphic sources of the earlier period give way in favour of Christian funerary inscriptions, which are by comparison disappointingly brief, or hagiographic sources in the form of local saints' lives or miracle collections. While the latter material is often rightly viewed with suspicion by historians because of its obvious bias and its tendency to conventional exaggeration, it clearly reflects the changed point of view. Several cities in the crucial period are well provided with evidence of this sort, which shows not only that they continued as vital centres but, even more importantly, how their urban life was now articulated. One or two have already been mentioned, such as Thessalonica in the early seventh century, known from the *Miracles of St. Demetrius*, composed by the archbishop of the city soon after AD 610 and vividly reflecting the dangers of invasion then facing the city; others include Seleucia in Cilicia, and late sixth-century Anastasioupolis in Galatia, known from the *Life* of St Theodore of Sykeon. Even having made all the necessary allowances, the picture that emerges from these and many comparable texts is of an urban life no less vital but quite different in kind and flavour from what we associate with the late antique city in the first part of the period, still with its municipal pride, its public spaces, its great buildings and its civic autonomy. Times had changed. A comparison has been made between cities at the end of our period and the decaying industrial towns of modern Britain. Plausible or not, at least this suggests some of the complexity of the changes that were underway.

## Urban violence

Late antique cities could be turbulent places. We have already encountered rioting in the context of religious division, especially in certain explosive urban centres such as Alexandria. When the word was given for the destruction or conversion of a temple, bishops often led the way in provoking the feelings of the crowd; the imperial authorities on the other hand are found trying to restrain such enthusiasm. But rioting in Constantinople was endemic in the fifth and sixth centuries. The most serious episode – not a religious disturbance – was the so-called Nika revolt of 532 (Chapter 5), when the emperor himself was ready to flee, and the disturbance was put down only at the cost of great

loss of life when imperial troops had been sent in under Belisarius. The immediate reasons for this episode had to do with the execution of some criminals
who belonged to the circus factions, the Blues and Greens, but it soon came
to focus on Justinian's unpopular ministers, especially the praetorian prefect
John the Cappadocian, whom the emperor hastily replaced. These are not
revolutionary uprisings, but short-lived explosions of violence against a highly
unstable background. While religious and political issues were of course likely
to be thrown up as soon as violence began, even if they had not actually trig-
gered it off, sustained movements for religious or political reform are not in
question in this period. Protests against this or that piece of imperial policy,
especially if it had to do with taxation or an unpopular minister, were common in Constantinople, and similar manifestations elsewhere mimicked those
of the capital, but urban violence in this period, though it was extremely common, did not turn into revolution.[65] Nor, though Procopius liked to think that
they were the work of the 'rabble', can these episodes be read in any simple
sense as expressions of the feelings of the poor or the masses. Only once is a
riot explicitly ascribed to the 'poor' (in 553, as a result of a debasement of the
bronze coinage – again the emperor immediately gave way), and riots about
bread or grain were relatively infrequent, thanks to the care which the authorities took to ensure the supply and keep the population quiet on this issue.[66]

Apart from the prejudice shown by Procopius and others, including Malalas, Menander Protector and Agathias, and the concern voiced in the anonymous sixth-century dialogue *On Political Science*,[67] there is no reason to think
that the better-off or middling parts of the urban population were any less
given to rioting than the really poor; many episodes were sparked off by hostility to individuals or passionate enthusiasm for chariot racing on the part of
all classes, and, as at Constantinople and Antioch, especially by members of
the 'factions' of Blues and Greens, the organized groups, effectively guilds,
of charioteers, performers, musicians and supporters who staffed the public entertainments of late antique cities, and the wider constituency of their
followers. Graffiti on seats at Aphrodisias and Alexandria vividly testify to
their widespread following. Association of the Blues and Greens with urban
violence began in the fifth century, and the level of instability, whether or
not associated with the 'parties', evidently rose all over the east in the sixth
century, reaching a peak with demonstrations in many cities towards the end
of the reign of Phocas in the early seventh century. Historians have often supposed that this could only be explained on the assumption that the Blues and
Greens were associated with particular religious or ideological standpoints,
but a strong rebuttal of this theory was mounted by Alan Cameron in the
1970s.[68] More recently Liebeschuetz has reviewed the evidence again and argued that the position was not quite so straightforward; the Blues and Greens
were not merely sporting hooligans, and while many of the recorded disturbances seem to have started in contexts of crowd and sporting excitement,
when there were serious issues, as in the overthrow of the Emperor Maurice
(602) and the turbulent reign of Phocas (602–10), the factions might well be

drawn in to take sides (Chapter 9). As Liebeschuetz points out, the factions could hardly fail to be drawn in, since 'after the army, the imperial administration and the church, they were easily the largest organizations in the Empire', with branches in every major city, large staffs and substantial patronage.[69] Emperors also favoured particular colours and the potential of the factions could be exploited to their own advantage by individuals, including members of the elite and the 'notables' who were now prominent in urban affairs. By the end of the sixth century, there were faction groupings even in small towns in Egypt, as we learn from the *Chronicle* of John of Nikiu and other sources.[70] Finally, the factions also acquired a military capacity and came to have a role in urban defence. The Blues and Greens were not political parties, and while their members might well adopt particular positions in specific cases, the factions as such followed no consistent policy. But in general, and despite the fact that our evidence is patchy, they seem to have taken on wider roles by the seventh century, and urban violence to have increased in level and frequency, a trend associated in general terms by Liebschuetz with the phenomenon of 'failing curial government'.[71]

It is true, as Whitby points out, that the level and frequency of factional disorders must be read chronologically, and that factions and their supporters were not infrequently involved in incidents of religious violence. But the ceremony and the public theatre that were the hallmarks of urban life in late antiquity, and which had their roots very far back in the Principate, had always been conducive to public manifestations that could easily turn into disorder. In the late antique period, not only did the emperor confront the people (and vice versa) in the Hippodrome at Constantinople, but provincial governors also behaved similarly in their local setting. Great churches were the scene of similar manifestations; here, too, large crowds often gathered in emotional circumstances, and passions could be easily inflamed. When rioting broke out, symbols of authority such as imperial or official statues, or the portraits of patriarchs and bishops, were frequently torn down or damaged. The people, or rather, some among them, acquired a real opportunity to express their views on public occasions, which they often did by chanting acclamations of the authorities, mixed in with political messages.

Chariot racing, and the context of the hippodrome, offered an obvious physical setting for such outbursts, and many riots began in the circus, but theatres were also frequently the scene of violent episodes. In both places a contributory factor was provided by the highly structured festivals and performances in late antique Greek cities, in which each social and professional group had its own designated place, as was the case in the theatre at Aphrodisias.[72] The so-called 'Brytae' had been abolished by Anastasius in 501 after episodes of violence; this involved aquatic displays or contests and dancing, and a similar festival held at Edessa was also abolished. However, festivals continued to be held in Constantinople and elsewhere in the sixth century, such as the Brumalia, celebrated in winter and known from several literary and documentary accounts. Choricius of Gaza describes such a festival at

Gaza, probably from the 530s, and such events provided a ready focus for crowd excitement; pantomimes always spelt trouble.[73] A remarkable example of organized crowd control is provided by the theatre claque known at Antioch in the late fourth century, but surely not unique to Antioch: these were professional cheerleaders who could manipulate audiences to powerful effect; since local governors were also expected to attend the theatre, they were often at the claque's mercy.[74] On the other hand, enthusiasm for star performers, especially charioteers, was also a major factor which could destabilise urban life: many contemporary epigrams celebrate famous charioteers, among them one of the most famous of all, Porphyrius, in whose honour as many as thirty-two are known. Two great statue bases survive, inscribed with these epigrams, which once bore his statues; they were erected, side by side with many other monuments, on the spina of the Hippodrome in Constantinople, round which the chariots raced.[75] To mark special feats, Porphyrius and his rivals might be commemorated in statues made of silver, gold, silver and bronze, or gold and bronze, the gifts of their loyal fans, the Blues and Greens,[76] and the peak of such commemoration, to judge from the surviving evidence, was reached under Justinian. The importance and prestige of the Hippodrome is indicated by the fact that it was also a showcase for some of the most famous of the many ancient statues collected in late antique Constantinople,[77] as well as the scene of several imperial accessions. The theatre at Aphrodisias remained in use in the sixth century, as is clear from the factional inscriptions, but early in the seventh century the stage building collapsed and was not repaired, and a wall-painting of the archangel Michael shows that at least part of the building was already being differently used.[78] Alan Cameron suggests that increasing financial difficulties are likely thereafter to have made the continued maintenance of chariot racing difficult. Procopius characteristically complains that Justinian closed down theatres, hippodromes and circuses so as to save money,[79] but while this may fit other indications, such as the fact that the circus at Carthage seems to have gone out of use during the sixth century, it is hardly the whole explanation. In fact factional disturbances continued in Egyptian towns and in Jerusalem, and into the seventh century, and even in Alexandria at the time of the Arab invasions.[80]

The early Byzantine city was a place of continual public confrontation, and the frequent mentions of rioting in our sources suggest that it was highly unstable. Ecclesiastical rivalries were just as likely to give rise to such episodes as others, and episcopal elections and other occasions were also accompanied by crowd participation and acclamations. But perhaps we should put urban riots in the same historiographical category as earthquakes: they are commonly recorded, but we have no very accurate way of judging their intensity except where the information happens to be especially detailed. Buildings such as the Senate House and the Baths of Zeuxippos, which housed great collections of ancient statuary in Constantinople, were burnt during the Nika revolt of 532, but the fate of their statues is less clear.[81] Late antique cities did not decline or collapse because of urban violence, and the riots were never fully revolutionary, even in the last years of Phocas. Rather, they were normally contained at an acceptable level, and Evelyne Patlagean has suggested that these public manifestations, ranging from the shouting of acclamations to full-fledged urban violence, in fact occupied a structural role in the overall consensus between government and governed, part of an uneasy but accepted balance whereby the authorities, on the one hand, supplied the people with both the essentials of life and the setting for the expression of opinion, and, on the other, came down with an iron grip when necessary, a collusion in the face of which the church sometimes took an independent role, but was more often a collaborator.[82] This consensus was fragile at best and broke down, in the west under pressure of external circumstances and in the east for more complex reasons, including the changes in the balance of urban leadership.

A final factor which needs to be emphasized is the vital role played by the government in the food-supply of major cities, especially Rome and Constantinople (Chapter 4), which reinforced the dependency of the population on the authorities, while at the same time encouraging and maintaining numbers of citizens at a large and potentially dangerous level. The system was highly organized, and left little scope for private contractors. The cost to the government of maintaining it was very great. In addition, it ensured that political factors continued to play a major role in the stability of the larger cities; it placed the government and the population of the capital in an artificial position of alternate confrontation and dependence, which could lead all too often to public disturbance. Furthermore, it rendered the capital highly vulnerable to any breakdown in supply. It was eventually external circumstances which brought about this breakdown, and with it a great reduction in the population at both Rome and Constantinople. Chris Wickham in particular has emphasized the huge impact on the general economy of the eastern Mediterranean as well as on Constantinople of the cessation of the *annona* in the early seventh century, and this was compounded for the capital by the damage done to the Aqueduct of Valens, not repaired until the next century, during the great siege of 626. At Rome, the distribution was continued after 476 by the church, though on a smaller scale, while at Constantinople, the fatal change came with the loss of Egypt, the main supplier of grain, to the Persians in the early seventh century, after which population contraction was rapid.[83] It is a useful corrective, when considering urban change in the period, to remember the high level of public investment in certain aspects of urban life, whether through the *annona* or through building programmes, which should warn us in turn that urban prosperity is not in itself a good indicator of the general prosperity or otherwise of the empire.

## Conclusion

Late antique and early Byzantine towns constitute a vibrant and exciting field of research and all generalizations run the risk of subsequent falsification. How far one can usefully discuss western and eastern Mediterranean together after the mid-sixth century is also open to dispute, but there is enough evidence to show that by the late sixth century at the latest, many – probably most – cities were experiencing fundamental changes; these changes had come earlier, and were felt more severely, in parts of the west. Nevertheless cities were not in a simple state of 'decline'. The old structures were not being broken down by movements from below; rather, the changes came about from a combination of factors, including changes in administration and state investment, the pressures of invasion and insecurity, and the growing diversion of resources to the church, with corresponding social changes. The proliferation of large churches in urban centres was a conspicuous feature, especially in the sixth century, but every village also had its small church, and the growing number of large and imposing monasteries and pilgrimage centres had a major social and economic impact on their setting. Some areas, such as the Judaean desert, saw the growth of a whole network of large and small such establishments, while powerful monastic leaders such as Cyril of Scythopolis under Justinian could play an important role in influencing affairs even in Constantinople.[84] Towns and countryside alike had profoundly changed, and both looked and felt different.

# 8

# THE EASTERN
# MEDITERRANEAN – A
# REGION IN FERMENT

The last chapter underlined the amount of recent scholarship devoted to the fate of towns, and the efforts of scholars to discover whether, and why, there may have been a 'decline' in the sixth century. Undoubtedly in the case of the east, much of the motivation for this lively interest derives from hindsight – from our awareness that the Arab conquests were just round the corner, and our knowledge that most of the eastern provinces were to be so quickly lost to the eastern empire. In a striking number of cases, the inhabitants of the cities we have been discussing simply surrendered them to the invaders. Now more than ever, given contemporary events, historians face the challenge of explaining the speed and ease of the Arab conquests, and it is natural to look for at least a partial answer in the state of the eastern provinces in the immediately preceding period. But a vibrant economic life has been revealed in recent work on the eastern provinces, and this, and the emergence of new approaches to Byzantine and early Islamic archaeology, have made the Near East in the sixth to eighth centuries one of the most fertile current areas of study. To that must be added a striking upsurge of interest in linguistic change and in the religious complexities of the region in this period. Chapter 9 will consider the Persian and Arab invasions, the situation of Jews in Palestine and elsewhere, and the religious conflicts of the seventh century which were felt in Palestine and Syria just as the Arabs armies arrived. The present chapter will be concerned with broader questions of settlement, the mix of languages, cultural expression and religion in the east, and the tense situation on the frontier and in these borderlands between Rome and Persia in the sixth century which led to the renewal of war between Byzantium and Persia and the successful Persian invasion of the early seventh century. The latter events, which ended with a great and unexpected victory for the Byzantines under the Emperor Heraclius, but were followed almost at once by the incursions from Arabia which we know as 'the Arab conquests', will be discussed in Chapter 9.

## Settlement and population

To what extent were long-term changes already taking place in the demographic structure of the east, the mix of ethnicities, and the relation of town to country, in the period before the seventh-century invasions? One striking feature is the progressive reliance of both Byzantium and Persia on Arab groups who based themselves not in cities, the traditional centres of Roman/Byzantine culture and the location of most of the army units in the later empire, but rather in desert encampments. The Ghassanids or Ghassan, with their ruling Jafnid elite, would congregate at the pilgrimage centre of St Sergius at Resafa or, it has been argued, at the shrine of John the Baptist at er-Ramthaniyye on the Golan Heights, while the pro-Sasanian Lakhmids, led by the Nasrids, had their base at al-Hira in modern Iraq. The earliest Arabic inscriptions use Aramaic script, but by the sixth century Arabic language and Arabic script were slowly coming into use alongside Greek, and church patronage by al-Mundhir is mentioned in the Syriac *Letter of the Archimandrites* of 569/70.[1] Kinda were another major Arab grouping, occupying large tracts of central Arabia in the fifth and sixth centuries; they were remembered as ruling a 'kingdom' in later Arabic sources, but were in fact clients of the south Yemeni state of Himyar (see below). Al-Harith (Arethas) the Kindite concluded a peace with Byzantium under Anastasius, and according to one account his descendant Kaisos received an embassy to the Ethiopians (as the new rulers of Himyar), Amerites and 'Saracens', headed by the historian Nonnosus, probably in 531, according to a summary preserved by Photius in the ninth century; both Arethas and Kaisos are called phylarchs, and Kaisos was being pressed by Byzantium to intervene against Persia. Two Sabean inscriptions confirm the domination of Himyar in central Arabia.[2] The presence of Arabs ('Saracens') both within and on the edge of Roman territory in the east had been familiar since the fourth century and before, and some had been Christianized at an early date; but under patronage from both Rome and Persia these 'federations' acquired a new sense of influence and identity. In the case of Ghassan, their relationship with Constantinople suffered a blow in the late sixth century when al-Mundhir fell from favour; eventually, however, both the pro-Roman and the pro-Persian groups gradually became Muslim.[3] During their period as Roman or Persian clients, both the Ghassanids and the Lakhmids were Christian, the Ghassan being Miaphysite, the Lakhmids becoming Nestorian when their king, Nu'man, converted in the late sixth century. The luxury of the Ghassanid court is remembered in Arabic literature, and their transition to Islam and absorption into the Umayyad state is a key question, though it is unlikely that they were patrons of the so-called 'desert castles' in the area, as has been argued.

At the same time a different phenomenon is emerging with increasing clarity in recent scholarship, namely the high density of settlement in certain areas from the late fifth century into the sixth. This is true of certain parts of southern Palestine, the Golan and especially the Negev, which reached its highest density of settlement, and presumably of population, at this point (Chapter 7). The villages of the limestone massif of northern Syria studied by Tchalenko, Tate and many others since (Chapter 7), also testify to a prosperous and dense habitation, and to intense cultivation in the hinterlands of

Antioch and Apamea. For once we also have evidence from papyri from Nessana in the south-west Negev, as well as archaeological evidence from urban centres such as Rehovot in the central Negev,[4] Oboda and Elusa, which also developed during this period, to set alongside the results of surveys. There is plentiful evidence of viticulture and olive-growing, as well as material evidence of elaborate irrigation methods for agriculture in this dry region, such as dams, aqueducts, cisterns and the like. The comparison with modern techniques for cultivating arid regions such as the Negev is very striking, although conclusions can be premature. Interestingly, the towns of this period in the Negev seem to have been more market and administrative centres for the surrounding countryside, which was thickly dotted with villages, than urban centres on the late classical model.

A similar pattern of settlement density can be traced in other ways. The impressive number of mosaic pavements surviving from churches, synagogues and other buildings from this period in Palestine demonstrate the level of investment in buildings, even if not general prosperity. The large city of Scythopolis (Bet Shean) shows no sign of declining until the city was hit by earthquake, probably in 749 (Chapter 7), and a bilingual balance from the city, inscribed in Greek and Arabic, seems to suggest that the local population had found a modus vivendi with the new elite of the Umayyad period, while a Greek inscription of 662 from Hammat Gader, on the east coast of the Sea of Galilee, uses dating by both the regnal year of the caliph Mu'awiya and the era of the former Greek city and Roman colony of Gadara. Reliable stratigraphy from excavation, which would yield better dating indicators, is admittedly often lacking, and surface finds may prove misleading. Yet population growth, development of towns and increased levels of cultivation and irrigation have been widely noted, not only in the Negev, but also in northern Syria and the Hauran. In contrast, there seems to have been a distinct falling away in many cases from the seventh century onwards, when, besides the effects of plague, the civil war under Phocas and the later invasions must also have taken their toll, together with a degree of emigration to the west. Some of the smaller and more remote of the many monasteries and hermitages in the Judaean desert seem to have fallen out of use in the seventh century, like the monastery of Khirbet ed-Deir, a cliff-side *coenobium* built in a linear fashion like those at Choziba, Spelaion and Theoctistus, though the large central ones survived into the Islamic period; a major factor in the reduction in number was the eventual disruption under new conditions to the impressive economic and market system which had previously enabled them to flourish so spectacularly.[5] All this precludes any straightforward equation of military investment with prosperity, and raises the question of how to explain the demographic increase.

Many, though not all, scholars have seen a downturn setting in before the seventh century.[6] This is still debated, and it is better not to imagine that there was a single unified late antique economy, even within the more prosperous east. Opinions vary, for instance, as to how much the Sasanian occupation of

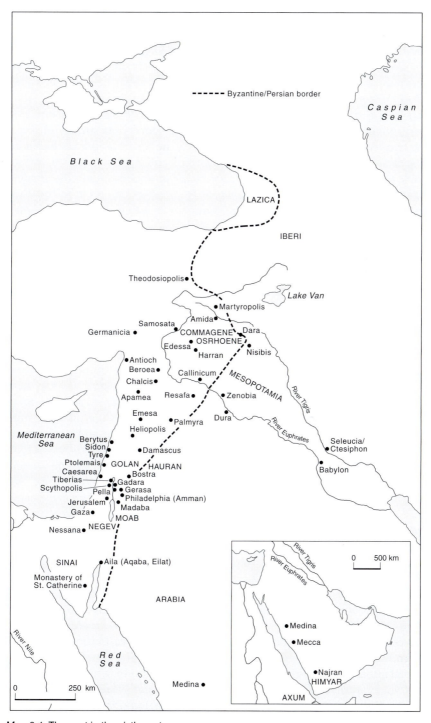

*Map 8.1* The east in the sixth century

Himyar in the 570s affected Byzantine maritime commerce in the Red Sea,[7] and there was variation even within specific areas such as the limestone massif or the area around the Judaean desert monasteries (below).

Various reasons have been put forward for prosperity in the east, among them the economic benefits of the pilgrim traffic (which included pilgrimage from Mesopotamia in modern Iraq, to the shrine of St Sergius at Resafa).[8] This was certainly helpful to the region, and had been so since the fourth century, but it cannot bear the weight that has sometimes been put on it. Similar patterns of increased population density are in any case observable elsewhere, for instance in Egypt. In the case of Palestine and Syria recent explanations look to long-distance trade as a major factor in understanding the changes in the region over the period; shipwreck archaeology based on finds off the coast of Israel is one indicator of the density of exchange in the sixth century, and of a falling-off in the seventh.[9]

Long-distance movement of commodities in connection with the *annona* has been much studied in recent years through the evidence from amphorae, and even though its main axis in the later part of our period was from Egypt and North Africa to Constantinople, it is now clear that other goods travelled in all directions, and that Palestine and Syria were producing not only olive oil but also wine on a large scale, amounting to a substantial surplus and source of local prosperity. Not only shipwreck evidence but also literary sources such as the seventh-century *Life of John the Almsgiver*, patriarch of Alexandria, show that early Byzantine ships were involved in extensive distribution networks across the Mediterranean and to and from the east, carrying a wide range of items from metalwork, glass and silverware to spices and perfumes. Cargoes of specialized items probably also made use of the *annona* ships on their return journey having delivered their original cargo. A classic example of private trade is provided by the sixth-century traveller and merchant known as Cosmas Indicopleustes ('he who sailed to India'), who described trading voyages to Ethiopia, the Red Sea, India and Sri Lanka in his *Christian Topography*,[10] but the material evidence tells a fuller story of long-distance and local exchange and the interaction of state and private.[11] This picture of extensive non-state production and distribution in the eastern provinces differs from that in the west, where the state-led *annona* accounted for a higher proportion of distribution, and it also reflects a different kind of settlement pattern, more urbanized and with more small producers still doing well, but fewer large estates.[12] Egypt, with its great landowning families, is indeed an exception to this pattern, though the interpretation of the evidence is controversial.[13] It ought to follow that the east was less affected when the *annona* ceased in the early seventh century, except that that coincided with the invasion and occupation of most of the east by the Persians; very little is known, however, about the actual impact of Persian rule (Chapter 9).

Older explanations for the prosperity of Syria and Palestine also appealed to the caravan trade which had been of major importance in accounting for the prosperity of Palmyra in the early empire, as we know from ample documentary evidence; the city suffered a decline when the rise of the Sasanian empire made free passage difficult, but eight churches are now known from late antique Palmyra, one of them a very large basilica of the sixth century and at least one a church built in the Umayyad period.[14] To take a further example from the north of the area, Sergiopolis (Resafa), the main Ghassanid centre, north-east of Palmyra, was not only a major religious site, the focus of pilgrimage to the shrine of St Sergius, but was also located on a major caravan route which made it an important site of fairs and markets as well as religious gatherings. Finally, it has long been supposed that it was trade that gave Mecca its importance in the lifetime of Muhammad; this has been vigorously questioned, but reasserted in recent scholarship based on archaeological evidence (albeit limited).[15] But as far as the eastern provinces are concerned, the caravan trade was only one contributor to regional prosperity in the sixth century when set against the broader picture revealed by amphorae and local archaeological evidence.

Constantinople in the sixth century was keen to build a wide sphere of influence among the kingdoms on the eastern fringes of the empire, and trade was certainly a factor in this.[16] In the early sixth century Yusuf, who had made himself king of Himyar (south Yemen), adopted an aggressive Judaism in a context of competition between Jews and Christians and of complex relationships with Byzantium and Axum, and took the opportunity to persecute Christians, including Byzantine merchants; expeditions were launched to remove him from Ethiopia (Axum), whose interests coincided with those of Constantinople. Byzantium was eager to maintain access to the southern trade route to the Far East, and concern for trade with Ethiopia and Arabia thus played a major role in Byzantine diplomatic relations with Axum and south Yemen in the early sixth century.[17] It is not surprising, then, that the controlled passage of merchandise was a major feature of the important treaty between Rome and Persia of 561; the third clause reads,

> Roman and Persian merchants of all kinds of goods, as well as similar tradesmen, shall conduct their business according to the established practice through the specified customs posts.
>
> (Menander, fr. 6, Blockley, *Menander the Guardsman*)

Silk was a particularly desirable commodity, and had been available to Byzantium only through Persia. According to Procopius, the (unsuccessful) Byzantine embassy to the Ethiopians in 531 offered them control of this trade as an inducement. However, according to a probably fanciful story also told by Procopius, Justinian later acquired some silk-worm eggs from Serinda, around modern Bokhara and Samarkand, allegedly in 552, with a group of monks as intermediaries.[18] Silk was become one of the most prestigious materials in elite Byzantine and medieval culture thereafter, and this story itself is indicative of the complex amalgam of military, diplomatic, religious and trading interests that went to make up Byzantine–Persian relations in the sixth century.

## Arabs in the Near East before Islam

The Arab federates were not merely military allies of the great powers (Chapter 9); they also acted as local patrons and influenced both religious and economic life. At Resafa again, a meeting point for semi-nomadic Arab pastoralists, a building traditionally identified as a *praetorium*, though decorated 'within the standard repertoire of fifth- and sixth-century church decoration', bears an inscription commemorating al-Mundhir, phylarch 570–81, with a standard Greek acclamation familiar from many inscriptions and graffiti: 'the fortune of al-Mundhir is victorious', or 'Long live al-Mundhir!'[19]

This al-Mundhir usefully held off attacks from the Arab allies of the Persians until he fell in 581 to long-standing imperial suspicion; it is interesting to find that an earlier stand-off between him and the emperor in Constantinople had been settled in 575 by an exchange of oaths at the tomb of St Sergius.[20] A complex balance existed in these regions between pastoral Arabs and monastic communities. We have already seen that there is a reference to a 'church' of al-Mundhir in the letter signed by 137 heads of anti-Chalcedonian monasteries. Such Arab influence could also make itself felt very directly, as when in the fifth century another Arab leader called, in Greek, Amorkesos (formerly subject to the Persians), had gained control of the island of Jotabe, possibly in the Gulf of Aqaba:

*Figure 8.1* The so-called 'praetorium' at Resafa

[He] left Persia and travelled to that part of Arabia adjacent to Persia. Setting out from here he made forays and attacks not upon any Romans, but upon the Saracens whom he encountered. He seized one of the islands belonging to the Romans, which was named Jotabe and, ejecting the Roman tax collectors, held the island himself and amassed considerable wealth through collecting taxes. When he had seized other villages nearby, Amorkesos wished to become an ally of the Romans and phylarch of the Saracens under Roman rule on the borders of Arabia Petraea.

(Malchus, fr. 1, Blockley)

The enterprising Amorkesos now sent Peter, 'the bishop of his tribe', to put his case to the Emperor Leo, who was not only persuaded, but invited Amorkesos to Constantinople, entertained him to dinner, presented him to the senate and gave him the title of *patricius*, much to the disapproval of the historian Malchus who tells the story. When Amorkesos left, the Emperor Leo gave him gifts and public money from the treasury, and he in return presented the emperor with 'a very valuable icon of gold set with precious stones'. The story shows very well the role played by Christianization in Byzantine diplomacy, as well as the techniques used to control border territories and manage local groups. At the end of the fifth century, however, Jotabe was recaptured by the governor of Palestine.[21] Also in the fifth century a certain Aspebetos, a pagan and a Persian subject, converted to Christianity after his son was healed by the monk Euthymius, and made Euthymius' monastery the centre of an ecclesiastical complex and tented settlement for Christian Arabs. Euthymius then requested and obtained the appointment of a bishop from the patriarch of Jerusalem, and with the patriarch's consent, Aspebetos was ordained bishop to care for these 'encampments'.[22] 'Saracens' also appear in Cyril of Scythopolis's *Life of St Sabas* both as the grateful recipients of Sabas's charity and as potential raiders on Christian monks; in the latter story, set in the wild area to the west of the Dead Sea, the prayers of the monks were answered when a chasm opened up in the earth and swallowed up the 'wicked barbarians'.[23]

The extent to which there was as yet an Arab self-definition is controversial. The epigraphic evidence is sparse, but an earlier and famous inscription from Nemara in southern Syria, dated to 328, and written in Arabic but in the Nabataean Aramaic script, is one of a small number of examples where Arabic is used. A certain Imru' al Qays describes himself in it as 'king of all the Arabs' (the reading is certain, if not the interpretation: the term could be geographical rather than ethnic). The term 'king' is also found in relation to the Lakhmids and Tanukh and the term 'Arab' was used by the Romans; for instance, in Justinian's *Novel* 102, which refers to the province of Arabia as 'the region of the Arabs'. There are a few examples from the sixth century of inscriptions in Arabic script, and the linguistic situation was clearly changing, a development in which the Ghassanids may have played a role. Drawing on this evidence and on the role of the Ghassanids in later Arab historical memory, Robert Hoyland has proposed an emergence of Arab identity in the pre-Islamic period on the lines of the ethnogenesis theory applied in the case of such groupings in the west (Chapter 2).[24] The Arabic sources also preserve a memory of heroic pre-Islamic poetry and aristocratic lifestyles. Arabic was becoming more widespread by the late sixth century, as seems to be indicated in the extraordinary cache of sixth-century papyri found in a room of the Petra Church at Petra in southern Jordan in 1993 (the very year when the first edition of this book was published), which consists of local documents written in Greek, as the accepted language of formal dealings, but evidently by people used to using a form of pre-Islamic Arabic.[25] This discovery, which includes a large number of texts dating from at least 513–592, has transformed not only the history of Petra as known hitherto, but also that of landholding practice and economic activity in the region, and of language use in the sixth century. Most are private documents, and record land transactions or wills, with donations to local churches or monasteries, made by all kinds of local people, many of whom bear civilian or military honorific titles, and who have Nabataean or more commonly Greek names, or both: one document records the marriage settlement of Theodoros, the son of Obadianos. The better-off among them own more than 50 hectares of land and lease some out to be worked by others, producing wheat, grapes and fruits. They used Arabic to name parts of their property, and in some cases the names are very close to those in use in the area today. These sensational papyri from Petra stand alongside the papyri from Nessana in the Negev discovered in the 1930s; however, the latter also contain literary material, including a Latin/Greek glossary of Virgil's *Aeneid*, and cover a later period, testifying to the continuance of a form of classical literary culture even into the Islamic period.[26]

## Local cultures, language and Hellenism

Thanks to the scholarship of the last two decades, the social, cultural and linguistic history of the Near East in late antiquity, not to mention its religions, can now be seen as immensely fluid. The language situation alone is described by Fergus Millar as an 'interplay of Greek with Semitic languages, whether Hebrew or various branches of Aramaic (Nabataean, Palmyrene, Jewish Aramaic, Syriac, Samaritan Aramaic, Christian Palestinian Aramaic (CPA)), with Egyptian (hieroglyphic, demotic or Coptic), with the languages and scripts of pre-Islamic Arabia, and finally with Arabic.' In the same volume Robert Hoyland tentatively includes this phenomenon within 'an efflorescence of a whole range of languages and scripts across the Roman Empire'.[27] Millar has insisted forcefully on the dominance of Greek as the accepted public and formal language of the eastern Roman empire (despite the continued use of Latin in certain contexts),[28] but in the Near East this was also a period of language formation, both oral and written, in which there was a wide range of language use and experience, from resort to paid translations up to (though probably not often) actual bilingualism.[29] But language and identity did not necessarily go together, let alone imply ethnicity, and indeed it is hard enough to clarify the development and inter-relation of the various languages and scripts known from the area, especially as our evidence is so unevenly spread. Syriac, the form of Aramaic from the region round Edessa, was unusual in that it became an important literary language during late antiquity, being used for many works of Christian theology and other kinds of Christian writing. An increasing influence of Greek can be seen in the Syriac writings of the sixth and seventh centuries, and there were many translations from one language into the other, especially of saints' lives and apocryphal works; many works circulated in several versions – Greek, Syriac, and sometimes Armenian, Georgian or, later, Arabic. However, few writers deployed both languages equally well themselves (they included bishop Rabbula of Edessa and his successor Ibas, both in the fifth century). Whether the use of Greek implies any kind of conscious Hellenism is hard to say. Funerary inscriptions from the Golan and from modern Jordan, for example, indicate that Greek was still in widespread use by individuals up to the seventh century, and many churches, including the fine churches at Jerash (Gerasa) in the so-called Decapolis, whose other cities included Philadelphia (modern Amman), were decorated with mosaic inscriptions in Greek verse as late as the middle of the eighth century and after. A mosaic with inscription in Greek from Umm er-Rasas (Kastron Mefaa), east of the Dead Sea and some 56 km south of Amman, dates from 718, though it has also been dated much later, and further construction, again with an inscription in Greek, in the same church is dated as late as 756. A range of the most important cities of the region are all named and depicted in mosaic, and from the sixth century we also have a mosaic map of Jerusalem itself in the church of St George at Madaba. Sophronius of Damascus, the future bishop of Jerusalem (d. 638), was able to compose poems in learned Greek verse to express his grief at the Persian conquest of Jerusalem in 614,[30] and the Nessana papyri show that a mastery of Greek was still thought desirable in much more remote places. Greek also continued to be the language of the Chalcedonian church in Jerusalem, and this continued in the Melkite church in the Islamic period. Similar questions surround the continued use of classical architectural forms and especially of classical iconographical themes, which continued to be used even in sixth-century and later church contexts in Jordan.[31]

These questions of language history have recently been studied, particularly in relation to documentary and epigraphic evidence as indicating history 'on the ground'. Similar issues arise in the increased use of Coptic in Egypt and its relation to Greek, and can be seen clearly in the very large numbers of Egyptian papyri.[32] In Syria, one important type of such evidence is provided by the signatures in records of church councils or other ecclesiastical documents such as the so-called *Letter of the Archimandrites* of 569 (above, Chapter 7). But fluidity or interplay is also evident in intellectual and religious spheres. Greek philosophy had been read at Edessa long before the fourth century, and Greek learning also penetrated to the famous schools at Nisibis and Seleucia-Ctesiphon and, later, Gundeshapur. In the late fourth century the Syriac Christian religious poet Ephraem moved from Nisibis to Edessa when the former was ceded to the Persians in 363. His highly metaphorical and imaginative poetry may strike a classical reader as very unfamiliar, and he expressed a lively contempt for everything Greek, i.e., pagan; but his work was quickly translated into Greek, and a large body of other material also exists in Greek under his name, which was later much cited in the Greek monastic literature. On the other hand, the culture of an important bishop such as Theodoret, bishop of Cyrrhus in northern Syria in the fifth century, was Greek; he wrote in Greek and owed his culture to the traditions of Greek rhetorical education, writing letters to officials and churchmen in rhetorical Greek and many other Greek works, including a refutation of heresies, even though many of his flock knew only Syriac; how much Syriac Theodoret knew himself is less certain, but his *Life* of Symeon the Elder was one of three such works: two in Greek and one in Syriac (Chapter 3). The culture of the Syrian city of Antioch, the second city in the eastern empire, was also essentially Greek; it was the earliest home of Christianity outside Judaea and the centre of one of the two major Greek schools of theology and biblical interpretation. At Jerusalem the bishop always preached in Greek, but an oral translation into Aramaic was provided during the liturgy when the pilgrim Egeria went there in 384. Even at Edessa, the very home of the great Syriac literary tradition in late antiquity, Greek was in use till late in the Islamic period.

To say that Greek was the dominant language, necessary for official transactions, is true, but can be misleading in that it may obscure the very widespread use of Greek even in non-official contexts. It is even more misleading to use acquaintance with Greek as a badge of identity.[33] The language of Jews in Palestine, for example, was Greek, and funerary inscriptions from the Golan and from modern Jordan, for example, indicate that Greek was still in widespread use by individuals up to the seventh century. Many churches, including the fine churches at Jerash (Gerasa) in the Decapolis, whose other cities included Philadelphia (modern Amman), were decorated with fine mosaic inscriptions in Greek verse as late as the middle of the eighth century and after. The administration and institutions of the empire placed an overlay of Greek on local conditions, but this had already been the case for centuries, since the foundations of Alexander the Great and the Seleucid empire that succeeded him. It is true that the literature in Syriac originated in a region considerably removed, and in certain ways very different, from the Hellenized coastal cities such as Caesarea, or indeed from much of Palestine, but distinctions between Greek and Semitic, whether applied to language or iconography, along ethnic or class lines can be very deceptive. An Arab dynasty ruled Edessa itself, and its affiliations can be clearly seen in the city's reliefs and mosaics. Yet the same city produced a third-century mosaic of Orpheus as well as a Syriac inscription. At Palmyra, with a bilingual culture in Greek and Palmyrene, the temple of Bel proclaims its Semitic roots, though like the cella of the temple of Ba'al Shamin, it was converted into a church.

The culture of the Near East in late antiquity was a mosaic which can only be interpreted by reference to local differentiation. In north-eastern Arabia, Aramaic appears from the second century BC onwards, and 'Nestorian' Christianity was well established there in late antiquity, with Syriac as its liturgical language;[34] there were also many Nestorians in south-eastern Arabia (Oman) when the area was under Sasanian rule before the Arab conquests.[35] Again, while Syriac was the main written language of the Persian Nestorian church (the Church of the East, for which see Chapter 9), Arabic was the spoken vernacular of the Christians in Arabia. The difficulty remains of matching modern notions of 'Arab', 'Syrian', 'Semitic' and other such terms, which are still entangled in a mesh of confusion and even prejudice, with the actual situation in our period. But what seems to be observable in late antiquity is a heightened awareness of and readiness to proclaim local traditions, with a consequent increase in their visibility.

In this context the application of the concept of Hellenism is much more difficult. Greek continued to be used as a literary language, and there is a huge volume of theological, hagiographical and other writing from the sixth and seventh centuries. The controversial bishop Severus of Antioch wrote in Greek, though his works survive in Syriac; Gaza was the centre both of monasticism and of a highly sophisticated Greek literary culture in the early sixth century,[36] while Procopius the historian came from Caesarea in Palestine. The monastic author Cyril of Scythopolis composed biographies of Palestinian monks, and

*Figure 8.2* The city of Scythopolis (Bet Shean), birthplace of the sixth-century monk and hagiographer Cyril of Scythopolis and other learned theologians. Scythopolis remained a flourishing city throughout the seventh century and into the eighth.

the later writers John Moschus, Sophronius, Maximus Confessor and Anastasius of Sinai, all writing in Greek, were monks in the region.

This Greek intellectual culture continued after the transition to Islamic rule, with the production of chronicles, saints' lives, apologetic works and many more; John of Damascus himself wrote in this tradition in the eighth century and the same period saw the creation of a great tradition of Greek hymnography. Much of this output presupposes the availability of a high level of traditional education, even if some of these writers also at times exploited the old but useful trope of the opposition of classical, i.e. pagan, culture to Christianity. Given such a context, including of course the role of Greek as the language of official and legal dealings, it is not surprising that it should have continued to be the language of government and bureaucracy under the

*Figure 8.3* The large refectory of the monastery of Martyrius in the Judaean desert near Jerusalem. The monastery was built in the late fifth century but the refectory dates from a century later. The modern building belongs to the settlement of Ma'ale Adumim.

Umayyads. The shift away from Greek that only becomes apparent in monasteries in the early ninth century reflects the move to Arabic that accompanied the change from Umayyad to Abbasid rule.

In art and iconography, we have seen that classicizing motifs and styles were freely used and if necessary adapted, often in very striking ways.[37] But whether contemporaries themselves had any concept of Hellenism is another matter entirely.

## Jews and Judaism

A substantial Jewish presence and corresponding Jewish influence are features of this area in Palestine itself and also more widely. In southern Arabia a substantial body of epigraphic material has shown that between 470 and 493 the kingdom of Himyar adopted a strongly monotheistic religious stance; Jews are attested in the fourth century and Jewish inscriptions begin in the fifth, with Christians also making an appearance. The kingdom came under direct Christian influence when after the episode at Najran it was subject to Axum, but it had already had a bishop in the reign of Anastasius[38] the presence and influence of both Jews and Christians in Arabia at the time of Muhammad provides an important context for the emergence of Islam (Chapter 9). The Babylonian Talmud emerged over a period of centuries within the Sasanian empire, and eventually overshadowed its Palestinian counterpart, and the Jewish diaspora is attested all over the eastern empire in synagogues and inscriptions. In Palestine itself a considerable Jewish population existed in the sixth century and on the eve of Islam, centred on Galilee and the Golan and with Tiberias as its main intellectual and religious centre. Some synagogues went out of use by the mid-sixth century, but many others continued to function until the early seventh century. We have already seen the astonishing richness of synagogue mosaics, which are still being revealed and interpreted, and this indicates a confident Jewish life in the context of the increasing preponderance of Christians. Nevertheless imperial legislation was becoming more intolerant by the sixth century. It has been suggested that the growing influence of imperial Christianity acted as a stimulus to others to crystallize their own religious identity. In the words of Seth Schwartz, 'Jewish life was transformed by Christian rule'; he goes on, 'the Jewish culture that emerged in late antiquity was radically distinctive and distinctively late antique – a product of the same political, social and economic forces that produced the same no less distinctive Christian culture of late antiquity'.[39] The development began with the imperial support for Christianity adopted by Constantine, which entailed a new attitude to contemporary Jews, as inheritors with Christians of the religious past of both religions, albeit having taken the wrong track. Constantine's successors were at the same time protective and restrictive in their approach, but gradually became more and more controlling. The Jewish patriarchate had been first limited in 415 and then abolished, and Justinian's legislation on the subject of Jews is distinctly negative. His *Novel* 146 (issued in

AD 553) prescribed the languages that should be used for synagogue readings, preferring the Septuagint translation for Greek, though commending that of Aquila on the grounds that it was the work of a gentile; the law makes clear that Judaism is in error and needs 'correction'. The broader context here is that of a return to the use of Hebrew among Jews in the sixth century, both in the diaspora and in Palestine, as well as an actual variety of Jewish language practice across the empire.[40] As the Christian empire became more repressive, Jews were classed alongside heretics and pagans in legislation, and even more forcefully in a mass of Christian writing. This trend led eventually to an enactment by Heraclius in the seventh century requiring all Jews to be baptised; this was repeated by Leo III in the eighth and Basil I in the ninth century, though it was a product of heightened animosity and resentment at the time and could hardly have been enforced (Chapter 9).

The Samaritans, with their centre on Mt Gerizim, where the Emperor Zeno built a church of the Theotokos on the site of their sacred precinct, were also subject to imperial repression, and rose up repeatedly in the fifth and sixth centuries; the uprisings were harshly put down, and Procopius claims that Justinian 'converted the Samaritans for the most part to a more pious way of life and has made them Christians'.[41] Jews had been the subject of hostility, and Judaism the target of stylized refutation in Christian apologetic writing, since as early as the second century, and were often depicted as malevolent and dangerous in saints' lives and other kinds of Christian writing. This tendency intensified as time went on, and reached a peak in the period of the Persian and Arab invasions, when Christian writers blamed the Jews of Palestine for helping the invaders and participating in the killing of Christians.[42]

Yet this increasing Christian pressure coincided with an efflorescence of Jewish life and, it would seem, of Jewish self-confidence, especially in Palestine. Jews appropriated many aspects of imperial Christianity and made it their own. Fifth-century Palestine was transformed by the building not only of large numbers of churches but also of synagogues, their decoration showing close parallels with Christian art (Chapter 7). Those who built them and worshipped in them ignored imperial prohibitions on building synagogues and clearly did not expect to suffer as a result.[43] Nor did they seem to have qualms about representational art, though this was to change. The flourishing Jewish life of Palestine was part of what Glen Bowersock calls the 'kind of miracle' of the late antique Near East, the Sepphoris synagogue a 'polyglot marvel, with inscriptions in Aramaic, Hebrew and Greek'[44] – though it was indeed a linguistic variety shared in many quite different and non-Jewish contexts. As we saw, late antiquity was also the period when the Palestinian and Babylonian Talmuds reached their final stages. However, the influence of the rabbis on everyday Jewish life, assumed in past scholarship, now seems much less evident (the parallelism with revisionist views of the actual impact of late Roman imperial legislation is obvious); Jews wanted to be distinctive, but they were also willing to adopt cultural expressions from wider society.[45] This did not protect them from occasional outbreaks of active Christian hostility, as had happened in the context of the arrival of relics of St Stephen on the island of Minorca in 417,[46] and many Christian bishops made it their business to stir up Christian suspicion. The attitudes of Christians towards Jews in Palestine also hardened, especially under the pressures of the seventh-century invasions, although much of this was expressed at a literary level. A corresponding process of increased Judaization has been seen by Seth Schwartz in synagogue art and in the emergence of the Hebrew poetic form of *piyyutim*, with its close relation to the rabbinic corpus;[47] this can be seen in turn as part of a resilience which meant that the Jewish presence survived the transition to Islamic rule, with Tiberias continuing to be a centre of Jewish learning and religious life under early Islam.[48] If true, this may also have been a contributing factor to the intense anti-Jewish rhetoric found in seventh-century and later Christian sources on the Persian and Arab invasions.

While the diffusion of synagogues in fifth- and sixth-century Palestine is indicative of a thriving village network, the same period saw extensive church building. How far Jews and Christians at this period tended to live in separate communities is a matter of controversy,[49] but village synagogues, like village churches, indicate the presence and willingness of donors to contribute on a large scale; as with donor inscriptions in churches, the economics of their construction were recorded, as at Bet Alfa and synagogues had treasuries. But the region was also the home of ascetics, some very famous and much-visited.

## The appeal of ascetics

In the late fourth and fifth centuries prominent westerners including Jerome and his friend Paula, who settled at Bethlehem, and the Younger Melania and her husband Pinianus travelled to the Holy Land and Melania founded a monastery on the Mount of Olives monasteries; the Empress Eudocia, wife of Theodosius II, travelled there with Melania in 438 and lived there for some years after 443. We have already encountered the stylite Symeon the Elder (d. 459) with his pillar at Qalaat Semaan in Syria (Chapter 3), and more than a century later, Symeon the Younger (d. 594), whose pillar was located outside Antioch on the so-called 'Wondrous Mountain', began his ascetic life by attaching himself to the community that had grown up around another stylite. According to his *Life* he was well informed about events in Antioch, knew of the death of the Lakhmid al-Mundhir in 553 and predicted the succession of Justin II in 565. Famous holy men like these were well connected and enjoyed elite patronage. They were very different from some of the ascetics who were the subjects of Theodoret's *Historia Religiosa* in the fifth century, some of whom practised exotic forms of personal abnegation such as living in cowsheds and eating grass.[50] Monasticism depended on ascetics; as we have seen, Cyril of Scythopolis in the sixth century also wrote of Euthymius and Sabas, monastic founders who were themselves ascetics, and the Judaean 'desert' was full of monasteries large and small, as well as hermitages and caves inhabited by individual holy men. The region was also the location for more fanciful stories about female ascetics who were repentant prostitutes and who disguised themselves as men in the ascetic life; particularly well-known examples are Pelagia, according to the story a courtesan from Antioch in the late fourth century, and Mary of Egypt, whose story is known in Latin in the sixth century, and who was said to have came originally from Alexandria to visit the Holy Sepulchre in Jerusalem and subsequently lived for many years in male disguise on the banks of the Jordan. Many versions of the story are known, including a Greek version attributed to Sophronius.[51] These are monastic stories, and John Moschus, who travelled with Sophronius and died in Rome in 619, was another Palestinian monastic writer in the late sixth century who collected anecdotes about such ascetics in Egypt, Palestine and Sinai in his *Spiritual Meadow*. Egypt, Palestine and Syria were thickly populated not only with monasteries but also with individual ascetics who spent long periods travelling or living in remote and difficult places; however, despite the ideology of isolation they were not totally cut off, and a delicate balance was preserved between the solitary life and interaction with others.

A sixth-century text which gives a vivid impression of monastic life in the area around Amida is John of Ephesus's *Lives of the Eastern Saints*, already referred to in Chapter 7, and indeed the ascetic ecosystem of the Near East in late antiquity is very well documented. It continued beyond the Arab conquests, and extended into Mesopotamia and regions further east in what is now Iraq. It also transcended language barriers; works were translated from and into a variety of languages – Greek, Syriac, Georgian, Latin, Arabic – which must be a sign of their extreme popularity, and of the vigour of the ascetic ideal, whether in living or historical examples or in stories. It was an ideal that found expression in the building and occupation of many monasteries, and which exercised a powerful effect on the minds and imagination of contemporaries. Over and above their personal ascetic struggle, these holy men and women played many roles in relation to their milieu. Some were local mediators in village society, according to the influential model set out by Peter Brown forty years ago,[52] others did live lives of near-total isolation, but others again were prominent leaders in their communities and beyond, or famous stars of the late antique world; we see the aged St Sabas in action in 518 when the decree came from Justin I to reinstate adherence to the Council of Chalcedon after the death of Anastasius, travelling to cities in the region, and later even to the court of Justinian, pleading the case of the church of Palestine after the damage done by the Samaritan revolt.[53] Justinian responded with tax remission, gold, restoration of burnt buildings, erection of a hospital and a new church of the Theotokos in Jerusalem (known as the Nea and shown on the mosaic map of Jerusalem at Madaba), and a portion of the tax revenues of the province for the buildings of fortifications to protect Sabas' monasteries. Eliciting patronage, including imperial patronage, and predicting the future, were just some of the essential gifts in the repertoire of such a holy man.

## Church councils and religious divisions

Monasteries and asceticism also crossed religious boundaries. The mainte-nance of Chalcedonian orthodoxy is a main theme in Cyril's *Lives*. Euthymius is credited with bringing the independent Empress Eudocia back to ortho-doxy, and had earlier instructed the bishop of the Saracens who attended the Council of Ephesus to follow Cyril of Alexandria and Acacius of Melitene in everything.[54] It was part of the agenda of hagiography to insist on the right doctrine of its subject, and Cyril provides a list of the heresies opposed by Euthymius; Euthymius supported the Council of Chalcedon (451), and Pal-estinian monasteries remained centres of Chalcedonianism (and, after the Council of 553, 'Neo-Chalcedonianism'), but Cyril's narrative reveals both the extent of anti-Chalcedonianism and the risk from his point of view that this opposition might prevail in the province.[55]

The struggle on the ground between pro- and anti-Chalcedonians occupied monks and bishops in the east throughout the late fifth and sixth centuries and later; the eastern provinces on the eve of Islam are often represented as if they were uniformly anti-Chalcedonian, but Sophronius and Maximus Confessor were only the most prominent among the defenders of Chalcedonian ortho-doxy in the seventh century in the very years of the Arab conquests (Chapter 9). The struggle involved local loyalties as well as relations with the imperial church. Bishops were required by the major councils to remove the names of those condemned as non-orthodox from the liturgical diptychs, as happened after the council of 553, but they also took independent action, and one of the central fields of dispute (and of confusion for ordinary people) was that of the sharing or denial of communion.[56] Monasteries and bishoprics and their people were also split, or, as we have seen, changed their positions, but the key moment came with the ordinations of bishops for the anti-Chalcedonians, and then by them of further anti-Chalcedonian bishops. Some were conse-crated in Constantinople and sent to Egypt, while others were given dioceses in other parts of the East but had to adopt an itinerant mode in the prevailing climate.[57] The sympathetic Empress Theodora and the Ghassanid phylarch al-Harith are credited with having fostered this initiative. A new hierarchy was thus initiated and was to last through periods of repression and even persecu-tion by the Chalcedonian government later in the sixth century. However, nei-ther Syria nor Palestine were by any means wholly anti-Chalcedonian, and in some cities, including Antioch and Edessa, and indeed Alexandria, there were competing groups and rival bishops; naturally personal rivalries and local fol-lowings were also involved. Justinian and his successors in Constantinople went on attempting to square the circle, and Heraclius was still trying to do the same in the seventh century with a new initiative – Monotheletism. This was, however, bitterly opposed by Chalcedonians in Palestine and led to the imperial condemnation and eventual deaths of Pope Martin I and Maximus Confessor (Chapter 9). But there were also divisions among the anti-Chalce-donians, and these often expressed themselves most bitterly within a single city or even a single monastery.[58] Anti-Chalcedonianism certainly had local manifestations and allegiances, but it cannot be maintained that it was a popular, ethnic or 'national' movement, and anti-Chalcedonian sentiment by no means coincided with Syriac Christianity. Throughout the reigns of Justin and Justinian the centres of the resistance were in Alexandria and Constantinople as much as, or even more than, they were in the Syrian countryside. It is not very surprising, however, if local interests started to turn the situation to their own advantage and claim the movement as their own, and one can see a powerful move in this direction in the energetic and extensive writing of men such as John of Tella.[59] Christianity was also well established within the Sasanian empire. The 'Nestorian' or dyophysite tradition identified with the School of Nisibis was strong, but by the sixth century it was not universal, as is demonstrated by the activities of Ahudemmeh,[60] and the treatment of Christians in Persia figured from time to time in Roman–Persian diplomacy in the late sixth century as it had since the time of Constantine.[61] Christians in the Persian empire also included Miaphysites, especially in western Mesopotamia,[62] and Christian discussion crossed political boundaries and spanned the territory of both empires. Public debates took place in Constantinople and Ctesiphon, under the patronage of both Justinian and Chosroes I, and also involved Manichaeans and Zoroastrians. East Syrian representatives were summoned to Constantinople in the early days of Justinian, and Chosroes held debates at his own court. Common themes were also debated in both places, such as the question of the eternity of the world, disputed by Christians, and debated also in sixth-century Alexandria, with Aristotelian logic as a shared technique.[63]

An enormous amount of documentation accompanied the councils and other meetings that attempted to settle the main christological and other divisions between Christians, and ranges from letters to individuals and dioceses to the formal acts of ecumenical councils. These documents are an invaluable source of information about the languages in use and the geographical spread of allegiances. A series of powerful articles by Fergus Millar has underlined the possibilities for the historian of this period in using this material.[64] It was a requirement of formal church councils that those present should indicate their assent to the decisions taken by signing a final agreed statement, and sanctions normally followed for those few who refused. The signatures are an invaluable source in themselves and are very revealing about language, the geographical range of bishoprics represented and (with caution) identity, and it is only relatively recently that they are being fully exploited by historians of late antiquity.

The meetings with anti-Chalcedonian easterners held in Constantinople in 532 (the so-called 'Conversations with the Syrian Orthodox')[65] were followed by Justinian's own initiative in the 540s to condemn the 'Three Chapters'; the fifth ecumenical council in 553 was called in order to try to deal with the resulting outcry (Chapter 5). Justinian's successor Justin II and his wife Sophia attempted again to bridge the divide between pro- and anti-Chalcedonians, with an unsuccessful meeting at Callinicum, but persecution followed, as it did again in 598–99. This was fruitless and any effects were temporary. Heraclius held meetings at Dvin to try to win round the Armenians even as he was struggling to meet the assault of Chosroes II's armies, and his Monothelete initiative in the 630s – yet another imperial attempt to win over the east – was met by hectic synodal activity in Palestine and Cyprus in which Sophronius was a major participant. The meeting known as the Lateran Synod held in Rome in 649, with prominent roles played by Maximus the Confessor and his supporters, was yet another powerful indicator of the extent of opposition to imperial policy. Its Acts, composed in Greek and only later translated into Latin, and written with heavy input from Maximus's own writings, are an indication of the level of tendentiousness as well as the sheer energy that was involved (Chapter 9). Yet the various meetings and synods mentioned here are for the most part only the more public and official; there were also countless local meetings, all with their own extensive records, preparatory materials and what we would now see as pubic relations. It is not surprising to find that in the major councils of the late seventh and eighth centuries the authenticity of evidence and materials cited in the discussions was such a serious concern that measures had to be put in place to try to verify them; nor is it surprising that in many cases they have come down to us in redacted versions which sometimes pose difficult problems of interpretation.[66]

## The eastern frontier

The study of the material remains of military installations in the east is an important factor in any consideration of the defence of the eastern provinces.[67] It is also closely connected with the development of a revised conception of frontiers as zones of influence and 'borderlands' (Chapter 2),[68] and with a better understanding of the relations between 'nomadic' and settled groups and of the use of local client forces. Nor does a frontier necessarily have to be linear: much of the very extensive building of fortifications under Anastasius and Justinian entailed building or strengthening garrison forts and fortifying cities well inside the conventional 'frontier'.

The build-up of Roman forces in the east had begun with Trajan's Parthian war of 106, which marked 'the beginning of an obsession which was to take a whole series of Roman emperors on campaign into Mesopotamia, and sometimes down as far as Seleucia and Ctesiphon on the Tigris'.[69] Under Septimius Severus in the early third century, two extra legions were created for service in the east, and five cities in the new province of Mesopotamia – Edessa, Carrhae, Resaina, Nisibis and Singara – were given the status of Roman colonies; eight legions were now stationed in the zone which stretched south from here to Arabia. Rome was soon faced with the strong military regime created by the Sasanians on its eastern borders and highly damaging incursions took place in the fourth century under Shapur I; Rome was obliged to make an expensive peace in 363 after the ill-fated Persian expedition of the Emperor

Julian, and ceded to Persia the important border city of Nisibis.[70] However, recent scholars have pointed out that for most of the period neither of the two empires seriously thought of trying to defeat the other or occupy territory on a large scale, and have argued that the Roman defence system was in fact much concerned with prestige, internal security and the policing of the border areas. Benjamin Isaac is not the only scholar to have argued that the military roads which are so conspicuous in this area, especially the strata Diocletiana, a road from north-east Arabia and Damascus to Palmyra and the Euphrates, and the earlier via nova Traiana, from Bostra to the Red Sea, were meant not as lines of defence, but rather as lines of communication. However, the need for an intensification of defences became acute when in the early sixth century the Persian shah Cavadh launched a major attack, with a damaging siege and capture of Amida in Mesopotamia in 502, vividly described in the Syriac chronicle attributed to a certain Joshua the Stylite.[71] People in the area who had managed to escape the Persian assault were tempted to flee, but the Syriac author Jacob of Serug wrote to all the cities nearby urging them to stay.[72] The same chronicle gives a striking picture, corroborated by Procopius' accounts of the Persian wars under Justinian, of the leadership bishops in eastern cities now provided in matters of defence, building fortifications, pleading the cause of their city with the emperor and negotiating with the Persians. They were not always successful: Megas, bishop of Beroea (Aleppo), had the unenviable task of trying to negotiate with Chosroes I when the latter was threatening Antioch in 540 and the Byzantine troops were wholly insufficient to defend it. Chosroes took 2,000 lbs of silver from Hierapolis and demanded ten *centenaria* to call off an attack on Antioch, but attacked Beroea (Aleppo) and sacked it in any case, and went on to sack Antioch. Orders had come from Constantinople not to hand over any money, and the city's patriarch, Ephraem, was thought to have favoured surrender.[73] Defence needs also went hand in hand with pleas for reduction of taxation. In 505–6 the generals Areobindus and Celer reported to the Emperor Anastasius that the border near Amida and Tella was in need of strengthening in order to fend off Persian attacks; as a result, orders were given to fortify the frontier site of Dara, a project in which the bishop of Amida was much involved, as is known from the anonymous continuation of the Syriac ecclesiastical history by bishop Zachariah of Mytilene; Procopius later contrived to give the credit for the massive fortifications of Dara to Justinian.[74] After the Persian assault on Amida the remaining population suffered badly from shortage of food, and the bishop went to Constantinople to plead with Anastasius for remission of taxes.[75] During the Persian wars of Justinian, and especially in the difficult years in the early 540s when Belisarius clearly did not have enough troops, bishops were even more active in their attempts to buy off the danger of a Persian siege, usually with large payments of silver (Chapter 5).

In the Sasanians, the Byzantines faced a rival power which was their equal in military capacity and at times capable of ruthless and aggressive campaigns against Roman territory. We have seen already the helplessness of the eastern cities when faced with the armies of Chosroes I, as well as the financial cost of peace to the Byzantine empire (Chapter 5). Very large payments were made by Byzantium to Persia over the course of the sixth century, and there are indications that Justinian found it difficult to maintain sufficient troops on the eastern frontier; the annual payment of 500 lbs of gold agreed in the great peace treaty of 561 was a considerable burden on Byzantium, and the treaty did not prevent war from breaking out again between the two sides.[76] Chosroes II (590–628) suffered a coup at home and owed his throne to the Emperor Maurice; he renewed the promise of freedom of religion to Christians within his kingdom who had been included in the peace of 561, and showed his attachment to the Christian shrine of St Sergius at Resafa with gifts when the saint answered his prayer that his Christian wife Shirin should conceive. Theophylact Simocatta records the long letter in Greek which the king sent to Sergius; Theophylact also tells how the king prayed before an image of the Theotokos carried by a Byzantine ambassador.[77] Nevertheless he proved just as ruthless an enemy as Chosroes I had been. Years before, the ageing Cavadh had proposed to Justin I that the latter adopt his son Chosroes I and so guarantee the latter's succession; this overture was taken very seriously on the Byzantine side and was formally discussed at a high-level diplomatic meeting on the frontier, but no agreement was reached; according to Procopius, who tells the story, the young Chosroes was deeply offended and vowed to make the Romans pay for this slight.[78] In real terms relations between the two empires and their rulers involved a complex interplay of mutual interest, balance of powers and (at times) overt hostility. Conquest as such was out of the question on the Byzantine side, but the Persian invasions of the early seventh century departed from previous precedent. The Persians not only delivered near-fatal blows to many Roman cities in Asia Minor, and stimulated flight among the Christian populations, especially the monks and clergy, of Palestine and Egypt, but also actually occupied and ruled the Byzantine east – if only through proxies – for nearly two decades (Chapter 9).

The Roman empire attempted to control and influence vast areas of the east, over a great swathe reaching from the northern Caucasus around to Egypt and beyond. It could not do this by arms alone, and the interconnection of mission and defence in late Roman policy in the east is a constant theme. This can be seen very clearly in the empire's dealings with the Caucasus, where the conversion to Christianity of Tzath the king of the Lazi under Justin I marked a deliberate departure from Persian clientship, and was correspondingly greeted with considerable pomp in Constantinople, including baptism, marriage to a noble Byzantine bride and the formal acceptance of a crown, Byzantine ceremonial robes of silk and many other gifts;[79] not surprisingly this was taken very badly by Cavadh, and proved to be merely an episode in the complex struggle for control of Lazica by Rome and Persia. The Lazi chafed under Roman control and appealed again to Persia, which duly invaded in 541 and received the submission of Tzath's successor Gubazes;[80] however, they found the Persians no better, and Lazica found itself a theatre of war in the late 540s.[81] Religion could be a useful tool for either side, but Byzantium was also committed to conversion, admittedly also potentially advantageous in diplomatic dealings, and the twin objects of conversion and defence are a theme of Procopius's *Buildings*, in which the foundation of new churches went hand in hand, as conspicuously in the case of his account of North Africa, with military installations.

The differences between east and west are great, but the eastern provinces in the seventh century shared with the fifth-century west the experience of external threats and the dangers of internal fragmentation. Changes in urban and rural settlement, Christianization, the interpenetration of Greek with local cultures and the impact of the military and fiscal needs of the Byzantine state are all very evident well before the last great Persian invasion of the early seventh century and the arrival in Syria of the followers of Muhammad. The story of the origins and expansion of Islam itself fall outside the compass of this book. Yet when the Muslims left Arabia and encountered Roman troops in Palestine and Syria, they found the Roman Near East already in a ferment of change.

# 9

# A CHANGED WORLD

### Renewed war with Persia

The peace of 561 did not last. Despite the Emperor Maurice's help to the young Chosroes II, the renewed war between Byzantium and Persia in the final years of the sixth century and the Persian invasion and conquest of Byzantine territory that followed in the early seventh century were devastating blows to the future of the empire. In 626 the Persians and the Avars joined in a siege of Constantinople that put the empire in a desperate situation and was very nearly successful, the Emperor Heraclius having taken the drastic step of leaving the capital to gather troops and to campaign.[1] The situation was very dangerous, and even before the siege started there were angry protests in the city about the price and supply of bread. The city's eventual delivery was ascribed to the intervention of the Virgin Mary:

> [God] by the welcome intercession of his undefiled Mother, who is in truth our Lady Mother of God and ever-Virgin Mary, with his mighty hand saved this humble city of his from the utterly godless enemies who encircled it in concert.
>
> (*Chron. Pasch.*, p. 169, trans. Whitby and Whitby)

The Virgin had become more and more prominent in religious consciousness; she was depicted in apse decoration and panel paintings, and after the siege she was now described in the guise of a general leading the inhabitants of Constantinople to victory.[2]

Success against the Persians by Heraclius in 628 and his restoration of the True Cross to Jerusalem in 630 was followed closely by the Arab invasions and Heraclius' decision to retreat from the east.[3] Despite lurid accounts of destruction in the Greek and Syriac sources, recent archaeological research indicates that neither the Persian nor the Arab invasions in Palestine and Syria left much trace on the ground, at least outside Jerusalem and its environs,[4] though the effects of Persian campaigns on Asia Minor cities such as Sardis may be a different matter (below). But the eastern empire ruled from Constantinople was greatly diminished; it only began to recover in the second half of the eighth century as a result of energetic imperial effort, and then in a form that was much changed in administrative and financial terms. It makes sense in many instances to see late antiquity as extending well into the Umayyad period, but this mainly eastern continuity should not obscure the drastic reduction and refocusing of the eastern empire which was also taking place. The 'Arab conquests' of the seventh century did not happen as quickly as the term suggests (though the early advance into Syria was dramatic), or without struggles and setbacks, but by the early eighth century the Mediterranean world was a very different place. The powerful Sasanian kingdom had fallen, and a new and powerful regime controlled the former Roman provinces in the east, Egypt and North Africa and much of Anatolia. Attempts on Constantinople, culminating in a potentially disastrous siege in 717–18, were repulsed. The Arabs failed in their hope of conquering Byzantium, but the emperors in Constantinople ruled a drastically reduced territory, the Muslims were already in Spain and the Mediterranean had become a dangerous place.[5]

## Rome and Persia from Justinian to Heraclius

We are well informed about the new campaigns conducted against the Sasanians by Justin II (565–78), Tiberius (578–82) and Maurice (582–602), Justinian's successors in the late sixth century, and about the final struggle between Rome and Persia in the years 603–30. In Greek, the history written by Menander Protector, which continued that of Agathias, is preserved only in fragments, but thanks to the interest in diplomacy shown by later Byzantine compilers, we have substantial sections relating to Byzantine–Persian relations under Justin II and Tiberius. The *Histories* of Theophylact Simocatta, written in the reign of Heraclius (AD 610–41), give a detailed account of the reign of the Emperor Maurice,[6] and there is a wide range of other sources, from the *Chronicon Paschale* and later chronicles to the epic poems which George of Pisidia wrote about Heraclius's wars. To these we can add a wealth of material in Syriac, especially chronicles, and the seventh-century Armenian chronicle attributed to the bishop Sebeos.[7] The Persian conquest and occupation of Jerusalem in 614 is very well documented by contemporaries, and later Greek, Syriac and Arabic sources are all important, especially for the years that saw the early stages of the Arab conquests and the end of the Sasanian kingdom.[8] This wealth of evidence is often difficult to use because much of it is fragmentary or written with a religious or partisan bias, while the problems surrounding the evidence for the early stages of Islam and the Arab conquests also give rise to extremely polarized positions among scholars. Not surprisingly, a huge amount of secondary literature has grown up, of which only the most important and the most helpful contributions can be referred to here. But again, this is a field in which there has been an explosion of recent scholarship, but also to which useful guides now exist.

Despite the 'Endless Peace' of 561, continuing grievances between the two powers emerged as soon as the usual embassy was sent to Chosroes after Justin II's succession in 565, and the new emperor adopted the same aggressive and defiant stance he had shown when approached by Avar envoys in Constantinople[9] and refused to accept what his envoys had agreed. Theophylact blames the emperor for the reopening of hostilities in 572, and a botched attempt at the assassination of the Ghassanid al-Mundhir and Justin's willingness to accept the persuasion of the Turks to go to war with Persia suggest that he was right to do so. The ecclesiastical historian Evagrius and other writers were also highly critical, the historian John of Epiphaneia stating that the real reason for hostilities was Justin's refusal to pay the agreed annual amount of gold according to the treaty. Justin's stance encouraged the Persarmenians to leave the side of Persia and join Rome (offering silk as an inducement, according to Gregory of Tours), thereby provoking the Persians.[10] The emperor's poor judgement continued during the hostilities, according to hostile reporters, when he interfered disastrously with the leadership of his generals, and later Justin was to launch a persecution of Miaphysites and to lapse into insanity on hearing the news of the loss of Dara (573), so that Tiberius and Justin's wife Sophia had to be given powers to rule. The result of this sorry episode for the Romans was that they had to pay a large sum and in addition agree a truce for five years with a very high level of annual payments.[11]

Chosroes took advantage of these gains to attack in Armenia, which fell outside the terms of the treaty, and then in Melitene, but was driven into retreat by Roman troops who were able to send Persian trophies (including war elephants) to Constantinople as a result.[12] Talks were renewed, and agreement had been reached when the Persians again defeated the Romans and went on the attack in Mesopotamia. The Romans, under the general Maurice (emperor from 582) fought back, together with al-Mundhir and the Ghassanids, despite suspicions of the latter's loyalty. The command passed to Philippicus, who defeated the Persians at Solachon in the Tur Abdin in 586, parading an image of Christ and the head of Symeon the Stylite which he obtained from Antioch.[13]

The two powers existed in an uneasy balance, with episodes of fighting and raiding alternating with short-term agreements, soon broken. Proxy war was also conducted between their respective clients, the Ghassan and Lakhm. Neither side won a clear or lasting advantage and the continuing warfare, which effectively lasted for over a century, was a serious drain on both sides, while cities, territories and the inhabitants of the contested areas were also losers. But the two powers also recognized each other's role. When in 590 the succession of Chosroes II was opposed by Bahram Chobin, the Persian king turned to the Roman emperor Maurice for help, and the latter not only assisted him but even called Chosroes his son; Roman and Persian forces fought together against the usurper.[14] As a result, Chosroes ceded to Rome not only Martyropolis and Dara but also parts of Armenia and Iberia (Georgia), and an unusual peace prevailed between the two empires for more than ten years.

The Byzantines and the Sasanians both ruled over vast areas with highly disparate populations and had much in common in terms of kingship and organization.[15] Christians, for example, constituted a substantial element in the Persian empire, and were embedded in the royal court.[16] Tensions

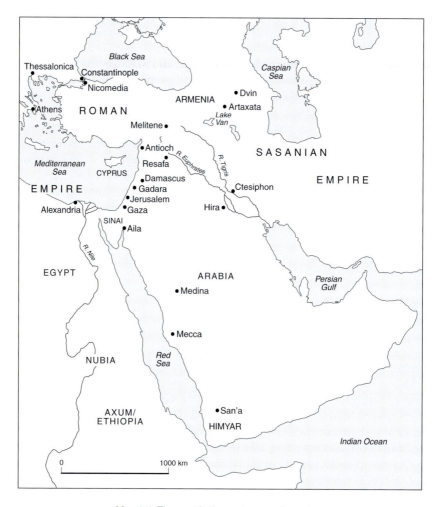

*Map 9.1* The east in the early seventh century

persisted with the Zoroastrian establishment, but by the end of the sixth century the religious ferment in the Near East as a whole was felt at the highest level. Imperial policy was also dictated by realism. What might seem a strange decision on the part of Maurice, to support his natural enemy rather than to profit from the internal discord in the Sasanian kingdom, as some urged, was both a demonstration of solidarity between kings and a hardheaded recognition of reality; neither side could or would aim at the total defeat of the other. Each side knew the strengths and weaknesses of the other from centuries of experience, and Maurice himself is credited with the *Strategikon*, a military manual discussing all aspects of late Roman warfare including the military characteristics of the Persians.[17]

This situation was soon to change. In 602 Maurice was deposed by Phocas, an army officer proclaimed by disaffected and ill-supplied troops in the Balkans. With Phocas outside Constantinople, the emperor called in the aid of the factions, but the Greens opted for Phocas, and Maurice was put to death with all his family.[18] For the last two decades the empire had also had to contend with assaults from the Avars and Slavs in the Balkans, and it was in this context that the soldiers raised Phocas as emperor. Chosroes took the opportunity to launch a major campaign against Byzantium on the pretext of avenging his adoptive father, parading Maurice's alleged surviving son Theodosius. Dara, only recently recovered by the Romans, was besieged and fell in 604 and this was followed by the capture of all the cities east of the Euphrates, Edessa, Harran, Callinicum and Circesium. The Persians were assisted from 609–10 by widespread disturbances in the Roman east involving the factions,[19] and the position of Phocas became more and more vulnerable. In this situation, Heraclius, the exarch of Africa, launched an expedition by sea which took Alexandria, the key port for the dispatch of the grain supply to the capital, and established itself on Cyprus; his son, also called Heraclius, was able to sail to Constantinople where he was welcomed, not least by the Green faction. In October 610 Heraclius became emperor, and Phocas was killed.

The Persian advance continued and Caesarea in Cappadocia was taken after a long siege; despite a Roman advance into Syria, the Persians moved south, taking Damascus and then Jerusalem in 614.[20] The patriarch and many of his people were taken with the True Cross to Ctesiphon, and according to Christian sources, the Persians sacked the city with great slaughter and deported many of its inhabitants. The fall of Jerusalem was followed by that of Alexandria (617), and Persian armies also stormed through Asia Minor, sacking Ephesus and Sardis and reaching Chalcedon. Palestine, Syria, Mesopotamia, Egypt and much of Asia Minor were under Persian control by 622, and the situation looked desperate for Constantinople, with attacks by the Avars and Slavs in the Balkans, an Avar siege of Thessalonica in 618 and the serious blow caused by the loss of the grain supply from Egypt.

## The Persian conquest of Jerusalem

The Persian advance and capture of Jerusalem provoked a bitter backlash against the Jews among Palestinian Christians, who blamed them for aiding the invaders. Christian sources, including the early-ninth century chronicle of Theophanes, important for this period, and the contemporary account attributed to Strategius, a monk of St Sabas, and surviving in Georgian and Arabic versions of the original Greek, the *Life* of George of Choziba, one of the Judaean desert monasteries, written soon after the events, and the narrative of the Armenian ps. Sebeos, are just some of the sources displaying a strong hostility to Jews.[21] Much of this anti-Jewish expression belongs to a long rhetorical tradition among Christian writers in late antiquity, but there is some reason to think that Jews in Palestine were courted at first by the

Persian invaders and even briefly entertained hopes of recovering the Temple Mount. Strategius' claim that Christians perished after being crammed by Jews into the Mamilla cistern in Jerusalem has been connected, plausibly or not, with physical evidence for burials.[22] Jewish apocalyptic flourished in this atmosphere, as did the recent genre of Hebrew liturgical poetry known as *piyyutim* (Chapter 8). Religious differences came to a head with the prospect of a change in the control of Jerusalem,[23] and in 632, after the restoration of the True Cross to Jerusalem, Heraclius decreed that all Jews must convert, a measure which came to little if anything, given its date, but which indicated and encouraged Christian anti-Jewish feeling. The genre of Christian apologetic dialogues between Christians and Jews, reviewing and refuting standard Jewish arguments against Christianity and invariably leading to the triumph of the Christian debaters, also flourished in the seventh and eighth centuries. In the anonymous *Quaestiones ad Antiochum ducem*, perhaps of the early eighth century, Christians are given arguments to use against Jews, or to reassure themselves, on topics such as the direction of prayer, circumcision, the veneration of created objects, the status of Christ, the destruction of the Jewish Temple and the superiority of Christianity.[24] A particularly striking, though not typical because less formulaic, example of the anti-Jewish dialogues is the so-called *Doctrina Jacobi nuper baptizati* of the 630s, telling of a converted Jew, which unusually contains much apparently circumstantial detail about Jewish communities in the eastern Mediterranean and Jacob's own involvement in factional disturbances.[25] A vivid impression of factional violence in various cities in the last days of Phocas is given by the Egyptian chronicler John of Nikiu (for whose work we depend on an extremely late Ethiopic translation from a lost Arabic paraphrase of the probably Coptic original), and while this is a difficult source on which to rely, many others confirm this picture of urban disturbances all round the Mediterranean, in which the factions joined in or sometimes took the lead (Chapter 7 above). Inscriptions at Ephesus, Oxyrhynchus and Alexandria confirm their importance and their bestowal of political support, and Phocas seems to have alienated the powerful Greens. The *Doctrina* also reflects this tense atmosphere when recounting the exploits of Jacob in his youth, before his conversion:

> [In the reign of Phocas], when the Greens, at the command of Kroukis, burned the Mese [in Constantinople] and had a bad time [cf. *Chron. Pasch.*, 695–6], I roughed up the Christians and fought them as incendiaries and Manichaeans. And when Bonosus at Antioch punished the Greens and slaughtered them [609], I went to Antioch … and, being a Blue and on the emperor's side, I beat up the Christians as Greens and called them traitors.
>
> (*Doctrina Jacobi* I.40)

The fall of Jerusalem and the capture of the empire's most precious relic, the True Cross, were matters of deep mourning for Christians and, as we saw, Sophronius, later patriarch of Jerusalem himself, composed poetic lamentations in the classical metre of anacreontics.[26] The joy when the Emperor Heraclius returned the Cross to Jerusalem in 630 was correspondingly great, and Sophronius and others did not fail to rejoice in what they saw as the discomfiture of the Jews.[27] But the Cross had been received in Ctesiphon with joy and celebration, not simply as a trophy of victory but also as a Christian symbol.

## Persian occupation and Roman recovery

Internal arrangements during the period of Persian occupation are hardly known, but papyrological evidence from Egypt suggests that little was changed and that the new rulers left existing administrative structures in place.[28] For the continued warfare we have detailed accounts in the *Chronicon Paschale*, the early ninth-century *Chronicle* of Theophanes (which draws on earlier sources), the poems of George of Pisidia and the Armenian writers ps. Sebeos and Movses Daskhurani, all of which have been covered in recent studies.[29] Peace having been made with the Avars in 620, Heraclius turned to gathering an army large enough to take on the Persians, melting down church treasures and a bronze ox that stood in the Forum Bovis in Constantinople. Despite winning a victory in battle, he soon had to return to confront the Avars, and agree to pay them a large annual subsidy before setting off again for Persarmenia. He dared to stay away from the capital during the dangerous Avar–Persian siege of 626, though he may have returned that winter. He had formed an alliance with the Turks and with them entered Persian territory; disaffected Persian nobles put Chosroes' son Cavadh on the throne and Chosroes was executed. Cavadh entered negotiations with Heraclius, and the latter announced his extraordinary success in a letter read out in St Sophia in May, 628.[30] Diplomatic conventions were maintained, and the new Persian shah addressed Heraclius as 'the most clement Roman emperor, our brother'. Peace was made in 629, with the Euphrates as the agreed border. The Sasanian kingdom lasted for two more decades, until 652, with the death of Yazdgerd III after a period of internal rivalry and confusion; the Persians continued to put up a resistance, but it was the Arabs, not the Romans, who defeated them. But the centuries-old threat which Persia had posed to Rome was over, and in 630 Heraclius triumphantly restored the True Cross to Jerusalem. The emperor's emotion is described by ps. Sebeos:

> [There was] the sound of weeping and wailing; their tears flowed from the awesome emotion of their hearts and from the rending of the entrails of the king, the princes, all his troops and the inhabitants of the city. No-one was able to sing the Lord's chants from the fearful and agonizing emotion of the king and the whole multitude.
>
> (Ps.Sebeos, 41, Thomson and Howard-Johnston, I, 90; II, 24)

Even if the Roman empire was better able to sustain the effort to defeat the Persians than many historians have assumed, the effects on the Roman economy as a whole of this prolonged warfare, alternating with periods of annual heavy payments, must have been very great, and the operational requirements in the east were also expensive and complex.[31] Meanwhile the Avars and Slavs were able to overrun western Illyricum and Greece and mount serious raids on Thessalonica; the city's survival was attributed to the intervention of St Demetrius in the *Miracles of St Demetrius*.[32] The Persian wars have been given a major role in the acute downturn in the fortunes of old classical cities, especially in Asia Minor, [33] but as we saw, recent archaeological work on Syria and Palestine suggests that the material impact of the Persian invasions there was limited (Chapter 7). There is, however, evidence that they provoked flight in some sectors of the population in the wanderings of Sophronius and Maximus Confessor, who settled in North Africa, the influx of monks and clergy from the east in Sicily and south Italy, the impact of which is still evident today in the churches and villages, and the case of St John the Almsgiver, who fled from Egypt to Cyprus, justifying his action in Scriptural terms. It may be dangerous to draw general conclusions from limited evidence, and warfare and conquest were not the only factors causing urban downturn, but the combined effects of the successful Persian and then Arab invasions caused disruption in particular places, brought negative economic consequences, ended the grain supply to the capital and detached large areas of territory and the tax base from the control of Constantinople.

## The Arab conquests and the coming of Islam

Scarcely had Heraclius returned to Constantinople after his entry into Jerusalem than another, and this time unforeseen, threat emerged in the east. Also in 630, Muhammad and his followers returned to Mecca from Medina, and Muhammad's leadership was established in Arabia. Muhammad himself died in 632, but Muslim raids into Palestine had begun by 634. It would seem in fact that a major advance was already taking place further south while Heraclius was occupied with the celebration of his victory over the Persians. Despite a defeat at Mu'ta in 629, largely at the hands of other Arab tribes, an Arab army took Tabuk in the northern Hejaz, whereupon three important Byzantine centres in eastern Palestina Tertia – Udruh and Aila (Aqaba), both legionary fortresses, as well as Jarba – simply surrendered, giving the Muslims access to southern Palestine. Again, the chronology of these events is hard to establish, but when the Muslims did reach the Negev and Gaza it seems clear that these areas were undefended, and they met relatively little resistance. Whatever the reasons, the infrastructure of defence which might have stopped the Muslims as they moved from Arabia into Palestine and Syria was absent.

The Arab advance was spectacular. Three battles took place between 634 and 637 at Ajnadayn, between Jerusalem and Gaza, Fihl (Pella), and the river Yarmuk. Damascus fell after a long siege, and according to tradition Jerusalem was dramatically handed over, according to Arabic sources, to the Caliph 'Umar I, walking on foot and dressed in dirty clothes to show his humility, by the patriarch Sophronius in 638; later tradition records the 'Covenant of Umar' with the people of Jerusalem. Alexandria fell in 642. The unfortunate Heraclius saw his armies defeated at the Yarmuk; bidding a famous farewell to Syria, as reported in later Syriac chronicles, he returned to Constantinople, where he died in 641. Alexandria was taken in the next year and the Arabs raided Cappadocia; they soon made damaging attacks on Cyprus and won a spectacular naval battle in the bay of Phoenix off the coast of Lycia in southern Asia Minor. They even reached the Bosphorus and threatened Constantinople, though this time they were forced to retreat. A few contemporaries recognized the importance of Muhammad, whom they regarded as a false prophet. In the 630s the *Doctrina Jacobi* cites a contemporary letter, supposedly from a Palestinian Jew called Abraham, according to whom a false prophet had appeared among the Saracens, foretelling the coming of the anointed one. Abraham asked a wise old man, expert in the Scriptures, about this, and the old man replied

> 'He is an imposter. Do the prophets come with swords and chariot? Truly these happenings today are the works of disorder.'

Abraham then made enquiries himself and was told that the prophet claimed to have the keys of paradise, which Abraham regarded as completely incredible and therefore as confirming the old man's words.[34] But at first the Byzantines were slow to realize that the invaders were other than 'Saracen' raiders with whom they had been familiar since the fourth century, and Christian sources emphasize their 'barbarian' ferocity. It is in general only later that Byzantine writers begin to show awareness of the religious content of Muhammad's teaching. The account given by the chronicler Theophanes (d. 817), based on an earlier eastern source, mixes hostility and slander with genuine observation:

> He taught his subjects that he who kills an enemy or is killed by an enemy goes to Paradise; and he said that this paradise was one of carnal eating and drinking and intercourse with women, and had a river of wine, honey and milk, and that the women were not like the ones down here, but different ones, and that the intercourse was long-lasting and the pleasure continuous; and other things full of profligacy and stupidity; also that men should feel sympathy for one another and help those who are wronged.
>
> (Theoph., *Chron.*, 334, Mango and Scott, 465)

Thus there was as yet little understanding, and there is a strong emphasis on the sufferings of the local populations in the written sources, especially those in Syriac. At the same time archaeological and other evidence suggests that the 'conquests' themselves did not at first represent a major break in continuity in the eastern Mediterranean provinces, especially as the Islamic rulers at first simply took over the main framework of the Byzantine administration and continued to use Greek-speaking officials to run it. The real change was to come only later, from the late seventh century onwards, and especially with the end of the Umayyad dynasty and transfer of government east to Baghdad in the mid-eighth century.

The course of the early conquests and the reasons behind them have been endlessly debated, and it has long been recognized that for contemporary sources we have to look to non-Islamic material; historical writing in Arabic took time to develop, and when it did it was based on oral material, including the *sira* (biographies of the Prophet), the *hadith* (acts and sayings of the Prophet) and *isnads* (reported 'chains' of witnesses), the nature of which is also controversial. Traditionalist modern accounts, and Muslim tradition itself, are based on a broad acceptance of this evidence, while revisionist approaches are strongly sceptical.[35] A more moderate position seems to be emerging, based on very detailed analysis of the Arabic writers, and giving weight to their presentation of pre-Islamic Arab culture, especially through the pre-Islamic Arabic poetry they preserve. Analysis of the events of the conquests themselves is coloured by these different approaches, with some arguing for a centrally controlled and determined programme of conquests driven by religious motives and others for more inchoate beginnings, with the systematic development of Islam itself seen as crystallizing only in the Syrian context. From the perspective of the Christian and Jewish populations of the Near East, and of the Byzantines in Constantinople, who were naturally preoccupied with the experience of defeat, it is not surprising if it took time to understand the phenomenon of emerging Islam. It seems unlikely that the anti-Jewish dialogues of the later seventh and eighth centuries were in fact veiled attacks on Islam, as has sometimes been argued. Rather, there seems to have been little actual awareness of the Qur'anic message before the later seventh century, and John of Damascus' eighth-century chapter on Islam (which he saw as a Christian heresy) is the first discussion in any detail; even then the passage is simply an extra chapter tacked on to the end of his listing of one hundred heresies.[36] Apocalyptic literature circulated in Greek and Syriac towards the end of the seventh century, but this was most concerned to place the defeat of the Roman empire within an eschatological frame.

A turning point came during the caliphate of Abd al-Malik (685–705) when a more aggressive line was adopted towards Christians, the Dome of the Rock was built on the site of the Jewish Temple (below) and a new non-figurative coinage was adopted. In 707 the great cathedral in Damascus, itself built over a Roman temple, and which had hitherto been used for prayer by both Christians and Muslims, was transformed into the Great Mosque that we see today.

By about 700, after decades of warfare, and certainly by 718, when the Arabs were already in Spain and a dangerous Arab siege of Constantinople was narrowly resisted, it was clear that the new rulers of the east were there to stay.

*Figure 9.1* The Great Mosque at Damascus (early eighth century), built on the site of a Christian church and Roman temple

### Christian religious divisions and religious reactions

The ordinations of Miaphysite clergy under Justinian had had the effect of creating a divided church and of giving the Miaphysites an established position. But as we have seen already, the east was not uniformly Miaphysite, even in strongly Miaphysite areas; the patriarchate of Antioch, for instance, passed several times between Chalcedonian and Miaphysite control, and there were both Miaphysite and orthodox communities in Edessa when Heraclius was there during his campaign. It has often been supposed, nevertheless, that the religious divisions among Christians aided the Arab conquests by reducing loyalty to Constantinople among the anti-Chalcedonians, and diverting attention from the need for defence, a theory for which there is little direct evidence.[37] If cities surrendered without fighting, it was because they had little choice, not because they preferred the Arabs to the Byzantines; they had faced very similar choices before – for instance, during the Persian wars of Chosroes I under Justinian – and behaved in similar ways when the alternative would have been a disastrous siege or violent capture. There was no shortage of military response in any case, and this was not in the hands of local clergy or local communities. It may be true that the Arab armies were motivated by a religious theory of the rewards of *jihad*, but Heraclius' wars were also seen by contemporaries as religious wars, and troops were spurred on by the use of Christian relics and images. The early Muslims were deeply divided themselves; the beginnings of Muslim rule outside Arabia were marked first by the *ridda* wars, or 'wars of apostasy' against the rule of Abu Bakr after Muhammad's death, then the murder of the Caliph 'Uthman in 656 and the coming to power of Mu'awiya in the context of the assassination of Muhammad's cousin and son-in-law 'Ali; this was followed by the death of the latter's son, Muhammad's grandson, Husayn, at Karbala in 680.[38] The murder of 'Uthman in particular (656) gave the Byzantines a breathing space and the chance to reorganize, but Heraclius had already begun the process of changing the army structure, and there was also work on the refortification of key coastal cities in Asia Minor.[39]

It is naturally tempting to imagine that after decades of warfare the Byzantines were in no condition to take on another enemy, but less easy to assess the actual military strength of the empire in the east; to the arguments that there had been a progressive reduction in defence and that Heraclius's campaign against the Persians in the 620s was only possible because of desperate recruiting measures, it may be responded that Byzantium was still capable of gathering and dispatching considerable forces both before and after the Arab conquests.[40] The contest was not all one-sided and the Muslims suffered several serious reverses. The late seventh and early eighth centuries were very difficult for the eastern empire, and there is also a gap in the coverage of the historical sources for about twenty years in the mid-seventh century, so that much detail remains obscure; one can imagine, however, that a serious lessening of the availability of elite education followed the loss of territory and the damage to cities. The state had lost a huge part of its tax-base and in the capital the Aqueduct of Valens which was essential for the city's water supply was not repaired after being damaged during the 626 siege, with a consequent dramatic downward impact on the population. The Emperor Constans II (641–68) moved his court to Sicily and was eventually assassinated. The Mediterranean became unsafe and open to the development of Arab piracy. But above all, Constantinople was not taken. The Byzantine state was much reduced and had to change its administrative, financial and military structures as a consequence. But its core institutions were able to adapt and survive.[41]

This was so despite the strength of the opposition, especially from the eastern provinces, to the efforts of Heraclius earlier in the century to find a solution to the christological divisions which still separated the church (Chapter 8). Miaphysites were not the only anti-Chalcedonians; the so-called 'Nestorians' also maintained that Christ had only one nature (the human), and the decisions of the Council of 553 had met with hostility in Italy. The successors of Justinian did not give up on their efforts to manage the situation, which was seen not only as politically dangerous but also as likely to bring divine punishment on the empire. The first formula was promoted by Heraclius in 633, soon after his success in restoring the Cross to Jerusalem, but Monoenergism, the theory that Christ had one 'energy', provoked opposition from Chalcedonians, and in 638 an imperial statement, the *Ekthesis*, displayed in St Sophia, proclaimed Monotheletism, the theory that Christ had a single will.[42] In the same year Sophronius, as patriarch of Jerusalem, surrendered the holy city to the Muslims, but he had already been a leader in orchestrating local meetings of bishops to oppose the innovation, and formally condemned the imperial religious policy.[43] Sophronius died, also in 638, and the opposition was continued by Maximus Confessor from his monastery in Carthage; in 645 Maximus publicly debated in Carthage with the former patriarch and Monothelete, Pyrrhus, and then left for Rome to organize the campaign from there (Chapter 8). The seventh-century popes were equally opposed to the imperial innovation, and both Pope Martin I and Maximus were arrested and taken to Constantinople for trial. Yet Monotheletism did not prevail. It was formally rejected by the Sixth Ecumenical Council held in Constantinople by the Emperor Constantine IV in 680–1. Not only was Maximus' reputation vindicated, but his theological writings established him as one of the most important of all Orthodox theologians.[44]

The seventh century was a period of intense and profound theological discussion, of which the central theme remained that of the nature of Christ. What did it mean that man was made in the image of Christ? How could the human and the divine natures of Christ be known? Did God suffer in the flesh in the crucifixion? Concerns had already been raised in the late sixth century about the cult of saints and their efficacy to intervene after death (Chapter 3), and a growing anxiety about religious images and especially depictions of Christ, and about the status of visual images as conveyors of truth, revealed itself in seventh-century writing, including the works of the monk Anastasius of Sinai and the anti-Jewish disputations. This debate and anxiety was part of the context for a prolonged argument in the next century about the status of images as compared with writing.[45] Sets of questions and answers on theological topics also survive from this period and are indicative of the need to explain issues of faith and practice in a situation that must often have seemed bewildering. It was in this crucial period that Maximus Confessor and after him Germanos, patriarch of Constantinople, 715–30, set out the symbolic understanding of the church and the liturgy that was to underpin eastern Orthodox thinking thereafter. As well as condemning Monotheletism, the Sixth Ecumenical Council in 681 recognized the degree of passion that had been aroused, and the likelihood of manipulation or falsification of evidence; the same concern was to persist in connection with the councils of the eighth century. Neither the fifth nor the sixth council had issued moral or pastoral canons and in 691 a further council was held in order to fill this gap, known as the Council in Trullo after the room in the palace where it met, or the 'Quinisext', after its status as an appendix to both the fifth and the sixth. Deep doctrinal divisions and the disturbance of church order that came with them also had profound ethical implications and church discipline needed to be reasserted. The intellectual and religious history of the period went together with its political and military history, and was frequently interwoven with it; it cannot be separated in modern accounts.

## Christians under Islam

At first little seemed to change in the provinces that were now part of the Umayyad caliphate. The rulers concentrated on military aims and on their

Arab and other Muslim followers, who received preferential treatment in the form of financial annuities, provision for their religious needs and settlement in new foundations. These included al-Kufa, very near to the Lakhmid centre at Hira, al-Basra and Wasit, all in Iraq, Fustat in Egypt and Kairouan in North Africa. Palestine and Syria were already highly urbanized and there and in north Mesopotamia such settlements were few; as under the Persians, the existing administration was largely left to run everything. But during the rule of Abd al-Malik (685–705), in the late seventh century a more forceful policy was adopted for the control of the Christian population and the assertion of Islam. The Dome of the Rock in Jerusalem built by Abd al-Malik carries anti-Christian verses round the inside of the dome,[46] and Christians were forbidden to parade the cross, figural motifs were removed from the coinage and Arabic replaced Greek as the language of administration. The change was clear. Some Christians longed for a restoration of idealized Roman rule, but in many ways community life continued as before. This included the intellectual activity of Christian writers in Syriac, who translated Greek texts and wrote on theology, mathematics and philosophy, in a tradition which was to continue for centuries. Jacob of Edessa (d. 708) was a prolific author who had been born in the territory of Antioch in about 633 and entered the monastery of Qenneshrin, travelled to Alexandria, became bishop of Edessa, but then spent his life in monasteries including Tell 'Adda, returning to Edessa for only a few months just before his death. Jacob produced works on grammar, history, exegesis, philosophy, liturgy, and collections of rules ('canons') and rulings on matters to do with Christian life under the Muslims, some in the form of answers to questions posed by others.[47] Just as earlier collections of questions and answers had dealt with the problems posed by intersectarian divisions among Christians such as the validity of the Eucharist if the elements had been consecrated by a 'heretic', so Jacob gave guidance to Christians about their necessary relations with Muslims in daily life. Thus a monk or deacon could participate in battle in the Muslim army if forced, but must not kill; priests may bless a Muslim; Christians may attend funerals of pagans and Jews.

Such were the day-to-day issues that faced all Christian communities, not only the Syrian Orthodox. In Egypt there is abundant papyrological evidence in Greek and Coptic for continuing Christian life in the early Islamic period.[48] In Palestine, the dyophysites who remained in communion with Chalcedonian orthodoxy were later known as 'Melkites', meaning those who supported the emperor, or the 'king'. Their centre remained the patriarchate of Jerusalem and the Palestinian monasteries, though they were certainly not confined to these areas, and John of Damascus and his disciple Theodore Abu Qurrah, bishop of Harran, who wrote in Arabic, were key theologians in the eighth and ninth centuries. In the major centres and in the higher echelons of the clergy, Greek continued in use among the Melkites, but by the ninth century the Palestinian monasteries were multilingual, and the wider Christian population in Palestine moved as easily from Aramaic to Arabic as monastic and ecclesiastical writers did from Greek.[49] The Church of the East, or Assyrian Christians, often wrongly labeled as Nestorians, stressed the human rather than the divine nature of Christ.[50] All these groups have survived until the present day.

In the sixth and seventh centuries the numerous monasteries of the Judaean desert were important centres, ranging from small hermitages to very large coenobia such as the monastery of Martyrius. Some remained in use until the nineteenth century, and St Sabas, east of Bethlehem, continues even today, though it has been extensively rebuilt and lost much of its monastic library to collectors in the nineteenth century. St Catherine's monastery at the foot of Mount Sinai is in a more isolated position and was able to maintain itself without interruption throughout the various vicissitudes of succeeding centuries. It still displays a letter supposedly from Muhammad, guaranteeing the freedom and protection of the monastery. St Catherine's also houses extraordinary collections of manuscripts and icons, and many more manuscripts were discovered in the course of restoration work in 1975. St Sabas is very differently positioned, not far from Bethlehem and within close reach of Jerusalem. In the eighth and ninth centuries it was a centre of learning and attracted monks with a wide variety of backgrounds and languages. By the ninth century Arabic was displacing Greek, but like St Catherine's, St Sabas remained in modern terms Greek Orthodox, i.e. Melkite. John of Damascus was almost certainly a monk at St Sabas, though the direct evidence for this is in fact rather slight, and St Sabas became a powerhouse for religious debates even in Constantinople in the eighth and ninth centuries.[51] Monasteries in Mesopotamia and the Tur Abdin also remained centres of learning for many centuries, and of these also some continue today.

The general condition of Christians and Jews under Islam has been much debated. As Peoples of the Book they were technically protected, but occupied a lesser status as non-Muslims and were subjected to various constraints including the poll-tax (*jizya*).[52] Christians naturally tended to produce stories of ill-treatment and even some accounts of martyrdoms at the hands of the Muslim authorities, whether of individuals or groups, such as the tale of the sixty martyrs of Gaza, soldiers imprisoned while defending the city of Gaza in 637, who subsequently refused to convert to Islam; but such cases were few in number, and the accounts are ideologically driven.[53] At the same time Christian communities in the Umayyad period were still engaging in church building and restoration, to the extent that the paradoxical term 'Umayyad churches' has been coined for the new or remodelled churches of this period. Robert Schick has produced long and impressive lists of churches that remained in use and churches that were newly built or restored in the period 640–813, as well as a corpus of sites, and some of the most spectacular and interesting of the mosaics already mentioned date from this period (Chapter 7).[54] The built landscape changed slowly. Church building work, as at Palmyra in Syria or at Umm er-Rasas in Jordan, coexisted with the so-called desert palaces and bath-houses (*qusur*) at Qasr al Hayr al-Gharbi, Qasr al-Hayr al-Sharqi, Hallabat or Qusayr

'Amra and elsewhere. The frescoes of Qusayr 'Amra in particular, in modern Jordan, with their depictions of six kings, four of them labelled in Greek and Arabic as rulers in the late antique Mediterranean world (Caesar, Roderic, Chosroes and the Negus), and combined with mythological and other scenes, are an extraordinary testimony to the breadth of cultural and artistic connections among the Umayyad elite.[55] It is not surprising to find a strong Sasanian artistic influence in these structures alongside the East Roman borrowings, whether in iconography or in the use of large-scale stucco decoration. Nor is it surprising that they were built in or at the edge of the 'desert', away from but within reach of the major urban centres; on one level they were retreats and country residences for their patrons, but they also tended to be located on main routes and on sites which facilitated communication with and control of the local tribes, and some had gardens or water installations. It is also possible to trace continuity of village settlement between the Roman and Umayyad periods in Transjordan and elsewhere.

The unevenness of available archaeological evidence means that it is harder to assess the impact of Umayyad rule on the major cities, though with some notable exceptions, especially Jerusalem and Amman, and at well-excavated sites such as Jerash, Pella and Umm Qays, and Muslims remained a small minority in the population as a whole. But it is clear that mosques, administrative and commercial structures were built in main and

*Figure 9.2* Nessana in the early 1990s. An important cache of sixth–seventh-century papyri in Greek, Latin, Syriac and Arabic was found here in 1935 during the excavation of one of the churches.

secondary centres including Jerusalem, Amman, Resafa, Tiberias, Jerash and Scythopolis.[56]

## Change and continuity in the east

It is certainly true that the emphasis on late antique continuity into the Islamic period in recent scholarship, with the 'break' usually seen as coinciding with the end of the Umayyads and removal of the capital to Baghdad in the eighth century, depends heavily on a concentration by late antique scholars on the eastern Mediterranean. Here too, however, deep changes came as a result of the Arab conquests, even if the conquests themselves left less trace on the archaeological record than previously assumed. The conquests also brought very serious consequences for the Byzantine state, and while Constantinople managed to escape being taken by the Avars and Persians and by the Arabs, it was dramatically diminished as a city by the eighth century. Even before that, the late seventh-century government went through very difficult times. Neither cultural nor economic explanations are in themselves sufficient to explain the changes that were taking place in the period; we must also bring in political and military factors, even while recognizing that the sixth to eighth centuries were a time of intense intellectual and religious ferment. I have earlier referred to this process as a 'redefinition of knowledge',[57] and indeed such was the acknowledged or unacknowledged goal of many Christian contemporaries. However, it is worth remembering that the need for such a redefinition arose from a situation of change, conflict and uncertainty in all parts of the Mediterranean world. Reactions were very diverse. One recent contribution refers to the sixth and seventh centuries as having 'witnessed the most protracted, detailed and fiercely contested debate on personhood and anthropology in human history – certainly in the history of the ancient world – as Christian, Jewish and ultimately Muslim monotheisms fought to define the various "orthodox" versions of their beliefs about God, man and the universe.'[58] The only way that the general history of this extraordinarily crucial period can truly be approached – including the issue of the 'end of antiquity' – is by rejecting an insistence on one factor over the others (economic over cultural history, for instance) and attempting instead to bring these different approaches together. That said, while this chapter has indeed been largely about the east, the Conclusion will address some of the wider (and contested) issues about the Mediterranean world in late antiquity.

# CONCLUSION

For a book that appeared in 1993, the choice of the title *The Mediterranean World in Late Antiquity* did not seem to need justification. Given the many publications that have subsequently appeared with the word 'Mediterranean' in their titles, it now indeed seems prescient.[1] It has been traditional to see the fall of the Roman empire, or at least 'the end of the ancient world', as marking a critical break in historical continuity in the history of the Mediterranean world. However, in their book, *The Corrupting Sea*,[2] Peregrine Horden and Nicholas Purcell present the history of the Mediterranean in terms of continuities, abiding structures and the *longue durée*. In this vision, geography and deeply ingrained social patterns matter more than events, and link all parts of the Mediterranean in commonality. Rather than emphasizing long-distance trading patterns and ruptures, Purcell and Horden lay stress on the continuation at all periods of small-scale connectivity. The ancient Mediterranean world belongs therefore to a system which links it to the Mediterranean worlds of later periods and even of today. Others have taken up this way of thinking and applied the term 'Mediterranean' to other seas ('other Mediterraneans'),[3] but the Purcell and Horden model explicitly disrupts the dominant emphasis on long-distance exchange as the marker of Mediterranean unity in late antiquity. The view of the Mediterranean world in the late Roman period as a more or less unified economic system is still to be found in other works; for instance, in Brent Shaw's comments on Chris Wickham's *Framing the Early Middle Ages*, a book with the sub-title *Europe and the Mediterranean, 400–800*. Shaw sees 'the Roman Mediterranean world-system' or 'Mediterranean world-system (MWS)' as a unified system that was being reconfigured, or indeed was fragmenting, before the end of Wickham's chosen period, i.e. by AD 800.[4] Michael McCormick's book, *Origins of the European Economy*, also takes a Mediterranean-wide view and focuses on long-distance trade and travel;[5] his findings point to a general downturn in cross-Mediterranean activity in the seventh century followed by an upturn by *c.* 900. This emphasis on long-distance shipping as an indicator of Mediterranean unity has been a powerful theme in the intense study of ceramics as evidence of trade and economic activity during the last generation, and while the study of amphorae in this sense dates only from the 1970s, the importance attached to cross-Mediterranean travel has been traditional since the Belgian historian Henri Pirenne denied the idea that the Roman empire ended with the barbarian invasions, and argued that the real break in Mediterranean culture, or as we would now say, the end of antiquity, came only with the Arab conquests in the seventh century; this, he argued, brought an end to long-distance trade as previously known, and transformed the Mediterranean into an 'Arab lake'.[6] In the 1970s and even into the 1980s, the 'Pirenne thesis' was still the basis of intense debate, and while the substance of the argument was transformed by the turn of the century in the scholarship towards the utilization of newly available ceramic and other archaeological evidence and the progressive refinement of dating techniques, the underlying agenda remained that of investigating the extent of cross-Mediterranean exchange.

Against this preoccupation with rupture and concentration on what they call 'high commerce' and its shipping lanes, Horden and Purcell introduced a sceptical note, pointing out that the Arab conquests in fact opened new networks; the notion of rupture is too simplistic.[7] A division has also opened up among historians of late antiquity between those who emphasize continuity and others, such as Peter Heather and Bryan Ward-Perkins, who vigorously re-emphasize the traditional 'fall' of the western empire in the fifth century, reintroduce the idea of barbarian invasion, and already think in term of a separated western Europe, two groups labelled by Ward-Perkins as 'continuists' and 'catastrophists'. The former look more to the east, and take a longer view of late antiquity, seeing it as embracing the emergence of Islam. That has been the thrust of the last two chapters. The emphasis on the continuity of late antiquity into the early Islamic period also has implications for the application of the Mediterranean model to the later Roman empire: after all, the Roman empire in this period was not limited to those provinces that bordered the Mediterranean, and the eastward emphasis adopted here and in much other recent work changes the focus even more. That tendency is carried further by historians who prefer to see the Roman empire in the context not of the Mediterranean alone, but of the whole of Eurasia.[8] In contrast, the 'catastrophist' view belongs within a scenario whose actual focus is on the origins of western Europe rather than the Mediterranean world.[9]

Meanwhile the end of empires has also re-emerged as a key topic for all periods, with the Roman empire as the paradigm by which others are judged. The comparator now is usually the 'American empire', as in Cullen Murphy's book, *Are we Rome? The End of an Empire and the Fate of America*, published in the United Kingdom with the uncompromising title, *The New Rome*.[10] A further way of approaching the issue is through explicit attention to comparative history, in particular through a comparison between Rome and China;[11] comparative history of this kind may be difficult, but it avoids the over-concentration on Europe (Euro-centrism) which has been criticized by many. Nevertheless, the problem of the end of the ancient world raises issues about east and west – where does the eastern empire fit, and does it belong with Europe? The question is more acute for the later Byzantine period,[12] but as

James O'Donnell has emphasized,[13] it is also sharply raised by the wars of Justinian and his attempt to restore unified Roman rule from Constantinople. The general question is brought into further relief by the fact that the Byzantines thought of themselves emphatically as 'Romans' even though their official and literary language, and so much of their culture, was Greek. There was no simple 'fall of the Roman empire': one could reasonably say that only part of the Roman empire 'fell', the western part, leaving what contemporaries thought of as Rome still intact. This is obscured by the current framing of the question in terms of a choice between decline or collapse on the one hand and continuity on the other.

Stress on a 'hard' periodization also raises the question of where to place the rise of Islam and the establishment of Arab Muslim rule in the eastern Mediterranean. Older scholarship – and some contemporary works – make a sharp divide between the late antique (or 'Byzantine') Near East and the Islamic period, a tendency which has been intensified in the past by the influence of boundaries between academic disciplines. However, attempts to break down these boundaries have been a feature of the scholarship of the last two decades, and the thinking of the 'continuity' or 'long late antiquity' school places the rise of Islam firmly in the late antique, i.e., in the Mediterranean, world.[14] The last two chapters have set out the context in which the first conquests took place, and emphasized religious, political and social factors in the pre-Islamic Near East which make the emergence of a new monotheistic religion more comprehensible. This approach is supported, as we have seen, by the striking lack of clear signs of dramatic change in the archaeological record. This is not to deny the power and originality of the new religion or its role in motivating state-formation but simply to insist that it emerged within a specific historical context.

Attempts to explain the fall of the Roman empire in the mid-twentieth century cast the debate in terms of two stark alternatives: either the empire collapsed because of internal factors, or it fell under the pressure of outside impact. Thus the French historian André Piganiol famously asserted in 1947 that the empire was 'assassinated', and in 1964 A.H.M Jones concluded that the main factors were external.[15] The Roman empire did not come to an end through revolutionary change. There was no uprising or popular impulse that brought about collapse, and in so far as class struggle existed (and there were certainly massive inequalities), it was for the most part passive and inert.[16] Though it has often been assumed that the lower classes and especially the non-Chalcedonians, were unwilling to continue fighting Constantinople's battles in the early seventh-century east, the actual reasons for the eventual loss of both western and eastern provinces were more numerous and more complex. It is more fruitful in the context of current research to look for changes in the balance of centre and periphery and at the shifting relations of local cultures and identities. Consideration of the *longue durée*, gradual and piecemeal change, is more helpful than the appeal to immediate causal factors. The extraordinary tenacity of the late Roman state can also too easily be forgotten in the search for explanations of its supposed decline and fall. Thus, while Justinian's wars may have overstretched the state economy, he was nevertheless able to sustain a massive war effort over a very long period and on several fronts, to establish a new and substantial Byzantine administrative and military system in the newly reconquered provinces of North Africa and Italy, to reclaim these provinces from Arian religious rule and build or remodel many churches, and to carry through an empire-wide building programme which was impressive on any estimate. That his successors experienced difficulties in maintaining his example was hardly surprising.

The empire was vulnerable to external developments as well as to its own internal problems. Not merely was it faced by extensive barbarian settlement in the west and the expensive and difficult Persian wars, in the east, followed by the Arab conquest. Changes in central Asia led in the fifth century to danger from the Huns, fortunately dissolved after the death of Attila, and later to the appearance of the Hephthalites, who threatened Constantinople at the end of the reign of Justinian. By this time the empire was already attempting to use the Avars to control other groups such as the Slavs in the Danubian regions. Corippus approvingly describes their haughty reception by Justin II at the beginning of his reign, but Justin's high-handedness to these and other potential enemies proved disastrous; large payments to the Avars by his successor Tiberius II (578–82) did not prevent them from becoming a major threat, or from besieging Constantinople in 626.[17] Needless to say, contemporaries had only a vague idea of the ethnic origins of the Avars and the Turks,[18] whose prominence in the late sixth century was followed in turn by the emergence, by the end of the seventh, of two other Turkic peoples, the Bulgars and the Khazars. Faced with these movements, the empire oscillated between trying to make alliances, backed up with payment of subsidies, and, when necessary, fighting. This was indeed the normal state of affairs, varying only in degree; war, not peace, was the norm, and when peace did prevail for a time it had usually been bought at a high cost.

Seen against this background, the 'decline' explanation appears inadequate. It is premised on the idea that it is reasonable to expect cultures and societies to be able to maintain themselves indefinitely in the same state. Phrases such as 'the end of classical antiquity' and the like assume an entity, 'classical antiquity', which is not itself liable to change. But societies do not exist in a vacuum. Changes in late antique urbanism have received enormous attention as indicators of decline or transformation; yet cities in antiquity, like cities now, did not exist in a steady state but were constantly being remodelled and adapted. Then, as now, the human environment was one of constant change. Myriads of small and large changes were taking place both within the vast territories of the empire and outside its borders: it is these changes taken together which have misleadingly been labelled 'decline'. Words such as 'decline' are irredeemably emotive, and it is not the historian's place to sit in moral judgement on his subject or to impose inappropriate classical norms.[19]

A different mode of explanation can be derived from recent work in anthropology, according to which complex societies tend of themselves to become ever more complex until finally they reach the point of collapse.[20] At first sight this avoids the difficulty of confusing explanations of change with descriptions of it. But it is not clear whether it really succeeds, or how appropriate a theory it is when applied to the Roman empire. A further danger in such generalizing explanations is that they may fail to take into account the actual historical variables – while it may be useful to see the Roman empire in comparison with other imperial systems, it was also a society *sui generis*, held together by a unique balance of factors which historians are still in the process of trying to understand. Similar issues arise in relation to comparisons between empires, which depend heavily on the specific points of comparison chosen. We must not lose sight of the particularity of late antiquity in the zeal to explain away the 'fall of the Roman empire'.

The present flow of research on the eastern provinces in late antiquity is indeed striking, but stems from the same preoccupation with acculturation and cultural change that lies behind comparable work on the west. The field is led by archaeology; archaeologists are giving more and more attention to studying the interaction of cultural systems and especially the process of acculturation. It is promising to see that an emphasis on ethnoarchaeology, the study of subcultures, and an emphasis on survey, landscape and small settlements lead them to take a longer and a broader view, and to turn less readily than before to literary sources for 'corroboration' of detailed hypotheses. Late antiquity – a period of cultural change and acculturation on a grand scale – offers tremendous scope in this direction, with consequent changes in how historians interpret the period and what questions they ask.

One such question is how far the influence of the state actually penetrated. Despite the political shifts, when seen from the longer perspective it is arguable that neither the establishment of the barbarian kingdoms in the west nor the Arab conquests brought the degree of change in the underlying social and economic structures of Europe that can be seen from the eleventh century onwards.[21] In northern Europe, one may point to a difference between the agricultural methods and crops more suitable to the heavy northern soil and colder climate of northern Germany and France and the wine- and oil-based economy of the Mediterranean; yet the same northern provinces, with the same ecology, had also been part of the Roman empire. In the east, both archaeologists and historians are agreed that the seventh-century Arab conquests in Palestine and Syria brought little real break in continuity. Much too much emphasis is still placed on the 'collapse' of the Roman empire and the 'transformation' of the classical world, and too little on the long-term continuities.

The search for the causes, in the traditional sense, of this 'transformation' also tends to obscure the particularity of individual experience in late antiquity, the range and variety of which in fact gives the period its undoubted imaginative appeal to modern eyes. A time of rapid change, when local structures were often more meaningful than the Roman state, when people could choose from a variety of allegiances, when differing cultural and mental systems jostled for pre-eminence, is, after all, something that we can all recognize, and with some of whose problems we might identify in the post-modern world. This was a time of change and of state-formation; new ways of constructing social identity were coming into being all round the Mediterranean, without as yet any certainty as to which ones would survive. History is about change, and those who are living in the middle of it are the last to recognize it for what it really is;[22] those who write about it from the vantage point of many centuries of hindsight need to be careful not to impose patterns and sharp breaks when the reality was very different.

The date of AD 700 suggested as an end point for this book is of course somewhat arbitrary, given the elasticity with which the concept of late antiquity is currently deployed. At the same time it acts as a marker to indicate that by the mid-eighth century, western Europe, Byzantium and the east looked different, and that each had undergone a period of sometimes painful adaptation. The coronation of Charlemagne as emperor by the pope in Rome on Christmas Day, AD 800, in one sense marked the transformation of the Frankish and Carolingian kingdom and asserted a theoretical equality with the empire at Constantinople that was underpinned by the dream of a possible marriage alliance with the Empress Irene. The eighth-century emperors of Byzantium had struggled with military defeat, depopulation of the capital and enormous loss of territory and achieved administrative, military and fiscal change. The divisions of loyalty which surrounded the eighth and ninth-century debate about religious images were not yet over, but the beginnings of intellectual revival in Byzantium were already apparent. In the east, the building of the new round city of Baghdad by the Caliph al-Mansur and its replacement of Damascus as the new capital of the Abbasid dynasty represented a cultural as well as a geographical move towards the east. We can continue to debate about when late antiquity came to an end, but each of these developments also presents new and different challenges for historians.

The last generation has seen an explosion of scholarship on late antiquity, accompanied by a debate about methodology which shows no sign of abating. The notion of a 'benign' late antiquity, with an emphasis on cultural continuity, has come under fire from several quarters, for its perceived lack of economic or administrative content, and for an over-optimistic approach which conceals the actual violence of the period. New approaches to barbarians and identity have also transformed scholarship on the west, and are in turn stimulating a return to older ideas in some quarters. Archaeology is central to these developments, and new discoveries and new research are changing the picture all the time. The debate about late antiquity is sometimes cast in terms of a tension between material culture, warfare and economic history on the one hand and cultural history on the other, but this opposition should be resisted: in a full history of the period all these approaches need to be included. Not only has the rich surviving textual and literary material proved an immensely fruitful field of study, but there has also been a new attention to theological and documentary texts such as the acts of the church councils, with the realization that such material is central to the general history of the period. Contemporaries engaged in fierce arguments and expressed themselves in strong language, which modern historians are learning belatedly to see for what it was. Now too, they are discovering the actual areas of common ground between polytheists and Christians, between different Christian groups, between Christians and Jews and Christians and Muslims. The parameters have well and truly changed.

# NOTES

## Introduction

1 All dates are AD/CE.

2 A forceful case is made for the predominance of Greek in the east in the fifth century (and later) by Fergus Millar, *A Greek Roman Empire. Power and Belief under Theodosius II (408–50)* (Berkeley: University of California Press, 2006), but Latin continued to be used in some official contexts, and still had a lively existence in intellectual circles in Constantinople in the sixth century (Chapter 5).

3 For this see Peter Heather and John Matthews, *The Goths in the Fourth Century*, Translated Texts for Historians 11 (Liverpool: Liverpool University Press, 1991).

4 James O'Donnell, *The Ruin of the Roman Empire* (London: Profile, 2009), argues that Theodoric and the Ostrogoths, rather than the empire run from Constantinople, were the true heirs to Roman values. See generally Paul Fouracre, ed., *The New Cambridge Medieval History I, c. 500–c. 700* (Cambridge: Cambridge University Press, 2005). Peter Brown, *The Rise of Western Christendom. Triumph and Diversity, AD 200–1000*, 2nd ed. (Oxford: Blackwell, 2003) is a wide-ranging and often thought-provoking treatment of these transitions.

5 This is the approach of G.W. Bowersock, Peter Brown and Oleg Grabar, eds., *Late Antiquity. A Guide to the Postclassical World* (Cambridge, Mass.: Harvard University Press, 1999); see Averil Cameron, 'The "long" late antiquity. A late-twentieth century model?', in T.P. Wiseman, ed., *Classics in Progress*, British Academy Centenary volume (Oxford, 2002), 165–91, and several of the articles in *Journal of Late Antiquity* 1.1 (2008).

6 See Bryan Ward-Perkins, *The Fall of Rome and the End of Civilization* (Oxford: Oxford University Press, 2005); Peter Heather, *The Fall of the Roman Empire* (London: Macmillan, 2005); *Empires and Barbarians. Migration, Development and the Birth of Europe* (Basingstoke: Macmillan, 2009).

7 See also his *The Inheritance of Rome. A History of Europe from 400 to 1000* (London: Allen Lane, 2009).

8 Heather, *Empires and Barbarians*, xvii; he casts his subject as 'the astounding transformation of barbarian Europe' (p. 9). The 'birth of Europe' is indeed another current issue.

9 See W.V. Harris, ed., *Rethinking the Mediterranean* (Oxford: Oxford University Press, 2005), and below, Conclusion.

10 M.I. Rostovzeff, *Social and Economic History of the Roman Empire*, 2nd ed. revised by P.M. Fraser (Oxford: Oxford University Press, 1957). Rostovzeff spent the rest of his academic life in the United States, at the universities of Madison, Wisconsin, and Yale.

11 On Jones's *Later Roman Empire* see David Gwynn, ed., *A.H.M. Jones and the Later Roman Empire* (Leiden: Brill, 2008); for discussion of Jones's chapter in *The Later Roman Empire* weighing up various explanations for the fall of the Roman empire, see Averil Cameron, 'A.H.M. Jones and the end of the ancient world', ibid., 231–50.

12 This has come in particular from Italian scholars; see A. Giardina, 'Esplosione di tardoantico', *Studi storici* 40 (1999), 157–80.

13 For orientation, see Luke Lavan and William Bowden, eds., *Theory and Practice in Late Antique Archaeology* (Leiden: Brill, 2003) the first volume in an important series, Late Antique Archaeology, in which seven volumes have so far appeared.

14 J. Elsner, *Art and the Roman Viewer. The Transformation of Art from the Pagan World to Christianity* (Cambridge: Cambridge University Press, 1995); *Imperial Rome and Christian Triumph: the Art of the Roman Empire AD 100–450* (Oxford: Oxford University Press, 1998); see also Eunice Dauterman Maguire and Henry Maguire, *Other Icons. Art and Power in Byzantine Secular Culture* (Princeton: Princeton University Press, 2007).

15 Luke Lavan, Ellen Swift and Toon Putzeys, eds., *Objects in Context, Objects in Use. Material Spatiality in Late Antiquity*, Late Antique Archaeology 5 (Leiden: Brill, 2007) presents material culture in a more dynamic relation to its contexts.

16 See on all these writers A.H. Merrills, *History and Geography in Late Antiquity* (Cambridge: Cambridge University Press, 2005); on Jordanes, W. Goffart, *The Narrators of Barbarian History (AD 550–800): Jordanes, Gregory of Tours, Bede and Paul the Deacon* (Princeton: Princeton University Press, 1988).

17 See W. Treadgold, *The Early Byzantine Historians* (Basingstoke: Palgrave Macmillan, 2007); Theophylact: Michael and Mary Whitby, *The History of Theophylact Simocatta*, trans. with introd. and notes (Oxford: Clarendon Press, 1986); Michael Whitby, *The Emperor Maurice and his Historian: Theophylact Simocatta on Persian and Balkan Warfare* (Oxford: Clarendon Press, 1988).

18 It becomes important in the later part of the period to know the religious orientation of our sources. 'Chalcedonian' indicates someone in the tradition of the Council of Chalcedon, 451; the term Miaphysite (also Monophysite) refers to those who emphasised the divine nature of Christ rather than the two equal natures: divine and human.

19 *The Acts of the Council of Chalcedon*, translated and with an introduction by Richard Price and Michael Gaddis, Translated Texts for Historians 45, 3 vols. (Liverpool: Liverpool University Press, 2005); *The Acts of Constantinople 553, with related texts from the Three Chapters Controversy*, translated with an introduction and notes by Richard Price, Translated Texts for Historians 51, 2 vols. (Liverpool: Liverpool University Press, 2009).

20 See, for instance, Hannah M. Cotton, Robert G. Hoyland, Jonathan J. Price and David L. Wasserstein, eds., *From Hellenism to Islam. Cultural and Linguistic Change in the Roman Near East* (Cambridge: Cambridge University Press, 2009).

21 This is the title of chapter 5 of Ward-Perkins, *The Fall of Rome*, which provides a graphic description. Liebeschuetz, *The Decline and Fall of the Roman City* also argues forcefully for 'decline' in the west at an earlier stage than in the east (where according to him it was also happening by the later sixth century).

22 Michael McCormick, *The Origins of the European Economy: Communications and Commerce, AD 300–900* (Cambridge: Cambridge University Press, 2001), and cf. P. Horden and N. Purcell, *The Corrupting Sea. A Study of Mediterranean History*, vol. I (Oxford: Blackwell, 2000), 153–60.

23 See Alan Walmsley, *Early Islamic Syria. An Archaeological Assessment* (London: Duckworth, 2007), and below, Chapter 9.

24 See Andrew Marsham, 'The early Caliphate and the inheritance of late antiquity (*c.* AD 610–*c.* AD 750)', in Philip Rousseau, ed., *A Companion to Late Antiquity* (Chichester: Wiley-Blackwell, 2009), 479–92.

25 See especially Harris, ed., *Rethinking the Mediterranean*; Brent D. Shaw, 'Challenging Braudel: a new vision of the Mediterranean', *Journal of Roman Archaeology* 14 (2001), 419–53; further, Conclusion.

26 The fourth century is covered in much more detail in D. Potter, *The Roman Empire at Bay AD 180–395* (London: Routledge, 2004), and see Stephen Mitchell, *History of the Later Roman Empire AD 284–641* (Oxford: Blackwell, 2007); more briefly, Averil Cameron, *The Later Roman Empire AD 284–430* (London: Fontana Press, 1993). The post-Constantinian period is covered in Averil Cameron and Peter Garnsey, eds., *The Late Empire, AD 337–425*, Cambridge Ancient History XIII (Cambridge: Cambridge University Press, 1994). See also

Rousseau, ed., *A Companion to Late Antiquity*; Scott Johnson, ed., *Handbook to Late Antiquity* (Oxford: Oxford University Press, 2011).

27 The reign of Diocletian is poorly documented, and has to be understood mainly on the basis of documentary and numismatic evidence: see Alan K. Bowman, 'Diocletian and the first tetrarchy, A.D. 284–305)', in Alan K. Bowman, Peter Garnsey and Averil Cameron, eds., *The Crisis of Empire, A.D. 193–337*, Cambridge Ancient History XII (Cambridge: Cambridge University Press, 2005), 67–89; Simon Corcoran, *The Empire of the Tetrarchs: Imperial Pronouncements and Government, AD 284–324*, rev. ed. (Oxford: Clarendon Press, 2000).

28 For instance, Peter Garnsey and Caroline Humfress, *The Evolution of the Late Antique World* (Cambridge: Orchard Academic, 2001); Clifford Ando, *The Matter of the Gods. Religion and the Roman Empire* (Berkeley: University of California Press, 2008). Constantine's early publicity explicitly emphasized descent from the third-century emperor Claudius Gothicus (268–70); on the model provided by Aurelian (270–75) see Alaric Watson, *Aurelian and the Third Century* (London: Routledge, 1999). On the historiography of the third-century 'crisis', see L. De Blois, 'The crisis of the third century A.D. in the Roman empire: a modern myth', in De Blois and J. Rich, eds., *The Transformation of Economic Life under the Roman Empire* (Amsterdam: J.C. Gieben, 2002), 204–17.

29 T.D. Barnes, *Constantine and Eusebius* (Cambridge, Mass.: Harvard University Press, 1981), is a classic work which by rehabilitating the evidence of Eusebius of Caesarea, presents Constantine as a firmly committed Christian, but disagreements continue; see now out of a huge literature Noel Lenski, ed., *The Cambridge Companion to the Age of Constantine* (Cambridge: Cambridge University Press, 2006); R. Van Dam, *The Roman Revolution of Constantine* (Cambridge: Cambridge University Press, 2007). In sharp contrast with the favourable accounts in Christian authors, Zosimus' *New History* II preserves a very hostile pagan version, claiming also that Constantine built new temples in Constantinople.

30 Eusebius, *Life of Constantine*, I. 41–42; the so-called 'Edict of Milan', declaring religious toleration and issued in connection with an uneasy meeting in Milan in the winter of 312–13 between Constantine and Licinius, promised religious toleration (Eusebius, *Ecclesiastical History* 10.5.2–14), but was hardly an innovation, since the persecution of Christians had already been called off by Galerius in 311 (Eusebius, *Historia Ecclesiastica* 8.17).

31 Theodoret, *Historia Ecclesiastica* I.6, 10. On the emperor's invitation see also Eus., *Life of Constantine* III.15 (commenting on the awe felt by the bishops at being invited to the imperial palace and the drawn swords of the guards).

32 For Constantius see especially T.D. Barnes, *Athanasius and Constantius: Theology and Politics in the Constantinian Empire* (Cambridge, Mass.: Harvard University Press, 1993).

33 Ammianus Marcellinus, *Histories*. 16.10. On Ammianus' historical technique see Timothy D. Barnes, *Ammianus Marcellinus and the Representation of Historical Reality* (Ithaca and London: Cornell University Press, 1998) and Gavin Kelly, *Ammianus Marcellinus, The Allusive Historian* (Cambridge: Cambridge University Press, 2008).

34 Amm., *Hist.* 20.4.

35 See Polymnia Athanassiadi, *Julian. An Intellectual Biography*, rev. ed. (London: Routledge, 1992); Rowland Smith, *Julian's Gods: Religion and Philosophy in the Thought and Action of Julian the Apostate* (London: Routledge, 1995); translated extracts with discussion, Samuel N.C. Lieu, *The Emperor Julian. Panegyric and Polemic*, 2nd ed. (Liverpool: Liverpool University Press, 1992); Shaun Tougher, *Julian the Apostate*, Debates and Documents in Ancient History (Edinburgh: Edinburgh University Press, 2007).

36 Amm., *Hist.* 23.1.2.

37 Amm., *Hist.* 25.5.1–7; 7.5–11.

38 Amm., *Hist.* 25.9.12. For the Emperor Valens see Noel Lenski, *Failure of Empire. Valens and the Roman State in the Fourth Century AD* (Berkeley: University of California Press, 2002).

39 See the discussion in John Matthews, *The Roman Empire of Ammianus* (London: Duckworth, 1989), 191–203. The challenger Procopius sought to mobilise his connection with the house of Constantine (Amm., *Hist.* 26.7.10).

40 Amm., *Hist.* 29.3.9; 29.1.27.

41 Amm., *Hist.* 28.1; they were followed by further trials at Antioch and elsewhere in the east: for the issues involved, see Matthews, *Roman Empire of Ammianus*, 209–17; Antioch and Scythopolis, 219–26. Ammianus on the cruelty of Valentinian, 29.3.8.

42 Amm., *Hist.* 31.1–4; so too Peter Heather, *The Fall of the Roman Empire. A New History* (Basingstoke: Macmillan, 2005), 151–67; see Chapter 2.

43 Amm., *Hist.* 31.12–13. See Matthews, *Roman Empire of Ammianus*, 167–89; Lenski, *Failure of Empire*, 334–67; Michael Kulikowski, *Rome's Gothic Wars* (Cambridge: Cambridge University Press, 2007), 137–43.

44 See Chapter 2; for a detailed introduction to the issues see Guy Halsall, *Barbarian Migrations and the Roman West* (Cambridge: Cambridge University Press, 2007), 376–568; on Adrianople and its antecedents, 165–80.

45 Key works include Walter Pohl, ed., *Kingdoms of the Empire. The Integration of Barbarians in Late Antiquity* (Leiden: Brill, 1997); Walter Pohl with Helmut Reimitz, eds., *Strategies of Distinction. The Construction of the Ethnic Communities, 300–800* (Leiden, Brill, 1998); Patrick T. Geary, *The Myth of Nations. The Medieval Origins of Europe* (Princeton: Princeton University Press, 2002); H.-W. Goetz, J. Jarnut and W. Pohl, eds., *Regna and Gentes. The Relationship between Late Antique and Early Medieval Peoples and Kingdoms in the Transformtion of the Roman World* (Leiden: Brill, 2003). Succinct statement of the issues with further bibliography in Rousseau, *A Companion to Late Antiquity*, 373–75; further, Chapter 2.

46 See Heather, *Empires and Barbarians*, 16–21.

47 See below, Chapter 2.

48 See, for instance, Stephen Mitchell and Geoffrey Greatrex, eds., *Ethnicity and Culture in Late Antiquity* (London and Swansea, 2000); Ralph Mathisen and Danuta Schanzer, eds., *Romans, Barbarians and the Transformation of the Roman World* (Farnham: Ashgate, 2011).

49 Heather, *Fall of the Roman Empire* (Heather returns to the theme, with more discussion of the revisionist approaches in *Empires and Barbarians*, asserting the greater importance of 'development' as opposed to 'migration, but still emphasising the role of violence and the key importance of the Huns); see also Ward-Perkins, *The Fall of Rome*. A stress on violence rather than integration is also the theme of Brent D. Shaw, 'War and violence', in Bowersock, Brown and Grabar, eds., *Late Antiquity*, 130–69.

50 Themistius, *Oration* 16.210 b–c.

51 See Alan Cameron, 'The last pagans of Rome', in William V. Harris, ed., *The Transformations of Urbs Roma in Late Antiquity* (Portsmouth, RI: Journal of Roman Archaeology, 1999), 109–21; id., *The Last Pagans of Rome* (Oxford: Oxford University Press, 2010).

52 See Neil McLynn, *Ambrose of Milan. Church and Court in a Christian Capital* (Berkeley: University of California Press, 1994); J.H.W.G. Liebeschuetz, *Ambrose of Milan. Political Letters and Speeches*, trans. with introduction and notes, with the assistance of Carole Hill, Translated Texts for Historians 43 (Liverpool: Liverpool University Press, 2005); however, see Alan Cameron, *The Last Pagans of Rome*, 39–46 for a sceptical view of the supposed clash between Symmachus and Ambrose.

53 On John Chrysostom see Wendy Mayer and Pauline Allen, eds., *John Chrysostom* (London: Routledge, 2000); J.H.W.G. Liebeschuetz, *Barbarians and Bishops. Army, Church and State in the Age of Arcadius and Chrysostom* (Oxford: Clarendon Press, 1990); on the importance of preaching in this period, see Mary B. Cunningham and Pauline Allen, eds., *Preacher and Audience. Studies in Early Christian and Byzantine Homiletics* (Leiden: Brill, 1998).

54 For the laws dealing with heretics, for which a precedent had been set by legislation against Manichaeism brought in by Diocletian and Maximian, see Caroline Humfress, *Orthodoxy and the Courts in Late Antiquity* (Oxford: Oxford University Press, 2007), 243–68. But the legal evidence is difficult to use, and does not straightforwardly support the common view that Christianity now became the only official religion of the empire: see the excellent discussion by Neil McLynn, 'Pagans in a Christian empire', in Rousseau, ed., *A Companion to Late Antiquity*, 572–87. Late Roman legislation and the law codes in particular have been the subject of several important recent discussions: see in particular John F. Matthews, *Laying Down the Law. A Study of the Theodosian Code* (New Haven: Yale University Press, 2000); Jill

Harries, *Law and Empire in Late Antiquity* (Cambridge: Cambridge University Press, 1999); Ralph Mathisen, ed., *Law, Society and Authority in Late Antiquity* (Oxford: Oxford University Press, 2001).

55  A point well made by Rita Lizzi Testa, 'The late antique bishop: image and reality', in Rousseau, *A Companion to Late Antiquity*, 523–38; see also for deconstruction of Theodosius' legislation Alan Cameron, *The Last Pagans of Rome*, 60–2.

56  Humfress, *Orthodoxy and the Courts*, 249.

57  The fundamental work on administrative and military organisation remains Jones, *Later Roman Empire*.

58  For this, see the thoughtful chapter by Thomas Graumann, 'The conduct of theology and the 'Fathers' of the Church', in Rousseau, *A Companion to Late Antiquity*, 539–55; below, Chapter 1.

# 1 Constantinople and the eastern empire

1  Foundation and subsequent history of Constantinople: C. Mango, *Le développement urbain de Constantinople (IVe–VIIe siècle)* (Paris: Boccard, 1985, rev. ed., 1990); G. Dagron, *Naissance d'une capitale: Constantinople et ses institutions de 330 à 451* (Paris: Presses universitaires de France, 1974). See also Cyril Mango and Gilbert Dagron, eds., with the assistance of Geoffrey Greatrex, *Constantinople and its Hinterland* (Aldershot: Variorum, 1985).

2  Eus., *Life of Constantine*, IV.51; see Introduction.

3  *Life of Constantine*, III.48; Zos., *New History* II.31.

4  Soz., *HE* VII.20.

5  Mango, *Le développement urbain*, 30; see ibid., 23–36 on Constantinople in the time of Constantine.

6  Eus., *Life of Constantine* III.54.2; see S. Bassett, *The Urban Image of Late Antique Constantinople* (Cambridge: Cambridge University Press, 2004).

7  At III.48 Eusebius claims that in Constantinople there were no 'images of the supposed gods which are worshipped in temples'; at IV.36 he reports a letter sent to him by the emperor ordering fifty copies of the Scriptures for the new city. The statues in the Hippodrome: Alan Cameron, *Porphyrius the Charioteer* (Oxford: Clarendon Press, 1973), 180–87. The early sixth-century poet Christodorus of Coptus wrote a verse description of the many such statues at the baths of Zeuxippus, burned in the Nika riot of 532; there was another concentration of classical statuary, including according to later accounts the Cnidian Aphrodite and other famous statues, at the 'Palace of Lausus' near the Mese.

8  Neither survives; for their construction and for Constantius's role, see C. Mango, 'Constantine's mausoleum and the translation of relics', *Byzantinische Zeitschrift* 83 (1990), 51–61 (= Cyril Mango, *Studies on Constantinople* [Aldershot: Variorum, 1993], V).

9  In a similar gesture, Ambrose boosted the status of Milan and his own position by publicly 'finding' the relics of the martyrs Gervasius and Protasius and depositing them in the new Basilica Ambrosiana at a tense moment in 386: Neil McLynn, *Ambrose of Milan. Church and Court in a Christian Capital* (Berkeley: University of California Press, 1994), 209–15.

10  Sozomen, *HE* VII.7; see on Gregory John McGuckin, *Saint Gregory of Nazianzus. An Intellectual Biography* (Crestwood, NY: St Vladimir's, 2001); S.J. Daly and J. Brian, *Gregory of Nazianzus* (London: Routledge, 2006).

11  See J.H.G. Liebeschuetz, *Barbarians and Bishops. Army. Church and State in the Age of Arcadius and Chrysostom* (Oxford: Oxford University Press, 1990); for Ulfila, 'missionary to the Goths', and the political aspects of their conversion, see Peter Heather and John Matthews, *The Goths in the Fourth Century*, Translated Texts for Historians 11 (Liverpool: Liverpool University Press, 1991), 135–53.

12  Liebeschuetz, *Barbarians and Bishops*, 165–70.

13  See Alan Cameron and Jacqueline Long, with a contribution by Lee Sherry, *Barbarians and Politics at the Court of Arcadius* (Berkeley: University of California Press, 1993), 91–102, dating

the speech to 398 and Synesius' departure to 400 and supposing that the surviving speech is not the one actually delivered before Arcadius (93); cf. Mitchell, *History of the Later Roman Empire*, 95–6.

14 Zos., *New Hist.*, 2.32; the classic discussion is by J. Durliat, *De la ville antique à la ville byzantine: le problème des subsistances* (Rome: École française de Rome, 1990).

15 Just how elaborate were the installations that provided the city's water supply is now clear: James Crow, Jonathan Bardill and Richard Bayliss, *The Water Supply of Byzantine Constantinople* (London: Society for the Promotion of Roman Studies, 2008).

16 The most straightforward introduction to the late Roman administrative system remains that of Jones, *Later Roman Empire* chaps. 13 and 16; the levers of power are discussed in Christopher Kelly, *Ruling the Later Roman Empire* (Cambridge, Mass.: Harvard University Press, 2004).

17 See Alan Cameron, *Claudian* (Oxford: Oxford University Press, 1970).

18 Peter Heather, *Goths and Romans, 332–489* (Oxford: Clarendon Press, 1991), 193–224; Liebeschuetz, *Barbarians and Bishops*, 55–85; H. Wolfram, *History of the Goths* (Berkeley: University of California Press, 1988), 150–61; id., *The Roman Empire and its Germanic Peoples* (Berkeley: University of California Press, 1997); see also Michael Kulikowski, *Rome's Gothic Wars from the Third Century to Alaric* (Cambridge: Cambridge University Press, 2007). Knowledge of these complicated events depends a good deal on the tendentious Latin poems of Claudian and the highly political, but allegorical and obscure *De Regno* by Synesius in Greek (summary: Cameron and Long, 103–106), both very difficult sources to use.

19 Zos. *New History*, V.37–51; VI. 6–13; Olympiodorus, frs 7, 11; Soz., *HE* IX.8.9.

20 Augustine's meditations on this theme are contained in his great work, the *City of God*, finished only some years later; Orosius' *History against the Pagans* answered the same questions in far simpler terms and was to become a textbook for the medieval west. See above all Peter Brown, *Augustine of Hippo*, new ed. with an epilogue (London: Faber, 2000). Note that at this period, and in this book, the terms 'orthodox' and 'catholic' mean roughly the same, i.e., 'not heretic'; though the term 'catholic' is more usually applied to the west it is not of course yet used in the sense of 'Roman Catholic', nor is 'orthodox' to be understood as having the same connotations as 'Eastern Orthodox' would today.

21 Now see Fergus Millar, *A Greek Roman Empire. Power and Belief under Theodosius II (408–450)* (Berkeley: University of California Press, 2006).

22 See Kenneth G. Holum, *Theodosian Empresses. Women and Imperial Dominion in Late Antiquity* (Berkeley: University of California Press, 1982); Alan Cameron, 'The empress and the poet', *Yale Classical Studies* 27 (1981), 272ff.; E.D. Hunt, *Holy Land Pilgrimage in the Later Roman Empire AD 312–460* (Oxford: Oxford University Press, 1982), 220–48.

23 Millar, *A Greek Roman Empire*, 7–13; on the Code, see John F. Matthews, *Laying Down the Law. A Study of the Theodosian Code* (New Haven: Yale University Press, 2000), with Jill Harries and Ian Wood, eds., *The Theodosian Code. Studies in the Imperial Law of Late Antiquity* (London: Duckworth, 1993), and Jill Harries, *Law and Empire in Late Antiquity* (Cambridge: Cambridge University Press, 1999), 59–69 (also on the importance of acclamation and public acceptance, on which see below).

24 See Liebeschuetz, *Barbarians and Bishops*, part III; on the complex sources, see 199–202; also id., 'Friends and enemies of John Chrysostom', in A. Moffatt (ed.), *Maistor* (Canberra; Australian Association for Byzantine Studies,1984), 85–111; J.N.D. Kelly, *Golden Mouth. The Story of John Chrysostom, Ascetic, Preacher, Bishop* (London: Duckworth, 1995); translated texts: Wendy Mayer and Pauline Allen, *John Chrysostom* (London: Routledge, 2000); Elizabeth A. Clark, *Jerome, Chrysostom and Friends* (Lewiston: Edwin Mellen Press, 1979).

25 Alexandria in late antiquity was a vibrant and important city: C. Haas, *Alexandria in Late Antiquity: Topography and Social Conflict* (Baltimore: Johns Hopkins University Press, 1997); Edward Watts, *City and School in Late Antique Athens and Alexandria* (Berkeley: University of California Press, 2006); id., *Riot in Alexandria. Tradition and Group Dynamics in Late Antique Pagan and Christian Communities* (Berkeley: University of California Press, 2010).

26 For the building, which also seems to have housed a library, see J.S. McKenzie, S. Gibson

and A.T. Reyes, 'Reconstructing the Serapeum from the archaeological evidence', *Journal of Roman Studies* 94 (2004), 35–63.

27  Below, Chapters 3 and 7, and see in general Michael E. Gaddis, *There is no Crime for those who have Christ. Religious Violence in the Christian Roman Empire* (Berkeley: University of California Press, 2005); H.A. Drake, ed., *Violence in Late Antiquity* (Aldershot: Ashgate, 2006), part IV; T.E. Gregory, *Vox Populi. Popular Opinion and Violence in the Religious Controversies of the Fifth Century AD* (Columbus, Ohio: Ohio State University Press, 1979). For the way in which the murder of Hypatia was treated by pagan and Christian writers (the sixth-century Neoplatonist Damascius, the church historian Socrates and the seventh-century chronicler John of Nikiu) see Edward Watts, 'The murder of Hypatia: acceptable or unacceptable violence?', in Drake, ed., *Violence in Late Antiquity*, 333–42.

28  See Chapters 5 and 8 below.

29  For the antecedents, with an emphasis on church councils, see Judith Herrin, *The Formation of Christendom* (Princeton: Princeton University Press, 1987).

30  The Greek hymn to the Virgin known as the Akathistos and usually ascribed to the sixth century is dated to the period after the Council of Ephesus by Leena Mari Peltomaa, *The Image of the Virgin in the Akathistos Hymn* (Leiden: Brill, 2001). It is often argued that the Empress Pulcheria particularly promoted the cult of the Virgin, and she was certainly an active influence: see e.g. Holum, *Theodosian Empresses*; V. Limberis, *Divine Heiress. The Virgin Mary and the Creation of Christian Constantinople* (London: Routledge, 1994); Kate Cooper, 'Empress and *Theotokos*. Gender and patronage in the christological controversy', in R. Swanson, ed., *The Church and Mary* (Woodbridge: Boydell and Brewer, 2004), 39–51; but see Richard Price, 'Marian piety and the Nestorian controversy', ibid., 31–38; C. Angelidi, *Pulcheria. La castità al potere (c. 399-c. 455)* (Milan: Jaca Book, 1996). She was certainly a powerful figure before and during the Council, and indeed later: see Liz James, *Empresses and Power in Early Byzantium* (Leicester: Leicester University Press, 2001).

31  On the Council and its Acts, see Thomas Graumann, '"Reading" the first council of Ephesus (431)', in Richard Price and Mary Whitby, eds., *Chalcedon in Context. Church Councils 400–700* (Liverpool: Liverpool University Press, 2009), 27–44; procedures at councils: Ramsay MacMullen, *Voting about God in Early Church Councils* (New Haven: Yale University Press, 2006).

32  See Millar, *A Greek Roman Empire*, chapter 5. An excellent succinct introduction to the councils of Ephesus I, II and Chalcedon is given in Richard Price and Michael Gaddis, *The Acts of the Council of Chalcedon* (Liverpool: Liverpool University Press, 2009), I, 17–51.

33  For Ibas/Hiba, see Robert Doran, *Stewards of the Poor. The Man of God, Rabbula and Hiba in Fifth-Century Edessa*, trans. with introduction and notes (Kalamazoo, MI: Cistercian Publications, 2006), 109–32. Parts of the proceedings are contained in the Acts of Chalcedon, which reviewed the decisions made in 449; otherwise the Acts of Ephesus II survive in two partial sixth-century Syriac translations, one a Miaphysite version highly favourable to Dioscorus: Fergus Millar, 'The Syriac Acts of the Second Council of Ephesus (449)', in Price and Whitby, eds., *Chalcedon in Context*, 45–69, especially 46–49; partial translation of the latter version in Doran, *Stewards of the Poor*, 133–88.

34  See Richard Price, 'The council of Chalcedon (451): a narrative', in Price and Whitby, eds., *Chalcedon in Context*, 70–91.

35  See Brent D. Shaw, 'African Christianity: disputes, definitions and "Donatists"', in Shaw, *Rulers, Nomads and Christians in Roman North Africa* (Aldershot: Variorum, 1995), XI; Brown, *Augustine of Hippo*, 330–39; Erika T. Hermanowicz, *Possidius of Calama. A Study of the North African Episcopate at the Time of Augustine* (Oxford: Oxford University Press, 2008).

36  See Pauline Allen, 'The definition and enforcement of orthodoxy', Cambridge Ancient History XIV, 811–34, at 815–18.

37  For Severus of Antioch see Pauline Allen and C.T.R. Hayward, *Severus of Antioch* (London: Routledge, 2004); Severus was also soon driven into exile, but has left important writings, originally in Greek but now preserved only in Syriac.

38  See J. Nelson, 'Symbols in context: rulers' inauguration rituals in Byzantium and the west in

the early middle ages', in D. Baker, ed., *The Orthodox Churches and the West* (Oxford: Blackwell, 1976), 97–118.

39 See on this Michael Whitby and Mary Whitby, *Chronicon Paschale, 284–628 AD* (Liverpool: Liverpool University Press, 1989), 113–14. Acclamations: C.M. Roueché, 'Acclamations in the later Roman empire: new evidence from Aphrodisias', *Journal of Roman Studies* 74 (1984), 181–99.

40 *Chron. Pasch.*, trans. Whitby and Whitby, 121.

41 Blues and Greens: Alan Cameron, *Porphyrius the Charioteer* (Oxford: Clarendon Press, 1973); id., *Circus Factions. Blues and Greens at Rome and Byzantium* (Oxford: Clarendon Press, 1976); C.M. Roueché, *Performers and Partisans at Aphrodisias in the Roman and Late Roman Periods* (London: Society for the Promotion of Roman Studies, 1992); for the factions in the early seventh century see Chapter 9 below.

42 Christopher Kelly, *Attila the Hun. Barbarian Terror and the Fall of the Roman Empire* (London: Vintage, 2009), 90–8.

43 See on the Vandals, A.H. Merrills, ed., *Vandals, Romans and Berbers. New Perspectives on Late Antique North Africa* (Aldershot: Ashgate, 2004), with bibliography. The economy of Vandal Africa has been a major theme in recent scholarship, as also have the dealings of the Arian Vandals, at times amounting to persecution, with their Catholic subjects, and especially the church: see Averil Cameron, 'Vandal and Byzantine Africa', Cambridge Ancient History XIII, 552–58; Andy Merrills and Richard Miles, *The Vandals* (Oxford: Wiley-Blackwell, 2010); Christopher Wickham, *The Inheritance of Rome. A History of Europe from 400 to 1000* (London: Allen Lane, 2009), 76–8.

44 For 476 see below, Chapter 2.

45 Galla Placidia had formerly been captured in the Visigothic sack of Rome in 410 and married to Athaulf (414).

46 For the Huns, see Kelly, *Attila the Hun*, with helpful bibliographical notes; Galla Placidia: 60–61, 79–81; on east-west relations in the early fifth century, see chaps. 6 and 7.

47 Malchus, frs 1, 3, 16, ed. R.C. Blockley, *The Greek Classicising Historians of the Later Roman Empire* I–II (Liverpool: Cairns, 1981, 1985). The sources for all these events are very scattered, the Greek histories of Priscus, Candidus and Malchus surviving only in fragments.

48 For Byzantine reactions to the fragmentation of the west see Walter E. Kaegi Jr., *Byzantium and the Decline of Rome* (Princeton: Princeton University Press, 1968).

## 2 The empire and the barbarians

1 According to Peter Heather, *Empires and Barbarians. Migration, Development and the Birth of Europe* (Basingstoke: Macmillan, 2009), 22, 'the invasion hypothesis is dead and buried'; for migration see 12–35. Heather's canvas in this book is broader than before, and this book takes in Slav movements and early medieval Europe as well as late antiquity. He has modified his earlier position to some extent in the light of the scholarship described in the text; nevertheless he keeps his main emphases, in particular his insistence on the instrumentality of the Huns: see Michael Kulikowski, *Rome's Gothic Wars from the Third Century to Alaric* (Cambridge: Cambridge University Press, 2007).

2 Trans. and comm. Charles C. Mierow, *The Gothic History of Jordanes* (Princeton, 1915). Discussion of the issues: Edward James, *Europe's Barbarians, AD 200–600* (Harlow, 2009); Guy Halsall, *Barbarian Migrations and the Roman West, 376–568* (London, 2003); see also W. Goffart, *The Narrators of Barbarian History (AD 550–800): Jordanes, Gregory of Tours, Bede and Paul the Deacon* (Princeton, 1988), with Andrew Merrills, *History and Geography in Late Antiquity* (Cambridge, 2005); above, Introduction.

3 For the sceptical view, see A. Gillett, ed., *On Barbarian Identity: Critical Approaches to Ethnicity in the Early Middle Ages* (Turnhout: Brepols, 2002).

4 An important stage in this process was marked by C.R. Whittaker, *Frontiers of the Roman Empire. A Social and Economic Study* (Baltimore: Johns Hopkins University Press, 1994). See

also the discussions in Ralph W. Mathisen and Hagith S. Sivan, eds. *Shifting Frontiers in Late Antiquity* (Aldershot: Variorum, 1996), introduction and Part I.

5 Procopius, *Wars* IV.1.1–8; Anon. Val. 37–38.

6 For eastern reactions: W.E. Kaegi Jr, *Byzantium and the Decline of Rome* (Princeton, NJ: Princeton University Press, 1968). Christopher Wickham, *The Inheritance of Rome. A History of Europe 400–1000* (London: Allen Lane, 2009), is an excellent guide (see his chapter 4 'Crisis and continuity, 400–550').

7 See below, and Wickham, *The Inheritance of Rome*, 102–4.

8 Sidonius was an accomplished author of poems and letters, whose attitude towards barbarian settlers became more and more pessimistic during the period from 450 to the 470s: see Jill Harries, *Sidonius Apollinaris and the Fall of Rome, AD 407–485* (Oxford: Clarendon Press, 1994).

9 Wickham, *The Inheritance of Rome*, 88; *Life of Severinus*, trans. L. Bieler (Washington, DC: Catholic University of America Press, 1965).

10 Heather, *Empires and Barbarians*, 246–56.

11 See Christopher Kelly, *Attila the Hun. Barbarian Terror and the Fall of the Roman Empire* (London: Bodley Head, 2009), 35.

12 Amm., *Hist.* 31.4f.; Eunapius, fr. 42; see Peter Heather, *Goths and Romans 332–489* (Oxford: Oxford University Press, 1991), chap. 4.

13 Olympiodorus, fr. 9; Zos., *New Hist.* V.26; Heather, *The Fall of the Roman Empire*, 192–9: four major incursions across the Rhine between 405 and 408.

14 Oros. VII.37; Zos. *New History*, VI. 2–3.

15 Ibid., 199.

16 Zos., *New Hist.* VI.10.

17 See I. Wood, 'The end of Roman Britain: continental evidence and parallels', in M. Lapidge and D. Dumville, eds., *Gildas: New Approaches* (Woodbridge, Suffolk: Boydell Press, 1984), 1–25; id., 'The fall of the western empire and the end of Roman Britain', *Britannia* 18 (1987), 251–62; R. Hodges, *The Anglo-Saxon Achievement* (London: Duckworth, 1989); S. Esmonde Cleary, *The Ending of Roman Britain* (London: Batsford, 1989).

18 Zos., *New Hist.* VI.6–13; above, Chapter 1.

19 Wickham, *The Inheritance of Rome*, 80–1.

20 Jordanes, *Getica*180ff.

21 John Vanderspoel, 'From empire to kingdoms in the late antique west', in Rousseau, ed., *A Companion to Late Antiquity*, 427–40; Wickham, *The Inheritance of Rome*, 82–87, with chapters 5–7; James, *Europe's Barbarians, AD 200–600*; P.S. Barnwell, *Emperors, Prefects and Kings. The Roman West, 395–565* (London: Duckworth, 1992); P.H. Sawyer and I.N. Wood, eds., *Early Medieval Kingship* (Leeds: University of Leeds, 1977).

22 See Ian Wood, *The Merovingian Kingdoms 450–751* (London: Longman, 1994); Edward James, *The Franks* (Oxford: Blackwell, 1988).

23 Trans. Penguin Classics; for the division of the kingdom between Clovis' four sons after his death see I. Wood, 'Kings, kingdoms and consent', in Sawyer and Wood, eds., *Early Medieval Kingship*, 6–29; the sixth-century historian Agathias includes a history of the Merovingian dynasty in his *Histories*, written early in the 570s (see Averil Cameron, *Agathias* (Oxford: Clarendon Press, 1970) 120–1).

24 On the Alamanni, see J. Drinkwater, *The Alamanni and Rome 213–496 (Caracalla to Clovis)* (Oxford: Oxford University Press, 2007).

25 See T.S. Brown, *Gentlemen and Officers. Imperial Administration and Aristocratic Power in Byzantine Italy AD 554–800* (London: British School at Rome, 1984); brief description in Christopher Wickham, *Early Medieval Italy: Central Power and Local Society, 400–1000* (London: Macmillan, 1981), 74–9; in general, Paul Fouracre, ed., *The New Cambridge Medieval History I, c. 500–700* (Cambridge: Cambridge University Press, 2005).

26 Cf. Wickham, *Early Medieval Italy*, 15: 'The holocaust in Italy came in the great age of wars, 535–93: the shifts of balance under the German rulers, first Odoacer (476–93) and then the Ostrogothic kings (490–553) were trivial by contrast.'

27 After 1,000 years, consuls now ceased to be appointed except when the office was taken by eastern emperors themselves: see Alan Cameron and Diane Schauer, 'The last consul. Basilius and his diptych', *Journal of Roman Studies* 72 (1982), 126–45.

28 Below, Chapter 5; see also J. Moorhead, 'Italian loyalties in Justinian's Gothic War', *Byzantion* 53 (1983), 575–96; id., 'Culture and power among the Ostrogoths', *Klio* 68 (1986), 112–22.

29 For a selection of the *Variae* see S.J.B. Barnish, *Cassiodorus: Variae*, translated with notes and introduction, Translated Texts for Historians 12 (Liverpool: Liverpool University Press, 1992); James W. Halporn, trans., *Cassiodorus, Institutions of Divine and Secular Learning and On the Soul*, with introduction by Mark Vessey, Translated Texts for Historians 42 (Liverpool: Liverpool University Press, 2004); James J. O'Donnell, *Cassiodorus* (Berkeley: University of California Press, 1979). Cassiodorus had been consul in 514, and became *magister officiorum*, praetorian prefect and *patricius*: *PLRE* II, 265–9.

30 This has been controversial: for discussion see Peter Heather, 'Cassiodorus and the rise of the Amals: genealogy and the Goths under Hun domination', *Journal of Roman Studies* 79 (1989), 103–28; Merrills, *History and Geography in Late Antiquity*, 100–15.

31 Procopius, *Wars* IV.1.32–34; *PLRE* II, 233–37; see Henry Chadwick, *Boethius* (Oxford: Oxford University Press, 1981); Margaret Gibson, ed., *Boethius. His Life, Thought and Influence* (Oxford: Blackwell, 1981).

32 See Mark Humphries, 'Italy, AD 425–605', Cambridge Ancient History XIII, 525–51; T.S. Burns, *A History of the Ostrogoths* (Bloomington, Indiana: Indiana University Press, 1984).

33 For the Visigoths at Toulouse see H. Wolfram, *History of the Goths*, trans. Thomas J. Dunlap (Berkeley: University of California Press, 1988), 172–242, and on the aftermath of Vouillé, 243–6.

34 See Roger Collins, *Early Medieval Spain. Unity in Diversity, 400–1000*, 2nd ed. (Basingstoke: Macmillan, 1995); understanding Visigothic involvement in Spain in the fifth century depends very much on the *Chronicle* of Hydatius: see R.W. Burgess, *The Chronicle of Hydatius and the Consularia Constantinopolitana*, ed., with an English translation (Oxford: Clarendon Press, 1993).

35 See Michael McCormick, *The Origins of the European Economy. Communications and Commerce, AD 300–900* (Cambridge: Cambridge University Press, 2001), to be read with Wickham, *Framing the Early Middle Ages*, 708–824. For further discussion see Conclusion, below.

36 Venantius: see Judith W. George, *Venantius Fortunatus. Personal and Political Poems*, trans. with notes and introduction, Translated Texts for Historians 23 (Liverpool: Liverpool University Press, 1995): R.A. Markus, *Gregory the Great and his World* (Cambridge: Cambridge University Press, 1997).

37 P.D. King, *Law and Society in the Visigothic Kingdom* (Cambridge: Cambridge University Press, 1972.), introduction.

38 Cf. Wickham, *The Inheritance of Rome*, 102–103; cf. 102 referring to 'a steady trend [from the fifth century] away from supporting armies by public taxation and towards supporting them by the rents deriving from private landowning'. The question of who owned the land and on what terms thus becomes the critical issue. In *Framing the Early Middle Ages*, 86, Wickham stresses that the fifth century marked only the beginning of the changes.

39 For a (somewhat polemical) account of this methodological change among archaeologists see Heather, *Empires and Barbarians*, 16–18; discussion of cemetery and other kinds of evidence, including place names, in Halsall, *Barbarian Migrations and the Roman West*, 152–61, 447–54.

40 The process is discussed in detail in Wickham, *Framing the Early Middle Ages*, 80–93.

41 Heather, *Goths and Romans*, e.g., 141.

42 For the implications of the gradual erosion of the Roman taxation system in the west see also Christopher Wickham, 'The other transition: from the ancient world to feudalism', *Past and Present* 103 (1984), 3–36; cf. id., *Framing the Early Middle Ages*, 84–92.

43 See R.C. Blockley, 'Subsidies and diplomacy: Rome and Persia in late antiquity', *Phoenix*

39 (1985), 62–74; E. Chrysos, 'Byzantine diplomacy, AD 300–800: means and ends', in J. Shepard and S. Franklin, eds., *Byzantine Diplomacy* (Aldershot: Ashgate, 1992), 25–39.

44 See on this J.H.W.G. Liebeschuetz, *Barbarians and Bishops. Army, Church and State in the Age of Arcadius and Chrysostom* (Oxford: Clarendon Press, 1990), 32–47.

45 Jordanes, *Get.* 146.

46 Zos., *New Hist.* V.36; Oros., *Hist.* VII.38; tariff; Zos., *New Hist.* V.41.

47 Hydatius, *Chron.* 69.

48 So Wickham, *The Inheritance of Rome*, 102.

49 See Jones, *Later Roman Empire*, I, 249–53.

50 Walter A. Goffart, *Barbarians and Romans, AS 418–584. The Techniques of Accommodation* (Princeton: Princeton University Press, 1980); Wickham, *Framing the Early Middle Ages*, 84–87; detailed discussion with bibliography in Halsall, *Barbarian Migrations*, 425–47.

51 See S.J.B. Barnish, 'Taxation, land, and barbarian settlement', *Papers of the British School at Rome* 54 (1986), 170–95; J.H.W.G. Liebeschuetz, 'Cities, taxes and the accommodation of the barbarians: the theories of Durliat and Goffart', in W. Pohl, ed., *Kingdoms of the Empire. The Integration of the Barbarians in Late Antiquity* (Leiden: Brill, 1997), 135–51.

52 Wickham, *Framing the Early Middle Ages*, 86: 'any model that supposes a smooth, merely administrative, changeover does violence to the evidence we have for the confusion of the fifth century'.

53 Stephen Mitchell, *A History of the Later Roman Empire, AD 284–641* (Oxford: Blackwell, 2007), 197.

54 Roger Collins, *Early Medieval Europe 300–1000* (Basingstoke: Macmillan, 1991).

55 See the excellent discussion by Andrew Fear, 'War and society', in Philip Sabin, Hans Van Wees and Michael Whitby, eds., *The Cambridge History of Greek and Roman Warfare* II: *Rome from the Late Republic to the Late Empire* (Cambridge: Cambridge University Press, 2007), 424–58. Ramsay MacMullen, *Corruption and the Decline of Rome* (New Haven: Yale University Press, 1988), Appendix A, 201–4, lists barbarians in the Roman army and in Appendix C, 209–17, instances of soldiers stationed in towns. Jones, *Later Roman Empire*, 606–86, remains essential on the late Roman army.

56 See Benjamin Isaac, 'The meaning of the terms "limes" and "limitanei" in ancient sources', *Journal of Roman Studies* 78 (1988), 125–47. They were not, as commonly supposed, a 'peasant militia' of questionable effectiveness: cf. A.D. Lee, 'Warfare and the state', in Sabin, Van Wees and Whitby, eds., *The Cambridge History of Greek and Roman Warfare*, II, 379–423, at 409.

57 For a generally positive view see now Hugh Elton, 'Military forces', in Sabin, Van Wees and Whitby, *The Cambridge History of Greek and Roman Warfare*, eds., II, 270–309.

58 Jones, *Later Roman Empire*, 207–8, 629–30; good discussion of the cost of the army and the implications of how soldiers were paid by Lee, 'Warfare and society', 401–412. M. Hendy, *Studies in the Byzantine Monetary Economy, c. AD 300–1450* (Cambridge: Cambridge University Press, 1985), 164–8, computes the cost of Justinian's army in North Africa on the basis of the figures given in the sources, and see on the size of the late Roman army Warren Treadgold, *Byzantium and its Army, 284–1081* (Stanford: Stanford University Press, 1995), 43–64; however, it is a dangerous procedure to rely on figures in the sources, which are notoriously unreliable: see Elton, 'Military forces', 284–86. For Justinian's wars and battles see also John Haldon, *The Byzantine Wars* (Stroud, 2001), 23–44.

59 So T.S. Parker, *Romans and Saracens. A History of the Arabian Frontier* (Winona Lake, Indiana: American Schools of Oriental Research, 1986); *The Roman Frontier in Central Jordan: Interim Report on the Limes Arabicus Project 1980–1985* (Oxford, BAR, 1987); discussion in Benjamin Isaac, 'The army in the Late Roman East', in Averil Cameron, ed., *States, Resources and Armies, the Byzantine and Early Islamic Near East III* (Princeton: Darwin Press, 1995), 125–55, at 137–45.

60 Elton, 'Military forces', 293.

61 *Contra* G.E.M. de Ste Croix, *The Class Struggle, in the Ancient Greek World. From the Archaic Age to the Arab Conquests* (London: Duckworth, 1981), 509–18; also Gibbon and many more recent historians: on this see Lee, 'Warfare and the state', 417.

62 See Lee, 'Warfare and the state', 396–98, with J.M. O'Flynn, *Generalissimos of the Western Roman Empire* (Edmonton, Alberta: University of Alberta Press, 1983).

63 Liebeschuetz, *Barbarians and Bishops*, 32–47.

64 For barbarian invasions as the key element (as opposed to internal or structural problems), the classic statement is that of André Piganiol, made at the end of his book, *L'Empire chrétien (325–395)* (Paris: Presses universitaires de France, 1947), 'the empire did not die a natural death, it was assassinated'; see Introduction.

65 For discussion see Elton, 'Military forces', 284–85 (*c.* 500,000 in the fourth century, *c.* 300,000 by the sixth); Jones, *Later Roman Empire* II, 1,042 seems to accept a figure of over 600,000; see also 679–80. On the *Notitia* see J.H. Ward, 'The Notitia Dignitatum', *Latomus* 33 (1974), 397–434.

66 See on this Elton, 'Military forces', 274–78, though with an emphasis on continuity. Michael Whitby, 'Recruitment in Roman armies from Justinian to Heraclius (ca. 565–615)', in Averil Cameron, ed., *States, Resources and Armies*, 61–124, emphasises the reliance on conscription and puts forward a robust assessment of military strength even at the end of our period (cf. 100 f. on the evidence of the late sixth-century *Strategikon* of Maurice). However Heraclius's recruitment for the war against Persia in the early seventh century involved a major effort, and by then there had been a retreat from the Danube region under pressure of repeated Slav migration and attacks (Chapter 9). David Potter, *Rome in the Ancient World. Romulus to Justinian* (London: Thames and Hudson, 2009), 317–34, gives a brief but thoughtful review of the post-Justinianic period and the (multiple) reasons for 'decline'.

67 See Benjamin Isaac, *The Limits of Empire. The Roman Army in the East* (Oxford: Oxford University Press, 1990, 1992); for the east see the spectacular photographs published by David Kennedy and Derrick Riley, *Rome's Desert Frontier from the Air* (London: Batsford, 1990); David Kennedy and Robert Bewley, *Ancient Jordan from the Air* (London: Council for British Research in the Levant, 2004); P. Freeman and D. Kennedy, eds., *The Defence of the Roman Empire in the East, I–II* (Oxford: BAR, 1986); D.H. French and C.S. Lightfoot, eds., *The Eastern Frontier of the Roman Empire, I–II* (Oxford: BAR, 1989) and see below, Chapter 9.

68 Trans. A. Fitzgerald (1930), II, 477.

69 Heather, *Empires and Barbarians*, is right to see this, and to include the migrations of the Slavs (and, he might have added, of Turkic peoples) as a continuation of the story. Similarly the apparently long-lived empire of Byzantium, which in a real sense lasted until 1453, nevertheless changed profoundly at various periods as the world around it also changed: Averil Cameron, *The Byzantines* (Oxford: Blackwell, 2006).

# 3 Christianization and its challenges

1 The traditional term 'paganism' (which I use at times for convenience) is a Christian invention and obscures the actual variety of cults and practice. For the actual continuance of pagan practice and thought see Ramsay MacMullen, *Christianity and Paganism in the Fourth to Eighth Centuries* (New Haven, 1997); F.R. Trombley, *Hellenic Religion and Christianization, c. 370–529*, 2 vols. (Leiden, 1993–94). Alan Cameron, *The Last Pagans of Rome* (Oxford: Oxford University Press, 2010), argues powerfully against the idea promoted in Christian sources of a stark struggle between Christianity and paganism (and defends his use of the term 'pagan' at 25–32).

2 David M. Gwynn and Suzanne Bangert, eds., *Religious Diversity in Late Antiquity*, Late Antique Archaeology 6 (Leiden: Brill, 2010); E. Rebillard and C. Sotinel, eds., *Les frontières du profane dans l'Antiquité tardive* (Rome: École française de Rome, 2010); Robert Markus, 'From Rome to the barbarian kingdoms (300–700)', in J. McManners, ed., *Oxford Illustrated History of Christianity* (Oxford: Oxford University Press, 1992), 62–91, at 62–73.

3 See e.g. Averil Cameron, *Christianity and the Rhetoric of Empire* (Berkeley: University of California Press, 1991); Dale B. Martin and Patricia Cox Miller, *The Cultural Turn in Late Ancient*

*Studies: Gender, Asceticism and Historiography* (Durham, NC: Duke University Press, 2005); Elizabeth A. Clark, *Reading Renunciation. Asceticism and Scripture In Early Christianity* (Princeton: Princeton University Press, 1999); ead., *History, Theory, Text. Historians and the Linguistic Turn* (Cambridge, Mass.: Harvard University Press, 2004). In general see now for comprehensive coverage Susan Ashbrook Harvey and David G. Hunter, eds., *The Oxford Handbook of Early Christian Studies* (Oxford: Oxford University Press, 2008).

4  See Averil Cameron, 'Education and literary culture, AD 337–425', Cambridge Ancient History XIII (Cambridge: Cambridge University Press, 1997), chap. 22, 665–707.

5  See also for different reasons Arnaldo Momigliano, ed., *The Conflict between Christianity and Paganism in the Fourth Century* (Oxford: Clarendon Press, 1963), Introduction.

6  Cambridge: Cambridge University Press, 1965.

7  Thus the period from the fourth to the seventh centuries was defined as an 'age of spirituality' in K. Weitzmann, ed., *The Age of Spirituality. Late Antique and Early Christian Art, Third to Seventh Century* (New York: Metropolitan Museum of Art, 1977), and the transition to Byzantine art has been seen in similar terms: E. Kitzinger, *Byzantine Art in the Making* (Cambridge, Mass.: Harvard University Press, 1977).

8  Vol 2: Charles and Luce Piétri, eds., *Naissance d'une chrétienté (250–430)* (Paris: Desclée, 1995); vol. 3: L. Piétri, ed., *Les églises d'Orient et d' Occident* (Paris: Desclée, 1998).

9  Cambridge: Cambridge University Press, 2007.

10  J. Rüpke, 'Early Christianity out of, and in, context', *Journal of Roman Studies* 99 (2009), 182–93 (reviewing vols. 1 and 2 of the *Cambridge History of Christianity*, and with much to commend in vol. 2 at 188–93).

11  Art. cit., 182.

12  For which see Peter Brown, 'Christianization and religious conflict', in Averil Cameron and Peter Garnsey, eds., *The Late Empire, AD 337–425*, The Cambridge Ancient History XIII (Cambridge, 1998), 632–64; id., *Authority and the Sacred: Aspects of the Christianisation of the Roman World* (Cambridge: Cambridge University Press, 2005); Kenneth Mills and Anthony Grafton, eds., *Conversion in Late Antiquity and Beyond* (Rochester, NY: University of Rochester Press, 2003); Rodney Stark, *The Rise of Christianity. A Sociologist Reconsiders History* (Princeton: Princeton University Press, 1996), for a controversial sociological approach, on which see the special issue of *JECS* 6.2 (1998); W.V. Harris, ed., *The Spread of Christianity in the First Four Centuries: Essays in Explanation* (Leiden: Brill, 2005).

13  For a useful corrective see John Curran, 'The conversion of Rome revisited', in Stephen Mitchell and Geoffrey Greatrex, eds., *Ethnicity and Culture in Late Antiquity* (London: Duckworth, 2000), 1–14.

14  The earliest of these may have been the church known as the Basilica Apostolorum (San Sebastiano), on the Via Appia, which became part of a large and elaborate complex. For a stimulating discussion of Christian funerary practice and martyrs' shrines see Ramsay MacMullen, *The Second Church. Popular Christianity, AD 200–400* (Atlanta: Society of Biblical Literature, 2009), with an appendix listing churches built before 400.

15  Some of these are included in the excellent collection of translated sources by Cyril Mango, *The Art of the Byzantine Empire 312–1453. Sources and Documents* (Englewood Cliffs, NJ: Prentice Hall, 1972, repr. Toronto: University of Toronto Press, 1986): cf. 24–25, prescriptions for what churches should be like; 27–29, the martyrium at Nyssa; 30, church of St Euphemia at Chalcedon; 32–39.

16  But see T.D. Barnes, *Early Christian Hagiography and Roman History* (Tübingen: Mohr Siebeck, 2010), 260–83, arguing against the authenticity of this well-known text.

17  See Daniel F. Caner, with contributions by Sebastian Brock, Richard M. Price and Kevin van Bladel, *History and Hagiography from the Late Antique Sinai*, Translated Texts for Historians 53 (Liverpool: Liverpool University Press, 2010), 18–19.

18  S. Apollinare Nuovo was the palace chapel of Theoderic, who made Ravenna his capital; some of its mosaic decoration was remodelled and the portrait of Justinian inserted when Gothic churches were reclaimed and catholic orthodoxy imposed after the Byzantine reconquest in 554 (Chapter 5): A. Urbano, 'Donation, dedication and *Damnatio memoriae*:

the Catholic reconciliation of Ravenna and the church of Sant' Apollinare Nuovo', *Journal of Early Christian Studies* 13 (2005), 71–110.

19 On the Roman churches, see H. Brandenburg, *Ancient Churches of Rome from the Fourth to the Seventh Century. The Dawn of Christian Architecture in the West* (Turnhout: Brepols, 2005).

20 Eus., *Life of Constantine*, III.50.

21 Cyril Mango, *Byzantine Architecture* (London: Faber/Electa, 1978), is a fine survey. There are many introductions to late antique and Byzantine art; see for instance Robin Cormack, *Byzantine Art* (Oxford: Oxford University Press, 2000), chapter 1. Thomas F. Mathews, *The Art of Byzantium* (London: George Weidenfeld and Nicolson Ltd, 1998), questions some traditional assumption, as does Jas Elsner, *Art and the Roman Viewer. The Transformation of Art from the Pagan World to Christianity* (Cambridge: Cambridge University Press, 1995).

22 For this church, and for the hymn in Syriac which celebrated it as symbolizing heaven, see Kathleen McVey, 'The domed church as microcosm: literary roots of an architectural symbol', *Dumbarton Oaks Papers* 37 (1983), 91–121.

23 See R.M. Harrison, *A Temple for Byzantium: the Discovery and Excavation of Anicia Juliana's Palace-church in Istanbul* (London: Harvey Miller, 1989) poem: *Anth. Pal.* I.10. See Gregory of Tours, *De gloria martyrum*, 102.

24 Marlia Mundell Mango, *Silver from Early Byzantium. The Kaper Koraon and Related Treasures* (Baltimore: Walters Art Gallery, 1986), 98, and see the introduction.

25 Personal communication from the excavator, Dr Grzegorz Majcherek.

26 See Claudia Rapp, *Holy Bishops in Late Antiquity. The Nature of Christian Leadership in an Age of Transition* (Berkeley: University of California Press, 2005); Andrea Sterk, *Renouncing the World yet Leading the Church: the Monk-Bishop in Late Antiquity* (Cambridge, Mass.: Harvard University Press, 2005); Peter Norton, *Episcopal Elections, 250–600. Hierarchy and Popular Will in Late Antiquity* (Oxford: Oxford University Press, 2007).

27 This is well brought out by Rita Lizzi Testa, 'The late antique bishop: image and reality', in Rousseau, ed., *A Companion to Late* Antiquity, 527–38.

28 Neil McLynn, *Ambrose of Milan. Church and Court in a Christian Capital* (Berkeley: University of California Press, 1994); J.H.W.G. Liebeschuetz, *Ambrose of Milan, Political Letters and Speeches*, Translated Texts for Historians 43 (Liverpool: Liverpool University Press, 2005).

29 The classic work on Augustine is Peter Brown's *Augustine of Hippo: A Biography*, new ed. (London: Faber, 2000); for the *Confessions* see the translation by Henry Chadwick (Oxford: Oxford University Press, 1991), and the excellent short introduction by Gillian Clark, *Augustine. The Confessions* (Cambridge: Cambridge University Press, 1993).

30 Theodoret: Theresa Urbainczyk, *Theodoret of Cyrrhus. The Bishop and the Holy Man* (Ann Arbor: University of Michigan Press, 2002); he wrote about these ascetics in his *Historia Religiosa*, trans. R.M. Price, *A History of the Monks of Syria by Theodoret of Cyrrhus* (Kalamazoo: Cistercian Publications, 1985). They included Symeon the Stylite the Elder, who spent decades living on top of a high pillar at Qalaat Semaan; for Symeon see also Robert Doran, *The Lives of Symeon Stylites* (Kalamazoo: Cistercian Publications, 1992).

31 R. Van Dam, *Leadership and Community in Late Antique Gaul* (Berkeley: University of California Press, 1985), 167, and in general on all these issues in the fifth-century west.

32 For Venantius see Judith W. George, *Venantius Fortunatus. A Latin Poet in Merovingian Gaul* (Oxford: Clarendon Press, 1992); ead., *Venantius Fortunatus: Personal and Political Poems*, Translated Texts for Historians 23 (Liverpool: Liverpool University Press, 1995).

33 For the patronage of western bishops, and their exploitation of relics for reasons of local prestige, see Peter Brown, *The Cult of the Saints. Its Rise and Function in Western Christianity* (London: SCM Press, 1981). There is a great deal of evidence for fifth- and sixth-century Gaul, where Caesarius of Arles (502–42) later exercised a more provincial but essentially similar role: see C.E. Stancliffe, *St. Martin and his Hagiographer. History and Miracle in Sulpicius Severus* (Oxford: Clarendon Press, 1983); Danuta Shanzer and Ian N. Wood, *Avitus of Vienne: Letters and Selected Prose*, Translated Texts for Historians 38 (Liverpool: Liverpool University Press, 2002); on Caesarius, see W. Klingshirn, *Caesarius of Arles. The Making of a Christian Community in Late Antique Gaul* (Cambridge: Cambridge University Press, 1994),

and *Caesarius of Arles: Life, Testament, Letters*, Translated Texts for Historians 19 (Liverpool: Liverpool University Press, 1994).

34 This is discussed in detail from the reign of Constantine onwards in an important though difficult book by G. Dagron, *Emperor and Priest. The Imperial Office in Byzantium*, Eng. trans. (Cambridge: Cambridge University Press, 2003).

35 The main account is by the ecclesiastical historian Rufinus (*HE* II.22–30), but this needs careful analysis: for discussion, see Johannes Hahn, Stephen Emmel and Ulrich Gotter, eds., *From Temple to Church. Destruction and Renewal of Local Cultic Topography in Late Antiquity* (Leiden: Brill, 2008); Edward J. Watts, *Riot in Alexandria. Tradition and Group Dynamics in Late Antique Pagan and Christian Communities* (Berkeley: University of California Press, 2010), 192–98: see Chapter 1.

36 G. Fowden, 'Bishops and temples in the eastern Roman empire, AD 320–435', *Journal of Theological Studies*, n.s. 29 (1978), 53–78; B. Caseau, 'The fate of rural temples in late antiquity and the Christianisation of the countryside', in William Bowden, Luke Lavan and Carlos Machado, eds., *Recent Research on the Late Antique Countryside*, Late Antique Archaeology 2 (Leiden: Brill, 2004), 105–44; ead., 'Sacred landscapes', in G.W. Bowersock, Peter Brown and Oleg Grabar, eds., *Late Antiquity. A Guide to the Post-Classical World* (Cambridge, Mass.: Harvard University Press, 1999), 21–59.

37 See Michael E. Gaddis, *There is no Crime for those who have Christ. Religious Violence in the Christian Roman Empire* (Berkeley: University of California Press, 2005); P. Chuvin, *A Chronicle of the Last Pagans*, Eng. trans., (Cambridge, Mass.: Harvard University Press, 1990).

38 See R.M. Price, *The Acts of the Council of Constantinople of 553, with Related Texts on the Three Chapters Controversy*, 2 vols., Translated Texts for Historians 51 (Liverpool: Liverpool University Press, 2009); C. Sotinel, 'Emperors and popes in the sixth century: the western view', in Michael Maas, ed., *The Cambridge Companion to the Age of Justinian* (Cambridge: Cambrdge University Press, 2005), 267–90; for the antecedents to the council of 553, Justinian's strenuous efforts to resolve matters and the vacillations and ill-treatment of Vigilius, see Celia Chazelle and Catherine Cubitt, eds., *The Crisis of the Oikoumene: the Three Chapters and the Failed Quest for Unity in the Sixth-Century Mediterranean* (Turnhout, 2007). Decision-making at church councils: Ramsay MacMullen, *Voting about God in Early Church Councils* (New Haven: Yale University Press, 2006).

39 See for a clear short treatment Michael Gaddis, 'The political church: religion and the state', in Rousseau, ed., *A Companion to Late Antiquity*, 511–24.

40 See now the full documentation from the council, translated with notes by R.M. Price, with Michael Gaddis, *The Acts of the Council of Chalcedon*, 3 vols. Translated Texts for Historians 45 (Liverpool: Liverpool University Press, 2009); Chapter 1 above.

41 See Chapters 5 and 8, with Susan Ashbrook Harvey, 'Remembering pain: Syriac historiography and the separation of the churches', *Byzantion* 58 (1988), 295–308.

42 See also the sixth-century treatise by Agapetus translated by Peter Bell, *Three Political Voices from the Age of Justinian*. Agapetus, *Advice to the Emperor, Dialogue on Political Science*, Paul the Silentiary, *Description of Hagia Sophia*, Translated Texts for Historians 52 (Liverpool: Liverpool University Press, 2009); Dagron, *Emperor and Priest*.

43 See Jones, *Later Roman Empire*, II, chapter 22 ('The church').

44 Eus., *Life of Constantine* III. 41–6.

45 See E.D. Hunt, *Holy Land Pilgrimage in the Later Roman Empire AD 312–460* (Oxford: Clarendon Press, 1982).

46 Socrates, *HE* VII.47; Clark, *Life of Melania*, 56; Evagrius, *HE* I.20.

47 *Life of Melania*, 58.

48 See Holum, *Theodosian Empresses*; Alan Cameron, 'The empress and the poet: paganism and politics at the court of Theodosius II', *Yale Classical Studies* 27 (1982), 272–89; Eudocia's verse inscription on the baths at Hammat Gader on the east coast of the Sea of Galilee: J. Green and Y. Tsafrir, 'Greek inscriptions from Hammat Gader: a poem by the Empress Eudocia and two building inscriptions', *Israel Exploration Journal* 32 (1982), 77–91.

49  On Theodora see Volker-Lorenz Menze, *Justinian and the Making of the Syrian Orthodox Church* (Oxford: Oxford University Press, 2008); Chapter 5 below.

50  Procopius, *Secret History* 17.5; cf. *Buildings* I.9.2; she is presented sympathetically by the Miaphysite writer John of Ephesus, see Menze, ibid.

51  See Virginia Burrus, ed., *Late Ancient Christianity* (Minneapolis: Fortress Press, 2005); Derek Krueger, ed., *Byzantine Christianity* (Minneapolis: Fortress Press, 2006), vols. 2 and 3 in the series A People's History of Christianity; cf. Kimberley Diane Bowes, *Private Worship, Public Values and Religious Change in Late Antiquity* (Cambridge: Cambridge University Press, 2008), focusing on private chapels and places of worship.

52  John of Ephesus, *HE* III.3.36.

53  *Sardis VII*, no. 19.

54  The extent to which the secondary literature has tended to be coloured by confessional approaches and assumptions of the 'triumph' of Christianity makes it difficult to deal with this issue, but see Trombley, *Hellenic Religion and Christianization, c. 370–529*; T.E. Gregory, 'The survival of paganism in Christian Greece: a critical survey', *American Journal of Philology* 107 (1986), 229–42; G.W. Bowersock, *Hellenism in Late Antiquity* (Cambridge: Cambridge University Press, 1990); Neil McLynn, 'Pagans in a Christian empire', in Rousseau, ed., *A Companion to Late Antiquity*, chapter 38, 572–87.

55  F.W. Trombley, 'Religious transition in sixth-century Syria', *Byzantinische Forschungen* 20 (1994), 153–95; Bowersock, *Hellenism in Late Antiquity*, 35–40. Pagan cult seems to have been continuing at Philae in Egypt in the 560s (P. Cair. Masp. I. 67004).

56  For Hellenism and the continuance of classical iconography, especially on mosaics, see Bowersock, *Hellenism in Late Antiquity*; below, Chapter 7.

57  Against the older notions of a 'pagan reaction', in late fourth-century Rome, and another in the 430s, see the powerful rebuttal by Alan Cameron, *The Last Pagans of Rome* (Oxford: Oxford University Press, 2010), with discussion of patronage and iconography at 691–742.

58  Rita Lizzi Testa, '*Augures et pontifices*: public sacral law in late antique Rome (fourth-fifth centuries AD', in Andrew Cain and Noel Lenski, eds., *The Power of Religion in Late Antiquity* (Farnham: Ashgate, 2009), 251–78; pagan priesthoods: Cameron, *Last Pagans*, 132–72.

59  Cyril Mango, 'Discontinuity with the classical past in Byzantium', in Margaret Mullett and Roger Scott, eds., *Byzantium and the Classical Tradition* (Birmingham: Centre for Byzantine Studies, University of Birmingham, 1981), 48–57, at 57.

60  See the *Life of Isidore*, by the Athenian Neoplatonist Damascius, trans. P. Athanassiadi, *Damascius, The Philosophical History* (Athens: Apamea Cultural Association, 1999); Zachariah of Mytilene, *Life of Severus*, trans. Lena Ambjörn (Piscataway, NJ: Gorgias Press, 2008).

61  *CJ* I, 5, 18.4; 11, 10 ('the sacrilegious foolishness of the Hellenes').

62  Evagrius, *HE* V.18; cf. John of Ephesus, *HE* III.27–35, V.37; Bowersock, *Hellenism in Late Antiquity*, 35ff.

63  See R.A. Markus, *The End of Ancient Christianity* (Cambridge: Cambridge University Press, 1990), 202–11, emphasizing the fact that what Caesarius called 'pagan' was often simply a matter of custom and habit. For the process of evangelization in northern Italy at the beginning of our period: Rita Lizzi, 'Ambrose's contemporaries and the Christianization of northern Italy', *Journal of Roman Studies* 80 (1990), 156–73.

64  See Ian Wood, *The Missionary Life. Saints and the Evangelisation of Europe, 400–1050* (Harlow: Longman, 2001); Richard Fletcher, *The Conversion of Europe. From Paganism to Christianity, 371–1386 AD* (London: Fontana, 1998).

65  See Caner, *History and Hagiography from the Late Antique Sinai*, 14–15.

66  *The Last Pagans of Rome*, 25–32.

67  Markus, *The End of Ancient Christianity*, 224–26 (an 'epistemological excision', a 'drainage of secularity').

68  See Guy G. Stroumsa, 'Christianity contested', in Casiday and Norris, eds., *Cambridge History of Christianity* 2, chap. 5. A key work arguing for a late 'parting of the ways' is Daniel Boyarin, *Border Lines. The Partition of Judaeo-Christianity* (Philadelphia: University of

Pennsylvania Press, 2004); see also Adam H. Becker and Annette Yoshiko Reed, eds., *The Ways that Never Parted. Jews and Christians in Late Antiquity and the Early Middle Ages* (Tübingen: Mohr Siebeck, 2003); L. Rutgers, *The Jews in Late Ancient Rome. Evidence of Cultural Interaction in the Roman Diaspora* (Leiden: Brill, 1995). For the torrent of Christian rhetoric directed at the conceptualisation of Judaism see Andrew S. Jacobs, *The Remains of the Jews. The Holy Land and Christian Empire in Late Antiquity* (Stanford: University of Stanford Press, 2004). Both Boyarin and Seth Schwartz, *Imperialism and Jewish Society 200 BCE to 640 CE* (Princeton: Princeton University Press, 2005), argue for the influence of Christian developments on Judaism in late antiquity.

69 See A. Chaniotis, 'The Jews of Aphrodisias: new evidence and old problems', *Scripta Classica Israelica* 21 (2002), 209–42.

70 Zodiac motifs were popular, and there is a striking mosaic of Orpheus from Gaza (though Orpheus is labelled as 'David'); recent excavations at Sepphoris have provided spectacular examples; further below, Chapter 7.

71 The fifth and sixth centuries were the great period of the establishment of monastic foundations in the west: Benedict of Nursia was a contemporary of Cassiodorus, Columba was active in Scotland in the sixth century and died and was buried at Iona in 597, while between his arrival in Gaul from Ireland, *c*. 575, and his death in 615, Columbanus was to found the great centres of Luxeuil and Bobbio.

72 For coenobitic organization, instituted by Pachomius, see Philip Rousseau, *Pachomius*, (Berkeley: University of California Press, 1985). Y. Hirschfeld, *The Judaean Desert Monasteries in the Byzantine Period* (New Haven: Yale University Press, 1992), based on both archaeological and literary evidence, gives a fascinating picture of life in the many monasteries of the Judaean desert in the fifth and sixth centuries, and for the complexities and the politics of late antique monasticism, see Daniel Caner, *Wandering, Begging Monks. Spiritual Authority and the Promotion of Monasticism in Late Antiquity* (Berkeley: University of California Press, 2002); the development of monasticism on Sinai, with individual cells and monastic centres, is well described by Caner, *History and Hagiography from the Late Antique Sinai*, introduction.

73 Trans. Gillian Clark, *Iamblichus. On the Pythagorean Life* Translated Texts for Historians 8 (Liverpool: Liverpool University Press, 1989).

74 See the wide range of extracts in V. Wimbush, ed., *Ascetic Behavior in Greco-Roman Antiquity: A Sourcebook* (Minneapolis: Fortress Press, 1990); Peter Brown, *The Body and Society. Men, Women and Sexual Renunciation in Early Christianity* (New York: Columbia University Press, 1988); Aline Rousselle, *Porneia: On Desire and the Body in Antiquity*, Eng. trans. (Oxford: Blackwell, 1988).

75 Leontius, *Life of Symeon the Fool*, 14; D. Krueger, *Symeon the Holy Fool: Leontius's Life and the Late Antique City* (Berkeley: University of California Press, 1996).

76 P. Brown, 'The rise and function of the holy man in late antiquity', *Journal of Roman Studies* 61 (1971), 80–101, reprinted with additions in his *Society and the Holy in Late Antiquity* (Berkeley: University of California Press, 1982), 103–52; for evaluation and reactions, see J. Howard-Johnston and P.A. Hayward, eds., *The Cult of Saints in Late Antiquity and the Middle Ages. Essays on the Contribution of Peter Brown* (Oxford: Oxford University Press, 1999).

77 Procopius, *Wars* I.7.5–11.

78 See A. Vööbus, *A History of Asceticism in the Syrian Orient*, 3 vols. (Louvain: CSCO, 1958– 88); S. Brock, 'Early Syrian asceticism', *Numen* 20 (1973), 1–19 (reprinted in his *Syriac Perspectives on Late Antiquity* (London: Variorum, 1984); Price, *A History of the Monks of Syria*.

79 The classic work for the west is Brown, *The Cult of the Saints*; see also S. Hackel, ed., *The Byzantine Saint* (London: Fellowship of St Alban and St Sergius, 1981).

80 A convenient list of these collections is provided in Scott Fitzgerald Johnson, *The Life and Miracles of Thekla. A Literary Study* (Cambridge, Mass: Center for Hellenic Studies, 2006), Appendix 2.

81 See P. Booth, 'Orthodox and heretic in the early Byzantine cult(s) of Saints Cosmas and Damian', in Peter Sarris, Matthew Dal Santo and Phil Booth, eds., *An Age of Saints? Conflict and Dissent in the Cult of Saints (300–1000 AD)* (Leiden: Brill, 2011); Matthew Dal Santo, 'Gregory

the Great and Eustratius of Constantinople: the *Dialogues on the Miracles of the Italian Fathers* as an apology for the cult of saints', *Journal of Early Christian Studies* 17.3 (2009), 421–57; G. Dagron, 'L'ombre d'un doute: l'hagiographie en question, VIe-XIe siècles', *Dumbarton Oaks Papers* 46 (1992), 59–68; John Haldon, in V.S. Crisafulli and J.W. Nesbitt, eds., *The Miracles of St Artemios. A Collection of Miracle Stories by an Anonymous Author of Seventh-Century Byzantium* (Leiden: Brill, 1997), 33–73.

82 For a good introduction see G. Vikan, *Byzantine Pilgrimage Art* (Washington DC: Dumbarton Oaks, 1982), with many examples. For Thekla souvenirs see also Stephen J. Davis, *The Cult of St Thecla. A Tradition of Women's Piety in Late Antiquity* (Oxford: Oxford University Press, 2001, 2008).

83 See the excellent study by Béatrice Caseau, 'Ordinary objects in Christian healing sanctuaries', in Luke Lavan, Ellen Swift and Toon Putzeys, eds., *Objects in Context, Objects in Use. Material Spatiality in Late Antiquity*, Late Antique Archaeology 5 (Leiden: Brill, 2007), 625–54.

84 See J. Herrin, 'Ideals of charity, realities of welfare. The philanthropic activity of the Byzantine church', in Rosemary Morris, ed., *Church and People in Byzantium* (Birmingham: Centre for Byzantine, Ottoman and Modern Greek Studies, 1990), 151–64; D.J. Constantelos, *Byzantine Philanthropy and Social Welfare*, 2nd rev. ed. (New Rochelle, NY: A.D. Caratzas, 1998).

85 See Peter Brown, *Poverty and Leadership in the Later Roman Empire* (Hanover, NH: Brandeis University Press, 2002); Margaret Atkins and Robin Osborne, eds., *Poverty in the Roman World* (Cambridge: Cambridge University Press, 2006), with five chapters dealing with late antiquity.

86 Jill Harries, '"Treasure in heaven": property and inheritance among the senators of late Rome', in E.M. Craik, ed., *Marriage and Property: Women and Marital Customs in History* (Aberdeen: Aberdeen University Press, 1984), 54–70.

87 See Richard Finn, *Almsgiving in the Later Roman Empire: Christian Promotion and Practice (313–450)* (Oxford: Oxford University Press, 2006).

88 See Clark, *Reading Renunciation*.

89 Evelyne Patlagean, *Pauvreté économique et pauvreté sociale à Byzance, IVe–VIIe siècles* (Paris: Mouton, 1977), 113–55, and cf. 181–96.

90 Trans. R. Davis, *The Book of Pontiffs (Liber Pontificalis)*, Translated Texts for Historians 6, rev. ed. (Liverpool: Liverpool University Press, 2000).

# 4 Late Roman society and economy

1 So A. Giardina, 'Esplosione di tardoantico', *Studi Storici* 40 (1999), 157–80; id., 'The transition to late antiquity', in W. Scheidel, I. Morris, R. Saller, eds., *The Cambridge Economic History of the Graeco-Roman World* (Cambridge: Cambridge University Press, 2007), 743–68.

2 See Averil Cameron, 'A.H.M. Jones and the end of the ancient world', in David M. Gwynn, ed., *A.H.M. Jones and the End of the Roman Empire* (Leiden: Brill, 2008), 231–49.

3 Ramsay MacMullen, *Corruption and the Decline of Rome* (New Haven: Yale University Press, 1988).

4 M.I. Rostovtzeff, *Social and Economic History of the Roman Empire*, Eng. trans., rev. P.M. Fraser (Oxford: Oxford University Press, 1957).

5 Perry Anderson, *Passages from Antiquity to Feudalism* (London: New Left Book Club, 1974).

6 G.E.M. De Ste Croix, *The Class Struggle in the Ancient Greek World: from the Archaic Age to the Arab Conquests* (London: Duckworth, 1981). For a recent discussion see A. Giardina, 'Marxism and historiography: perspectives on Roman history', in Chris Wickham, ed., *Marxist History-Writing for the Twenty-First Century* (Oxford: Oxford University Press for the British Academy, 2007), 15–31.

7 See for instance A.H.M. Jones's articles on the colonate and taxation in P. Brunt, ed., *The Roman Economy* (Oxford: Blackwell, 1974); Rostovtzeff, *Social and Economic History of the Roman Empire*, chapter 12, and cf., e.g., C.G. Starr, *The Roman Empire, 27 BC to AD 476: A*

*Study in Survival* (Oxford: 1982), 164–5: 'politically the structure of the Later Roman Empire is one of the grimmest of all ancient times'; 'to modern man, the corrupt, brutal regimentation of the Later Empire appears as a horrible example of the victory of the state over the individual'. Peter Brown's review discussion of Jones, *Later Roman Empire*, in his *Religion and Society in the Age of St. Augustine* (London: Faber, 1972), 46–73, is still worth reading, and on Jones's views on taxation and the late Roman economy see Bryan Ward-Perkins, 'Jones and the Late Roman economy', in David M. Gwynn, ed., *A.H.M. Jones and the Later Roman Empire* (Leiden: Brill, 2008), 193–212.

8 J. Banaji, *Agrarian Change in Late Antiquity. Gold, Labour and Aristocratic Dominance*, rev. ed. (Oxford: Oxford University Press, 2007); Peter Sarris, *Economy and Society in the Age of Justinian* (Cambridge: Cambridge University Press, 2006).

9 *De mortibus persecutorum* 7.

10 As argued by e.g. A.H.M. Jones, 'Over-taxation and the decline of the Roman Empire', in Brunt, ed., *The Roman Economy*, 82–9.

11 Christopher Wickham's *Framing the Early Middle Ages. Europe and the Mediterranean 400–800* (Oxford: Oxford University Press, 2005) is an outstanding work which deals with both east and west in a comparative perspective, and see further below.

12 Moses Finley, *The Ancient Economy* (Berkeley and Los Angeles: University of California Press, 1973), 2nd rev. ed. (London: Hogarth, 1985).

13 Cf. Peter Garnsey and Caroline Humfress, *The Evolution of the Late Antique World* (Cambridge: Orchard Academic, 2001); Simon Price and Peter Thonemann, *The Birth of Classical Europe. A History from Troy to Augustine* (London: Allen Lane, 2010).

14 However, a controversial book by Peter F. Bang, *The Roman Bazaar. A Comparative Study of Trade and Markets in a Tributary Empire* (Cambridge: Cambridge University Press, 2008), insists on the inapplicability of the market model, and see id., 'The ancient economy and new institutional economics', review article on Scheidel, Morris and Saller, eds., *The Cambridge Economic History of the Greco-Roman World*, in *Journal of Roman Studies* 99 (2009), 194–206.

15 See for instance Walter Scheidel and Steven J. Friesen, 'The size of the economy and the distribution of income in the Roman empire', *Journal of Roman Studies* 99 (2009), 61–91; Alan K. Bowman and Andrew Wilson, eds., *Quantifying the Roman Economy. Methods and Problems* (Oxford: Oxford University Press, 2009).

16 On the methodological issues see Wickham, *Framing the Early Middle Ages*, 700–8.

17 On which see Banaji, *Agrarian Change in Late Antiquity* and Sarris, *Economy and Society in the Age of Justinian*.

18 R. MacMullen, 'Late Roman slavery', *Historia* 36 (1987), 359–82; C.R. Whittaker, 'Circe's pigs: from slavery to serfdom in the later Roman world', *Slavery and Abolition* 8 (1987), 87–122; Y. Rotman, *Byzantine Slavery and the Mediterranean World*, Eng. trans. (Cambridge, Mass.: Harvard University Press, 2009).

19 Noel Lenski, 'Captivity, slavery and cultural exchange between Rome and the Germans from the first to the seventh century CE', in Catherine M. Cameron, ed., *Invisible Citizens. Captives and their Consequences* (Salt Lake City: University of Utah Press, 2008), 80–109.

20 W. Klingshirn, 'Charity and power: Caesarius of Arles and the ransoming of captives in sub-Roman Gaul', *Journal of Roman Studies* 75 (1985), 183–203.

21 For discussion of this difficult topic, see Cam Grey, 'Contextualising *colonatus*: the origin of the Later Roman empire', *Journal of Roman Studies* 97 (2007), 155–75, especially 156–61, responding to J.-M. Carrié, 'Le "colonat du Bas-Empire": un mythe historiographique?', *Opus* 1 (1982), 351–71, and in turn A.J.B. Sirks (who writes as a Roman lawyer), 'The colonate in Justinian's reign', *Journal of Roman Studies* 98 (2008), 120–43, responding to Grey; see also A. Marcone, *Il colonato tardoantico nella storiografia moderna* (Como: Edizioni New Press, 1988); Giardina, 'The transition to late antiquity'. Labour and social relations in the late Roman world are discussed in Part III of Cambridge Ancient History XIII, pp. 277–370, and by Bryan Ward-Perkins in vol. XIV for the period 425-*c*. 600, at 315–91.

22 Grey, art. cit., 159.

23 So for instance A.H.M. Jones, 'The caste system in the Roman empire', in Brunt, ed., *The Roman Economy*, 396–418; id., 'The Roman colonate', in ibid., 293–307.

24 *CJ* XI.48.21.1; 50.2.3; 52.1.1; Grey, art. cit., 172–73.

25 See Sirks, art. cit., 143.

26 See R. MacMullen, 'Judicial savagery in the Roman empire', *Chiron* 16 (1986), 147–66.

27 On this see Peter Brown, *Poverty and Leadership in the Later Roman Empire* (Hanover, NH: University Press of New England, 2002); almsgiving: Richard Finn, *Almsgiving in the later Roman Empire: Christian Promotion and Practice (313–450)* (New York: Oxford University Press, 2006); above, Chapter 3.

28 For the post-Roman west see Peter Heather, 'State, lordship and community in the west (*c.* AD 400–600)', in Cambridge Ancient History XIV, 437–68. Chris Wickham, 'The other transition: from the ancient world to feudalism', *Past and Present* 103 (1984), 3–36, is a classic discussion of transition.

29 See John Haldon, 'Economy and administration: how did the empire work?', in Rousseau, ed., *A Companion to Late Antiquity*, 28–59, at 53.

30 *CJ* I.55.8, 11; Jones, *Later Roman Empire* I, 758 (in a section headed 'The decline of the councils'). See J.H.W.G. Liebeschuetz, *The Decline and Fall of the Roman City* (Oxford: Oxford University Press, 2001), chap. 3, 'Post-curial civic government', 104–36 and further below.

31 *De Mag.* I.28.

32 Jones, *Later Roman Empire* I, 748; see 740–57.

33 Eusebius, *Life of Constantine* IV.1; see Peter Heather, 'New men for new Constantines? Creating an imperial elite in the eastern Mediterranean', in Paul Magdalino, ed., *New Constantines* (Aldershot: Variorum, 1994), 1–10, also discussing the curial class and the new office-holding bureaucracy (with obvious parallels with the Augustan regime).

34 For examples, and for the geographical spread of senatorial landowning, see Wickham, *Framing the Early Middle Ages*, 162–4.

35 *Hist.* 14.6, 28.4.

36 For discussion, see Ward-Perkins, *Cambridge Ancient History* XIV, 369–77, discussing e.g. C.R. Whittaker, 'Late Roman trade and traders', in P. Garnsey, K. Hopkins and C.R. Whittaker, eds, *Trade in the Ancient Economy* (London: Chatto and Windus, 1983), 163–81; further below.

37 See Banaji, *Agrarian Change in Late Antiquity* and Sarris, *Economy and Society in the Age of Justinin*, and see below; cf. Sarris, 197 (of the evidence from papyri): 'production on the great estates was highly commodified: labour was rationally and flexibly organised, with workers being directed between estate properties; a certain amount of specialisation would appear to have characterised the holdings which the estate comprised, and the surplus produced by the in-hand seems to have been marketed, presumably via the various estate-owned shops and warehouses attested in the sources. Both conceptually and practically, estate management was highly monetised.'

38 Peter Brown, 'Aspects of the Christianization of the Roman aristocracy', *Journal of Roman Studies* 51 (1961), 1–11, is still basic.

39 So too Ramsay MacMullen, *Corruption and the Decline of Rome* (New Haven: Yale University Press, 1988).

40 Christopher Kelly, *Ruling the Later Roman Empire* (Cambridge, Mass.: Belknap Press of Harvard University Press, 2004), discusses the nuances and complexities of the Late Roman system.

41 For the oath see C. Pazdernik, 'The trembling of Cain: religious power and institutional culture in Justinianic oath-making', in Andrew Cain and Noel Lenski, eds., *The Power of Religion in Late Antiquity* (Farnham: Ashgate, 2009), 143–54, and for payment for clergy offices see Sabine R. Huebner, 'Currencies of power: the venality of offices in the Later Roman Empire', ibid., 167–79.

42 *Nov.* 6 (535); *Nov.* 123 (546).

43 Procopius, *Secret History*, 21.9f.; *Nov.* 49.1: governors were now to be selected by the bishops, *possessores* and prominent local residents. The *Synecdemus* of Hierocles, a document in

Greek dating from early in Justinian's reign but based on earlier material, gives a list of eastern provinces and their governors, which can now be supplemented from the *Prosopography of the Later Roman Empire*: see Charlotte M. Roueché, 'The functions of the Roman governor in Late Antiquity: some observations' and 'Provincial governors and their titulature in the sixth century', *Antiquité tardive* 5 (1998), 31–36, 83–89.

44  See A. Wallace-Hadrill, ed., *Patronage in Ancient Society* (London: Routledge, 1989), in particular Peter Garnsey and Greg Woolf, 'Patronage of the rural poor', at 162–6. For patronage in late antiquity see Peter Brown, *Power and Persuasion in Late Antiquity. Towards a Christian Empire* (Madison, Wisc.: University of Wisconsin Press, 1992).

45  Garnsey and Woolf, art. cit., 167.

46  *CTh* 11.24.6.

47  *CJ* XI.54.1, AD 468.

48  Jones, *Later Roman Empire* I, 468–9 (and in general on finance, 411–69).

49  See R.C. Blockley, 'Subsidies and diplomacy: Rome and Persia in late antiquity', *Phoenix* 39 (1985), 62–74; further, Chapter 9.

50  *CJ* 11.1.1; *CJ* 12.2.2.

51  Jones, *Later Roman Empire* II, 1045, 'the basic economic weakness of the empire was that too few producers supported too many idle mouths'. One must remember that Jones believed that the late Roman army had doubled in size since the Principate (ibid., 1046).

52  Jones, *Later Roman Empire* I, 691–705; at Rome there were also free distributions of pork and of oil, the former causing some awkward problems of supply.

53  See Peter Garnsey, 'Grain for Rome', in Garnsey, Hopkins and Whittaker, eds., *Trade in the Ancient Economy*, 118–30; J. Durliat, *De la ville antique à la ville byzantine: le problème des subsistences* (Rome: École française de Rome, 1990); B. Sirks, *Food for Rome. The Legal Structure of the Transportation and Processing of Supplies for the Imperial Distributions in Rome and Constantinople* (Amsterdam: Gieben, 1991).

54  See Wickham, *Framing the Early Middle Ages*, 710–15.

55  Wickham, 716–18, also discussing the relationship between commercial exchange and the 'fiscal movement of goods'.

56  For all this section see Ward-Perkins, Cambridge Ancient History XIV, 377–81.

57  See Jones, *Later Roman Empire* I, 438–48; for the money supply, especially in the east, see C. Morrisson and J.P. Sodini, 'The sixth-century economy' in Angeliki E. Laiou, ed., *The Economic History of Byzantium, From the Seventh through the Fifteenth Century*, 3 vols. (Washington, DC: Dumbarton Oaks, 2002), I, 171–219, at 212–19; a good short survey of both economy and money in the sixth-century east can also be found in Angeliki E. Laiou and Cécile Morrisson, *The Byzantine Economy* (Cambridge: Cambridge University Press, 2007), 22–38, cf. 38–42 on the theory of a downturn after *c.* 550.

58  An overall discussion can be found in Liebeschuetz, *Decline and Fall of the Roman City*, and see Chapter 7 below.

59  See Chris Wickham, 'Marx, Sherlock Holmes and late Roman commerce', *Journal of Roman Studies* 78 (1988), 190–3, who provides a good introduction to the fundamental Italian work by A. Carandini and others, especially C. Panella, 'Le merci: produzioni, itinerari e destini', in A. Giardina, ed., *Società romana e impero tardoantico* III (Bari: Laterza, 1986), 431–59; see also Carandini, ibid., 3–19, for a more theoretical exposition; and C. Panella, 'Gli scambi nel Mediterraneo Occidentale dal IV al VII secolo dal punto di vista di alcune "merci", in *Hommes et richesses dans l' empire byzantin* (Paris: Lethielleux, 1989) I, 129–41. See John Hayes, *Late Roman Pottery* (London: British School at Rome, 1972; *Supplement*, 1980); S. Kingsley and M. Decker, eds., *Economy and Exchange in the East Mediterranean during Late Antiquity* (Oxford: Oxbow, 2001); Sean A. Kingsley, *Shipwreck Archaeology of the Holy Land. Processes and Parameters* (London: Duckworth, 2004).

60  For the prosperity of North Africa in the pre-Vandal period and for the increasing scale of senatorial holdings there, see C. Lepelley, *Les cités de l'Afrique romaine au Bas-Empire*, I–II (Paris: Études augustiniennes, 1979–81); id., 'Peuplement et richesses de l'Afrique romaine tardive', in Morrisson and Lefort, eds, *Hommes et richesses dans l'empire byzantin* I, 17–30. The

Vandal conquest 'broke the tax spine' (Wickham, *Framing the Early Middle Ages*, 711), but exchange continued (ibid., 722). Differences between the western and eastern Mediterranean: ibid., 709, 713–14.

61 See *Framing the Early Middle Ages*, 708–20, 'The Mediterranean world system'; further, Conclusion.

62 Ibid., 716–17.

63 For example Niall Ferguson, *Colossus. The Rise and Fall of the American Empire* (London: Allen Lane, 2004); Cullen Murphy, *Are we Rome? The End of an Empire and the Fate of America* (Boston: Houghton Mifflin Co, 2007).

# 5 Justinian and reconquest

1 Jones, *Later Roman Empire* I, chapter 9, and E. Stein, *Histoire du Bas-Empire*, II, rev. J.-R.Palanque (Paris: Desclée de Brouwer, 1949, repr. Amsterdam: Hakkert, 1968), remain basic; Michael Maas, ed., *The Cambridge Companion to the Age of Justinian* (Cambridge: Cambridge University Press, 2005) is a valuable up-to-date guide, and see also Averil Cameron, 'Justin I and Justinian', in *Cambridge Ancient History* XIV, 63–85; John Moorhead, *Justinian* (London: Longman, 1994); J.A.S. Evans, *The Age of Justinian. The Circumstances of Imperial Power* (London: Routledge, 1996); Averil Cameron, 'Gibbon and Justinian', in Rosamond McKitterick and Roland Quinault, eds., *Edward Gibbon and Empire* (Cambridge: Cambridge University Press, 1997), 34–52.

2 For a clear introduction see Caroline Humfress, 'Law and legal practice in the age of Justinian' in Maas, ed., *Companion to the Age of Justinian*, 161–5.

3 For Tribonian and his activity, see Tony Honoré, *Tribonian* (London: Duckworth, 1978). Jurists were allowed to translate the *Digest* into Greek, but only if they kept very closely to the Latin text.

4 Humfress, 'Law and legal practice', 171–6.

5 See Michael Maas, 'Roman history and Christian ideology in Justinianic reform legislation', *DOP* 40 (1986), 17–31.

6 See Averil Cameron, *Procopius and the Sixth Century* (London: Duckworth, 1985) and further below. The *Wars* were completed in AD 553–4. Despite some voices of disagreement, it still seems most likely that the *Buildings* dates from 554 and the *Secret History* from 550–51; this apparent contradiction is made easier to explain by the fact that the note of criticism of the regime in the *Wars* grows more obvious in the last two books.

7 For the *Buildings*, see below and further, Chapter 7.

8 By Anthony Kaldellis, *Procopius of Caesarea. Tyranny, History and Philosophy at the End of Antiquity* (Philadelphia, PA: University of Pennsylvania Press, 2004).

9 See Peter Bell, *Three Political Voices from the Age of Justinian. Agapetus*, Advice to the Emperor, *Dialogue on Political Science*, Paul the Silentiary, *Description of Hagia Sophia*, Translated Texts for Historians 52 (Liverpool: Liverpool University Press, 2009); D.J. O'Meara, *Platonopolis: Platonic Political Philosophy in Late Antiquity* (Oxford: Oxford University Press, 2003); John the Lydian: Michael Maas, *John Lydus and the Roman Past. Antiquarianism and Politics in the Age of Justinian* (London: Routledge, 1992).

10 See Averil Cameron, 'Vandal and Byzantine Africa', *Cambridge Ancient History* XIV (Cambridge: Cambridge University Press, 2000), 552–69 and further below and Chapter 7.

11 See John Moorhead, *The Roman Empire Divided, 400–700* (London: Longmans, 2001); Neil Christie, *The Lombards: the Ancient Longobards* (Oxford: Blackwell, 1995). Italy: see E. Zanini, *Le Italie byzantine. Territorio, insediamenti ed economia nella provincia bizantina d'Italia (VI–VIII secolo)* (Bari: Edipuglia, 1998).

12 Honoré, *Tribonian*, chap.1. Measures against pagans: *CJ* I, 5, 18.4; 11, 10 ('the sacrilegious foolishness of the Hellenes'); the patrician Phocas, the *quaestor sacri palatii* Thomas and the ex-prefect Asclepiodotus were all put on trial; Asclepiodotus committed suicide, and so did Phocas when he was tried again on the same charge in AD 546.

13  For discussion of the former view, see Cameron, *Procopius*, chap. 2; the latter view is expressed in E. Kitzinger, *Byzantine Art in the Making* (Cambridge, Mass.: Harvard University Press, 1977).

14  Proc., *Buildings* I.10.16 (Belisarius presenting the spoils of Italy and Africa to Justinian and Theodora); Corippus, *In laudem Iustini minoris*, I, 276–89 (pall decorated with Justinian as victor trampling on the Vandal king with Libya and old Rome); II, 121–23 ('Justinian was everywhere', with 'the story of his triumphs' recorded on gold vessels).

15  Proc., *Wars* IV.9.1.

16  On Justinian as a theologian, see Angelo di Berardino, *Patrology. The Eastern Fathers from the Council of Chalcedon (451) to John of Damascus (d.750)*, Eng. trans. (Cambridge: James Clarke and Co., 2006), 53–92. For the relations of Justinian with the eastern churches see Volker-Lorenz Menze, *Justinian and the Making of the Syrian Orthodox Church* (Oxford: Oxford University Press, 2008). Displaced Miaphysite monks and clergy living in Constantinople: see Susan Ashbrook Harvey, *Asceticism and Society in Crisis. John of Ephesus and the Lives of the Eastern Saints* (Berkeley: University of California Press, 1990), 86ff.; not only were they protected by the Empress Theodora, who lodged them in part of the imperial palace, but were also allegedly visited by the emperor for the purpose of theological discussions.

17  Michael Whitby, *The Ecclesiastical History of Evagrius Scholasticus*, Translated Texts for Historians 33 (Liverpool: Liverpool University Press, 2000), IV.39; see below.

18  See Cameron, *Procopius*, chapter 14; Procopius's most fundamental (and classic) criticism of Justinian is that the emperor was a dangerous innovator, a charge which Procopius also laid against Justinian's great rival and enemy, Chosores I.

19  See J.W. George, 'Vandal poets in their context', in A.H. Merrills, ed., *Vandals, Romans and Berbers. New Perspectives on Late Antique North Africa* (Aldershot: Ashgate, 2004), 133–43.

20  Proc., *Wars* III.10–12.

21  Proc., *Wars* IV.9; V.4–5; Amalasuntha was pro-Roman and wanted her son to be brought up like a Roman prince, which annoyed the Goths (Proc., *Wars* 2.1–22, 4.4); for her knowledge of Greek and Latin: see S.B. Barnish, *Cassiodorus: Variae*, Translated Texts for Historians 12 (Liverpool: Liverpool University Press, 1992), XI.1.6 'she is fluent in the splendour of Greek oratory; she shines in the glory of Roman eloquence', and see introduction, ix–xiv.

22  The episode is vividly described in the seventh-century *Chronicon Paschale* (Easter Chronicle) as well as by Procopius and Malalas: Procopius, *Wars* I.24.7–58; Malalas, *Chron.*, 473–77; *Chron. Pasch.*, trans. with commentary by Michael and Mary Whitby, *Chronicon Paschale, 284–628 AD*, Translated Texts for Historians 7 (Liverpool: Liverpool University Press, 1989), 112–27; G. Greatrex, 'The Nika riot: a reappraisal', *Journal of Hellenic Studies* 117 (1997), 60–86. The loss of life is estimated at 30,000 by Malalas, fr. 46 and 50,000 by John the Lydian, *De Mag.* III.70.

23  See Whitby and Whitby, 113, for the source of this dialogue.

24  Proc., *Wars* III.20.1.

25  See Averil Cameron, 'Vandal and Byzantine Africa', 552–69, at 559. One of the main sources for North Africa under the Vandals is the Latin account by a local bishop, Victor of Vita, of the alleged sufferings of the Catholic church and population at the hands of the Arian Vandals; see John Moorhead, *Victor of Vita: History of the Vandal Persecution*, Translated Texts for Historians 10 (Liverpool: Liverpool University Press, 1992).

26  See Maas, 'Roman history and Christian ideology'.

27  For Rome and Persia, see Beate Dignas and Engelbert Winter, *Rome and Persia in Late Antiquity: Neighbours and Rivals* (Cambridge: Cambridge University Press, 2007), and Geoffrey Greatrex and Samuel N.C. Lieu, *The Roman Eastern Frontier and the Persian Wars, Part II, AD 363–630. A Narrative Sourcebook* (London: Routledge, 2002).

28  Agathias, *Hist.* II.30–31; see further, Chapter 6.

29  For Malalas, see Elizabeth Jeffreys, Michael Jeffreys and Roger Scott, with Brian Croke, *The Chronicle of John Malalas* (Melbourne: Australian Association for Byzantine Studies, 1986); Elizabeth Jeffreys, with Brian Croke and Roger Scott, *Studies in John Malalas* (Sydney: Australian Association for Byzantine Studies, 1990).

30  Proc., *Wars* II.7; further Chapter 8 below.
31  G. Downey, *A History of Antioch in Syria. From Seluecus to the Arab Conquest* (Princeton, NJ: Princeton University Press, 1961), 533–46; Greatrex and Lieu, *The Roman Eastern Frontier II*, 104–6.
32  Proc., *Wars* II.22–3.
33  Justinian, *Edict* IX.3; there was also an immediate rise in prices (*Nov.* 122, AD 544).
34  Recent bibliography: Lester K. Little, ed., *Plague and the End of Antiquity. The Pandemic of 541–750* (Cambridge: Cambridge University Press, 2007); Dionysios Ch. Stathakapoulos, *Famine and Pestilence in the Late Roman and Early Byzantine Empire. A Systematic Survey of Subsistence Crises and Epidemics* (Aldershot: Ashgate, 2004). Mischa Meier, *Das andere Zeitalter Justinians. Kontingenzerfahrung und Kontingengenzbewältigung im 6. Jahr. n. Chr.* (Göttingen: Vandenhoeck & Ruprecht, 2003), lays heavy stress of this and other contingent events in explaining sixth-century history.
35  Peregrine Horden, 'The Mediterranean plague in the age of Justinian', in Philip Rousseau, ed., *A Companion to Late Antiquity* (Chichester: Wiley-Blackwell, 2009), 134–60, an energetic and sceptical treatment by a historian of Byzantine medicine.
36  *Wars* II.24.f.
37  Peace terms and status of Christians: Greatrex and Lieu, *The Roman Eastern Frontier II*, 131–34; see Sebastian Brock, 'Christians in the Sasanid empire: a case of divided loyalties', *Studies in Church History* 18 (1982), 1–19, reprinted in id., *Syriac Perspectives on Late Antiquity* (London: Variorum, 1984), VI; below, Chapter 8.
38  For the numbers and the military difficulties during the Gothic wars, see E.A. Thompson, 'The Byzantine conquest of Italy: military problems', in id., *Romans and Barbarians. The Decline of the Western Empire* (Madison: University of Wisconsin Press: 1982), 77–91; brief overall discussion: A.D. Lee, 'The empire at war', in Maas, ed., *Companion to the Age of Justinian*, 113–33.
39  Proc., *Wars* VII.38.
40  See Cameron, *Procopius*, 195–7.
41  Agathias' *Histories*, trans. J. Frendo (Berlin: de Gruyter, 1975); Averil Cameron, *Agathias* (Oxford: Clarendon Press, 1970); W. Treadgold, *The Early Byzantine Historians* (Basingstoke: Palgrave Macmillan, 2007), 279–90; Procopius: Cameron, *Procopius*, 54–5, 189–90. Procopius' disillusionment shows clearly in *Wars* VII–VIII.
42  S.T. Stevens, A.V. Kalinowski and H. van der Leest, *Bir Ftouha. A Pilgrimage Complex at Carthage*, Journal of Roman Archaeology supplement 59 (Providence, RI: Journal of Roman Archaeology, 2005).
43  Chapter 3 above; the materials from the council are translated by Richard M. Price, *The Acts of Constantinople 553, with related texts from the Three Chapters Controversy*, translated with an introduction and notes, Translated Texts for Historians 51, 2 vols. (Liverpool: Liverpool University Press, 2009).
44  Celia Chazelle and Catherine Cubitt, eds., *The Crisis of the Oikoumene: the Three Chapters and the Failed Quest for Unity in the Sixth-Century Mediterranean* (Turnhout: Brepols, 2007); Theodore of Mopsuestia died in 428, before Ephesus I, but like the other two theologians his work was controversial in the fifth century (Chapter 1).
45  His discussions with the 'Syrian orthodox' in Constantinople in 532 had collapsed in the context of the Nika revolt of 532 and a synod called in 536 represented a swing back to Chalcedonians, as a result of which Severus of Antioch was anathematized and his books ordered to be burned. Another issue that arose, especially after 536, involved the teachings of the third-century writer Origen, which were especially divisive among the Chalcedonian monasteries of Palestine represented by S. Sabas, and Origen was condemned posthumously in 553. For all these complex events, and the theological policy of Justinian's reign, see A. Grillmeier, with Theresia Hainthaler, *Christ in the Christian Tradition* 2.2. *The Church of Constantinople in the Sixth Century*, Eng. trans. (London: Mowbray, 1995), 317–473.
46  For a strongly anti-eastern view see James J. O'Donnell, *The Ruin of the Roman Empire* (London: Profile, 2009); for the attitudes of the Roman population in Italy see Thompson, 'The

Byzantine conquest of Italy: public opinion', in id., *Romans and Barbarians*, 92–109; J. Moorhead, 'Italian loyalties during Justinian's Gothic war', *Byzantion* 53 (1983), 575–96.

47 CJ I.27.

48 CJ I.27.2.

49 John Troglita's campaigns, in difficult conditions for the Byzantine heavy cavalry and culminating in 548, are the subject of Corippus's *Iohannis*, eight books of Latin hexameters; for a detailed treatment of Romans and Berbers in North Africa, see Y. Modéran, *Les Maures et l'Afrique romaine (IVe–VIIe siècle)* (Rome: École française de Rome, 2003), with 585–644 on 533–48. It was the Berbers themselves who sent envoys to Belisarius for ceremonial recognition, not the other way round (Proc., *Wars* III.25.3–8; Modéran, 586); when they rebelled just as Belisarius was departing for Constantinople with his captives and also his own elite guard, it came as a shock (Proc., *Wars* IV.8.9), but the Berbers justified it in a letter to the general Solomon on the grounds that Belisarius had let them down (*Wars* IV.11.9–12).

50 Modéran, *Les Maures*, 668–81.

51 CJ I.27.

52 *Wars* II.8.25.

53 So also Modéran, 587, on the unpreparedness of the easterners for the task.

54 Yvette Duval, *Loca sanctorum Africae: le culte des martyrs en Afrique du IVe au VII siècle* (Rome: École française de Rome, 1982).

55 Modéran, *Les Maures*, 645–68.

56 See Walter E. Kaegi, *Muslim Expansion and Byzantine Collapse in North Africa* (Cambridge: Cambridge University Press, 2010), using Arabic sources, and see especially chapter 2 on the tendency of Maghrebi historians to stress the role of the local ('autochthonous') population in relation to the Arab conquests rather than the Byzantine presence.

57 See the collection of papers edited by C.M. Roueché in *Antiquité tardive* 8 (2000), 7–180. The *Buildings* is an extended panegyric, and parts of it, especially book I on Constantinople, fulfil the conventions of the genre, although other parts consist only of lists of sites; its unevenness makes it likely that it was unfinished and its status as a text must always be remembered when using it to provide historical information. It is also far from comprehensive, even in the fuller sections.

58 See e.g. B. Croke and J. Crow, 'Procopius on Dara', *Journal of Roman Studies* 73 (1983), 143–59, with L.M. Whitby, 'Procopius' description of Martyropolis' (*De Aedificiis* 3.2.10–14)', *Byzantinoslavica* 45 (1984), 177–82; id., 'Procopius and the development of Roman defences in upper Mesopotamia', in P. Freeman and D. Kennedy, eds., *The Defence of the Roman and Byzantine East* (Oxford, BAR, 1986), 717–35; id., 'Procopius's description of Dara (*Buildings* 2.1–3)', in ibid., 737–83. For Justinian's building in Greece, see Timothy E. Gregory, 'Fortification and urban design in early Byzantine Greece', in R.L. Hohlfelder, ed., *City, Town and Countryside in the Early Byzantine Era*, New York, 1982, 43–64; and for Illyricum, Frank E. Wozniak, 'The Justinianic fortification of Interior Illyricum', in ibid., 199–209. For the works on the Persian frontier and the Black Sea coast, where the status of Lazica was a matter for contention between Byzantium and Persia see James Howard-Johnston, 'Procopius, Roman defences north of the Taurus and the new fortress of Citharizon', in D.H. French and C.S. Lightfoot, eds., *The Eastern Frontier of the Roman Empire*, 2 vols. (Oxford: BAR, 1989), 203–29 at 217.

59 See Modéran, *Les Maures*, 596–604; D. Pringle, *The Defence of Byzantine Africa, from Justinian to the Arab Conquest. An Account of the Military History and Archaeology of the African Provinces in the Sixth and Seventh Centuries*, 2 vols. (Oxford: BAR, 1981, 2001); J. Durliat, *Les dédicaces d'ouvrages de défense dans l'Afrique byzantine* (Rome: École française de Rome, 1981); D. Mattingly and R.B. Hitchner, 'Roman Africa: an archaeological review', *Journal of Roman Studies* 85 (1995), 165–213, at 209–63; a very important recent study is Anna Leone, *Changing Townscapes in North Africa from Late Antiquity to the Arab Conquest* (Bari: Edipuglia, 2007).

60 Proc., *Buildings* VI.4–5.

61 *Buildings* V.6; see Y. Tsafrir, 'Procopius and the Nea church in Jerusalem', *Ant. Tard.* 8 (2000), 149–64.

62 *Buildings* V.8.9.

63 See Cameron, *Procopius*, 96–8; Daniel E. Caner, *History and Hagiography from the Late Antique Sinai*, Translated Texts for Historians 53 (Liverpool: Liverpool University Press, 2010), 273–82, translates and comments on Procopius' account and that of the tenth-century Arabic writer Eutychius of Alexandria (Sa'id ibn Batriq).

64 Robin Cormack, *Byzantine Art* (Oxford: Oxford University Press, 2000), 48–51; the mosaic dates from between 548, when Theodora died, and 565, when Justinian died himself.

65 See Timothy E. Gregory, 'Procopius on Greece', *Ant.tard.* 8 (2000), 105–14.

66 Garth Fowden, *Empire to Commonwealth. Consequences of Monotheism in Late Antiquity* (Princeton: Princeton University Press, 1993).

67 For the change in atmosphere see Roger Scott, 'Malalas, the *Secret History* and Justinian's propaganda', *Dumbarton Oaks Papers* 39 (1985), 99–109.

68 Proc., *Wars* I.25; *Secret History* 17.38f.

69 See Peter Bell, *Social Conflict in the Age of Justinian* (Oxford: Oxford University Press, 2011); further Chapter 7.

70 For Italy and Spain see Moorhead, *The Roman Empire Divided*, 133–55; the Balkans, the site according to Procopius of 600 fortresses: ibid., 163–71; for the exarchate, see T.S. Brown, *Gentlemen and Officers. Imperial Administration and Aristocratic Power in Byzantine Italy AD 554–800* (Rome: British School at Rome, 1984).

71 Roger Collins, *Early Medieval Spain. Unity in Diversity, 400–1000* (London: Macmillan, 1983), 38.

72 See Brown, *Gentlemen and Officers*, chaps 1 and 2.

73 See Deborah Mauskopf Deliyannis, *Ravenna in Late Antiquity* (Cambridge: Cambridge University Press, 2010).

74 For this see Judith Herrin, *The Formation of Christendom* (Oxford: Blackwell, 1987), 121–5.

75 It is a question whether or not Procopius actually counts Justinian's reign from 518, as argued by the editor of Procopius, J. Haury: see R. Scott, 'Justinian's coinage, the Easter reforms and the date of the *Secret History*', *Byzantine and Modern Greek Studies* 11 (1987) 215–21; Cameron, *Procopius*, 9.

76 *Secret History* 23.20f.

77 See Cameron, *Procopius*, 62ff., and especially chap 13.

78 The apologetic *Life of Eutychius*, written after his death by the deacon Eustratius, and the Syriac *Ecclesiastical History* by John of Ephesus, are the main sources: see Averil Cameron, 'Eustratius's Life of the Patriarch Eutychius and the Fifth Ecumenical Council', in J. Chrysostomides, ed., *Kathegetria. Essays Presented to Joan Hussey for her 80th Birthday*, (Camberley: Porphyrogenita, 1988), 225–47; ead., 'The Life of the Patriarch Eutychius: models of the past in the late sixth century', in G. Clarke, ed., *Reading the Past in Late Antiquity* (Rushcutters Bay: Australian National University Press, 1990), 205–23.

79 For all three see Bell, *Three Political Voices*.

80 For an overview with bibliography see Joseph D. Alchermes, 'Art and architecture in the age of Justinian', in Maas, *Companion to the Age of Justinian*, 343–75.

81 See Averil and Alan Cameron, 'The Cycle of Agathias', *Journal of Hellenic Studies* 86 (1966), 6–25; Claudia Rapp, 'Literary culture under Justinian', in Maas, ed., *Companion to the Age of Justinian*, 376–97.

82 Procopius, *Buildings* I. 1.22ff.; Paul the Silentiary. *Description of Hagia Sophia*; translations: Mango, *Art*, 72–102; see Bell, *Three Political Voices*, 189–212; Mary Whitby, 'The occasion of Paul the Silentiary's *Ekphrasis* of S. Sophia', *Classical Quarterly* 35 (1985), 215–28; Paul Magdalino and Ruth Macrides, 'The architecture of ekphrasis: the construction and context of Paul the Silentiary's poem on S. Sophia', *Byzantine and Modern Greek Studies* 12 (1988), 47–82.

83 On Romanos see Derek Krueger, *Writing and Holiness. The Practice of Authorship in the Early Christian East* (Philadelphia, PA: University of Pennsylvania Press, 2004), chapter 8.

84 For Latin writers in Constantinople, see Averil Cameron, 'Roman studies in sixth-century

Constantinople', in Philip Rousseau and Manolis Papoutsakis, eds., *Transformations of Late Antiquity. Essays for Peter Brown* (Aldershot, 2009), 15–36.

85 See also Sarris, *Economy and Society in the Age of Justinian*, for emphasis on the fiscal exhaustion of the state in the post-Justinianic period.

## 6 Late antique culture and private life

1 See André Burguière, *The Annales School: an Intellectual History*, Eng. trans. (Ithaca, NY: Cornell University Press, 2009), especially chap. 9.

2 Especially in his *Power and Persuasion in Late Antiquity. Towards a Christian Empire* (Madison, Wisc.: University of Wisconsin Press, 1992), and see Averil Cameron, 'Redrawing the map: Christian territory after Foucault', *JRS* 76 (1986), 266–71.

3 See for example K. Weitzmann, ed., *Age of Spirituality. A Symposium* (New York: Metropolitan Museum of Art, 1980). Peter Brown, *The Making of Late Antiquity* (Cambridge, Mass.: Harvard University Press, 1978), poses the question of how and why an enhanced spirituality developed in the fourth century.

4 Brown, *The Making of Late Antiquity*, 21.

5 For discussion of this concept see *Antiquité tardive* 9 (2001), containing a collection of papers edited by J.-M. Carrié and Gisella Cantino Wataghin, with the overall title *La 'démocratisation de la culture' dans l'antiquité tardive*.

6 The first published volume in the series was Ralph W. Mathisen and Hagith S. Sivan, *Shifting Frontiers in Late Antiquity* (Aldershot: Variorum, 1996); the most recent at the time of writing, the seventh in the series, is Andrew Cain and Noel Lenski, eds., *The Power of Religion in Late Antiquity* (Farnham: Ashgate, 2009).

7 Noel Lenski, 'Introduction: power and religion on the frontier of late antiquity', in Cain and Lenski, eds., *The Power of Religion in Late Antiquity*, 1–17, at 5.

8 Among North American writers on late antiquity an important role has been played by Elizabeth A. Clark, not only in her own writing but also through the lead she has given through editorship of the *Journal of Early Christian Studies* and in the North American Patristic Society; cf. especially her *Reading Renunciation: Asceticism and Scripture in Early Christianity* (Princeton: Princeton University Press, 1999), with Dale B. Martin and Patricia Cox Miller, eds., *The Cultural Turn in Late Ancient Studies. Gender, Asceticism and Historiography* (Durham, NC: Duke University Press, 2005).

9 Some Byzantinists, in a debate led by art historians, tend to emphasize the difference: see Leslie Brubaker, 'Critical approaches to art history', in Elizabeth Jeffreys, ed., *The Oxford Handbook of Byzantine Studies* (Oxford: Oxford University Press, 2008), 59–66; Liz James, ed., *Art and Text in Byzantine Culture* (Cambridge: Cambridge University Press, 2007).

10 Peter Brown's *Augustine of Hippo* (London: Faber, 1967; new ed. with epilogue, 2000) remains classic; short introduction by Henry Chadwick, *Augustine* (Oxford: Oxford University Press, 1986); *Confessions*, trans. Henry Chadwick (Oxford: Oxford University Press, 1991); see Gillian Clark, *Augustine. The Confessions* (Cambridge: Cambridge University Press, 1993).

11 Robert A. Kaster, *Guardians of Language. The Grammarian and Society in Late Antiquity* (Berkeley: University of California Press, 1988) provides a prosopography of Latin *grammatici* (teachers of grammar, which preceded rhetoric in a young person's education) from the fourth to sixth centuries; a great deal is known about education in late fourth-century Antioch, especially through the letters of Libanius, on which see Raffaella Cribiore, *The School of Libanius in Late Antique Antioch* (Princeton: Princeton University Press, 2007), and about Alexandria, on which see Christopher Haas, *Alexandria in Late Antiquity, Topography and Social Conflict* (Baltimore: Johns Hopkins University Press, 1997) and Edward J. Watts, *City and School in Late Antique Athens and Alexandria* (Berkeley: University of California Press, 2006).

12 See P. Lemerle, *Byzantine Humanism*, Eng. trans. (Canberra: Australian Association for Byzantine Studies, 1986), 63–4.

13 Gaza: B. Bitton Ashkelony and A. Kofsky, eds., *Christian Gaza in Late Antiquity* (Leiden: Brill, 2004).

14 See Edward J. Watts, *Riot in Alexandria. Tradition and Group Dynamics in Late Antique Pagan and Christian Communities* (Berkeley: University of California Press, 2010); P. Chuvin, *A Chronicle of the Last Pagans* (Eng. trans., Cambridge, Mass.: Harvard University Press, 1990), 105–11; Alexandria was favoured by the elite of Aphrodisias for the education of their sons: Charlotte Roueché, *Aphrodisias in Late Antiquity* (London: Society for the Promotion of Roman Studies, 1989), 85–93. The evidence of Zachariah Scholasticus, viewed sceptically by Alan Cameron, is defended by Watts, *Riot in Alexandria*, Appendix 2.

15 See Watts, *Riot in Alexandria*, 5–7. More than twenty of these halls have already been uncovered.

16 See Alan Cameron, 'The empress and the poet', in id., *Literature and Society in the Early Byzantine World* (London: Variorum, 1985), III; T.E. Gregory, 'The remarkable Christmas homily of Kyros Panopolites', *Greek, Roman and Byzantine Studies* 16 (1975), 317–24; Bowersock, *Hellenism in Late Antiquity*, 63–5.

17 In general, see Averil Cameron, *Christianity and the Rhetoric of Empire*, and for the centrality of *paideia* in late antique society see Brown, *Power and Persuasion in Late Antiquity*.

18 Proc., *Wars* V.1.2.

19 Claudia Rapp, *Holy Bishops in Late Antiquity. The Nature of Christian Leadership in an Age of Transition* (Berkeley: University of California Press, 2005), 188–95.

20 Cameron, 'The empress and the poet'.

21 For the interconnection between iconographical themes on mosaics and in poetry see G.W. Bowersock, *Mosaics as History. The Near East from Late Antiquity to Islam* (Cambridge, Mass.: The Belknap Press of Harvard University Press, 2006); mythological themes continued to be used in late antiquity in many forms of literature and art, including silverware and on sarcophagi: for one example see Alan Cameron, 'The young Achilles in the Roman world', *Journal of Roman Studies* 99 (2009), 1–22; Bowersock, *Hellenism in Late Antiquity*, 64f.; Nonnus: ibid., 62; Alan Cameron, *Last Pagans of Rome*, 700–2.

22 See the classic article by Alan Cameron, 'Wandering poets: a literary movement in Byzantine Egypt', in *Literature and Society in the Early Byzantine World*, I. For Dioscorus against the Greek and Coptic background of Middle Egypt in the late sixth century: L.B. MacCoull, *Dioscorus of Aphrodito. His Work and his World* (Berkeley and Los Angeles: University of California Press, 1988); Bowersock, *Hellenism in Late Antiquity*, 66.

23 See Chapter 9.

24 Bitton-Ashkelony and Kofsky, eds., *Christian Gaza in Late Antiquity*, with which compare the same authors' study of monastic culture there, *The Monastic School of Gaza* (Leiden: Brill, 2006); Bowersock, *Mosaics as History*, 32, 56, 58, 62; synagogue mosaics: Chapter 7 below.

25 See David Woods, 'Late antique historiography: a brief history of time', in Rousseau, ed. *A Companion to Late Antiquity*, 357–75; G. Marasco, ed., *Greek and Roman Historiography in Late Antiquity* (Leiden: Brill, 2003); W. Treadgold, *The Early Byzantine Historians* (Basingstoke: Palgrave Macmillan, 2007).

26 Alan Cameron, 'The date and identity of Macrobius', *Journal of Roman Studies* 56 (1966), 25–38.

27 M. Rosenblum, *Luxorius. A Latin Poet among the Vandals* (New York: Columbia University Press, 1961). Biblical epic: Michael Roberts, *Biblical Epic and Rhetorical Paraphrase in Late Antiquity* (Liverpool: F. Cairns, 1985).

28 See Michael Roberts, *The Jeweled Style. Poetry and Poetics in Late Antiquity* (Ithaca, NY: Cornell University Press, 1989), with the essays in Patricia Cox Miller, *The Poetry of Thought in Late Antiquity. Essays in Imagination and Religion* (Aldershot: Ashgate, 2001). For the reuse of old material in late antique architecture, inappropriately as it might seem to a modern viewer, see B. Brenk, 'Spolia from Constantine to Charlemagne: Aesthetics versus ideology,' *Dumbarton Oaks Papers* 41 (1987), 103–9; J. Elsner, 'From the culture of spolia to the cult of relics: the Arch of Constantine and the genesis of late antique forms', *Papers of the British School at Rome* 68 (2000), 149–84.

29  A less positive view of late antique literary culture is expressed by J.H.W.G. Liebeschuetz, *The Decline and Fall of the Roman City* (Oxford: Oxford University Press, 2001).

30  Among recent work that of Richard Sorabji is especially important: see his *Time, Creation and the Continuum: Theories in Antiquity and the Early Middle Ages* (London: Variorum, 1983), and the papers edited by him in *Philoponus and the Rejection of Aristotelian Science* (London: Duckworth, 1987) and *Aristotle Transformed. The Ancient Commentators and their Influence*, (London: Duckworth, 1990).

31  At Apamea, elaborate fourth-century mosaics of Socrates with six sages, Odysseus' return, Kallos (the personification of Beauty) and Cassiopeia were subsequently built over when the cathedral was constructed. For these and the mosaics from New Paphos in Cyprus, also depicting Cassiopeia, and the birth of Dionysos, see Bowersock, *Hellenism in Late Antiquity*, chap. 4 and id., *Mosaics as History*.

32  Trans. Mark Edwards, *Neoplatonic Saints. The Lives of Plotinus and Proclus by their Students*, Translated Texts for Historians 35 (Liverpool: Liverpool University Press, 2000); see G. Fowden, 'The pagan holy man in late antique society', *Journal of Hellenic Studies* 102 (1982), 33–59; and for possible archaeological evidence for philosophical teaching at Athens, see Alison Frantz, *The Athenian Agora XXIV. Late Antiquity A.D. 267–700* (Princeton, NJ: Princeton University Press, 1988), especially 56–8, 82–92.

33  For this, see the essays in H.J. Blumenthal and R.A. Markus, eds, *Neoplatonism and Early Christian Thought* (London: Variorum, 1981). The thought of Boethius, expressed in his *Consolation of Philosophy*, was also deeply imbued with Neoplatonic ideas (see Chapter 2).

34  Malalas, *Chronicle*, trans. Jeffreys, 264; Damascius: see P. Athanassiadi, *Damascius, The Philosophical History* (Athens: Apamea Cultural Association, 1999).

35  *Hist.* II.30–1.

36  Edward Watts, 'Justinian, Malalas and the end of Athenian philosophical teaching in AD 529', *Journal of Roman Studies* 94 (2004), 168–82; id., *City and School in Late Antique Athens and Alexandria*; Dominic J. O'Meara, *Platonopolis. Platonic Political Philosophy in Late Antiquity* (Oxford: Oxford University Press, 2005). Simplicius at Harran: I. Hadot, 'The life and work of Simplicius in Greek and Arabic sources', in Sorabji, ed., *Aristotle Transformed*, 275–303, following M. Tardieu, 'Sabiens coraniques et "Sabiens" de Harran', *Journal asiatique* 274 (1986), 1–44.

37  See B. Dignas and E. Winter, *Rome and Persia in Late Antiquity. Neighbours and Rivals* (Cambridge: Cambridge University Press, 2007), 264.

38  For Neoplatonism in Palestinian monastic circles in the sixth century, see I. Perczel, 'Pseudo-Dionysius and Palestinian Origenism', in J. Patrich, ed., *The Sabaite Heritage in the Orthodox Church from the Fifth Century to the Present* (Leuven: Peeters, 2001), 261–82.

39  Henry Chadwick, 'Philoponus, the Christian theologian', in Sorabji, ed., *Philoponus*, 41–56; see also Sorabji, 'John Philoponus', ibid., 1–40.

40  See Robert Browning, *Medieval and Modern Greek*, 2nd ed. (Cambridge: Cambridge University Press, 1983).

41  See Averil Cameron, 'Education and literary culture, AD 337–425', *Cambridge Ancient History* XIII, 665–707, at 698–707; Frances Young, Lewis Ayres and Andrew Louth, eds., *Cambridge History of Early Christian Literature* (Cambridge: Cambridge University Press, 2004).

42  Many examples also show literary affinities with contemporary lives of pagan men: see Averil Cameron, *Christianity and the Rhetoric of Empire*, esp. chap. 3; Tomas Hägg and Philip Rousseau, eds., with the assistance of Christian Høgel, *Greek Biography and Panegyric in Late Antiquity* (Berkeley: University of California Press, 2000).

43  See on this Elizabeth Jeffreys, 'Malalas' world-view', and Roger Scott, 'Malalas and his contemporaries', in E. Jeffreys, B. Croke and R. Scott, eds., *Studies in John Malalas* (Sydney: Australian Association for Byzantine Studies, 1990), 55–86.

44  See D. Burton-Christie, *The Word in the Desert. Scripture and the Quest for Holiness in Early Christian Monasticism* (New York: Oxford University Press, 1993); R.M. Price, *A History of the Monks of Syria* (Kalamazoo, Mich.: Cistercian Publications, 1985); Georgia Frank, *The*

*Memory of the Eyes. Pilgrims to Living Saints in Christian Late Antiquity* (Berkeley: University of California Press, 2000).

45 See Cameron, *Christianity and the Rhetoric of Empire*, chap. 6.

46 The Italian historian Santo Mazzarino used the term 'democratisation of culture': see J.-M. Carrié and Gisella Cantino Wataghin, eds., *La 'démocratisation de la culture, dans l'antiquité tardive*, in *Antiquité tardive* 9 (2001).

47 See E. Kitzinger, 'The cult of images in the period before Iconoclasm', *Dumbarton Oaks Papers* 8 (1954), 85–150; Nilus: Cyril Mango, *The Art of the Byzantine Era 312–1453. Sources and Documents* (Englewood Cliffs, JN: Prentice Hall, 1972, repr. Toronto, 1986), 33.

48 For icons, see Averil Cameron, 'Images of authority: elites and icons in late sixth-century Byzantium', *Past and Present* 84 (1979), 3–25; 'The language of images: the rise of icons and Christian representation', in Averil Cameron, *Changing Cultures in Early* Byzantium (Aldershot: Variorum, 1996), XII; Chapter 9 below.

49 L. Cracco Ruggini, 'The ecclesiastical histories and the pagan historiography: providence and miracles', *Athenaeum* n.s. 55 (1977), 107–26; ead., 'Il miracolo nella cultura del tardo impero: concetto e funzione', in *Hagiographie, Cultures et Sociétés, IVe–XIIe siècles* (Paris: Études augustiniennes, 1981), 161–204; Averil Cameron, *Christianity and the Rhetoric of Empire*, chap. 6.

50 See Richard Finn, *Asceticism in the Greco-Roman World* (Cambridge: Cambridge University Press, 2009), 9–32.

51 See É. Rebillard, *The Care of the Dead in Late Antiquity*, Eng. trans. (Ithaca, NY: Cornell University Press, 2009); shorter treatment by Rebillard in Rousseau, *A Companion to Late Antiquity*, 220–31 ('The church, the living and the dead').

52 See Kate Cooper, 'Gender and the fall of Rome', in Rousseau, ed., *A Companion to Late Antiquity*, 187–200, at 192.

53 Melania: Elizabeth A. Clark, *The Life of Melania the Younger* (New York: Edwin Mellen Press, 1984); on the issues, see the excellent introduction by Judith Evans-Grubbs, 'Late Roman marriage and family relationships', in Rousseau, ed., *A Companion to Late Antiquity*, 201–19 (for Melania, see 208–9).

54 Many of the substantial corpus of surviving letters tell us nothing directly on the subject, and are semi-public and literary in character; however, see.Evans-Grubbs, art. cit., for a discussion based explicitly on personal narratives (Evans-Grubbs, 201). The best source of actual private letters is the papyri, which often preserve fragments of letters written to each other by ordinary people, though these too can sometimes be difficult to interpret.

55 The problem of the evidence is discussed by E. Patlagean, *Pauvreté économique et pauvreté sociale à Byzance, IVe–VIIe siècles* (Paris: Mouton, 1977), 145–55.

56 Brent D. Shaw, 'Latin funerary epigraphy and family life in the later Roman empire', *Historia* 33 (1984), 457–97; contraception: id.,'The family in late antiquity: the experience of Augustine', *Past and Present* 115 (1987), 3–51, at 44–7; infanticide and sale of infants: ibid., 43f. R. Stark, *The Rise of Christianity. A Sociologist Reconsiders History* (Princeton: Princeton University Press, 1995) puts forward the theory of a demographic increase among Christians on the grounds that they cared for the sick and did not practise infanticide; this seems over-simplistic.

57 *City of God*, 19.16.

58 See Shaw, 'The family in late antiquity', 10f. and esp. 28–38; Evans-Grubbs, art. cit., 213–17.

59 Kate Cooper, *The Virgin and the Bride. Idealized Womanhood in Late Antiquity* (Cambridge, Mass.: Harvard University Press, 1996), and cf. ead., *The Fall of the Roman Household* (Cambridge: Cambridge University Press, 1997) and Kate Cooper and Julia Hillner, eds., *Religion, Dynasty and Patronage in Early Christian Rome 300–900* (Cambridge; Cambridge University Press, 2007).

60 But there is much late antique material in Arietta Papaconstantinou and Alice-Mary Talbot, eds., *Becoming Byzantine. Children and Childhood in Byzantium* (Washington, DC: Dumbarton

Oaks, 2009), and see Cecily Hennessy, *Images of Children in Byzantium* (Farnham: Ashgate, 2008).

61  Shaw, 'The family in late antiquity', 39.

62  See Gillian Clark, *Women in Late Antiquity: Pagan and Christian Lifestyles* (Oxford: Clarendon Press, 1993); A. Arjava, *Women and Law in Late Antiquity* (Oxford: Clarendon Press, 1996). Useful discussion of the role played by women in the process of Christianization in Elizabeth A. Castelli, 'Gender, theory and *The Rise of Christianity*: a response to Rodney Stark', *Journal of Early Christian Studies* 6.2 (1998), 227–57.

63  See Elizabeth A. Clark, *Jerome, Chrysostom and Friends*, 2nd ed. (Lewiston: Edwin Mellen Press, 1982).

64  Palladius, *Lausiac History* 36.6–7, trans. Meyer; cited by P. Brown, *The Body and Society. Men, Women and Sexual Renunciation in Early Christianity* (New York: Columbia University Press, 1988), 378.

65  See Averil Cameron, *Christianity and the Rhetoric of Empire*, 165ff. For the tangled mix of ideas and associations surrounding the concept of Mary in relation to women see Elaine Pagels, *Adam, Eve and the Serpent* (London: Weidenfeld and Nicolson, 1988); Averil Cameron, 'Virginity as metaphor', in Averil Cameron, ed., *History as Text* (London: Duckworth, 1989), 184–205; Aline Rousselle, *Porneia. On Desire and the Body in Antiquity*, Eng. trans. (Oxford: Blackwell, 1989).

66  The Greek title *Theotokos* ('bearer of God') was officially accorded to Mary at Ephesus I, and the Akathistos hymn, which became the basis of much later eastern homiletic and devotion to the Virgin is dated to the fifth century by Leena Mari Peltomaa, *The Image of the Virgin Mary in the Akathistos Hymn* (Leiden: Brill, 2001). For the later development of the cult of the Virgin in the east, see Chapter 9.

67  For this and other examples see Benedicta Ward, *Harlots of the Desert* (Oxford: Mowbray, 1987); cf. Sebastian P. Brock and Susan Ashbrook Harvey, *Holy Women of the Syrian Orient* (Berkeley: University of California Press, 1987).

68  For the eastern empire see Joëlle Beaucamp, *Le statut de la femme à Byzance (4e–7e siècle) I. Le droit impérial* (Paris: Diffusion de Boccard, 1990), II. *Les pratiques sociales* (Paris: Diffusion de Boccard, 1992), drawing on the papyrological evidence. For Roman women under Germanic rule, see Cooper, 'Gender and the fall of Rome', 197–8.

69  See Virginia Burrus, *Begotten, Not Made: Conceiving Manhood in Late Antiquity* (Stanford: Stanford University Press, 2000); for Kate Cooper, Christianization also implies a redefinition of earlier ideals of Roman manliness, with the household as the locus of gender challenges to both men and women; see Cooper, 'Gender and the fall of Rome'; ead., 'Approaching the holy household', *Journal of Early Christian Studies* 15 (2007), 131–42.

70  Shaun Tougher, ed., *Eunuchs in Antiquity and Beyond* (London: Duckworth, 2002); Kathryn Ringrose, *The Perfect Servant. Eunuchs and the Social Construction of Gender in Byzantium* (Chicago, Ill; University of Chicago Press, 2003).

71  For some publications specifically directed at this field, see e.g. Michael Grünbart, Ewald Kislinger, Anna Muthesius and Dionysios Stathakopoulos, eds., *Material Culture and Well-being in Byzantium (400–1453)* (Vienna: Verlag der Österreichischen Akademie der Wissenschaften, 2007); Luke Lavan, Ellen Swift and Toon Putzeys, eds., *Objects in Context, Objects in Use. Material Spatiality in Late Antiquity*, Late Antique Archaeology 5 (Leiden: Brill, 2007); some studies focus on particular aspects, though not from a material culture perspective, e.g. Susan Ashbrook Harvey, *Scenting Salvation: Ancient Christianity and the Olfactory Imagination* (Berkeley: University of California Press, 2006); B. Caseau, 'Christian bodies: the senses and early Byzantine Christianity', in Liz James, ed., *Desire and Denial in Byzanrtium*, Publications of the Society for the Promotion of Byzantine Studies 6 (Aldershot: Ashgate, 1999), 101–10.

72  Above, n. 9, and cf. also Leslie Brubaker and John Haldon, *Byzantium in the Iconoclast Era (c. 680–850). The Sources: An Annotated Survey* (Aldershot: Ashgate, 2001).

73  Cf. the controversial work of A. Gell, *Art and Agency: an Anthropological Theory* (Oxford: Clarendon Press, 1998), with Robin Osborne and Jeremy Tanner, eds., *Art's Agency and Art History* (Oxford: Blackwell, 2007).

74 See Averil Cameron, *Christianity and the Rhetoric of Empire*, esp. chap. 6; Brown, *Power and Persuasion in Late Antiquity*, chap. 4.

# 7 Urban change and the late antique countryside

1 For discontinuity: C. Mango, *Byzantium. The Empire of New Rome* (London: Weidenfeld and Nicolson, 1980), chap. 3, 'The disappearance and revival of cities', with bibliography at 310–11; W. Brandes, *Die Städte Kleinasiens im 7. und 8. Jahrhundert* (Berlin: Akademie Verlag, 1989); see now Helen Saradi, 'Towns and cities', in Elizabeth Jeffreys, with John Haldon and Robin Cormack, eds., *The Oxford Handbook of Byzantine Studies* (Oxford: Oxford University Press, 2008), 317–27; ead., *The Byzantine City in the Sixth Century: Literary Images and Historical Reality* (Athens: Society of Messenian Archaeological Studies, 2006), with the review by L. Lavan, 'What killed the ancient city? Chronology, causation and traces of continuity', *Journal of Roman Archaeology* 22 (2009), 803–12, with Ine Jacobs, *The Classical City in Late Antiquity* (Leuven: Peeters, 2010). For cities in the Near East see further below.

2 All such figures have their problems: for a succinct survey of current thinking on population size and demography from the fourth to seventh centuries see Dionysios Stathakopoulos, 'Population, demography and disease', in Jeffreys, with Haldon and Cormack, eds., *The Oxford Handbook of Byzantine Studies*, 309–16, at 309–11.

3 Fourth-century Antioch is one case where we have the evidence to see this relation in action: see the study by J.H.W.G. Liebeschuetz, *Antioch. City and Imperial Administration in the Later Roman Empire* (Oxford: Oxford University Press, 1972). For Antioch in later periods, see G. Downey, *A History of Antioch in Syria* (Princeton: Princeton University Press, 1961), with J.H.W.G. Liebeschuetz and H. Kennedy, 'Antioch and the villages of northern Syria in the fifth and sixth centuries AD: trends and problems', *Nottingham Medieval Studies* 23 (1988), 65–90 (reprinted in J.H.W.G. Liebeschuetz, *From Diocletian to the Arab Conquest* (London: Variorum, 1990), XVI); id., 'The view from Antioch: from Libanius via John Chrysostom to John Malalas and beyond', *Cristianesimo nella Storia* 31 (2009), 441–70. Another example is the less well-known site of Sagalassos: see H. Vanhaverbeke, F. Martens and M. Waelkens, 'Another view on late antiquity: Sagalassos (SW Anatolia), its suburbium and its countryside in late antiquity', in A.G. Poulter, ed., *The Transition to Late Antiquity on the Danube and Beyond* (Oxford: Oxford University Press for the British Academy, 2007), 611–48.

4 J. Lefort, C. Morrisson and J.P. Sodini, *Les villages dans l'empire byzantin, IVe–XVe siècle* (Paris: Lethielleux, 2005); M. Kaplan, *Byzance: villes et campagnes* (Paris: Éditions Picard, 2006).

5 See the useful collection of studies in William Bowden, Luke Lavan and Carlos Machado, eds., *Recent Research on the Late Antique Countryside*, Late Antique Archaeology 2 (Leiden: Brill, 2003).

6 Good discussion by A.G. Poulter, 'The transition to late antiquity', in Poulter, ed., *The Transition to Late Antiquity in the Danube and Beyond*, 1–50, at 41–6.

7 T. Potter, *The Changing Landscape of South Etruria* (London: Elek, 1979).

8 P. Leveau, *Caesarea de Maurétanie: une ville romaine et ses campagnes* (Rome: École français de Rome, 1984). Another region which has benefited from archaeological survey work is Kasserine in modern Tunisia.

9 See J. Bintliff, 'The contribution of regional survey to the late antiquity debate: Greece in its Mediterranean context', in Poulter, ed., *The Transition to Late Antiquity on the Danube and Beyond*, 649–78.

10 G. Tchalenko, *Villages antiques de la Syrie du nord*, I–III (Paris: P. Geuthner, 1953–58); see G. Tate, *Les campagnes de la Syrie du Nord du IIe au VII siècle: un exemple d'expansion démographique et économique à la fin de l'antiquité* (Paris: P. Geuthner, 1992); J.-M. Dentzer, ed., *Le Hauran* I (Paris: P. Geuthner, 1985–86), II (Beyrouth: Institut Français d'Archéologie du Proche-Orient, 2003). On this debate, see Bintliff, art. cit., 654–57; C. Foss, 'The Near Eastern countryside in late antiquity', in J.H. Humphrey, ed., *The Roman and Byzantine Near East:*

*Some Recent Archaeological Work* (Ann Arbor, MI: Journal of Roman Archaeology, 1995), 213–34.

11 For which see Vanhaverbeke, Martens and Waelkens, 'Another view on late antiquity: Sagalassos (SW Anatolia), its suburbium and its countryside in late antiquity'.

12 C. Mango, *Le développement urbain de Constantinople (IVe–VIIe siècle)* (Paris: Boccard, 1985, rev. ed., 1990) shows, largely from textual evidence, how gradually the city actually took shape; see above, Chapter 1.

13 See Jonathan Bardill and John W. Hayes, 'Excavations beneath the peristyle mosaic in the Great Palace of the Byzantine emperors: the pottery from site D, 1936', *Cahiers archéologiques* 50 (2002), 27–40.

14 See James Crow, Jonathan Bardill and Richard Bayliss, with additional contributions by Paolo Bono and with the assistance of Dirk Krausmüller and Robert Jordan, *The Water Supply of Byzantine Constantinople* (London: Society for the Promotion of Roman Studies, 2008).

15 Jonathan Bardill, *Brickstamps of Constantinople* (Oxford: Oxford University Press, 2004).

16 For the late antique inscriptions of Aphrodisias, see C.M. Roueché, *Aphrodisias in Late Antiquity* (London: Society for the Promotion of Roman Studies, 1989), *Performers and Partisans at Aphrodisias* (London: Society for the Promotion of Roman Studies, 1993).

17 R.R.R. Smith, 'Late Roman philosopher portraits from Aphrodisias', *Journal of Roman Studies* 80 (1990), 127–55; on the late antique sculpture of Aphrodisias see also R.R.R. Smith, with Sheila Dillon et al., *Roman Portrait Statuary at Aphrodisias* (Mainz am Rhein: Verlag Philipp von Zabern, 2006), and the volumes of *Aphrodisias Papers* edited by Smith and others since 1990.

18 See A. Chaniotis, 'The conversion of the temple of Aphrodite at Aphrodisias in context', in Johannes Hahn, Stephen Emmel and Ulrich Gotter, eds., *From Temple to Church. Destruction and Renewal of Local Cultic Topography in Late Antiquity* (Leiden: Brill, 2008), 243–73, emphasizing the religious complexity of the city's population.

19 Ephesus: see Clive Foss, *Ephesus after Antiquity. A Late Antique, Byzantine and Turkish City* (Cambridge: Cambridge University Press, 1979); for recent work there under the auspices of the Austrian Academy of Sciences, see S. Ladstätter and A. Pülz, 'Ephesus in the late Roman and early Byzantine period: changes in its urban character from the third to the seventh century AD', in Poulter, ed., *The Transition to Late Antiquity on the Danube and Beyond*, 391–433. The fine remains at Apamea give some idea of its life as a centre of late antique philosophical and religious culture, for one aspect of which see Polymnia Athanassiadi, 'Apamea and the Chaldaean oracles: a holy city and a holy book', in A. Smith, *The Philosopher and Society in Late Antiquity* (Swansea: Classical Press of Wales, 2005), 116–43.

20 For some of the deficiencies in available archaeological evidence, see Poulter, 'The transition to late antiquity', in Poulter, ed., *The Transition to Late Antiquity in the Danube and Beyond*, at 26.

21 See above, Chapter 5; the papers edited by C.M. Roueché, ed., *De aedificiis. Le texte de Procope et les réalités*, *Antiquité tardive* 8 (2001), 7–180, bring out some of the problems inherent in relating this work to the surviving material evidence.

22 For sixth-century Carthage and other North African sites, see Anna Leone, *Changing Townscapes in North Africa from Late Antiquity to the Arab Conquest* (Bari: Edipuglia, 2007), 154–78. The methodological problems involved in using Procopius' lists of *phrouria* in the Balkans are discussed by Archibald Dunn, 'Continuiity and change in the Macedonian countryside: from Gallienus to Justinian', in Bowden, Lavan and Machado, eds., *Recent Research on the Late Antique Countryside*, 535–86, at 575–80, and J.-P. Sodini, 'The transformation of cities in late antiquity within the provinces of Macedonia and Epirus', in Poulter, ed., *The Transition to Late Antiquity*, 311–36, at 314–15.

23 See Y. Tsafrir and G. Foerster, 'Urbanism at Scythopolis-Bet Shean in the fourth to seventh centuries', *Dumbarton Oaks Papers* 51 (1997), 85–146. The massive earthquake of AD 747–48 has also been thought to be the cause of damage at other Decapolis cities including Pella, Gadara, Abila and Capitolias: Liebeschuetz, *Decline and Fall of the Roman City*, 297.

24 See K.W. Russell, 'The earthquake chronology of Palestine and northwest Arabia from the 2nd through the mid-8th century AD', *Bull. American Schools of Oriental Research* 260 (1985), 37–60. M. Meier, *Das andere Zeitalter Iustinians. Kontingenzerfahrung und Kontingenzbewältigung im 6. Jahrhundert n. Chr.* (Göttingen: Vandenhoeck und Ruprecht, 2003), approaches the history of the sixth century through a study of catastrophes, including plague and earthquake; see Chapter 5 above for the problems surrounding the Justinianic plague.

25 Useful introductions: S. Barnish, 'The transformation of classical cities and the Pirenne debate', *Journal of Roman Archaeology* 2 (1989), 385–400; M. Whittow, 'Ruling the late Roman and early Byzantine city: a continuous history', *Past and Present* 129 (1990), 3–29 (an optimistic view based mainly on the Near East); see also out of a large bibliography G.P. Brogiolo and B. Ward-Perkins, eds., *The Idea and Ideal of the Town between Late Antiquity and the Early Middle Ages* (Leiden: Brill, 1999). Most of these urban settlements were small by modern standards and the terms 'city' and 'town' are often used more or less interchangeably in modern archaeological literature, bypassing the legal and administrative issues connected with cities and city status (on which see Christopher Kelly, *Ruling the Later Roman Empire* (Cambridge, Mass.: Belknap Press of the Harvard University Press, 2004)).

26 J.H.W.G. Liebeschuetz, *The Decline and Fall of the Roman City* (Oxford: Oxford University Press, 2001), is not afraid to use the term 'decline' and sees this as setting in before the end of the fifth century in the west and already during the sixth century in the east; see also Bryan Ward-Perkins, *The Fall of Rome and the End of Civilization* (Oxford: Oxford University Press, 2005), Chapter VI, 124–37.

27 For the process seen on a grand scale in the high empire, see G.M. Rogers, *The Sacred Identity of Ephesos* (London: Routledge, 1991).

28 *Buildings* V.2.1–5, describing Helenopolis in Bithynia.

29 *Buildings* IV. 1.19–27; the identification is not universally accepted due to the lack of epigraphic confirmation: see B. Bavant, 'Caricin Grad and the changes in the nature of urbanism in the central Balkans in the sixth century', in Poulter, ed., *The Transition to Late Antiquity on the Danube and Beyond*, 337–74; however, assuming it is correct, Procopius' description now seems nearer the mark than was earlier thought.

30 Denys Pringle, 'Two fortified sites in Byzantine Africa: Aïn Djelloula and Henchir Sguidan', *Antiquité tardive* 10 (2002), 269–90; Proc., *Buildings* VI.6.17–18.

31 See Kaegi, *Muslim Expansion and Byzantine Collapse*, 106–12.

32 Nicopolis was founded in the second century AD with grid plan and public buildings on the model of the cities of Asia Minor; destroyed by the Huns in the fifth century, it was rebuilt after 450 on very different lines. For discussion see M. Whittow, 'Nicopolis ad Istrum: backward and Balkan?', in Poulter, ed., *Transition to Late Antiquity*, 375–89, with A.G. Poulter, *Nicopolis ad Istrum: A Roman, Late Roman and early Byzantine City* (London: Society for the Promotion of Roman Studies, 1995).

33 See Whittow, art. cit., 386 with Sodini, 'The transformation of cities in late antiquity in the provinces of Macedonia and Epirus', and J. Crow, 'Amida and Tropaeum Traiani: a comparison of late antique fortress cities on the Lower Danube and Mesopotamia', in Poulter, ed., *The Transition to Late Antiquity*, 435–55.

34 See T.E. Gregory, 'Fortification and urban design in early Byzantine Greece', in R.L. Hohlfelder, ed., *City, Town and Countryside in the Early Byzantine Era* (Boulder: Columbia University Press, 1982), 54–5. Others may have retreated to the islands: Sinclair Hood, 'Isles of refuge in the early Byzantine period', *Annals of the British School at Athens* 65 (1970), 37–45.

35 See now F. Curta, *The Making of the Slavs: History and Archaeology of the Lower Danube Region, c. 500–700* (Cambridge, 2001); good short exposition in S. Mitchell, *A History of the Later Roman Empire, AD 284–641* (Oxford: Blackwell, 2007), 405–8.

36 D. Metcalf, 'The Slavonic threat to Greece', *Hesperia* 31 (1962), 134–57; id., 'Avar and Slav invasions into the Balkan peninsula (*c.* 575–625): the nature of the numismatic evidence', *Journal of Roman Archaeology* 4 (1991), 140–8. The extent of Slav occupation in Greece in the early Middle Ages is hard to establish and has been highly controversial in the context of the history of modern Greece.

37  See C. Foss, 'The Persians in Asia Minor and the end of antiquity', *English Historical Review* 367 (1975), 721–47; id., 'The Persians in the Roman Near East (602–630 AD)' *Journal of the Royal Asiatic Society*, ser. 3.13 (2003), 149–70; Chapter 9 below.

38  Very useful indications in A. Augenti, *Città e Porti dall'Antichità al Medievo* (Rome: Carocci, 2010). This paragraph very briefly summarizes some of the material presented at a conference on the western Mediterranean economy in the seventh century, held in Oxford in March, 2011, organized by Vivien Prigent and Arietta Papaconstantinou.

39  Proc., *Buildings* II.10.2–25. Antioch was earthquake-prone; there were several in the fourth century and a particularly severe one in 458, but Evagrius makes it clear that its effects were felt chiefly in the quarter known as the 'New City', where colonnaded streets, a tetrapyle and the circus were damaged (Evagrius, *HE* II.12–15). John Malalas and Procopius claim that 250,000 or even 300,000 people died in the 526 earthquake (Malal, p. 420.6; Proc., *Wars* II.14.6) these figures are hardly credible. For Antioch, see also C. Kontoleon, ed., *Antioch. The Last Ancient City* (Princeton: Princeton University Press, 2001); I. Sandwell and J. Huskinson, eds., *Culture and Society in Later Roman Antioch* (Oxford: Oxbow, 2004).

40  Evagrius, *HE* VI.8.

41  Cathedral: Evagr., *HE* VI.8); Gregory: John of Ephesus, III.27–34 (also Heliopolis/ Ba'albek), V.17; Liebeschuetz, *Decline and Fall of the Roman City*, 262–69; 'the view from Antioch', 466–7.

42  Hugh Kennedy, 'From Polis to Madina: urban change in late antique and early Islamic Syria', *Past and Present* 106 (1985), 3–27; 'Antioch: from Byzantium to Islam and back again', in Rich, ed., *The City in Late Antiquity*, 181–98; C. Foss, 'Syria in transition, AD 550–750: an archaeological approach', *Dumbarton Oaks Papers* 51 (1997), 189–269; critical discussion: Alan Walmsley, *Early Islamic Syria. An Archaeological Assessment* (London: Duckworth, 2007), 34–45, 126–29. See also J. Alchermes, 'Spolia in Roman cities of the Late Empire: legislative rationales and architectural re-use', *Dumbarton Oaks Papers* 48 (1994), 167–78.

43  See Walmsley, *Early Islamic Syria*, 45–7.

44  Caesarea: Robert L. Vann, 'Byzantine street construction at Caesarea Maritima', in Hohlfelder, ed., *City, Town and Countryside*, 167–70. An imperial inscription guarantees the identification of the impressive remains of the Nea church at Jerusalem: N. Avigad, 'A building inscription of the Emperor Justinian and the Nea in Jerusalem', *Israel Exploration Journal* 27 (1977), 145–51; see Proc., *Buildings*, V.6.1.

45  See Whittow, 'Ruling the late Roman and early Byzantine city', 13–15; general survey of building in the Near East: L. Di Segni, 'Epigraphic documentation on building in the provinces of Palestina and Arabia, 4th–7thc', in J.H. Humphrey, ed., *The Roman and Byzantine Near East* 2, JRS supp. Series 31 (Portsmouth, RI: Journal of Roman Archaeology, 1999), 149–78. For the mosaics, see G.W. Bowersock, *Hellenism in Late Antiquity* (Ann Arbor: University of Michigan Press, 1990), chap. 6; id., *Mosaics as History: The Near East from Late Antiquity to Islam* (Cambridge, Mass.: The Belknap Press of Harvard University Press, 2006); M. Piccirillo, *The Mosaics of Jordan*, ed. Patricia M. Bikai and Thomas A. Dailey (Amman, Jordan: American Center of Oriental Research, 1992); Liebeschuetz, *Decline and Fall of the Roman City*, 298–9. Greek inscriptions also indicate building and repairs in churches from the seventh and early eighth-centuries at sites in modern Israel and at Gaza: Leah Di Segni, 'Greek inscriptions in transition from the Byzantine to the Early Islamic Period', in Hannah M. Cotton, Robert G. Hoyland, Jonathan J. Price and David J. Wasserstein, eds., *From Hellenism to Islam. Cultural and Linguistic Change in the Roman Near East* (Cambridge: Cambridge University Press, 2009), 352–73, at 358–9.

46  Z. Weiss, with contributions from E. Netzer et al., *The Sepphoris Synagogue. Deciphering an Ancient Message through its Archaeological and Socio-Historical Contexts* (Jerusalem: Israel Exploration Society and Institute of Archaeology, Hebrew University of Jerusalem, 2005); 'Artistic trends and contact between Jews and 'others' in late antique Sepphoris: recent research', in David M. Gwynn and Susanne Bangert, eds., *Religious Diversity in Late Antiquity* (Leiden: Brill, 2010), 167–88; see also Jas Elsner, 'Archaeologies and agendas: reflections on late ancient Jewish art and early Christian art', *Journal of Roman Studies* 93 (2001), 114–28; David

Milson, *Art and Architecture of the Synagogue in Late Antique Palestine: In the Shadow of the Church* (Leiden: Brill, 2007); Fergus Millar, 'Narrative and identity in mosaics from the late Roman Near East: pagan, Jewish and Christian', in Yaron Z. Eliav, Elise A. Friedland and Sharon Herbert, eds., *The Sculptural Environment of the Roman Near East. Reflections on Culture, Ideology and Power* (Leuven: Peeters, 2008), 225–56.

47  Whittow, 'Ruling the late Roman and early Byzantine city', 17 (part of a general argument from the silver treasures of Syrian churches, for which see also Chapter 3).

48  See T.J.W. Wilkinson, *Town and Country in S. E. Anatolia. I. Settlement and Land Use at Kurban Höyük* (Chicago, Ill.: Oriental Institute of the University of Chicago, 1990) 117f., 131–2, arguing for 'precipitous decline' in settlement resulting from the Persian and Islamic invasions.

49  See D. Krueger, *Symeon the Holy Fool. Leontius's Life and the Late Antique City* (Berkeley: University of California Press, 1996); *Miracles of St Demetrius*: see R. Cormack, *Writing in Gold* (London: George Philip, 1985), chap. 2; text, ed. P. Lemerle, *Les plus anciens recueils des miracles de Saint Démétrius*, 2 vols, (Paris: Éditions du CNRS, 1979–81); Theodore of Sykeon: S. Mitchell, *Anatolia; Land, Men and Gods in Asia Minor*, 2 vols. (Oxford: Oxford University Press, 1995), II, 122–50.

50  Mango, *Byzantium. The Empire of New Rome*, 68–9, lays great emphasis on the presumed demographic effects; contra, Whittow, 'Ruling the late Roman and early Byzantine city', 13, and for a reasoned argument against over-reliance on the literary evidence see J. Durliat, 'La peste du VIe siècle', in *Hommes et richesses dans l'empire byzantin* I (Paris: Lethielleux, 1989), 107–19. Cemeteries in the west do, however, seem to show such traces.

51  Y. Hirschfeld, *The Judaean Desert Monasteries in the Byzantine Period* (New Haven, Conn.: Yale University Press, 1992), 228, drawing on the *Life* of the saint by Cyril of Scythopolis.

52  For south-east Palestine and Arabia see S. Thomas Parker, *Romans and Saracens. A History of the Arabian Frontier* (Winona Lake: American Schools of Oriental Research, 1986), and above, Chapter 2; however, the identification of some of the frontier installations is disputed: for discussion see Greg Fisher, 'A new perspective on Rome's desert frontier', *Bulletin of the American Schools of Oriental Research* 336 (2004), 49–60.

53  Liebeschuetz, *Decline and Fall of the Roman City*, 274 f.; Michael Whitby, 'Factions, bishops, violence and urban decline' in Jens-Uwe Krause and Christian Witschel, eds., *Die Stadt in der Spätantike – Niedergang oder Wandel?*, Historia Einzelschrift 190 (Stuttgart: Franz Steiner Verlag, 2006), 441–61, at 456.

54  See Béatrice Caseau, 'The fate of rural temples in late antiquity and the Christianisation of the countryside', in Bowen, Lavan and Machado, eds., *Recent Research on the Late Antique Countryside*, 105–44, an excellent discussion of evidence that often needs to be carefully interpreted, with Chapter 3 above; the faltering and uncertain, though ultimately successful narrative of the Christianization of pagan religious buildings is also emphasized in ead., 'Sacred landscapes', in G.W. Bowersock, Peter Brown and Oleg Grabar, eds., *Late Antiquity. A Guide to the Post-classical World* (Cambridge, Mass.: Harvard University Press, 1999), 21–59.

55  The increased civic role of bishops: Liebeschuetz, *Decline and Fall of the Roman City*, chap. 4, 137–68; see Chapter 3.

56  See I. Ševčenko and N.P. Ševčenko, *The Life of St. Nicholas of Sion* (Brookline, Mass.: Hellenic College Press, 1984), paras 52–5. Slaughtering and offering up oxen, which then provided feasts, seems to have been one of Nicholas' specialities – see paras 87–91, and he was also good at financing church restoration and ensuring good crops (paras 91–5); cf. C. Foss, 'Cities and villages of Lycia in the life of St Nicholas of Sion', *Greek Orthodox Theological Review* 36 (1991), 303–37.

57  For the manifestation of this change in the evidence from Egypt, see R. Alston, 'Urban population in late Roman Egypt and the end of the ancient world', in W. Scheidel, ed., *Debating Roman Demography* (Leiden: Brill, 2001), 161–204, at 193–5; it included the increasing amounts of land owned by monasteries. Alston sees a gradual erosion of traditional urban centres in Egypt from the seventh century onwards in favour of more rural conditions, without a single dominant cause.

58  See J.-M. Spieser, 'L'évolution de la ville byzantine de l'époque paléo-chrétienne à l'iconoclasme', in *Hommes et richesses* I, 97–106, esp. 102–6.

59  See A. Laniado, *Recherches sur les notables municipaux dans l'Empire protobyzantin* (Paris: Centre d'histoire et de civilisation de Byzance, 2002); in the sixth century, Justinian was still legislating to try to maintain the membership of city councils; but see above, Chapter 4, on the debate.

60  Discussion in Jones, *Later Roman Empire* II, 757–63; Liebeschuetz, *Decline and Fall of the Roman City*, chap. 3, 104–36, 'Post-curial civic government'; variety of terms used: ibid., 112–13.

61  As emphasized by Whittow, 'Nicopolis ad Istrum', 380–5, who writes of their having built up 'portfolios of assets', and thus 'adapted and survived'; some, such as the Apiones so well known from Egyptian papyri, did much better than that, and for these great landowners see J. Banaji, *Agrarian Change in Late Antiquity: Gold, Labour and Aristocratic Dominance*, rev. ed. (Oxford: Oxford University Press, 2007); P. Sarris, *Economy and Society in the Age of Justinian* (Oxford: Oxford University Press, 1999, 2006).

62  See M.C. Mundell Mango, *Silver from Early Byzantium. The Kaper Koraon and Related Treasures* (Baltimore: Walters Art Gallery, 1986), 3–6, 11–15.

63  See J.P.C. Kent and K.S. Painter, *Wealth of the Roman World, AD 300–700* (London: British Museum Publications, 1977); cf. David Buckton, ed., *Byzantium. Treasures of Byzantine Art and Culture from British Collections* (London: British Museum Press, 1994), 30–69.

64  Susan Ashbrook Harvey, *Asceticism and Society in Crisis: John of Ephesus and the 'Lives of the Eastern Saints'* (Berkeley: University of California Press, 1990); more emphasis on the social and economic details in the work in Frank R. Trombley, 'Religious transition in sixth-century Syria', *Byzantinische Forschungen* 20 (1994), 153–94, at 154–67, 194.

65  For urban violence and its social and economic causes in the general context of late antique urbanism, see Patlagean, *Pauvreté économique et pauvreté sociale*, 203–31; in the context of late antique cities in the east, Liebeschuetz, *Decline and Fall of the Roman City*, chap. 8, 'Conflict and Disorder in the East', 249–83; Whitby, 'Factions, bishops, violence and urban decline'.

66  Ibid., 216–17.

67  Peter M. Bell, *Thee Political Voices from the Age of Justinian – Agapetus, Advice to the Emperor, Dialogue on Political Science, Paul the Silentiary, Description of Hagia Sophia* (Liverpool: Liverpool University Press, 2009); see Peter Bell, *Social Conflict in the Age of Justinian* (Oxford: Oxford University Press, 2011).

68  Alan Cameron, *Circus Factions. Blues and Greens at Rome and Byzantium* (Oxford: Clarendon Press, 1976).

69  Liebeschuetz, *Decline and Fall of the Roman City*, 277.

70  Liebeschuetz, *Decline and Fall of the Roman City*, 269–72; for some reservations see Whitby, 'Factions, bishops, violence and urban decline'; John of Nikiu: below Chapter 9.

71  Liebeschuetz, *Decline and Fall of the Roman City*, 256; for the factions, see ibid., 255–76; Whitby, 'Factions, bishops, violence and urban decline', 445–6.

72  A wealth of epigraphic and other evidence is cited in Roueché, *Performers and Partisans at Aphrodisias*.

73  *Or.* XIII; for an identification of the Brytae, the Edessene festival and the Maiuma, a night festival also involving water and lewd dancing, which had been previously banned for similar reasons and then revived, see Geoffrey Greatrex and John W. Watt, 'One, two or three feasts? The Brytae, the Maiuma and the May festival at Edessa', *Oriens Christianus* 83 (1999), 1–21.

74  Cameron, *Circus Factions*, 237ff., citing Liebeschuetz, *Antioch*, 210f.

75  Alan Cameron, *Porphyrius the Charioteer* (Oxford: Clarendon Press, 1973) discusses the evidence and provides an ingenious reconstruction of the monuments; for factional violence see 232–3.

76  Ibid., 214–22.

77  Nearly all are known only from later literary sources: Sarah Bassett, *The Urban Image of Late*

*Antique Constantinople* (Cambridge: Cambridge University Press, 2004), provides a catalogue of known Hippodrome statuary at 212–32.

78  R. Cormack, 'The wall-painting of St. Michael in the theatre', in R.R.R. Smith, and Kenan T. Erim, eds., *Aphrodisias Papers* 2 (Ann Arbor, Michigan: Dept of Classical Studies, University of Michigan, 1991), 109–22.

79  *Secret History*, 26.8–9.

80  Liebeschuetz, *Decline and Fall of the Roman City*, 253–5; Blues and Greens continued to exist in Byzantium, where they still played a role in the racing in the Hippodrome at Constantinople, and came to be part of the ceremonial surrounding the emperors.

81  Bassett, *The Urban Image of Late Antique Constantinople*, chap. 6, 'Justinian and antiquity', 121–36, arguing for a progressive shift in patronage from a classical to an ecclesiastical focus.

82  Patlagean, *Pauvreté économique et pauvreté sociale*, 215. Acclamations: C.M. Roueché, 'Acclamations in the later Roman empire: new evidence from Aphrodisias', *Journal of Roman Studies* 74 (1984), 181–99; the reception of the Theodosian Code was greeted by acclamations by the senate (all recorded), and the practice continued in Byzantine court ceremonial.

83  End of the free bread distribution in Constantinople: *Chron. Pasch.* s.a. 617: 'in this year the recipients of the state bread were requested for 3 coins for each loaf as a levy. And after everyone had provided this, straightway in the month August of the same indiction 6 the provision of this state bread was completely suspended'.

84  Hirschfeld, *The Judaean Desert Monasteries in the Byzantine Period*; J. Patrich, *Sabas, Leader of Palestinian Monasticism: A Comparative Study in Eastern Monasticism, Fourth to Seventh Centuries* (Washington, DC: Dumbarton Oaks, 1995); John Binns, *Ascetics and Ambassadors of Christ. The Monasteries of Palestine, 314–641* (Oxford: Clarendon Press, 1994); *Lives of the Monks of Palestine by Cyril of Scythopolis* (Kalamazoo: Cistercian Publications, 1991).

# 8  The eastern Mediterranean – a region in ferment

1  From a large bibliography, see Fergus Millar, 'Christian monasticism in Roman Arabia at the birth of Mahomet', *Semitica et Classica* 2 (2009), 97–115, at 105; 'Arabs' and 'Saracens': id., 'The Theodosian empire (408–50) and the Arabs: Saracens or Ishmaelites?', in E. Gruen, ed., *Cultural Borrowings and Ethnic Appropriations in Antiquity* (Stuttgart: Franz Steiner, 2005), 297–314.

2  A Byzantine embassy sent by Justinian to Himyar and to the Ethiopians (Axum) with a similar aim in 531 is also mentioned by Proc., *Wars* I.19–20, and one to Axum by Malalas, *Chon.*, XVIII.56. Given its strategic position, it is not surprising that both Byzantium and Axum interested themselves in Himyar in the early sixth century. The literary sources for Himyar are complex, but see the helpful collection of discussions in Joëlle Beaucamp, Françoise Briquel-Chatonnet and Christian Julien Robin, eds., *Juifs et chrétiens en Arabie aux Ve et VIe siècles: regards croisés sur les sources* (Paris: Association des amis du Centre d'histoire et civilisation de Byzance, 2010), and further below.

3  See Greg Fisher, *Between Empires. Arabs, Romans and Sasanians in Late Antiquity* (Oxford: Oxford University Press, 2011). A great deal has been written recently about Arabs and the rise of Arabic in the Roman empire before Islam; see I. Shahid, *Rome and the Arabs. A Prolegomenon to the Study of Byzantium and the Arabs* (Washington, DC: Dumbarton Oaks, 1984); *Rome and the Arabs in the Fifth Century* (Washington, DC: Dumbarton Oaks, 1989); *Rome and the Arabs in the Sixth Century*, 2 vols. (Washington, DC: Dumbarton Oaks, 1995, 2002), with M. Whittow, 'Rome and the Jafnids: writing the history of a 6th-century tribal dynasty', in J.H. Humphrey, ed., *The Roman and Byzantine Near East. Some Recent Archaeological Research* 2 (Portsmouth, RI: Journal of Roman Archaeology, 2002), 207–24; R.G. Hoyland, *Arabia and the Arabs. From the Bronze Age to the Coming of Islam* (London: Routledge, 2001), and further below and Chapter 9.

4 Y. Tsafrir et al., *Excavations at Rehovot-in-the-Negev* I, Qedem 25 (Jerusalem: Institute of Archaeology, Hebrew University, 1988).

5 See Y. Hirschfeld, *The Judaean Desert Monasteries in the Byzantine Period* (New Haven: Yale University Press, 1982); id., *The Early Byzantine Monastery at Khirbet ed-Deir in the Judaean Desert. The Excavations in 1981–1987*, Qedem 38 (Jerusalem: Hebrew University, 1999). On the monastery of St Sabas during the Persian invasions see Chapter 9.

6 See B. Ward-Perkins, 'Land, labour and settlement', and 'Specialized production and exchange', in Cambridge Ancient History XIV, 315–44, 346–91; Cécile Morrisson and J.-P. Sodini, 'The sixth-century economy', in Angeliki E. Laiou, ed., *The Economic History of Byzantium* (Washington, DC, 2002), 3 vols., 171–220; contrast J. Banaji, *Agrarian Change in Late Antiquity. Gold, Labour and Aristocratic Dominance*, rev. ed. (Oxford: Oxford University Press, 2007), arguing for an increasing dominance of large estates, on which see also below.

7 For continuity: Marlia Mundell Mango, 'Byzantine maritime trade with the east (4th–7th centuries)', *ARAM* 8 (1996), 139–63.

8 Known particularly from the *History* of Ahudemmeh, the sixth-century bishop of Beth 'Arbaya and Miaphysite 'metropolitan of the East': see Elizabeth Key Fowden, *The Barbarian Plain. Saint Sergius between Rome and Iran* (Berkeley: University of California Press, 1999), 121–6.

9 Sean A. Kingsley, *Shipwreck Archaeology of the Holy Land. Processes and Parameters* (London: Duckworth, 2004); population increase: C. Dauphin, *La Palestine byzantine: peuplement et populations* (Oxford: Archaeopress, 1998).

10 W. Wolska-Conus, *La topographie chrétienne de Cosmas Indicopleustes* (Paris: Presses universitaires de France, 1962).

11 See Ward-Perkins, 'Specialisation, trade and prosperity. An overview of the economy of the late antique eastern Mediterranean', in Sean Kingsley and Michael Decker, eds., *Economy and Exchange in the Eastern Mediterranean during Late Antiquity* (Oxford: Oxbow, 2001), 167–78; Angeliki E. Laiou and Cécile Morrisson, eds., *The Byzantine Economy* (Cambridge: Cambridge University Press, 2007), 35–8. Peregrine Horden and Nicholas Purcell, *The Corrupting Sea* (Oxford: Blackwell, 2000), 153–60, argue against excessive emphasis on long-distance traffic ('shipping lanes') and for the persistence of small-scale connectivity, despite what they call 'the early medieval depression' of the seventh to ninth centuries.

12 See Kingsley and Decker, eds., *Economy and Exchange in the East Mediterranean*, especially the papers by Kingsley (Palestinian wine trade), Decker (north Syria), Marlia Mundell Mango (non-ceramic evidence for trade) and Bryan Ward-Perkins (methodological observations and limitations of amphorae evidence). For trade see also Marlia Mundell Mango, ed., *Byzantine Trade, 4th–12th Centuries* (Farnham: Ashgate, 2009).

13 See R.S. Bagnall, *Egypt in Late Antiquity* (Princeton: Princeton University Press, 1993); id., ed., *Egypt in the Byzantine World, 300–700* (Cambridge: Cambridge University Press, 2007): emphasis on large estates: Banaji, *Agrarian Change*; P. Sarris, *Economy and Society in the Age of Justinian* (Cambridge: Cambridge University Press, 2006); C. Zuckerman, *Du village à l'empire: autour du register fiscal d'Aphrodito, 525–526* (Paris: Association des amis du Centre d'histoire et civilisation de Byzance, 2004); against Banaji, G. Ruffini, *Social Networks in Byzantine Egypt* (Cambridge: Cambridge University Press, 2008), especially on Oxyrhynchus and Aphrodito.

14 I owe this information to the kindness of the excavator, Dr Grzegorz Majcherek.

15 Against: P. Crone, *Meccan Trade and the Rise of Islam* (Princeton: Princeton University Press, 1987); but see Andrew Marsham, 'The early Caliphate and the inheritance of late antiquity (*c.* AD 610–*c.* AD 750)', in Philip Rousseau, ed., *A Companion to Late Antiquity* (Chichester, UK: Wiley-Blackwell, 2009), 479–92, at 482–83; James Howard-Johnston, *Witnesses to a World Crisis: Historians and Histories of the Middle East in the Seventh Century* (Oxford: Oxford University Press, 2010), 398–402, 452, and Crone, 'Quraysh and the Roman army: making sense of the Meccan leather trade', *Bulletin of the School of Oriental and African Studies* 70 (2007), 63–88 (possibility of Meccans producing leather for the Roman army).

16 See G. Fowden, *Empire to Commonwealth. Consequences of Monotheism in Late Antiquity* (Cambridge: Cambridge University Press, 1993).

17 The important role of the south Arabian kingdom of Himyar (Yemen) in early-sixth-century religious and diplomatic history has been strikingly revealed in the epigraphy of the region in addition to the texts already well-known: further below.

18 Proc., *Wars* VIII.17.1–8; Geoffrey Greatrex and Samuel N.C. Lieu, *The Roman Eastern Frontier and the Persian Wars, Part II, AD 363–630. A Narrative Sourcebook* (London: Routledge, 2002), 129.

19 See Fowden, *Barbarian Plain*, 149–73 (a 'tribal church' functioning also as an audience chamber); other Ghassanid churches and sites, including Jabiya in the Hauran, ibid., 143–4.

20 Fowden, *Barbarian Plain*, 172; John Eph., *HE* III.6.4.

21 For similar dealings with Arab tribes under Justinian, see Procopius, *Wars* I.19.8–13 (Abukarib), with M. Sartre, *Trois études sur l'Arabie romaine et byzantine*, Coll. Latomus 178 (Brussels: Revue d'études latines, 1982).

22 Cyril of Scythopolis, *Lives of the Monks of Palestine*, tr. R.M. Price (Kalamazoo, MI: Cistercian Publications, 1991), 18.24–25. Both passages are cited by Robert G. Hoyland, 'Arab kings, Arab tribes and the beginnings of Arab historical memory in late Roman epigraphy', in Hannah M. Cotton, Robert G. Hoyland, Jonathan J. Price and David J. Wasserstein, eds., *From Hellenism to Islam. Cultural and Linguistic Change in the Roman Near East* (Cambridge: Cambridge University Press, 2007), 374–400.

23 *Life of Sabas* 14, in Price, *Lives of the Monks of Palestine*, 106.

24 Robert G. Hoyland, 'Epigraphy and the linguistic background to the Qur'an', in G.S. Reynolds, ed., *The Qur'an in its Historical Context* (London: Routledge, 2008), 51–69, with id., 'Arab kings Arab tribes and the beginnings of Arab historical memory'. Hoyland argues for a widespread use of both spoken and written Arabic across the Near East by the seventh century; on the issue of identity, see also Fisher, *Between Empires*. The origins of the Arabic script are the subject of much debate, but Hoyland provides a clear introduction to the question, and see M.A. Macdonald, ed., *The Development of Arabic as a Written Language*, supplement to the Proceedings of the Seminar for Arabian Studies 40 (Oxford; Archaeopress, 2010).

25 The papyri are still in the course of publication, but have already yielded important results for the working of law as well as for the social and linguistic milieu of pre-Islamic Petra: see the review article by H. Sivan, *Journal of Late Antiquity* 1.1 (2008), 197–9; for late antique Petra, including the evidence from the papyri, see the comprehensive article by Zbigniew T. Fiema, 'Late-antique Petra and its hinterland: recent research and new interpretations', in J.H. Humphrey, ed., *The Roman and Byzantine Near East* 3, JRA supp series 49 (Portsmouth, RI: Journal of Roman Archaeology, 2002), 191–252, with 219 on the language of the papyri.

26 L. Casson, E.L. Hettich, *Excavations at Nessana* II. *The Literary Papyri* (Princeton: Princeton University Press, 1950); C.J. Kraemer, *Excavations at Nessana* III. *The Non-Literary Papyri* (Princeton: Princeton University Press, 1958).

27 Fergus Millar, 'Introduction', in Cotton, Hoyland, Price and Wasserstein, eds., *From Hellenism to Islam*, 1–12, at 2; Hoyland, 'Arab kings, Arab tribes', 375.

28 Especially in *A Greek Roman Empire. Power and Belief under Theodosius II (AD 408–450)* (Berkeley: University of California Press, 2006), but also in a series of powerful articles; for Egypt, see Arietta Papaconstantinou, '"What remains behind": Hellenism and Romanitas in Christian Egypt after the Arab conquest', in Cotton, Hoyland, Price and Wasserstein, eds., *From Hellenism to Islam*, 447–66.

29 For the latter, see J.N. Adams, M. Janse and Simon Swain, eds., *Bilingualism in Ancient Society: Language Contact and the Written Word* (Oxford: Oxford University Press, 2002).

30 M. Gigante, ed., *Sophronii Anacreontica* (Rome: Gismondi, 1957).

31 See Glen W. Bowersock, *Hellenism in Late Antiquity* (Ann Arbor: University of Michigan Press, 1990); M. Piccirillo, *The Mosaics of Jordan* (Amman: American Center of Oriental Research, 1992); for pagan/classical themes in synagogue mosaics see Chapter 7.

32 Arietta Papaconstantinou, *Languages and Literature of Early Christianity: Coptic* (Paris:

Lavoisier, 2009); ead., ed., *The Multilingual Experience in Egypt, from the Ptolemies to the Abbasids* (Farnham: Ashgate, 2010).

33 For some of these issues, see Fergus Millar, 'Empire, community and culture in the Roman Near East: Syrians, Jews and Arabs', *Journal of Jewish Studies*, 38 (1987), 143–604; 'Linguistic co-existence in Constantinople: Greek and Latin (and Syriac) in the Acts of the Synod of 536 C.E.', *Journal of Roman Studies* 99 (2009), 92–103.

34 See David Potts, *The Arabian Gulf in Antiquity* II (Oxford: Clarendon Press, 1990), 221, 227, 241ff. Christian and Jewish communities continued to exist in the area after the coming of Islam (221, n. 105).

35 Ibid., 339.

36 D. Westberg, *Celebrating with Words: Studies in the Rhetorical Works of the Gaza School* (Uppsala, 2010).

37 See especially Bowersock, *Hellenism in Late Antiquity*.

38 For the monotheistic epigraphy of Himyar, see I. Gajda, '*Le royaume de Himyar à l'époque monothéiste* (Paris: de Boccard, 2009), with ead., 'Quel monothéisme en Arabie du Sud ancienne?', in Beaucamp, Briquel-Chatonnet and Robin, eds., *Juifs et chrétiens en Arabie aux Ve et VIe siècles*, 107–22; Himyar came under Sasanian rule in the early 570s; for Himyar in the Arabic tradition, see Howard-Johnston, *Witnesses to a World Crisis*, 396–98.

39 Seth Schwartz, *Imperialism and Jewish Society, 200 B.C.E. to 640 C.E.* (Princeton: Princeton University Press, 2001), 180, 184.

40 Tessa Rajak, *Translation and Survival. The Greek Bible of the Ancient Jewish Diaspora* (Oxford: Oxford University Press, 2009), 302–3, 307.

41 Shimon Dar, 'Archaeological aspects of Samaritan research in Israel', in David M. Gwynn and Susanne Bangert, eds., *Religious Diversity in Late Antiquity* (Leiden: Brill, 2010), 189–98; Proc., *Buildings* V.7.16; Cyril of Scythopolis, *Life of S. Sabas*, 70.

42 For an introduction to this massive literature in the context of the particular circumstances of the seventh century, see Averil Cameron, 'Blaming the Jews: the seventh-century invasions of Palestine in context', *Travaux et Mémoires* 14 (Mélanges Gilbert Dagron) (2002), 57–78, with ead., 'Jews and heretics – a category error?', in Adam H. Becker and Annette Yoshiko Reed, eds., *The Ways that Never Parted. Jews and Christians in Late Antiquity and the Early Middle Ages* (Tübingen: Mohr Siebeck, 2003). 345–60; further, Chapter 9 below.

43 This self-confidence is brought out in G.W. Bowersock, *Mosaics as History* (Cambridge, Mass.: The Belknap Press of Harvard University Press, 2006), with a thoughtful discussion of the widespread manifestation of Jewish and Christian iconoclasm in the region in the early Islamic period at 91–111, and see also Steven Fine, *Art and Judaism in the Greco-Roman World: Towards a New Jewish Archaeology* (Cambridge: Cambridge University Press, 2005), though see also below.

44 Ibid., 120, 119.

45 Schwartz, *Imperialism and Jewish Society*, 199–202, cf. also 182–3 on the changed scholarly approaches on the issue.

46 Ibid., 197–7; S. Bradbury, *Severus of Minorca: Letter on the Conversion of the Jews* (Oxford: Clarendon Press, 1996).

47 Schwartz, *Imperialism and Jewish Society*, chapter 9, 'Judaization', 240–74.

48 Tiberias before the Arab conquests had been the seat of the Jewish patriarchs and was the home of the Palestinian Talmud and the *piyyutim*: Schwartz, ibid., 205.

49 See Benjamin Isaac, 'Inscriptions and religious identity in the Golan', in Humphrey, ed., *The Roman and Byzantine Near East* 2, 179–88.

50 R.M. Price, *A History of the Monks of Syria* (Kalamazoo: Cistercian Publications, 1985).

51 See Benedicta Ward, *Harlots of the Desert: A Study of Repentance in Early Monastic Sources* (Oxford: Mowbray, 1987); Sebastian P. Brock and Susan Ashbrook Harvey, *Holy Women of the Syrian Orient* (rev. ed., Berkeley: University of California Press, 1998).

52 Peter Brown, 'The rise and function of the holy man in late antiquity', *Journal of Roman studies* 16 (1971), 80–101; see James Howard-Johnston and Paul Fouracre, eds., *The Cult of Saints*

*in Late Antiquity and the Middle Ages. Essays on the Contribution of Peter Brown* (Oxford: Oxford University Press, 1999).

53  Cyril of Scythopolis, *Life of S. Sabas*, 60, 61,71–4; while in Constantinople Sabas allegedly predicted the recovery of Rome and Africa by Justinian.

54  *Life of Euthymius*, 30, 20.

55  Ibid., 27; Euthymius memorably admitted that he had 'not read in detail everything that this council has examined and enacted', but that he regarded it as orthodox.

56  See on all of this Volker-Lorenz Menze, *Justinian and the Making of the Syrian Orthodox Church* (Oxford: Oxford University Press, 2008), and for a survey of the events leading up the separation between Chalcedonians and anti-Chalcedonians in the sixth century L. Van Rompay, 'Society and community in the Christian East', in Michael Maas, ed., *The Cambridge Companion to the Age of Justinian* (Cambridge: Cambridge University Press, 2005), 239–66. See also Philip Wood, *'We have no King but Christ.' Christian Political Thought in Greater Syria on the Eve of the Arab Conquest (c. 400–585)* (Oxford: Oxford University Press, 2010).

57  Van Rompay, 248–52.

58  Ibid., 253.

59  Ibid., 255–7; see Volker L. Menze and Kutlu Akalin, *John of Tella's Profession of Faith. The Legacy of a Sixth-Century Syrian Orthodox Bishop* (Piscataway, NJ: Gorgias Press, 2009).

60  School of Nisibis: Adam Becker, *Fear of God and the Beginning of Wisdom. The School of Nisibis and Christian Scholastic Culture in Late Antique Mesopotamia* (Philadelphia, Pa: University of Pennsylvania Press, 2006); id., *Sources for the History of the School of Nisibis*, trans. with introduction and notes, Translated Texts for Historians 50 (Liverpool: Liverpool University Press, 2008).

61  In general, see S.P. Brock, 'Christians in the Sasanian empire: a case of divided loyalties', in id., *Syriac Perspectives on Late Antiquity* (London: Variorum, 1984), VI; further, Chapter 9.

62  See also Michael Morony, *Iraq after the Muslim Conquest* (Princeton: Princeton University Press, 1984), 372–6. In his *Lives of the Eastern Saints*, John of Ephesus, himself a Miaphysite, 'portrays [the Persian empire] as a land teeming with well-trained, argumentative heretics', i.e., Nestorians and Manichaeans: see Joel Thomas Walker, *The Legend of Mar Qardagh. Narrative and Christian Heroism in Late Antique Iraq* (Berkeley: University of California Press, 2006), 176.

63  See Walker, op.cit., chapter 3. Aristotelian logic was also taught at the School of Nisibis: Walker, 175.

64  See Fergus Millar, 'Repentant heretics in fifth-century Lydia: identity and literacy', *Scripta Classica Israelica* 23 (2004), 111–30; 'The Syriac Acts of the Second Council of Ephesus (449)', in Richard Price and Mary Whitby, eds., *Chalcedon in Context, Church Councils 400–700* (Liverpool: Liverpool University Press, 2009), 45–69; id., 'Christian monasticism in Roman Arabia'; id., 'Linguistic co-existence in Constantinople'.

65  See S.P. Brock, 'The conversations with the Syrian Orthodox under Justinian (532)', in Brock, *Studies in Syriac Christianity: History, Literature and Theology* (London: Variorum, 1992), XIII.

66  Averil Cameron, 'Texts as weapons: polemic in the Byzantine dark ages', in Alan Bowman and Greg Woolf, eds., *Literacy and Power in the Ancient World*, (Cambridge: Cambridge University Press, 1994), 198–215.

67  Key works include Benjamin Isaac, *The Limits of Empire. The Roman Army in the East*, rev. ed. (Oxford: Clarendon Press, 1992); Philip Freeman and David Kennedy, eds,, *The Defence of the Roman and Byzantine East I–II* (Oxford: BAR, 1986); S. Thomas Parker, *Romans and Saracens. A History of the Arabian Frontier* (Winona Lake: American Schools of Oriental Research, 1986), and see Jodi Magness, 'Redating the forts at Ein Boqeq, Upper Zohar and other sites in SE Judaea, and the implications for the nature of the *Limes Palaestinae*', in Humphrey, ed., *The Roman and Byzantine Near East* 2, 189–206. Useful historical survey, maps and splendid pictures in David Kennedy and Derrick Riley, *Rome's Desert Frontier from the Air* (Sheffield: Dept of Archaeology and Prehistory, Sheffield University, 1989).

68  See Greg Fisher, 'A new perspective on Rome's desert frontier', *Bulletin of the American Schools of Oriental Research* 336 (2004), 49–60; for the wider eastern context see Geoffrey

Greatrex, 'Byzantium and the east in the sixth century', in Maas, ed., *Companion to the Age of Justinian*, 477–509.

69  Fergus Millar, 'Empire, community and culture', 143–64 at 145f.

70  For translated texts and detailed discussion, see Greatrex and Lieu, *The Roman Eastern Frontier, II*; see also Beate Dignas and Engelbert Winter, *Rome and Persia in Late Antiquity. Neighbours and Rivals* (Cambridge: Cambridge University Press, 2007).

71  *The Chronicle of Pseudo-Joshua the Stylite*, trans. with notes and introduction by Frank R. Trombley and John W. Watt, Translated Texts for Historians 32 (Liverpool: Liverpool University Press, 2000).

72  Ibid., 54, pp. 63–4.

73  Malalas, *Chron.* 405; Greatrex and Lieu, *The Roman Eastern Frontier II*, 103.

74  Ps. Josh. Styl., 90, with Trombley and Watts, 109–10; on the remains at Dara, see Michael Whitby, 'Procopius' description of Dara (*Buildings* II.1–3)', in Freeman and Kennedy, eds., *The Defence of the Roman and Byzantine East I*, 737–83.

75  Ps. Josh. Styl., 78, p. 95, with notes.

76  Greatrex, 'Byzantium and the east in the sixth century', 500, 503.

77  Theophylact, *Hist.* V. 1.14–15, trans. Michael and Mary Whitby; see Michael Whitby, *The Emperor Maurice and his Historian. Theophylact Simocatta on Persian and Balkan Warfare* (Oxford: Clarendon Press, 1988), 292–304.

78  Proc., *Wars* I.11.23–50.

79  Greatrex, 'Byzantium and the east in the sixth century', 491, 493 f., 496–98; Tzath: Malalas, *Chron.* 340–1; Greatrex and Lieu, *The Roman Eastern Frontier II*, 79–80.

80  Ibid., 115; Proc. *Secret History* 2.29–31.

81  Proc., *Wars* II.28.18–24.


# 9  A changed world

1  See James Howard-Johnston, 'The siege of Constantinople in 626', in C. Mango and G. Dagron, eds., *Constantinople and its Hinterland* (Aldershot: Ashgate, 2005), 131–42; *Chron. Pasch.*, s.a. 626, trans. Whitby and Whitby, pp. 169–81.

2  Little survives from Constantinople itself, but for the early Roman icons, see M. Vassilaki, ed., *Mother of God. Representations of the Virgin in Byzantine Art* (Milan: Skira, 2000), with ead., ed., *Images of the Mother of God. Perceptions of the Theotokos in Byzantium* (Aldershot: Ashgate, 2004); for the Virgin and Constantinople see Bissera V. Pentcheva, *Icons and Power. The Mother of God in Byzantium* (University Park, Pa: University of Pennsylvania Press, 2006).

3  For the reign of Heraclius, see Walter E. Kaegi, *Heraclius, Emperor of Byzantium* (Cambridge University Press, 2003); Gerrit J. Reinink and Bernard H. Stolte, eds., *The Reign of Heraclius. Crisis and Confrontation 9610–641* (Leuven: Peeters, 2002).

4  See Robert Schick, *The Christian Communities of Palestine from Byzantine to Islamic Rule. A Historical and Archaeological Study* (Princeton: Darwin Press, 1995), 33–48.

5  The argument for a 'new world order' is forcefully put by James Howard-Johnston, *Witnesses to a World Crisis: Historians and Histories of the Middle East in the Seventh Century* (Oxford: Oxford University Press, 2010), especially 510–16.

6  Menander Protector: R.C. Blockley, *The History of Menander the Guardsman* (Liverpool: F. Cairns, 1985); Theophylact: see Michael and Mary Whitby, *The History of Theophylact Simocatta*, trans. with introduction and notes (Oxford: Clarendon Press, 1986); Michael Whitby, *The Emperor Maurice and his Historian. Theophylact Simocatta on Persian and Balkan Warfare* (Oxford; Clarendon Press, 1988).

7  Howard-Johnston, *Witnesses to a World Crisis*, subjects these sources to a very detailed treatment, and many extracts are set out in Geoffrey Greatrex and Samuel N.C. Lieu, *The Roman Eastern Frontier and the Persian Wars, Part II, AD 363–630* (London: Routledge, 2002), chaps. 10–16; see also Beate Dignas and Engelbert Winter, *Rome and Persia in Late Antiquity. Neighbours and Rivals* (Cambridge: Cambridge University Press, 2007). For ps. Sebeos, see R.W.

Thomson and James Howard-Johnston, with the assistance of Tim Greenwood, *The Armenian History attributed to Sebeos* I–II, Translated Texts for Historians 31 (Liverpool: Liverpool University Press, 1999), and for the Syriac chronicles see Andrew Palmer, *The Seventh-Century in the West-Syrian Chronicles*, Translated Texts for Historians 15 (Liverpool: Liverpool University Press, 1993).

8  For the non-Islamic sources on early Islam, see the important study by Robert Hoyland, *Seeing Islam as Others Saw It. A Survey and Evaluation of Christian, Jewish and Zoroastrian Writings on Early Islam* (Princeton: Darwin Press, 1997).

9  As recorded in Corippus' Latin panegyrical poem on his accession: see Averil Cameron, *Flavius Cresconius Corippus, In Laude Iustini minoris libri IV* (London: Athlone Press, 1976), III.151 ff.

10  Greatrex and Lieu, *The Roman Eastern Frontier II*, 135–42; the Roman sources all assume the desirability of an aggressive anti-Persian policy, though it is not obvious that out and out aggression was always the actual aim: see Benjamin Isaac, 'The army in the late Roman East: the Persian wars and the defence of the Byzantine provinces', in Averil Cameron, ed., *States, Resources and Armies*, (Princeton: Darwin Press, 1995), 125–51, at 125–9.

11  Ibid., 142–53.

12  Theophylact, *Hist.* III.14.10–11; John of Biclar, a. 575.

13  Theophylact, *Hist.* II.3–4; Evagrius, *HE* I.13; for the battle, see John Haldon, *The Byzantine Wars. Battles and Campaigns of the Byzantine Era* (Stroud: Tempus, 2001), 52–6.

14  Theophylact, *Hist.* V.3; Greatrex and Lieu, *The Roman Eastern Frontier II*, 173–4.

15  See Matthew Canepa, *The Two Eyes of the Earth. Art and Ritual of Kingship between Rome and Sasanian Iran* (Berkeley: University of California Press, 2009), with rich bibliography.

16  Theophylact records the interest Chosroes showed in an icon of the Theotokos, who appeared to him and told him she was giving him victory (Theophylact, *Hist.* V.15.9–10). His marriage to the Christian Shirin became the subject of later romances: see Dignas and Winter, *Rome and Persia in Late Antiquity*, 225–31.

17  Trans. George T. Dennis, *Maurice's Strategikon: Handbook of Byzantine Military Strategy* (Philadelphia: University of Pennsylvania Press, 1984); the work draws on earlier material but also uses official and documentary sources: Philip Rance, 'Battle', in Philip Sabin, Hans van Wees and Michael Whitby, eds., *The Cambridge History of Greek and Roman Warfare II* (Cambridge University Press, 2007), 347–48.

18  Theophylact, *Hist.* 8.7.8–9.12.

19  *Chron. Pasch.*, s.a. 609; see below.

20  The chronology of these years is difficult to establish: Greatrex and Lieu, *The Roman Eastern Frontier II*, chap. 13, especially 182–3; Howard-Johnston, *Witnesses to a World Crisis*, 436–45, provides a narrative, and see Thomson and Howard-Johnston, *Armenian History*, xxii–xxv; Mark Whittow, *The Making of Orthodox Byzantium 600–1025* (London: Macmillan, 1996), 69–95, 'The fall of the old order'.

21  See Averil Cameron, 'Blaming the Jews: the seventh-century invasions of Palestine in context', *Travaux et Mémoires* 14 (*Mélanges Gilbert Dagron*) (2002), 57–78; Howard-Johnston, *Witnesses to a World Crisis*, 164–71; Hoyland, *Seeing Islam as Others Saw It*, 78–87; B. Flusin, *Saint Anastase le Perse et l'histoire de la Palestine au début du VIIe siècle*, 2 vols. (Paris: Éditions du CNRS, 1992).

22  Cameron, 'Blaming the Jews', 62; discussion, G. Avni, 'The Persian conquest of Jerusalem (614 CE): an archaeological assessment', *Bulletin of the American Schools of Oriental Research* 357 (2010), 35–48, arguing for minimal evidence of destruction.

23  A more political explanation for this anti-Jewish sentiment is proposed by David M. Olster, *Roman Defeat, Christian Response and the Literary Construction of the Jew* (Philadelphia: University of Pennsylvania Press, 1994).

24  Migne, *PG* 28. 589–700; the fact that it also defends the veneration of religious images (chaps. 39–41) suggests that this part at least must date from the second half of the seventh century at the earliest.

25 See G. Dagron and V. Déroche, 'Juifs et chrétiens dans l'Orient du VIIe siècle', *Travaux et Mémoires* 11 (1991), 17–273.

26 M. Gigante, ed., *Sophronii Anacreontica* (Rome: Gismondi, 1957).

27 *Anacr.* 18: however, 'anti-semitism' (Howard-Johnston, *Witnesses to a World Crisis*, 174) does not seem an appropriate term.

28 So Howard-Johnston, *Witnesses to a World Crisis*, 440–1; see also Schick, *Christian Communities*.

29 For these and other sources see Greatrex and Lieu, *The Roman Eastern Frontier II*, 198–228; for Theophanes, see Cyril Mango and Roger Scott, eds., *The Chronicle of Theophanes Confessor. Byzantine and Near Eastern History, AD 284–813* (Oxford: Clarendon Press, 1997); George of Pisidia: Mary Whitby, 'George of Pisidia's presentation of the Emperor Heraclius and his campaigns: variety and development', in Reinink and Stolte, eds., *The Reign of Heraclius*, 157–73; ead., 'Defender of the Cross: George of Pisidia on the Emperor Heraclius and his deputees', in Mary Whitby, ed., *The Propaganda of Power: The Role of Panegyric in Late Antiquity* (Leiden: Brill, 1998), 247–73: Movses Daskhurani: Howard-Johnston, *Witnesses to a World Crisis*, 105–13.

30 *Chron. Pasch.* s.a. 628; for all these events see Greatrex and Lieu, *The Roman Eastern Frontier, Part II*, 198–228.

31 For the latter, see Frank R. Trombley, 'The operational methods of the late Roman army in the Persian war of 572–591', in Ariel S. Lewin and Pietrina Pellegrini, eds., *The Late Roman Army in the Near East from Diocletian to the Arab Conquest*, BAR international ser. 1717 (Oxford: BAR, 2007), 321–56.

32 Ed. P. Lemerle, *Les plus anciens recueils des miracles de saint Démétrius*, 2 vols. (Paris: Editions du CNRS, 1979, 1981).

33 E.g. C. Foss, 'The Persians in Asia Minor and the end of classical antiquity', *English Historical Review* 90 (1975), 721–47; 'The fall of Sardis in 616 and the value of evidence', *Jahrbuch der österr. Byzantinischen Gesellschaft* 24 (1975), 11–22; 'Archaeology and the "twenty cities" of Byzantine Asia', *American Journal of Archaeology* 81 (1977), 469–86, cf. 469 'the empire was savagely overrun by the Sassanian Persians'; 'The Persians in the Roman Near East (602–630 AD)', *Journal of the Royal Asiatic Society*, ser. 3. 13 (2003), 149–70.

34 Patricia Crone and Michael Cook, *Hagarism. The Making of the Islamic World* (Cambridge: Cambridge University Press, 1977), 3–4.

35 See for detailed discussion, based mainly on the Arabic sources: F.M. Donner, *The Early Islamic Conquests* (Princeton: Princeton University Press, 1981), 128–55; and see W.E. Kaegi Jr, *Byzantium and the Early Islamic Conquests* (Cambridge: Cambridge University Press, 1992). Political history of the early Islamic state: Hugh Kennedy, *The Prophet and the Age of the Caliphates. The Islamic Near East from the Sixth to the Eleventh Century* (London: Longman, 1986); sceptics and revisionists: Patricia Crone and Michael Cook, *Hagarism: The Making of the Islamic World* (Cambridge: Cambridge University Press, 1977): Gerald Hawting, *The Idea of Idolatry and the Emergence of Islam. From Polemic to History* (Cambridge: Cambridge University Press, 1999); A. Noth and L.I. Conrad, *The Early Islamic Historical Tradition: A Source-Critical Study* (Princeton: Darwin Press, 1999). The memory of pre-Islamic Arab identity: Robert G. Hoyland, *Arabia and the Arabs from the Bronze Age to the Coming of Islam* (London: Routledge, 2001). Howard-Johnston, *Witnesses to a World Crisis*, launches a forceful defence of the reliability of the historical record in Arabic and the idea that the conquests were centrally planned and driven by religion.

36 Ed. R. Le Coz, *Jean Damascène, Écrits sur l'Islame*, Sources chrétiennes 383 (Paris: Cerf, 1992); cf. Andrew Louth, *St John Damascene. Tradition and Originality in Byzantine Theology* (Oxford: Oxford University Press, 2002); Hoyland, *Seeing Islam as Others Saw It*, 485–9.

37 See Kaegi, *Byzantium and the Early Islamic Conquests*, 265–9; John Moorhead, 'The Monophysite response to the Arab invasions', *Byzantion* 51 (1981), 579–91.

38 Modern Shi'ism claims to represent the true Islamic tradition and the claims of the Prophet's family to the succession.

39 'Uthman and Constans II: Howard-Johnston, *Witnesses to a World Crisis*, 483; the

introduction of the new military themes was gradual, but Heraclius seems to have started the process: see John Haldon, 'Seventh-century continuities: the *Ajnad* and the "thematic myth"', in Cameron, ed., *States, Resources and Armies*, 379–425.

40  For the first view, see Benjamin Isaac, 'The army in the late Roman East: the Persian wars and the defence of the Byzantine provinces', in Cameron, ed., *States, Resources and Armies*, 125–51; against: Michael Whitby, 'Recruitment in Roman armies from Justinian to Heraclius (ca. 565–615)', ibid., 61–124; Howard-Johnston, *Witnesses to a World Crisis*.

41  See Whittow, *The Making of Orthodox Byzantium*, 96–133; John F. Haldon, *Byzantium in the Seventh Century* (Cambridge: Cambridge University Press, 1990); Averil Cameron, *The Byzantines* (Oxford: Blackwell, 2006).

42  Theoph., 329–30, Mango and Scott, 460; Theophanes attributes the new ideas to the influence on the emperor of Sergius of Constantinople, Athanasius of Antioch and Cyrus of Phasis.

43  Sources for the Monothelete controversy: Friedhelm Winkelmann, *Der monenergetisch-monotheletische Streit*, Berliner byzantinische Studien 6 (Frankfurt am Main: Peter Lang, 2001), giving an idea of the intensity of the debate; changing sides was not uncommon, as happened in the case of the ex-patriarch Pyrrhus. Contacts between Rome and Palestine: Schick, *Christian Communities*, 61; Sophronius as defender of orthodoxy: Pauline Allen, *Sophronius of Jerusalem and Seventh-Century Heresy. The Synodical Letter and Other Documents* (Oxford: Oxford University Press, 2009).

44  See Andrew Louth, *Maximus the Confessor* (London: Routledge, 1996); Pauline Allen and Bronwen Neil, eds., *Maximus the Confessor and his Companions. Documents from Exile* (Oxford: Oxford University Press, 2002); above, chapter 8.

45  For these issues, see Averil Cameron, 'The language of images; icons and Christian representation', in Diana Wood, ed. *The Church and the Arts*, Studies in Church History 28 (Oxford: Blackwell, 1992), 1–42; Anna Kartsonia, *Anastasis. The Making of an Image* (Princeton: Princeton University Press, 1986); G. Dagron, 'Holy images and likeness', *Dumbarton Oaks Papers* 45 (1991), 23–33; there are excellent general guides in French and English: G. Dagron, 'L'Église et la chrétienté byzantines entre les invasions et l'iconoclasme (VIIe-début VIIIe siècle)', in G. Dagron, P. Riché, A. Vauchez, eds., *Histoire du christianisme des origines à nos jours IV. Évêques, moines empereurs (610–1054)* (Paris: Desclée, 1993), 9–91; Jean-Robert Armogathe, Pascal Montaubin and Michel-Yves Perrin, eds., *Histoire générale du christianisme des origines au XVe siècle* I (Paris: Presses universitaires de France, 2010), 551–752; Andrew Louth, 'The emergence of Byzantine Orthodoxy, 600–1095', in Thomas F.X. Noble and Julia M.H. Smith, eds., *The Cambridge History of Christianity 3. Early Medieval Christianities, c. 600–c. 1100* (Cambridge: Cambridge University Press, 2010), 46–64.

46  See Julian Raby and Jeremy Johns, eds., *Bayt al-Maqdis*, 2 vols. (Oxford: Oxford University Press, 1992, 1999); Oleg Grabar, *The Dome of the Rock* (Cambridge, Mass.: The Belknap Press of Harvard University Press, 2006); see for Abd al-Malik's other measures G.R.D. King, 'Islam, iconoclasm and the declaration of doctrine', *Bulletin of the School of Oriental and African Studies* 48 (1985), 267–77.

47  See Bas ter Haar Romeny, ed., *Jacob of Edessa and the Syriac Culture of his Day* (Leiden: Brill, 2008), especially Robert Hoyland, 'Jacob and early Islamic Edessa', ibid., 11–24.

48  See A. Papaconstantinou, *Le culte des saints en Egypte: des Byzantins aux Abbassides* (Paris: CNRS Editions, 2001).

49  K. Leeming, 'The adoption of Arabic as a liturgical language by the Palestinian Melkites', *ARAM* 15 (2003), 239–46; Milka Rubin, 'Arabization versus Islamization in the Palestinian Melkite community during the early Muslim period', in Ariel Kofsky and Guy G. Stroumsa, eds., *Sharing the Sacred. Religious Contacts and Conflicts in the Holy Land* (Jerusalem: Yad Izhak Ben Zvi, 1998), 149–62; Sidney H. Griffith, *Arabic Christianity in the Monasteries of Ninth-Century Palestine* (Aldershot: Variorum, 1992); cf. id., *The Church in the Shadow of the Mosque. Christians and Muslims in the World of Islam* (Princeton: Princeton University Press, 2008).

50  For the interplay of Christian identities in this period, see Philip Wood, *'We have no King but*

*Christ'*; 'Nestorians' also spread to the far east and were officially welcomed to China in the 630s, as recorded on an eighth-century stele in Chinese and Syriac found at Xian.

51  For a sceptical approach to John of Damascus' connection with St Sabas see M.-F. Auzépy, 'De la Palestine à Constantinople (VIIIe – IXe siècles): Étienne le Sabaïte et Jean Damascène', *Travaux et Mémoires* 12 (1994), 183–218. Stephen the Sabaite was a monk of St Sabas in the late seventh century, and his *Life*, written by Leontius in Greek, 807, and translated into Arabic and Georgian, contains many details about the monastery, but is curiously silent on the famous theologian: see Hoyland, *Seeing Islam as Others Saw It*, 109–10; see also 480–4 on the difficulties surrounding the biography of John of Damascus.

52  The situation of Jews under Islam has become in some quarters highly emotive, with the use of the concept of 'dhimmitude', but see Mark R. Cohen, *Under Crescent and Cross: the Jews in the Middle Ages*, rev. ed. (Princeton: Princeton University Press, 2008).

53  Schick, *Christian Communities of Palestine*, 171–2; a well-known, though isolated, case of an individual was that of Peter of Capitolias (Beit Ras), put to death under Al-Walid I in 715: ibid., 173–4.

54  Ibid., chap. 6, 112–23; corpus of sites: 227–484.

55  Garth Fowden, *Qusayr Amra. Art and the Umayyad Elite in Late Antique Syria* (Berkeley: University of California Press, 2004).

56  Alan Walmsley, *Early Islamic Syria: An Archaeological Assessment* (London: Duckworth, 2007), 76–90.

57  Averil Cameron, 'Byzantium in the seventh century: the search for redefinition', in J. Fontaine and J. Hillgarth, eds., *The Seventh Century: Change and Continuity* (London: Warburg Institute, 1992), 250–76.

58  Kate Cooper and Matthew Dal Santo, 'Boethius, Gregory the Great and the Christian "afterlife" of classical dialogue', in Simon Goldhill, ed., *The End of Dialogue in Antiquity* (Cambridge: Cambridge University Press, 2008), 173–89, at 187, and see Averil Cameron, *Changing Cultures in Early Byzantium* (Aldershot: Variorum, 1996).

# Conclusion

1  For this phenomenon, see especially Susan Alcock, 'Alphabet soup in the Mediterranean basin: the emergence of the Mediterranean serial', in William V. Harris, ed., *Rethinking the Mediterranean* (Oxford: Oxford University Press, 2005), 314–36.

2  Peregrine Horden and Nicholas Purcell, *The Corrupting Sea: A Study of Mediterranean History* (Oxford: Blackwell, 2000); see Brent D. Shaw, 'Challenging Braudel: a new vision of the Mediterranean', *Journal of Roman Archaeology* 14 (2001), 419–53; Harris, ed., *Rethinking the Mediterranean*; Irad Malkin, ed., *Mediterranean Paradigms and Classical Antiquity* (London: Routledge, 2005); David Abulafia, ed., *The Mediterranean in History* (London: Thames and Hudson, 2003); id., *The Great Sea. A Human History of the Mediterranean* (London: Penguin, 2011).

3  David Abulafia, 'Mediterraneans', in Harris, ed., *Rethinking the Mediterranean*, 64–93.

4  Brent D. Shaw, 'After Rome. Transformations of the early Mediterranean world', *New Left Review* 51 (May/June 2008), 89–114.

5  Michael McCormick, *Origins of the European Economy. Communications and Commerce AD 300–900* (Cambridge: Cambridge University Press, 2001).

6  Henri Pirenne, *Mahomet et Charlemagne* (Paris: Félix Alcan, 1937); see the review by Peter Brown, '*Mohammed and Charlemagne* by Henri Pirenne', in id., *Society and the Holy in Late Antiquity* (Berkeley: University of California Press, 1982), 63–79. As Brown points out, though the book appeared only in 1937, Pirenne had expressed his ideas from as early as 1922.

7  Horden and Purcell, *The Corrupting Sea*, 169–72; cf. on 'high commerce' 365–76; 'early medieval depression', 153–60.

8  See Ian Morris and Walter Scheidel, eds., *The Dynamics of Ancient Empires. State Power from Assyria to Byzantium* (Oxford: Oxford University Press, 2009); Walter Scheidel, ed., *Rome and China. Comparative Perspectives on Ancient World Empires* (Oxford: Oxford University Press, 2009).

9 See Averil Cameron, *The Byzantines* (Oxford: Blackwell, 2006), preface. For the deceptiveness of a concentration on cities, especially evident in the bibliography on medieval Europe, but as we have seen also a central theme for the late antique east, see Horden and Purcell, *The Corrupting Sea*, chap. 4, with 533–54.

10 See Cullen Murphy, *Are we Rome? The End of an Empire and the Fate of America* (Boston: Houghton Mifflin Co., 2007) (= *The New Rome. The End of an Empire and the Fate of America* (Thriplow: Icon, 2008)); cf. e.g. Niall Ferguson, *Colossus. The Rise and Fall of the American Empire* (London: Allen Lane 2004).

11 See Morris and Scheidel, eds., *The Dynamics of Ancient Empires*; Scheidel, *Rome and China*. The comparison itself is not new: it was pursued in the 1970s for the high Roman empire by Keith Hopkins, and is a feature of an influential work of the 1980s, Michael Mann's *Sources of Social Power 1. A History of Power from the Beginning to AD 1760* (Cambridge: Cambridge University Press, 1986), where, however, China is compared unfavourably with Rome (for Mann's Eurocentric approach see Chris Wickham, 'Historical materialism, historical sociology', *New Left Review* 171 (1988), 63–78.

12 See Averil Cameron, 'The Absence of Byzantium', *Nea Hestia*, Jan., 2008, 4–59 (English and Greek).

13 James O'Donnell, *The Ruin of the Roman Empire* (London: Profile, 2009).

14 See e.g. Glen Bowersock, Peter Brown, Oleg Grabar, eds., *Late Antiquity. A Guide to the Post-Classical World* (Cambridge, Mass.: Harvard University Press, 1999), and cf. the series Studies in Late Antiquity and Early Islam, published by the Darwin Press, Princeton since 1992. See also Aziz al-Azmeh, *The History of Allah: Islam in Late Antiquity* (forthcoming), with id., *Muslim Kingship: Power and the Sacred in Muslim, Christian and Pagan Polities* (London 1997); Thomas Sizgorich, *Violence and Belief in Late Antiquity. Militant Devotion in Christianity and Islam* (Philadelphia: University of Pennsylvania Press, 2009).

15 For further discussion of the range of views and the various answers given by scholars of the period, see Averil Cameron, 'A.H.M. Jones and the end of the ancient world', in D.H. Gwynn, ed., *A.H.M. Jones and the Later Roman Empire*, Brill's Series on the Early Middle Ages 15 (Leiden and Boston: Brill, 2008), 231–49; ead., 'Thoughts on the Introduction to *The Conflict between Paganism and Christianity in the Fourth Century*, in Peter Brown, Rita Lizzi Testa, eds., Pagans and Christians in the Roman Empire. The Breaking of a Dialogue (IVth–VIth century A.D.), Proceedings of the International Conference at the Monastery of Bose (October 2008) (LIT Verlag: Münster, 2011), 39–54.

16 Despite G.E.M. de Ste. Croix, *The Class Struggle in the Ancient Greek World* (London: Duckworth, 1981).

17 Jones, *Later Roman Empire*, I, 304–7.

18 See Theophylact, *Hist.*,VII.7.6.ff., with Michael Whitby, *The Emperor Maurice and his Historian* (Oxford: Oxford University Press, 1988), 315–17; F. Curta, with the assistance of R. Kavalev, ed., *The Other Europe in the Middle Ages: Avars, Bulgars, Khazaras and Cumans* (Leiden: Brill, 2007).

19 To quote one recent scholar: 'one must accept that the term "decline" should be abandoned, along with its correlate, "prosperity", and other emotionally laden terms such as "conquest", "desolation", "nomad invasion", or even the more benign "squatters"' (Donald Whitcomb, *Journal of Roman Archaeology* 22 (2009), 827–31, at 831).

20 Cf. Greg Woolf, 'World-systems analysis and the Roman empire', *Journal of Roman Archaeology* 3 (1990), 44–58; cf. the related idea of 'overstretch' (Paul Kennedy, *The Rise and Fall of the Great Powers. Economic Change and Military Conflict from 1500 to 2000* (New York: Random House, 1987).

21 For the latter, see e.g. R.I. Moore, *The First European Revolution, c. 970–1215* (Oxford: Blackwell, 2000).

22 Though contemporaries who experienced the strains in the seventh-century east also searched for causes, as is emphasized by Leslie Brubaker and John Haldon, *Byzantium in the Iconoclast Era, c. 680–850. A History* (Cambridge: Cambridge University Press, 2011), 18–22.

# BIBLIOGRAPHY

## Basic and general works

Armogathe, Jean Robert, Montaubin, Pascal, and Perrin, Michel-Yves, eds., *Histoire générale du christianisme des origines au XVe siècle* I (Paris: Presses universitaires de France, 2010)

Bowersock, G.W., Brown, Peter, and Grabar, Oleg, eds., *Late Antiquity. A Guide to the Postclassical World* (Cambridge, Mass.: Harvard University Press, 1999)

Cameron, Averil, and Garnsey, Peter, eds., *The Late Empire, AD 337–425*, Cambridge Ancient History XIII (Cambridge: Cambridge University Press, 1994)

Cameron, Averil, Ward-Perkins, Bryan, and Whitby, Michael, *Late Antiquity: Empire and Successors, AD 425–600*, Cambridge Ancient History XIV (Cambridge: Cambridge University Press, 2000)

Casiday, A., and Norris, F.W., eds., *Cambridge History of Christianity* II (Cambridge: Cambridge University Press, 2007)

Dagron, G., Riché, P., and Vauchez, A., eds., *Évêques, moines, empereurs (610–1054), Histoire du christianisme des origines à nas jours* IV (Paris: Deschée, 1993).

di Berardino, Angelo, *Patrology. The Eastern Fathers from the Council of Chalcedon (451) to John of Damascus (d.750),* Eng. trans. (Cambridge: James Clarke and co., 2006)

Dignas, Beate, and Winter, Engelbert, *Rome and Persia in Late Antiquity: Neighbours and Rivals* (Cambridge: Cambridge University Press, 2007)

Fouracre, Paul, ed., *The New Cambridge Medieval History I, c. 500–c. 700* (Cambridge: Cambridge University Press, 2005)

Giardina, A., ed., *Società romana e impero tardoantico*, 4 vols. (Bari: Laterza, 1986)

Greatrex, Geoffrey, and Lieu, Samuel N.C., *The Roman Eastern Frontier and the Persian Wars, Part II, AD 363–630. A Narrative Sourcebook* (London: Routledge, 2002)

Harvey, Susan Ashbrook, and Hunter, David G., eds., *The Oxford Handbook of Early Christian Studies* (Oxford: Oxford University Press, 2008)

Jeffreys, Elizabeth, with Haldon, John, and Cormack, Robin, eds., *The Oxford Handbook of Byzantine Studies* (Oxford: Oxford University Press, 2008)

Johnson, Scott Fitzgerald., ed., *Handbook to Late Antiquity* (Oxford: Oxford University Press, 2011).

Jones, A.H.M., *The Later Roman Empire 284–602. A Social, Economic and Administrative Survey*, 3 vols. (Oxford: Blackwell, 1964)

—— *The Decline of the Ancient World* (London: Longman, 1966)

Maas, Michael, ed., *The Cambridge Companion to the Age of Justinian* (Cambridge: Cambrdge University Press, 2005)

Mango, Cyril, *The Art of the Byzantine Empire 312–1453. Sources and Documents* (Englewood Cliffs, NJ: Prentice Hall, 1972, repr. Toronto: University of Toronto Press, 1986)

Mitchell, Stephen, *History of the Later Roman Empire AD 284–641* (Oxford: Blackwell, 2007)

Noble, Thomas F.X., and Smith, Julia M.H., eds., *The Cambridge History of Christianity 3. Early Medieval Christianities, c. 600-c. 1100* (Cambridge: Cambridge University Press, 2010)

Pietri, Charles, and Pietri, Luce, eds., *Naissance d'une chrétienté (250–430), Histoire du christianisme des origines à nos jours* II (Paris: Desclée, 1995)

Pietri, L., ed., *Les églises d'Orient et d' Occident, Histoire du christianisme des origines à nos jours* III (Paris: Desclée, 1998)

Rousseau, Philip, ed., with the assistance of Raithel, Jutta, *A Companion to Late Antiquity* (Chichester: Wiley-Blackwell, 2009)

Stein, E., *Histoire du Bas-Empire*, II, rev. J.-R.Palanque (Paris: Desclée de Brouwer, 1949, repr. Amsterdam: Hakkert, 1968)

Weitzmann, Kurt, ed., *The Age of Spirituality. Late Antique and Early Christian Art, Third to Seventh Century* (New York: Metropolitan Museum of Art, 1977)

Wickham, Christopher, *Framing the Early Middle Ages. Europe and the Mediterranean, 400–800* (Oxford: Oxford University Press, 2005)

—— *The Inheritance of Rome. A History of Europe from 400 to 1000* (London: Allen Lane, 2009)

Young, Frances, Ayres, Lewis, and Louth, Andrew, eds., *Cambridge History of Early Christian Literature* (Cambridge: Cambridge University Press, 2004)

## Secondary literature

Abulafia, David, *The Great Sea. A Human History of the Mediterranean* (London: Penguin, 2011)

Abulafia, David, ed., *The Mediterranean in History* (London: Thames and Hudson, 2003)

Adams, J.N., Janse, M., and Swain, Simon, eds., *Bilingualism in Ancient Society: Language Contact and the Written Word* (Oxford: Oxford University Press, 2002)

al-Azmeh, Aziz, *The History of Allah: Islam in Late Antiquity* (forthcoming)

—— *Muslim Kingship: Power and the Sacred in Muslim, Christian and Pagan Polities* (London: I.B. Tauris, 1997)

Alchermes, Joseph D., 'Spolia in Roman cities of the Late Empire: legislative rationales and architectural re-use', *Dumbarton Oaks Papers* 48 (1994), 167–78

—— 'Art and architecture in the age of Justinian', in Maas, *Companion to the Age of Justinian*, 343–75

Alcock, Susan, 'Alphabet soup in the Mediterranean basin: the emergence of the Mediterranean serial', in Harris, ed., *Rethinking the Mediterranean*, 314–36

Allen, Pauline, 'The definition and enforcement of orthodoxy', in Cameron, Ward-Perkins and Whitby, eds., Cambridge Ancient History XIV, 811–34

—— *Sophronius of Jerusalem and Seventh-Century Heresy. The Synodical Letter and Other Documents* (Oxford: Oxford University Press, 2009)

Allen, Pauline, and Neil, Bronwen, eds., *Maximus the Confessor and his Companions. Documents from Exile* (Oxford: Oxford University Press, 2002)

Allen, Pauline, and C.T.R. Hayward, *Severus of Antioch* (London: Routledge, 2004)

Alston, R., 'Urban population in late Roman Egypt and the end of the ancient world', in Scheidel, ed., *Debating Roman Demography*, 161–204

Ambjörn, Lena, *The Life of Severus by Zachariah of Mytilene*, translated with introduction (Piscataway, NJ: Gorgias Press, 2008)

Anderson, Perry, *Passages from Antiquity to Feudalism* (London: New Left Book Club, 1974)

Ando, Clifford, *The Matter of the Gods. Religion and the Roman Empire* (Berkeley: University of California Press, 2008)

Angelidi, C., *Pulcheria. La castità al potere (c. 399–c. 455)* (Milan: Jaca Book, 1996)

Arjava, A., *Women and Law in Late Antiquity* (Oxford: Clarendon Press, 1996)

Athanassiadi, Polymnia, *Julian. An Intellectual Biography*, rev. ed. (London: Routledge, 1992)

—— *Damascius, The Philosophical History* (Athens: Apamea Cultural Association, 1999)

—— 'Apamea and the Chaldaean oracles: a holy city and a holy book', in Smith, ed., *The Philosopher and Society in Late Antiquity*, 116–43

Atkins, Margaret, and Osborne, Robin, eds., *Poverty in the Roman World* (Cambridge: Cambridge University Press, 2006)

Augustine, *Confessions*, trans. with an introduction and notes by Henry Chadwick (Oxford: Oxford University Press, 1991)

Auzépy, M.-F., 'De la Palestine à Constantinople (VIIIe – IXe siècles): Étienne le Sabaïte et Jean Damascène', *Travaux et Mémoires* 12 (1994), 183–218

Avni, G., 'The Persian conquest of Jerusalem (614 CE): an archaeological assessment', *Bulletin of the American Schools of Oriental Research* 357 (2010), 35–48

Bagnall, R.S., *Egypt in Late Antiquity* (Princeton: Princeton University Press, 1993)

Bagnall, R.S., ed., *Egypt in the Byzantine World, 300–700* (Cambridge: Cambridge University Press, 2007)

Baker, D., ed., *The Orthodox Churches and the West* (Oxford: Blackwell, 1976)

Banaji, J., *Agrarian Change in Late Antiquity. Gold, Labour and Aristocratic Dominance*, rev. ed. (Oxford: Oxford University Press, 2007)

Bang, Peter F., *The Roman Bazaar. A Comparative Study of Trade and Markets in a Tributary Empire* (Cambridge: Cambridge University Press, 2008)

—— 'The ancient economy and new institutional economics', *Journal of Roman Studies* 99 (2009), 194–206

Bardill, Jonathan, *Brickstamps of Constantinople* (Oxford: Oxford University Press, 2004)

Barnes, T.D., *Constantine and Eusebius* (Cambridge, Mass.: Harvard University Press, 1981)

—— *Athanasius and Constantius: Theology and Politics in the Constantinian Empire* (Cambridge, Mass: Harvard University Press, 1993)

—— *Ammianus Marcellinus and the Representation of Historical Reality* (Ithaca and London: Cornell University Press, 1998)

—— *Early Christian Hagiography and Roman History* (Tübingen: Mohr Siebeck, 2010)

Barnish, S.J.B., 'Taxation, land, and barbarian settlement', *Papers of the British School at Rome* 54 (1986), 170–95

—— 'The transformation of classical cities and the Pirenne debate', *Journal of Roman Archaeology* 2 (1989), 385–400

—— *Cassiodorus: Variae*, translated with notes and introduction, Translated Texts for Historians 12 (Liverpool: Liverpool University Press, 1992)

Barnwell, P.S., *Emperors, Prefects and Kings. The Roman West, 395–565* (London: Duckworth, 1992)

Bassett, S., *The Urban Image of Late Antique Constantinople* (Cambridge: Cambridge University Press, 2004)

Bavant, B., 'Caricin Grad and the changes in the nature of urbanism in the central Balkans in the sixth century', in Poulter, ed., *The Transition to Late Antiquity on the Danube and Beyond*, 337–74

Beaucamp, Joëlle, *Le statut de la femme à Byzance (4e–7e siècle) I. Le droit impérial: II. Les pratiques sociales* (Paris: Diffusion de Boccard, 1990, 1992)

Beaucamp, Joëlle, Briquel-Chatonnet, Françoise, and Robin, Christian Julien, eds., *Juifs et chrétiens en Arabie aux Ve et VIe siècles: regards croisés sur les sources*, Centre de recherché d'histoire at civilisation de Byzance, Monographies 32, *Le massacre de Najrân II* (Paris: Association des amis du Centre de l'histoire et civilisation de Byzance, 2010)

Becker, Adam, *Fear of God and the Beginning of Wisdom. The School of Nisibis and Christian Scholastic Culture in Late Antique Mesopotamia* (Philadelphia, Pa: University of Pennsylvania Press, 2006)

—— *Sources for the History of the School of Nisibis*, trans. with introduction and notes, Translated Texts for Historians 50 (Liverpool: Liverpool University Press, 2008)

Becker, Adam H., and Reed, Annette Yoshiko, eds., *The Ways that Never Parted. Jews and Christians in Late Antiquity and the Early Middle Ages* (Tübingen: Mohr Siebeck, 2003)

Bell, Peter, *Three Political Voices from the Age of Justinian.* Agapetus, *Advice to the Emperor, Dialogue on Political Science,* Paul the Silentiary, *Description of Hagia Sophia,* Translated Texts for Historians 52 (Liverpool: Liverpool University Press, 2009)

—— *Social Conflict in the Age of Justinian* (Oxford: Oxford University Press, 2011)

Bintliff, J., 'The contribution of regional survey to the late antiquity debate: Greece in its Mediterranean context', in Poulter, ed., *The Transition to Late Antiquity on the Danube and Beyond,* 649–78

Bitton-Ashkelony, B., and Kofsky, A., *The Monastic School of Gaza* (Leiden: Brill, 2006)

Bitton-Ashkelony, B., and Kofsky, A., eds., *Christian Gaza in Late Antiquity* (Leiden: Brill, 2004)

Blockley, R.C., *The Greek Classicising Historians of the Later Roman Empire* I–II (Liverpool: Cairns, 1981, 1985)

—— 'Subsidies and diplomacy: Rome and Persia in late antiquity', *Phoenix* 39 (1985), 62–74

—— *The History of Menander the Guardsman* (Liverpool: F. Cairns, 1985)

Blumenthal, H.J., and Markus, R.A., eds, *Neoplatonism and Early Christian Thought* (London: Variorum, 1981)

Bowes, Kimberley Diane, *Private Worship, Public Values and Religious Change in Late Antiquity* (Cambridge: Cambridge University Press, 2008)

Bowden, William, Lavan, Luke, and Machado, Carlos, eds., *Recent Research on the Late Antique Countryside,* Late Antique Archaeology 2 (Leiden: Brill, 2004)

Bowersock, G.W., *Hellenism in Late Antiquity* (Cambridge: Cambridge University Press, 1990)

—— *Mosaics as History. The Near East from Late Antiquity to Islam* (Cambridge, Mass.: The Belknap Press of Harvard University Press, 2006)

Bowman, Alan K., 'Diocletian and the first tetrarchy, A.D. 284–305', in Bowman, Alan K., Garnsey, Peter, and Cameron, Averil, eds., *The Crisis of Empire, A.D. 193–337,* Cambridge Ancient History XII (Cambridge: Cambridge University Press, 2005), 67–89

Bowman, Alan, and Woolf, Greg, eds., *Literacy and Power in the Ancient World* (Cambridge: Cambridge University Press, 1994)

Bowman, Alan K., and Wilson, Andrew, eds., *Quantifying the Roman Economy. Methods and Problems* (Oxford: Oxford University Press, 2009).

Boyarin, Daniel, *Border Lines. The Partition of Judaeo-Christianity* (Philadelphia: University of Pennsylvania Press, 2004)

Bradbury, S., *Severus of Minorca: Letter on the Conversion of the Jews* (Oxford: Clarendon Press, 1996)

Brandenburg, H., *Ancient Churches of Rome from the Fourth to the Seventh Century. The Dawn of Christian Architecture in the West* (Turnhout; Brepols, 2005)

Brandes, W., *Die Städte Kleinasiens im 7. und 8. Jahrhundert* (Berlin: Akademie Verlag, 1989)

Brenk, B., 'Spolia from Constantine to Charlemagne: aesthetics versus ideology', *Dumbarton Oaks Papers* 41 (1987), 103–09

Brock, S., 'Early Syrian asceticism', *Numen* 20 (1973), 1–19 (reprinted in his *Syriac Perspectives on Late Antiquity* (London: Variorum, 1984), I

—— 'Christians in the Sasanid empire: a case of divided loyalties', *Studies in Church History* 18 (1982), 1–19, reprinted in id., *Syriac Perspectives on Late Antiquity* (London: Variorum, 1984), VI

—— 'The conversations with the Syrian Orthodox under Justinian (532)', in Brock, *Studies in Syriac Christianity: History, Literature and Theology* (London: Variorum, 1992), XIII

Brock, Sebastian P., and Harvey, Susan Ashbrook, *Holy Women of the Syrian Orient* (Berkeley: University of California Press, rev. ed., 1988)

Brogiolo, G.P., and Ward-Perkins, B., eds., *The Idea and Ideal of the Town between Late Antiquity and the Early Middle Ages* (Leiden: Brill, 1999)

Brown, Peter, 'Aspects of the Christianization of the Roman aristocracy', *Journal of Roman Studies* 51 (1961), 1–11

—— *The World of Late Antiquity* (London: Thames and Hudson, 1971)

—— 'The rise and function of the holy man in late antiquity', *Journal of Roman studies* 61 (1971), 80–101

—— *Religion and Society in the Age of St. Augustine* (London: Faber, 1972)

—— *The Making of Late Antiquity* (Cambridge, Mass.: Harvard University Press, 1978)

—— *The Cult of the Saints. Its Rise and Function in Western Christianity* (London: SCM Press, 1981)

—— 'The rise and function of the holy man in late antiquity', *Journal of Roman Studies* 61 (1971), 80–101, reprinted with additions in his *Society and the Holy in Late Antiquity* (Berkeley: University of California Press, 1982), 103–52

—— 'Mohammed and Charlemagne by Henri Pirenne', in *Society and the Holy in Late Antiquity* (Berkeley: University of California Press, 1982), 63–79

—— *The Body and Society. Men, Women and Sexual Renunciation in Early Christianity* (New York: Columbia University Press, 1988)

—— 'Christianization and religious conflict', in Cameron and Garnsey, eds., Cambridge Ancient History XIII, 632–64

—— *Power and Persuasion in Late Antiquity. Towards a Christian Empire* (Madison, Wisc.: University of Wisconsin Press, 1992)

—— *Augustine of Hippo*, new ed. with an epilogue (London: Faber, 2000)

—— *Poverty and Leadership in the Later Roman Empire* (Hanover, NH: Brandeis University Press, 2002)

—— *The Rise of Western Christendom. Triumph and Diversity, AD 200–1000*, 2nd ed. (Oxford: Blackwell, 2003)

—— *Authority and the Sacred: Aspects of the Christianisation of the Roman World* (Cambridge: Cambridge University Press, 2005)

Brown, Peter, and Testa, Rita Lizzi, eds., Pagans and Christians in the Roman Empire. The Breaking of a Dialogue (IVth–VIth Century A.D.), Proceedings of the International Conference at the monastery of Bose (October 2008) (LIT Verlag: Munster, 2011)

Brown, T.S., *Gentlemen and Officers. Imperial Administration and Aristocratic Power in Byzantine Italy AD 554–800* (London: British School at Rome, 1984)

Browning, Robert, *Medieval and Modern Greek*, 2nd ed. (Cambridge: Cambridge University Press, 1983)

Brubaker, Leslie, 'Critical approaches to art history', in Jeffreys, ed., *The Oxford Handbook of Byzantine Studies*, 59–66

Brubaker, Leslie, and Haldon, John, *Byzantium in the Iconoclast Era (c. 680–850). The Sources: An Annotated Survey* (Aldershot: Ashgate, 2001)

—— *Byzantium in the Iconoclast Era, c. 680–850. A History* (Cambridge: Cambridge University Press, 2011)

Brunt, P., ed., *The Roman Economy* (Oxford: Blackwell, 1974)

Buckton, David, ed., *Byzantium. Treasures of Byzantine Art and Culture from British Collections* (London: British Museum Press, 1994)

Burgess, R.W., *The Chronicle of Hydatius and the Consularia Constantinopolitana*, ed. with an English translation (Oxford: Clarendon Press, 1993)

Burguière, André, *The Annales School: an Intellectual History*, Eng. trans. (Ithaca, NY: Cornell University Press, 2009)

Burns, T.S., *A History of the Ostrogoths* (Bloomington, Indiana: Indiana University Press, 1984)

Burrus, Virginia, *Begotten, Not Made: Conceiving Manhood in Late Antiquity* (Stanford: Stanford University Press, 2000)

Burrus, Virginia, ed., *Late Ancient Christianity*, A People's History of Christianity 2 (Minneapolis: Fortress Press, 2005)

Burton-Christie, D., *The Word in the Desert. Scripture and the Quest for Holiness in Early Christian Monasticism* (New York: Oxford University Press, 1993)

Cain, Andrew, and Lenski, Noel, eds., *The Power of Religion in Late Antiquity* (Farnham: Ashgate, 2009)

Cameron, Alan, 'The date and identity of Macrobius', *Journal of Roman Studies* 56 (1966), 25–38

—— *Claudian* (Oxford: Oxford University Press, 1970)

—— *Porphyrius the Charioteer* (Oxford: Clarendon Press, 1973)

—— *Circus Factions. Blues and Greens at Rome and Byzantium* (Oxford: Clarendon Press, 1976)

—— 'The empress and the poet', *Yale Classical Studies* 27 (1981), 272–89

—— 'Wandering poets: a literary movement in Byzantine Egypt', in Cameron, Alan, *Literature and Society in the Early Byzantine World*, (London: Variorum, 1985) I

—— 'The last pagans of Rome', in William V. Harris, ed., *The Transformations of Urbs Roma in Late Antiquity* (Portsmouth, RI: Journal of Roman Archaeology, 1999), 109–21

—— 'The young Achilles in the Roman world', *Journal of Roman Studies* 99 (2009), 1–22

—— *The Last Pagans of Rome* (Oxford: Oxford University Press, 2010)

Cameron, Alan, and Schauer, Diane, 'The last consul. Basilius and his diptych', *Journal of Roman Studies* 72 (1982), 126–45

Cameron, Alan, and Long, Jacqueline, with a contribution by Sherry, Lee, *Barbarians and Politics at the Court of Arcadius* (Berkeley: University of California Press, 1993)

Cameron, Averil, *Agathias* (Oxford: Clarendon Press, 1970)

—— *Flavius Cresconius Corippus, In Laudem Iustini minoris libri IV* (London: Athlone Press, 1976)

—— 'Images of authority: elites and icons in late sixth-century Byzantium', *Past and Present* 84 (1979), 3–25

—— *Procopius and the Sixth Century* (London: Duckworth, 1985)

—— 'Redrawing the map: early Christian territory after Foucault', *Journal of Roman Studies* 76 (1986), 266–71

—— 'Eustratius's Life of the Patriarch Eutychius and the Fifth Ecumenical Council', in Chrysostomides, ed., *Kathegetria*, 225–47

—— 'Virginity as metaphor', in Averil Cameron, ed., *History as Text* (London: Duckworth, 1989), 184–205

—— 'The Life of the Patriarch Eutychius: models of the past in the late sixth century', in Clarke, ed., *Reading the Past in Late Antiquity*, 205–23

—— *Christianity and the Rhetoric of Empire* (Berkeley: University of California Press, 1991)

—— 'The language of images; icons and Christian representation', in Wood, ed. *The Church and the Arts*, 1–42

—— *The Later Roman Empire AD 284–430* (London: Fontana Press, 1993, 2012)

—— 'Texts as weapons: polemic in the Byzantine dark ages', in Bowman and Woolf, eds., *Literacy and Power in the Ancient World*, 198–215

—— 'The language of images: the rise of icons and Christian representation', in Averil Cameron, *Changing Cultures in Early Byzantium*, XII

—— 'Gibbon and Justinian', in McKitterick and Quinault, eds., *Edward Gibbon and Empire*, 34–52

—— 'Education and literary culture, AD 337–425', in Cameron and Garnsey, eds., Cambridge Ancient History XIII, 665–707

—— *Changing Cultures in Early Byzantium* (Aldershot: Variorum, 1996)

—— 'Justin I and Justinian', in Cameron, Ward-Perkins and Whitby, eds., Cambridge Ancient History XIV, 63–85

—— 'Vandal and Byzantine Africa', in Cameron, Ward-Perkins and Whitby, eds., ibid., 552–8

—— 'The 'long' late antiquity. A late-twentieth century model?', in T.P. Wiseman, ed., *Classics in Progress*, British Academy Centenary volume (Oxford, 2002), 165–91

—— 'Blaming the Jews: the seventh-century invasions of Palestine in context', *Travaux et Mémoires* 14 (Mélanges Gilbert Dagron) (2002), 57–78

—— 'Jews and heretics – a category error?', in Becker and Reed, eds., *The Ways that Never Parted*, 345–60

—— 'A.H.M. Jones and the end of the ancient world', in Gwynn, ed., *A.H.M. Jones and the Later Roman Empire*, 231–50

—— *The Byzantines* (Oxford: Blackwell, 2006)

—— 'The Absence of Byzantium', *Nea Hestia* (Jan., 2008), 4–59 (English and Greek)

—— 'Roman studies in sixth-century Constantinople', in Philip Rousseau and Manolis Papoutsakis, eds., *Transformations of Late Antiquity. Essays for Peter Brown* (Aldershot, 2009), 15–36

—— 'Thoughts on the Introduction to *The Conflict between Paganism and Christianity in the Fourth Century*', in Brown and Testa, eds., *Pagans and Christians in the Roman Empire*, 39–54

Cameron, Averil, ed., *States, Resources and Armies, The Byzantine and Early Islamic Near East III* (Princeton: Darwin Press, 1995)

Cameron, Averil and Cameron, Alan, 'The Cycle of Agathias', *Journal of Hellenic Studies* 86 (1966), 6–25

Cameron, Catherine M., ed., *Invisible Citizens. Captives and their Consequences* (Salt Lake City: University of Utah Press, 2008)

Canepa, Matthew, *The Two Eyes of the Earth. Art and Ritual of Kingship between Rome and Sasanian Iran* (Berkeley: University of California Press, 2009)

Caner, Daniel F., *Wandering, Begging Monks. Spiritual Authority and the Promotion of Monasticism in Late Antiquity* (Berkeley: University of California Press, 2002)

Caner, Daniel F., with contributions by Sebastian Brock, Richard M. Price and Kevin van Bladel, *History and Hagiography from the Late Antique Sinai*, Translated Texts for Historians 53 (Liverpool: Liverpool University Press, 2010)

Carrié, J.-M., 'Le "colonat du Bas-Empire": un mythe historiographique?', *Opus* 1 (1982), 351–71

Carrié, J.-M., and Cantino Wataghin, Gisella , eds., *La 'démocratisation de la culture' dans l'antiquité tardive*, Antiquité tardive 9 (2001)

Caseau, Béatrice, 'Christian bodies: the senses and early Byzantine Christianity', in James, ed., *Desire and Denial in Byzantium,* 101–10

—— 'Sacred landscapes', in Bowersock, Brown and Grabar, eds., *Late Antiquity. A Guide to the Post-Classical World*, 21–59

—— 'The fate of rural temples in late antiquity and the Christianisation of the countryside', in Bowden, Lavan, and Machado, eds., *Recent Research on the Late Antique Countryside*, 105–44

—— 'Ordinary objects in Christian healing sanctuaries', in Lavan, Swift, and Putzeys, eds., *Objects in Context, Objects in Use,* 625–54

Casson, L., and Hettich, E.L., eds., *Excavations at Nessana* II. *The Literary Papyri* (Princeton: Princeton University Press, 1950)

Castelli, Elizabeth A., 'Gender, theory and *The Rise of Christianity*: a response to Rodney Stark', *Journal of Early Christian Studies* 6.2 (1998), 227–57

Chadwick, Henry, *Boethius* (Oxford: Oxford University Press, 1981)

—— *Augustine* (Oxford: Oxford University Press, 1986)

—— 'Philoponus, the Christian theologian', in Sorabji, ed., *Philoponus*, 41–56

Chaniotis, A., 'The Jews of Aphrodisias: new evidence and old problems', *Scripta Classica Israelica* 21 (2002), 209–42

—— 'The conversion of the temple of Aphrodite at Aphrodisias in context', in Hahn, Emmel and Gotter, eds., *From Temple to Church,* 243–73

Chazelle, Celia, and Cubitt, Catherine, eds., *The Crisis of the Oikoumene: the Three Chapters and the Failed Quest for Unity in the Sixth-Century Mediterranean* (Turnhout: Brepols, 2007)

Christie, Neil, *The Lombards: the Ancient Longobards* (Oxford: Blackwell, 1995)

*The Chronicle of Pseudo-Joshua the Stylite*, trans. with notes and introduction by Frank R. Trombley and John W. Watt, Translated Texts for Historians 32 (Liverpool: Liverpool University Press, 2000)

Chrysos, E., 'Byzantine diplomacy, AD 300–800: means and ends', in Shepard and Franklin, eds., *Byzantine Diplomacy*, 25–39

Chrysostomides, J., ed., *Kathegetria. Essays Presented to Joan Hussey for her 80th Birthday* (Camberley: Porphyrogenita, 1988)

Chuvin, P., *A Chronicle of the Last Pagans*, Eng. trans. (Cambridge, Mass.: Harvard University Press, 1990)

Clark, Elizabeth A., *Jerome, Chrysostom and Friends* (Lewiston: Edwin Mellen Press, 1979)

—— *The Life of Melania the Younger*, introduction, translation and commentary (New York: Edwin Mellen Press, 1984)

—— *Reading Renunciation. Asceticism and Scripture In Early Christianity* (Princeton: Princeton University Press, 1999)

—— *History, Theory, Text. Historians and the Linguistic Turn* (Cambridge, Mass.: Harvard University Press, 2004)

Clark, Gillian, *Iamblichus. On the Pythagorean Life* Translated Texts for Historians 8 (Liverpool: Liverpool University Press, 1989)

—— *Augustine. The Confessions* (Cambridge: Cambridge University Press, 1993)

—— *Women in Late Antiquity: Pagan and Christian Lifestyles* (Oxford: Clarendon Press, 1993)

Clarke, G., ed., *Reading the Past in Late Antiquity* (Rushcutters Bay: Australian National University Press, 1990)

Cleary, S. Esmonde, *The Ending of Roman Britain* (London: Batsford, 1989)

Cohen, Mark R., *Under Crescent and Cross: the Jews in the Middle Ages*, rev. ed. (Princeton: Princeton University Press, 2008)

Collins, Roger, *Early Medieval Europe 300–1000* (Basingstoke: Macmillan, 1991)

—— *Early Medieval Spain. Unity in Diversity, 400–1000*, 2nd ed. (Basingstoke: Macmillan, 1995)

Constantelos, D.J., *Byzantine Philanthropy and Social Welfare*, 2nd rev. ed. (New Rochelle, NY: A.D. Caratzas, 1998)

Cooper, Kate, 'Empress and *Theotokos*. Gender and patronage in the christological controversy', in Swanson, ed., *The Church and Mary*, 39–51

—— *The Virgin and the Bride. Idealized Womanhood in Late Antiquity* (Cambridge, Mass.: Harvard University Press, 1996)

—— *The Fall of the Roman Household* (Cambridge: Cambridge University Press, 1997)

—— 'Approaching the holy household', *Journal of Early Christian Studies* 15 (2007), 131–42

—— 'Gender and the fall of Rome', in Rousseau, ed., *A Companion to Late Antiquity*, 187–200

Cooper, Kate, and Hillner, Julia, eds., *Religion, Dynasty and Patronage in Early Christian Rome 300–900* (Cambridge; Cambridge University Press, 2007)

Cooper, Kate, and Dal Santo, Matthew, 'Boethius, Gregory the Great and the Christian "after-life" of classical dialogue', in Goldhill, ed., *The End of Dialogue in Antiquity*, 173–89

Corcoran, Simon, *The Empire of the Tetrarchs: Imperial Pronouncements and Government, AD 284–324*, rev. ed. (Oxford: Clarendon Press, 2000)

Cormack, Robin, *Writing in Gold* (London: George Philip, 1985)

—— 'The wall-painting of St. Michael in the theatre', in Smith and Erim, eds., *Aphrodisias Papers* 2, 109–22

—— *Byzantine Art* (Oxford: Oxford University Press, 2000)

Cotton, Hannah M., Hoyland, Robert G., Price, Jonathan I., and Wasserstein, David L., eds., *From Hellenism to Islam. Cultural and Linguistic Change in the Roman Near East* (Cambridge: Cambridge University Press, 2009)

Cracco Ruggini, L., 'The ecclesiastical histories and the pagan historiography: providence and miracles', *Athenaeum* n.s. 55 (1977), 107–26

—— 'Il miracolo nella cultura del tardo impero: concetto e funzione', in *Hagiographie, Cultures et Sociétés, IVe–XIIe siècles* (Paris: Études augustiniennes, 1981), 161–204

Craik, E.M., ed., *Marriage and Property: Women and Marital Customs in History* (Aberdeen: Aberdeen University Press, 1984)

Cribiore, Raffaella, *The School of Libanius in Late Antique Antioch* (Princeton: Princeton University Press, 2007)

Crisafulli, J.S., and Nesbitt, J.W., eds., *The Miracles of St Artemios. A Collection of Miracle Stories by an Anonymous Author of Seventh-Century Byzantium* (Leiden: Brill, 1997)

Croke, B., and Crow, J., 'Procopius on Dara', *Journal of Roman Studies* 73 (1983), 143–59

Crone, Patricia, *Meccan Trade and the Rise of Islam* (Princeton: Princeton University Press, 1987)

—— 'Quraysh and the Roman army: making sense of the Meccan leather trade', *Bulletin of the School of Oriental and African Studies* 70 (2007), 63–88

Crone, Patricia, and Cook, Michael, *Hagarism: The Making of the Islamic World* (Cambridge: Cambridge University Press, 1977)

Crow, James, 'Amida and Tropaeum Traiani: a comparison of late antique fortress cities on the Lower Danube and Mesopotamia', in Poulter, ed., *The Transition to Late Antiquity*, 435–55

Crow, James, Bardill, Jonathan, and Bayliss, Richard, *The Water Supply of Byzantine Constantinople* (London: Society for the Promotion of Roman Studies, 2008)

Cunningham, Mary B., and Allen, Pauline, eds., *Preacher and Audience. Studies in Early Christian and Byzantine Homiletics* (Leiden: Brill, 1998)

Curran, John, 'The conversion of Rome revisited', in Mitchell and Greatrex, eds., *Ethnicity and Culture in Late Antiquity*, 1–14

Curta, F., *The Making of the Slavs: History and Archaeology of the Lower Danube Region, c. 500–700* (Cambridge, 2001)

Curta, F., with the assistance of R. Kavalev, ed., *The Other Europe in the Middle Ages: Avars, Bulgars, Khazaras and Cumans* (Leiden: Brill, 2007)

Dagron, G., *Naissance d'une capitale: Constantinople et ses institutions de 330 à 451* (Paris: Presses universitaires de France, 1974)

—— 'Holy images and likeness', *Dumbarton Oaks Papers* 45 (1991), 23–33

—— 'L'ombre d'un doute: l'hagiographie en question, VIe-XIe siècles', *Dumbarton Oaks Papers* 46 (1992), 59–68

—— 'L'Église et la chrétienté byzantines entre les invasions et l'iconoclasme, VIIe-début VIIIe siècle', in Dagron, Riché, and Vauchez, eds., *Histoire du christianisme IV. Évêques, moines empereurs (610–1054)*, 9–91

—— *Emperor and Priest. The Imperial Office in Byzantium*, Eng. trans. (Cambridge: Cambridge University Press, 2003)

Dagron, G., and Déroche, V., 'Juifs et chrétiens dans l'Orient du VIIe siècle', *Travaux et Mémoires* 11 (1991), 17–273

Dal Santo, Matthew, 'Gregory the Great and Eustratius of Constantinople: the *Dialogues on the Miracles of the Italian Fathers* as an apology for the cult of saints', *Journal of Early Christian Studies* 17.3 (2009), 421–57

Daly, S.J., and Brian J., *Gregory of Nazianzus* (London: Routledge, 2006)

Davis, R. *The Book of Pontiffs (Liber Pontificalis)*, Translated Texts for Historians 6, rev. ed. (Liverpool: Liverpool University Press, 2000)

Dar, Shimon, 'Archaeological aspects of Samaritan research in Israel', in Gwynn and Bangert, eds., *Religious Diversity in Late Antiquity*, 189–98

Dauphin, C., *La Palestine byzantine: peuplement et populations* (Oxford: Archaeopress, 1998)

Davis, Stephen J., *The Cult of St Thecla. A Tradition of Women's Piety in Late Antiquity* (Oxford: Oxford University Press, 2001, 2008)

De Blois, L., 'The crisis of the third century A.D. in the Roman empire: a modern myth', in De Blois, L., and Rich, J., eds., *The Transformation of Economic Life under the Roman Empire* (Amsterdam: J.C. Gieben, 2002), 204–17

Deliyannis, Deborah Mauskopf, *Ravenna in Late Antiquity* (Cambridge: Cambridge University Press, 2010)

Dennis, George T., *Maurice's Strategikon: Handbook of Byzantine Military Strategy* (Philadelphia: University of Pennsylvania Press, 1984)

Dentzer, J.-M., ed., *Le Hauran* I (Paris: P. Geuthner, 1985–86), II (Beyrouth: Institut Français d'Archéologie du Proche-Orient, 2003)

de Ste Croix, G.E.M., *The Class Struggle, in the Ancient Greek World. From the Archaic Age to the Arab Conquests* (London: Duckworth, 1981)

Di Segni, L., 'Epigraphic documentation on building in the provinces of Palestina and Arabia, 4th–7thc', in Humphrey, ed., *The Roman and Byzantine Near East* 2, 149–78

—— 'Greek inscriptions in transition from the Byzantine to the Early Islamic Period', in Cotton, Hoyland, Price, and Wasserstein, eds., *From Hellenism to Islam. Cultural and Linguistic Change in the Roman Near East*, 352–73

Donner, F.M., *The Early Islamic Conquests* (Princeton: Princeton University Press, 1981)

Doran, Robert, *The Lives of Symeon Stylites* (Kalamazoo: Cistercian Publications, 1992)

—— *Stewards of the Poor. The Man of God, Rabbula and Hiba in Fifth-Century Edessa*, trans. with introduction and notes (Kalamazoo, MI: Cistercian Publications, 2006)

Downey, G., *A History of Antioch in Syria. From Seleucus to the Arab Conquest* (Princeton, NJ: Princeton University Press, 1961)

Drake, H.A., ed., *Violence in Late Antiquity* (Aldershot: Ashgate, 2006)

Drinkwater, J., *The Alamanni and Rome 213–496 (Caracalla to Clovis)* (Oxford: Oxford University Press, 2007)

Dunn, Archibald, 'Continuiity and change in the Macedonian countryside: from Gallienus to Justinian', in Bowden, Lavan and Machado, eds., *Recent Research on the Late Antique Countryside*, 535–86

Durliat, J., *Les dédicaces d'ouvrages de défense dans l'Afrique byzantine* (Rome: École française de Rome, 1981)

—— *De la ville antique à la ville byzantine: le problème des subsistances* (Rome: École française de Rome, 1990)

Duval, Yvette, *Loca sanctorum Africae: le culte des martyrs en Afrique du IVe au VII siècle* (Rome: École française de Rome, 1982)

Edwards, Mark, *Neoplatonic Saints. The Lives of Plotinus and Proclus by their Students*, Translated Texts for Historians 35 (Liverpool: Liverpool University Press, 2000)

Eliav, Yaron Z., Friedland, Elise A., Herbert, Sharon, eds., *The Sculptural Environment of the Roman Near East. Reflections on Culture, Ideology and Power* (Leuven: Peeters, 2008)

Elsner, J., *Art and the Roman Viewer. The Transformation of Art from the Pagan World to Christianity* (Cambridge: Cambridge University Press, 1995)

—— *Imperial Rome and Christian Triumph: the Art of the Roman Empire AD 100–450* (Oxford: Oxford University Press, 1998)

—— 'From the culture of spolia to the cult of relics: the Arch of Constantine and the genesis of late antique forms', *Papers of the British School at Rome* 68 (2000), 149–84

—— 'Archaeologies and agendas: reflections on late ancient Jewish art and early Christian art', *Journal of Roman Studies* 93 (2001), 114–28

Evans, J.A.S., *The Age of Justinian. The Circumstances of Imperial Power* (London: Routledge, 1996)

Evans-Grubbs, Judith, 'Late Roman marriage and family relationships', in Rousseau, ed., *A Companion to Late Antiquity*, 201–19

Fear, Andrew, 'War and society', in Sabin, Van Wees and Whitby, eds., *The Cambridge History of Greek and Roman Warfare* II, 424–58

Ferguson, Niall, *Colossus. The Rise and Fall of the American Empire* (London: Allen Lane, 2004)

Fiema, Zbigniew T., 'Late-antique Petra and its hinterland: recent research and new interpretations', in Humphrey, ed., *The Roman and Byzantine Near East* 3, 191–252

Fine, Steven, *Art and Judaism in the Greco-Roman World: Towards a New Jewish Archaeology* (Cambridge: Cambridge University Press, 2005)

Finley, *The Ancient Economy* (Berkeley and Los Angeles: University of California Press, 1973, 2nd rev. ed. (London: Hogarth, 1985)

Finn, Richard, *Almsgiving in the Later Roman Empire: Christian Promotion and Practice (313–450)* (Oxford: Oxford University Press, 2006)

Fisher, Greg, 'A new perspective on Rome's desert frontier', *Bulletin of the American Schools of Oriental Research* 336 (2004), 49–60

—— *Between Empires. Arabs, Romans and Sasanians in Late Antiquity* (Oxford: Oxford University Press, 2011)

Fletcher, Richard, *The Conversion of Europe. From Paganism to Christianity, 371–1386 AD* (London: Fontana, 1998)

Flusin, B., *Saint Anastase le Perse et l'histoire de la Palestine au début du VIIe siècle*, 2 vols. (Paris: Éditions du CNRS, 1992)

Foss, Clive, 'The Persians in Asia Minor and the end of antiquity', *English Historical Review* 367 (1975), 721–47

—— 'The fall of Sardis in 616 and the value of evidence', *Jahrbuch der österr. Byzantinischen Gesellschaft* 24 (1975), 11–22

—— 'Archaeology and the "twenty cities" of Byzantine Asia", *American Journal of Archaeology* 81 (1977), 469–86

—— *Ephesus after Antiquity. A Late Antique, Byzantine and Turkish City* (Cambridge: Cambridge University Press, 1979)

—— 'Cities and villages of Lycia in the Life of St Nicholas of Sion', *Greek Orthodox Theological Review* 36 (1991), 303–37

—— 'Syria in transition, AD 550–750: an archaeological approach', *Dumbarton Oaks Papers* 51 (1997), 189–269

—— 'The Near Eastern countryside in late antiquity', in Humphrey, ed., *The Roman and Byzantine Near East,* 213–34

—— 'The Persians in the Roman Near East (602–630 AD)' *Journal of the Royal Asiatic Society*, ser. 3.13 (2003), 149–70

Fowden, Elizabeth Key, *The Barbarian Plain. Saint Sergius between Rome and Iran* (Berkeley: University of California Press, 1999)

Fowden, Garth, 'Bishops and temples in the eastern Roman empire, AD 320–435', *Journal of Theological Studies*, n.s. 29 (1978), 53–78

—— 'The pagan holy man in late antique society', *Journal of Hellenic Studies* 102 (1982), 33–59

—— *Empire to Commonwealth. Consequences of Monotheism in Late Antiquity* (Princeton: Princeton University Press, 1993)

—— *Qusayr Amra. Art and the Umayyad Elite in Late Antique Syria* (Berkeley: University of California Press, 2004)

Frank, Georgia, *The Memory of the Eyes. Pilgrims to Living Saints in Christian Late Antiquity* (Berkeley: University of California Press, 2000)

Frantz, Alison, *The Athenian Agora XXIV. Late Antiquity, A.D. 267–700* (Princeton, NJ: Princeton University Press, 1988)

Freeman, P., and Kennedy, D., eds. *The Defence of the Roman Empire in the East, I–II* (Oxford: BAR, 1986)

French, D.H., and Lightfoot, C.S., eds., *The Eastern Frontier of the Roman Empire, I–II* (Oxford: BAR, 1989)

Gaddis, Michael E., *There is no Crime for those who have Christ. Religious Violence in the Christian Roman Empire* (Berkeley: University of California Press, 2005)

—— 'The political church: religion and the state', in Rousseau, ed., *A Companion to Late Antiquity*, 511–24

Gajda, I., *Le royaume de Himyar à l'époque monothéiste* (Paris: de Boccard, 2009)

—— 'Quel monothéisme en Arabie du Sud ancienne?', in Beaucamp, Briquel-Chatonnet and Robin, eds., *Juifs et chrétiens en Arabie aux Ve et VIe siècles*, 107–22

Garnsey, Peter, 'Grain for Rome', in Garnsey, Hopkins, and Whittaker, eds., *Trade in the Ancient Economy*, 118–30

Garnsey, P., Hopkins, K., and Whittaker, C.R., eds., *Trade in the Ancient Economy* (London: Chatto and Windus, 1983)

Garnsey, Peter, and Humfress, Caroline, *The Evolution of the Late Antique World* (Cambridge: Orchard Academic, 2001)

Geary, Patrick T., *The Myth of Nations. The Medieval Origins of Europe* (Princeton: Princeton University Press, 2002)

Gell, A., *Art and Agency: an Anthropological Theory* (Oxford: Clarendon Press, 1998)

George, Judith W., *Venantius Fortunatus. A Latin Poet in Merovingian Gaul* (Oxford: Clarendon Press, 1992)

—— *Venantius Fortunatus. Personal and Political Poems*, trans. with notes and introduction, Translated Texts for Historians 23 (Liverpool: Liverpool University Press, 1995)

—— 'Vandal poets in their context', in Merrills, ed., *Vandals, Romans and Berbers*, 133–43

Giardina, A., 'Esplosione di tardoantico', *Studi storici* 40 (1999), 157–80

—— 'The transition to late antiquity', in Scheidel, Morris, and Saller, eds., *The Cambridge Economic History of the Graeco-Roman World*, 743–68

—— 'Marxism and historiography: perspectives on Roman history', in Wickham, ed., *Marxist History-Writing for the Twenty-First Century*, 15–31

Gibson, Margaret, ed., *Boethius. His Life, Thought and Influence* (Oxford: Blackwell, 1981)

Gigante, M., ed., *Sophronii Anacreontica* (Rome: Gismondi, 1957)

Gillett, A., ed., *On Barbarian Identity: Critical Approaches to Ethnicity in the Early Middle Ages* (Turnhout: Brepols, 2002)

Goetz, H.-W., Jarnut, J., and Pohl, W., eds., *Regna and Gentes. The Relationship between Late Antique and Early Medieval Peoples and Kingdoms in the Transformation of the Roman World* (Leiden: Brill, 2003)

Goffart, Walter A., *Barbarians and Romans, AD 418–584. The Techniques of Accommodation* (Princeton: Princeton University Press, 1980)

—— *The Narrators of Barbarian History (AD 550–800): Jordanes, Gregory of Tours, Bede and Paul the Deacon* (Princeton: Princeton University Press, 1988)

Goldhill, Simon, ed., *The End of Dialogue in Antiquity* (Cambridge: Cambridge University Press, 2008)

Grabar, Oleg, *The Dome of the Rock* (Cambridge, Mass.: The Belknap Press of Harvard University Press, 2006)

Graumann, Thomas, 'The conduct of theology and the "Fathers" of the Church', in Rousseau, *A Companion to Late Antiquity*, 539–55

—— '"Reading" the first council of Ephesus (431)', in Price and Whitby, eds., *Chalcedon in Context*, 27–44

Greatrex, G., 'The Nika riot: a reappraisal', *Journal of Hellenic Studies* 117 (1997), 60–86

—— 'Byzantium and the east in the sixth century', in Maas, ed., *Companion to the Age of Justinian*, 477–509.

Greatrex, G., and Watt, John W., 'One, two or three feasts? The Brytae, the Maiuma and the May festival at Edessa', *Oriens Christianus* 83 (1999), 1–21

Green, J., and Tsafrir, Y., 'Greek inscriptions from Hammat Gader: a poem by the Empress Eudocia and two building inscriptions', *Israel Exploration Journal* 32 (1982), 77–91

Gregory, Timothy E., 'The remarkable Christmas homily of Kyros Panopolites', *Greek, Roman and Byzantine Studies* 16 (1975), 317–24

—— *Vox Populi. Popular Opinion and Violence in the Religious Controversies of the Fifth Century AD* (Columbus, Ohio: Ohio State University Press, 1979)

—— 'Fortification and urban design in early Byzantine Greece', in Hohlfelder, ed., *City, Town and Countryside in the Early Byzantine Era*, 43–64

—— 'The survival of paganism in Christian Greece: a critical survey', *American Journal of Philology* 107 (1986), 229–42

—— 'Procopius on Greece', *Ant.tard.* 8 (2000), 105–14

Grey, Cam, 'Contextualising *colonatus*: the origin of the Later Roman empire', *Journal of Roman Studies* 97 (2007), 155–75

Griffith, Sidney H., *Arabic Christianity in the Monasteries of Ninth-Century Palestine* (Aldershot: Variorum, 1992)

—— *The Church in the Shadow of the Mosque. Christians and Muslims in the World of Islam* (Princeton: Princeton University Press, 2008)

Grillmeier, A., with Hainthaler, Theresia, *Christ in the Christian Tradition 2.2. The Church of Constantinople in the Sixth Century*, Eng. trans. (London: Mowbray, 1995)

Grünbart, Michael, Kislinger, Ewald, Muthesius, Anna, and Stathakopoulos, Dionysios, eds., *Material Culture and Well-Being in Byzantium (400–1453)* (Vienna: Verlag der Österreichischen Akademie der Wissenschaften, 2007)

Gruen, E., ed., *Cultural Borrowings and Ethnic Appropriations in Antiquity* (Stuttgart: Franz Steiner, 2005)

Gwynn, David, M., ed., *A.H.M. Jones and the Later Roman Empire* (Leiden: Brill, 2008)

Gwynn, David, and Bangert, Suzanne, eds., *Religious Diversity in Late Antiquity*, Late Antique Archaeology 6 (Leiden: Brill, 2010)

Hägg, Tomas, and Rousseau, Philip, eds., with the assistance of Christian Høgel, *Greek Biography and Panegyric in Late Antiquity* (Berkeley: University of California Press, 2000)

Haas, C., *Alexandria in Late Antiquity: Topography and Social Conflict* (Baltimore: Johns Hopkins University Press, 1997)

Hackel, S., ed., *The Byzantine Saint* (London: Fellowship of St Alban and St Sergius, 1981)

Hadot, I., 'The life and work of Simplicius in Greek and Arabic sources', in Sorabji, ed., *Aristotle Transformed*, 275–303

Hahn, Johannes, Emmel, Stephen, and Gotter, Ulrich, eds., *From Temple to Church. Destruction and Renewal of Local Cultic Topography in Late Antiquity* (Leiden: Brill, 2008)

Haldon, John F., *Byzantium in the Seventh Century* (Cambridge: Cambridge University Press, 1990)

—— 'Seventh-century continuities: the *Ajnad* and the "thematic myth"', in Averil Cameron, ed., *States, Resources and Armies*, 379–425

—— *The Byzantine Wars. Battles and Campaigns of the Byzantine Era* (Stroud: Tempus, 2001)

—— 'Economy and administration: how did the empire work?', in Rousseau, ed., *A Companion to Late Antiquity*, 28–59

Halporn, James W., trans., *Cassiodorus, Institutions of Divine and Secular Learning and On the Soul*, with introduction by Mark Vessey, Translated Texts for Historians 42 (Liverpool: Liverpool University Press, 2004)

Halsall, Guy, *Barbarian Migrations and the Roman West, 376–568* (London, 2003)

Harries, Jill, '"Treasure in heaven": property and inheritance among the senators of late Rome', in Craik, ed., *Marriage and Property*, 54–70

—— *Sidonius Apollinaris and the Fall of Rome, AD 407–485* (Oxford: Clarendon Press, 1994)

—— *Law and Empire in Late Antiquity* (Cambridge: Cambridge University Press, 1999)

Harries, Jill, and Wood, Ian, eds., *The Theodosian Code. Studies in the Imperial Law of Late Antiquity* (London: Duckworth, 1993)

Harris, W.V., ed., *Rethinking the Mediterranean* (Oxford: Oxford University Press, 2005)

—— ed., *The Spread of Christianity in the First Four Centuries: Essays in Explanation* (Leiden: Brill, 2005)

Harrison, R.M., *A Temple for Byzantium: the Discovery and Excavation of Anicia Juliana's Palace-Church in Istanbul* (London: Harvey Miller, 1989)

Harvey, Susan Ashbrook, 'Remembering pain: Syriac historiography and the separation of the churches', *Byzantion* 58 (1988), 295–308

—— *Asceticism and Society in Crisis. John of Ephesus and the Lives of the Eastern Saints* (Berkeley: University of California Press, 1990)

—— *Scenting Salvation: Ancient Christianity and the Olfactory Imagination* (Berkeley: University of California Press, 2006)

Hawting, Gerald, *The Idea of Idolatry and the Emergence of Islam. From Polemic to History* (Cambridge: Cambridge University Press, 1999)

Hayes, John, *Late Roman Pottery* (London: British School at Rome, 1972; *Supplement*, 1980)

Heather, Peter, 'Cassiodorus and the rise of the Amals: genealogy and the Goths under Hun domination', *Journal of Roman Studies* 79 (1989), 103–28

—— *Goths and Romans, 332–489* (Oxford: Clarendon Press, 1991)

—— 'New men for new Constantines? Creating an imperial elite in the eastern Mediterranean', in Magdalino, ed., *New Constantines*, 1–10

—— 'State, lordship and community in the west (c. AD 400–600)', in Cameron, Garnsey, and Whitby, eds., Cambridge Ancient History XIV, 437–68

—— *The Fall of the Roman Empire. A New History* (Basingstoke: Macmillan, 2005)

—— *Empires and Barbarians. Migration, Development and the Birth of Europe* (Basingstoke: Macmillan, 2009)

Heather, Peter, and Matthews, John, *The Goths in the Fourth Century*, Translated Texts for Historians 11 (Liverpool: Liverpool University Press, 1991)

Hendy, M., *Studies in the Byzantine Monetary Economy, c. AD 300–1450* (Cambridge: Cambridge University Press, 1985)

Hennessy, Cecily, *Images of Children in Byzantium* (Farnham: Ashgate, 2008)

Hermanowicz, Erika T., *Possidius of Calama. A Study of the North African Episcopate at the Time of Augustine* (Oxford: Oxford University Press, 2008)

Herrin, Judith, *The Formation of Christendom* (Princeton: Princeton University Press, 1987)

—— 'Ideals of charity, realities of welfare. The philanthropic activity of the Byzantine church', in Morris, ed., *Church and People in Byzantium*, 151–64

Hirschfeld, Y., *The Judaean Desert Monasteries in the Byzantine Period* (New Haven: Yale University Press, 1992)

—— *The Early Byzantine Monastery at Khirbet ed-Deir in the Judaean Desert. The Excavations in 1981–1987*, Qedem 38 (Jerusalem: Hebrew University, 1999)

Hodges, R., *The Anglo-Saxon Achievement* (London: Duckworth, 1989)

Hohlfelder, R.L., ed., *City, Town and Countryside in the Early Byzantine Era* (New York, 1982)

Holum, Kenneth G., *Theodosian Empresses. Women and Imperial Dominion in Late Antiquity* (Berkeley: University of California Press, 1982)

*Hommes et richesses dans l'empire byzantine* I, *IVe–VIIe siècle* (Paris: Lethielleux, 1989)

Honoré, Tony, *Tribonian* (London: Duckworth, 1978)

Hood, Sinclair, 'Isles of refuge in the early Byzantine period', *Annals of the British School at Athens* 65 (1970), 37–45

Horden, Peregrine, 'The Mediterranean plague in the age of Justinian', in Rousseau, ed., *A Companion to Late Antiquity*, 134–60

Horden, Peregrine, and Purcell, Nicholas, *The Corrupting Sea. A Study of Mediterranean History, vol. I* (Oxford: Blackwell, 2000)

Howard-Johnston, James, 'Procopius, Roman defences north of the Taurus and the new fortress of Citharizon', in French and Lightfoot, eds., *The Eastern Frontier of the Roman Empire*, 203–29

—— 'The siege of Constantinople in 626', in Mango and Dagron, eds., *Constantinople and its Hinterland*, 131–42

—— *Witness to a World Crisis. Historians and Histories of the Middle East in the Seventh Century* (Oxford, Oxford University Press, 2010)

Howard-Johnston, J., and Hayward, P.A., eds., *The Cult of Saints in Late Antiquity and the Middle Ages. Essays on the Contribution of Peter Brown* (Oxford: Oxford University Press, 1999)

Hoyland, Robert G., *Seeing Islam as Others Saw It. A Survey and Evaluation of Christian, Jewish and Zoroastrian Writings on Early Islam* (Princeton: Darwin Press, 1997)

—— *Arabia and the Arabs. From the Bronze Age to the Coming of Islam* (London: Routledge, 2001)

—— 'Arab kings, Arab tribes and the beginnings of Arab historical memory in late Roman epigraphy', in Cotton, Hoyland, Price, and Wasserstein, eds., *From Hellenism to Islam*, 374–400

—— 'Jacob and early Islamic Edessa', in Romeny, Bas ter Haar, ed., *Jacob of Edessa and the Syriac Culture of his Day*, 11–24

—— 'Epigraphy and the linguistic background to the Qur'an', in Reynolds, ed., *The Qur'an in its Historical Context*, 51–69

Huebner, Sabine R., 'Currencies of power: the venality of offices in the Later Roman Empire', in Cain and Lenski, eds., *The Power of Religion in Late Antiquity*, 167–79

Humfress, Caroline, *Orthodoxy and the Courts in Late Antiquity* (Oxford: Oxford University Press, 2007)

Humphrey, J.H., ed., *The Roman and Byzantine Near East: Some Recent Archaeological Work*, JRA supp. series 14 (Ann Arbor, MI: Journal of Roman Archaeology, 1995)

—— ed., *The Roman and Byzantine Near East* 2, JRA supp. series 31 (Portsmouth, RI: Journal of Roman Archaeology, 1999)

—— ed., *The Roman and Byzantine Near East* 3, JRA supp series 49 (Portsmouth, RI: Journal of Roman Archaeology, 2002)

Humphries, Mark, 'Italy, AD 425–605', in Cameron and Garnsey, eds., Cambridge Ancient History XIII, 525–51

Hunt, E.D., *Holy Land Pilgrimage in the Later Roman Empire AD 312–460* (Oxford: Oxford University Press, 1982)

Isaac, Benjamin, 'The meaning of the terms "limes" and "limitanei" in ancient sources', *Journal of Roman Studies* 78 (1988), 125–47

—— *The Limits of Empire. The Roman Army in the East* (Oxford: Oxford University Press, 1990, 1992)

—— 'The army in the Late Roman East', in Averil Cameron, ed., *States, Resources and Armies*, 125–55

—— 'Inscriptions and religious identity in the Golan', in Humphrey, ed., *The Roman and Byzantine Near East* 2, 179–88

Jacobs, Andrew S., *The Remains of the Jews. The Holy Land and Christian Empire in Late Antiquity* (Stanford: University of Stanford Press, 2004)

Jacobs, Ine, *The Classical City in Late Antiquity* (Leuven: Peeters, 2010)

James, Edward, *The Franks* (Oxford: Blackwell, 1988)

—— *Europe's Barbarians, AD 200–600* (Harlow, 2009)

James, Liz, *Empresses and Power in Early Byzantium* (Leicester: Leicester University Press, 2001)

—— *Art and Text in Byzantine Culture* (Cambridge: Cambridge University Press, 2007)

James, Liz, ed., *Desire and Denial in Byzantium*, Publications of the Society for the Promotion of Byzantine Studies 6 (Aldershot: Ashgate, 1999)

Jeffreys, Elizabeth, Jeffreys, Michael, and Scott, Roger, with Croke, Brian, *The Chronicle of John Malalas* (Melbourne: Australian Association for Byzantine Studies, 1986)

Jeffreys, Elizabeth, with Croke, Brian, and Scott, Roger, *Studies in John Malalas* (Sydney: Australian Association for Byzantine Studies, 1990)

Johnson, Scott Fitzgerald, *The Life and Miracles of Thekla. A Literary Study* (Cambridge, Mass: Center for Hellenic Studies, 2006)

Jones, A.H.M., 'Over-taxation and the decline of the Roman Empire', in Brunt, ed., *The Roman Economy*, 82–89

—— 'The Roman colonate', ibid., 293–307

—— 'The caste system in the Roman empire', ibid, 396–418

Kaegi Jr., Walter E., *Byzantium and the Decline of Rome* (Princeton: Princeton University Press, 1968)

—— *Byzantium and the Early Islamic Conquests* (Cambridge: Cambridge University Press, 1992)

—— *Heraclius, Emperor of Byzantium* (Cambridge: Cambridge University Press, 2003)

—— *Muslim Expansion and Byzantine Collapse in North Africa* (Cambridge: Cambridge University Press, 2010)

Kaldellis, Anthony, *Procopius of Caesarea. Tyranny, History and Philosophy at the End of Antiquity* (Philadelphia, Pa: University of Pennsylvania Press, 2004)

Kaplan, M., *Byzance: villes et campagnes* (Paris: Éditions Picard, 2006)

Kartsonis, Anna, *Anastasis. The Making of an Image* (Princeton: Princeton University Press, 1986)

Kaster, Robert A., *Guardians of Language. The Grammarian and Society in Late Antiquity* (Berkeley: University of California Press, 1988)

Kelly, Christopher, *Ruling the Later Roman Empire* (Cambridge, Mass.: Harvard University Press, 2004)

—— *Attila the Hun Barbarian Terror and the Fall of the Roman Empire* (London: Vintage, 2009)

Kelly, Gavin, *Ammianus Marcellinus, The Allusive Historian* (Cambridge: Cambridge University Press, 2008)

Kelly, J.N.D., *Golden Mouth. The Story of John Chrysostom, Ascetic, Preacher, Bishop* (London: Duckworth, 1995)

Kennedy, David, and Riley, Derrick, *Rome's Desert Frontier from the Air* (London: Batsford, 1990)

Kennedy, David, and Bewley, Robert, *Ancient Jordan from the Air* (London: Council for British Research in the Levant, 2004)

Kennedy, Hugh, 'From Polis to Madina: urban change in late antique and early Islamic Syria', *Past and Present* 106 (1985), 3–27

—— *The Prophet and the Age of the Caliphates. The Islamic Near East from the Sixth to the Eleventh Century* (London: Longman, 1986)

—— 'Antioch: from Byzantium to Islam and back again', in Rich, ed., *The City in Late Antiquity*, 181–98

Kennedy, Paul, *The Rise and Fall of the Great Powers. Economic Change and Military Conflict from 1500 to 2000* (New York: Random House, 1987)

Kent, J.P.C., and Painter, K.S., *Wealth of the Roman World, AD 300–700* (London: British Museum Publications, 1977)

King, G.R.D., 'Islam, iconoclasm and the declaration of doctrine', *Bulletin of the School of Oriental and African Studies* 48 (1985), 267–77

King, P.D., *Law and Society in the Visigothic Kingdom* (Cambridge: Cambridge University Press, 1972)

Kingsley, Sean A., *Shipwreck Archaeology of the Holy Land. Processes and Parameters* (London: Duckworth, 2004)

Kingsley, Sean A., and Decker, Michael, eds., *Economy and Exchange in the Eastern Mediterranean during Late Antiquity* (Oxford: Oxbow, 2001)

Kitzinger, E., 'The cult of images in the period before Iconoclasm', *Dumbarton Oaks Papers* 8 (1954), 85–150

—— *Byzantine Art in the Making* (Cambridge, Mass.: Harvard University Press, 1977)

Klingshirn, W., 'Charity and power: Caesarius of Arles and the ransoming of captives in sub-Roman Gaul', *Journal of Roman Studies* 75 (1985), 183–203

—— *Caesarius of Arles. The Making of a Christian Community in Late Antique Gaul* (Cambridge: Cambridge University Press, 1994)

—— *Caesarius of Arles: Life, Testament, Letters*, Translated Texts for Historians 19 (Liverpool: Liverpool University Press, 1994)

Kofsky, Ariel, and Stroumsa, Guy G., eds., *Sharing the Sacred. Religious Contacts and Conflicts in the Holy Land* (Jerusalem: Yad Izhak Ben Zvi, 1998)

Kontoleon, C., ed., *Antioch. The Last Ancient City* (Princeton: Princeton University Press, 2001)

Kraemer, C.J., Jr., ed., *Excavations at Nessana* III. *The Non-Literary Papyri* (Princeton: Princeton University Press, 1958)

Krause, Jens-Uwe, and Witschel, Christian, eds., *Die Stadt in der Spätantike – Niedergang oder Wandel?*, Historia Einzelschrift 190 (Stuttgart: Franz Steiner Verlag, 2006)

Krueger, Derek, *Symeon the Holy Fool: Leontius's Life and the Late Antique City* (Berkeley: University of California Press, 1996)

—— *Writing and Holiness. The Practice of Authorship in the Early Christian East* (Philadelphia, Pa: University of Pennsylvania Press, 2004)

Krueger, Derek, ed., *Byzantine Christianity*, A People's History of Christianity 3 (Minneapolis: Fortress Press, 2006)

Kulikowski, Michael, *Rome's Gothic Wars* (Cambridge: Cambridge University Press, 2007)

Ladstätter, S., and Pülz, A., 'Ephesus in the late Roman and early Byzantine period: changes in its urban character from the third to the seventh century AD', in Poulter, ed., *The Transition to Late Antiquity on the Danube and Beyond*, 391–433

Laiou, Angeliki E., ed., *The Economic History of Byzantium. From the Seventh through the Fifteenth Century*, 3 vols. (Washington, DC: Dumbarton Oaks, 2002)

Laiou, Angeliki E., and Morrisson, Cécile, *The Byzantine Economy* (Cambridge: Cambridge University Press, 2007)

Laniado, A., *Recherches sur les notables municipaux dans l'Empire protobyzantin* (Paris: Centre d'histoire et de civilisation de Byzance, 2002)

Lapidge, Michael, and Dumville, D., eds., *Gildas: New Approaches* (Woodbridge, Suffolk: Boydell Press, 1984)

Lavan, Luke, 'What killed the ancient city? Chronology, causation and traces of continuity', *Journal of Roman Archaeology* 22 (2009), 803–12

Lavan, Luke, and Bowden, William, eds., *Theory and Practice in Late Antique Archaeology*, Late Antique Archaeology 1 (Leiden: Brill, 2003)

Lavan, Luke, Swift, Ellen and Putzeys, Toon, eds., *Objects in Context, Objects in Use. Material Spatiality in Late Antiquity*, Late Antique Archaeology 5 (Leiden: Brill, 2007)

Le Coz, R., *Jean Damascène, Écrits sur l'Islam,* Sources chrétiennes 383 (Paris: Cerf, 1992)

Leeming, K., 'The adoption of Arabic as a liturgical language by the Palestinian Melkites', *ARAM* 15 (2003), 239–46

Lefort, J., Morrisson, C., and Sodini, J.P., *Les villages dans l'empire byzantin, IVe-XVe siècle* (Paris: Lethielleux, 2005)

Lemerle, P., *Les plus anciens recueils des miracles de saint Démétrius*, 2 vols. (Paris: Editions du CNRS, 1979, 1981)

Lenski, Noel, *Failure of Empire. Valens and the Roman State in the Fourth Century AD* (Berkeley: University of California Press, 2002)

—— 'Captivity, slavery and cultural exchange between Rome and the Germans from the first to the seventh century CE', in Cameron, ed., *Invisible Citizens. Captives and their Consequences*, 80–109

Lee, A.D., 'Warfare and the state', in Sabin, Van Wees, and Whitby, eds., *The Cambridge History of Greek and Roman Warfare* II, 379–423

—— 'The empire at war', in Maas, ed., *Companion to the Age of Justinian*, 113–33

Lemerle, Paul, *Byzantine Humanism*, Eng. trans. (Canberra: Australian Association for Byzantine Studies, 1986)

Lenski, Noel, ed., *The Cambridge Companion to the Age of Constantine* (Cambridge: Cambridge University Press, 2006)

Leone, Anna, *Changing Townscapes in North Africa from Late Antiquity to the Arab Conquest* (Bari: Edipuglia, 2007)

Lepelley, C., *Les cités de l'Afrique romaine an Bas-Empire*, I–II (Paris: Études augustiniennes, 1979–81)

—— 'Peuplement et richesses de l'Afrique romaine tardive', in Morrisson and Lefort, eds., *Hommes et richesses dans l'empire byzantin* I, 17–30

Leveau, P., *Caesarea de Maurétanie: une ville romaine et ses campagnes* (Rome: École français de Rome, 1984)

Lewin, Ariel S., and Pellegrini, Pietrina, eds., *The Late Roman Army in the Near East from Diocletian to the Arab Conquest*, BAR international ser. 1717 (Oxford: BAR, 2007)

Liebeschuetz, J.H.W.G., *Antioch. City and Imperial Administration in the Later Roman Empire* (Oxford: Oxford University Press, 1972)

—— 'Friends and enemies of John Chrysostom', in A. Moffatt, ed., *Maistor* (Canberra; Australian Association for Byzantine Studies, 1984), 85–111

—— *Barbarians and Bishops. Army, Church and State in the Age of Arcadius and Chrysostom* (Oxford: Clarendon Press, 1990)

—— 'Cities, taxes and the accommodation of the barbarians: the theories of Durliat and Goffart', in Pohl, ed., *Kingdoms of the Empire*, 135–51

—— *The Decline and Fall of the Roman City* (Oxford: Oxford University Press, 2001)

—— *Ambrose of Milan. Political Letters and Speeches*, trans. with introduction and notes, with the assistance of Carole Hill, Translated Texts for Historians 43 (Liverpool: Liverpool University Press, 2005)

—— 'The view from Antioch: from Libanius via John Chrysostom to John Malalas and beyond', *Cristianesimo nella Storia* 31 (2009), 441–70

Liebeschuetz, J.H.W.G., and Kennedy, H., 'Antioch and the villages of northern Syria in the fifth and sixth centuries AD: trends and problems', *Nottingham Medieval Studies* 23 (1988), 65–90 (reprinted in J.H.W.G. Liebeschuetz, *From Diocletian to the Arab Conquest* (London: Variorum, 1990), XVI)

Lieu, Samuel N.C., *The Emperor Julian. Panegyric and Polemic*, 2nd ed. (Liverpool: Liverpool University Press, 1992)

*Life of Severinus*, trans. L. Bieler (Washington, DC: Catholic University of America Press, 1965)

Limberis, V., *Divine Heiress. The Virgin Mary and the Creation of Christian Constantinople* (London: Routledge, 1994)

Little, Lester K., ed., *Plague and the End of Antiquity. The Pandemic of 541–750* (Cambridge: Cambridge University Press, 2007)

Lizzi, Rita, 'Ambrose's contemporaries and the Christianization of northern Italy', *Journal of Roman Studies* 80 (1990), 156–73 (see also Testa, Rita Lizzi)

Louth, Andrew, *Maximus the Confessor* (London: Routledge, 1996)

—— *St John Damascene. Tradition and Originality in Byzantine Theology* (Oxford: Oxford University Press, 2002)

—— 'The emergence of Byzantine Orthodoxy, 600–1095', in Noble and Smith, eds., *The Cambridge History of Christianity 3*, 46–64

Maas, Michael, 'Roman history and Christian ideology in Justinianic reform legislation', *Dumbarton Oaks Papers* 40 (1986), 17–31

—— *John Lydus and the Roman Past. Antiquarianism and Politics in the Age of Justinian* (London: Routledge, 1992)

MacCoull, L.B., *Dioscorus of Aphrodito. His Work and his World* (Berkeley and Los Angeles: University of California Press, 1988)

Macdonald, M.A., ed., *The Development of Arabic as a Written Language*, supplement to the Proceedings of the Seminar for Arabian Studies 40 (Oxford; Archaeopress, 2010)

MacMullen, Ramsay, 'Judicial savagery in the Roman empire', *Chiron* 16 (1986), 147–66

—— 'Late Roman slavery', *Historia* 36 (1987), 359–82

—— *Corruption and the Decline of Rome* (New Haven: Yale University Press, 1988)

—— *Christianity and Paganism in the Fourth to Eighth Centuries* (New Haven, 1997)

—— *Voting about God in Early Church Councils* (New Haven: Yale University Press, 2006)

—— *The Second Church. Popular Christianity, AD 200–400* (Atlanta: Society of Biblical Literature, 2009)

Magdalino, Paul, ed., *New Constantines* (Aldershot: Variorum, 1994)

Magdalino, Paul, and Macrides, Ruth, 'The architecture of ekphrasis: the construction and context of Paul the Silentiary's poem on S. Sophia', *Byzantine and Modern Greek Studies* 12 (1988), 47–82

Magness, Jodi, 'Redating the forts at Ein Boqeq, Upper Zohar and other sites in SE Judaea, and the implications for the nature of the *Limes Palaestinae*', in Humphrey, ed., *The Roman and Byzantine Near East* 2, 189–206

Maguire, Eunice Dauterman, and Maguire, Henry, *Other Icons. Art and Power in Byzantine Secular Culture* (Princeton: Princeton University Press, 2007)

Malkin, Irad, ed., *Mediterranean Paradigms and Classical Antiquity* (London: Routledge, 2005)

Mango, C., *Byzantine Architecture* (London: Faber/Electa, 1978)

—— *Byzantium. The Empire of New Rome* (London: Weidenfeld and Nicolson, 1980)

—— 'Discontinuity with the classical past in Byzantium', in Mullett and Scott, eds., *Byzantium and the Classical Tradition*, 48–57

—— 'Constantine's mausoleum and the translation of relics', *Byzantinische Zeitschrift* 83 (1990), 51–61 (= Cyril Mango, *Studies on Constantinople* (Aldershot: Variorum, 1993), V).

—— *Le développement urbain de Constantinople (IVe–VIIe siècle)* (Paris: Boccard, 1985, rev. ed., 1990)

Mango, Cyril, and Dagron, Gilbert, eds., with the assistance of Greatrex, Geoffrey, *Constantinople and its Hinterland* (Aldershot: Variorum, 1985)

Mango, Cyril, and Scott, Roger, eds., *The Chronicle of Theophanes Confessor. Byzantine and Near Eastern History, AD 284–813* (Oxford: Clarendon Press, 1997)

Mango, Marlia Mundell, *Silver from Early Byzantium. The Kaper Koraon and Related Treasures* (Baltimore: Walters Art Gallery, 1986)

—— 'Byzantine maritime trade with the east 4th–7th centuries', *ARAM* 8 (1996), 139–63

Mango, Marlia Mundell, ed., *Byzantine Trade, 4th–12th Centuries* (Farnham: Ashgate, 2009)

Mann, Michael, *The Sources of Social Power* 1. *A History of Power from the Beginning to AD 1760* (Cambridge: Cambridge University Press, 1986)

Marasco, G., ed., *Greek and Roman Historiography in Late Antiquity* (Leiden: Brill, 2003)

Marcone, A., *Il colonato tardoantico nella storiografia moderna* (Como: Edizioni New Press, 1988)

Markus, R.A., *The End of Ancient Christianity* (Cambridge: Cambridge University Press, 1990)

—— 'From Rome to the barbarian kingdoms (300–700)', in McManners, ed., *Oxford Illustrated History of Christianity*, 62–91

—— *Gregory the Great and his World* (Cambridge: Cambridge University Press, 1997).

Marsham, Andrew, 'The early Caliphate and the inheritance of late antiquity (c. AD 610-c. AD 750)', in Rousseau, ed., *A Companion to Late Antiquity*, 479–92

Martin, Dale B., and Miller, Patricia Cox, *The Cultural Turn in Late Ancient Studies: Gender, Asceticism and Historiography* (Durham, NC: Duke University Press, 2005)

Matthews, John F., *The Roman Empire of Ammianus* (London: Duckworth, 1989)

—— *Laying Down the Law. A Study of the Theodosian Code* (New Haven: Yale University Press, 2000)

Mathews, Thomas F., *The Art of Byzantium* (London: George Weidenfeld and Nicolson Ltd, 1998)

Mathisen, Ralph, ed., *Law, Society and Authority in Late Antiquity* (Oxford: Oxford University Press, 2001)

Mathisen, Ralph W., and Sivan, Hagith S., eds. *Shifting Frontiers in Late Antiquity* (Aldershot: Variorum, 1996)

Mathisen, Ralph, and Schanzer, Danuta, eds., *Romans, Barbarians and the Transformation of the Roman World* (Farnham: Ashgate, 2011)

Matthews, John F., *Laying Down the Law. A Study of the Theodosian Code* (New Haven: Yale University Press, 2000)

Mattingly, D., and Hitchner, R.B., 'Roman Africa: an archaeological review', *Journal of Roman Studies* 85 (1995), 165–213

Mayer, Wendy, and Allen, Pauline, eds., *John Chrysostom* (London: Routledge, 2000)

McCormick, Michael, *The Origins of the European Economy: Communications and Commerce, AD 300–900* (Cambridge: Cambridge University Press, 2001)

McGuckin, John, *Saint Gregory of Nazianzus. An Intellectual Biography* (Crestwood, NY: St Vladimir's, 2001)

McKenzie, J.S., Gibson, S., and Reyes, A.T., 'Reconstructing the Serapeum from the archaeological evidence', *Journal of Roman Studies* 94 (2004), 35–63

McKitterick, Rosamond, and Quinault, Roland, eds., *Edward Gibbon and Empire* (Cambridge: Cambridge University Press, 1997)

McLynn, Neil, *Ambrose of Milan. Church and Court in a Christian Capital* (Berkeley: University of California Press, 1994)

—— 'Pagans in a Christian empire', in Rousseau, ed., *A Companion to Late Antiquity*, 572–87

McManners, J., ed., *Oxford Illustrated History of Christianity* (Oxford: Oxford University Press, 1992)

McVey, Kathleen, 'The domed church as microcosm: literary roots of an architectural symbol', *Dumbarton Oaks Papers* 37 (1983), 91–121

Meier, Mischa, *Das andere Zeitalter Justinians. Kontingenzerfahrung und Kontingengenzbewältigung im 6. Jahr. n. Chr.* (Göttingen: Vandenhoeck & Ruprecht, 2003)

Menze, Volker-Lorenz, *Justinian and the Making of the Syrian Orthodox Church* (Oxford: Oxford University Press, 2008)

Menze, Volker-Lorenz, and Akalin, Kutlu, *John of Tella's Profession of Faith. The Legacy of a Sixth-Century Syrian Orthodox Bishop* (Piscataway, NJ: Gorgias Press, 2009)

Merrills, A.H., *Vandals, Romans and Berbers. New Perspectives on Late Antique North Africa* (Aldershot: Ashgate, 2004)

—— *History and Geography in Late Antiquity* (Cambridge: Cambridge University Press, 2005)

Merrills, Andy, and Miles, Richard, *The Vandals* (Oxford: Wiley-Blackwell, 2010)

Metcalf, D., 'The Slavonic threat to Greece', *Hesperia* 31 (1962), 134–57

—— 'Avar and Slav invasions into the Balkan peninsula (c. 575–625): the nature of the numismatic evidence', *Journal of Roman Archaeology* 4 (1991), 140–48

Mierow, Charles, C., *The Gothic History of Jordanes* (Princeton: Princeton University Press, 1915)

Millar, Fergus, 'Empire, community and culture in the Roman Near East: Syrians, Jews and Arabs', *Journal of Jewish Studies*, 38 (1987), 143–604

—— 'Repentant heretics in fifth-century Lydia: identity and literacy', *Scripta Classica Israelica* 23 (2004), 111–30

—— 'The Theodosian empire (408–50) and the Arabs: Saracens or Ishmaelites?', in Gruen, ed., *Cultural Borrowings and Ethnic Appropriations in Antiquity*, 297–314

—— *A Greek Roman Empire. Power and Belief under Theodosius II (408–50)* (Berkeley: University of California Press, 2006)

—— 'The Syriac Acts of the Second Council of Ephesus (449)', in Price and Whitby, eds., *Chalcedon in Context*, 45–69

—— 'Narrative and identity in mosaics from the late Roman Near East: pagan, Jewish and Christian', in Eliav, Friedland and Herbert, eds., *The Sculptural Environment of the Roman Near East,* 225–56

—— 'Christian monasticism in Roman Arabia at the birth of Mahomet', *Semitica et Classica* 2 (2009), 97–115

—— 'Linguistic co-existence in Constantinople: Greek and Latin (and Syriac) in the Acts of the Synod of 536 C.E.', *Journal of Roman Studies* 99 (2009), 92–103

Miller, Patricia Cox, *The Poetry of Thought in Late Antiquity. Essays in Imagination and Religion* (Aldershot: Ashgate, 2001)

Mills, Kenneth, and Grafton, Anthony, eds., *Conversion in Late Antiquity and Beyond* (Rochester, NY: University of Rochester Press, 2003)

Milson, David, *Art and Architecture of the Synagogue in Late Antique Palestine: In the Shadow of the Church* (Leiden: Brill, 2007)

Mitchell, Stephen, *Anatolia; Land, Men and Gods in Asia Minor,* 2 vols. (Oxford: Oxford University Press, 1995)

Mitchell, Stephen, and Greatrex, Geoffrey, eds., *Ethnicity and Culture in Late Antiquity* (London and Swansea: Duckworth, 2000)

Modéran, Yves, *Les Maures et l'Afrique romaine (IVe–VIIe siècle)* (Rome: École française de Rome, 2003)

Momigliano, Arnaldo, ed., *The Conflict between Christianity and Paganism in the Fourth Century* (Oxford: Clarendon Press, 1963)

Moore, R.I., *The First European Revolution, c. 970–1215* (Oxford: Blackwell, 2000)

Moorhead, John, 'The Monophysite response to the Arab invasions', *Byzantion* 51 (1981), 579–91

—— 'Italian loyalties in Justinian's Gothic War', *Byzantion* 53 (1983), 575–96

—— 'Culture and power among the Ostrogoths', *Klio* 68 (1986), 112–22

—— *Victor of Vita: History of the Vandal Persecution,* Translated Texts for Historians 10 (Liverpool: Liverpool University Press, 1992)

—— *Justinian* (London: Longman, 1994)

—— *The Roman Empire Divided, 400–700* (London: Longmans, 2001)

Morony, Michael, *Iraq after the Muslim Conquest* (Princeton: Princeton University Press, 1984)

Morris, Ian, and Scheidel, Walter, eds., *The Dynamics of Ancient Empires. State Power from Assyria to Byzantium* (Oxford: Oxford University Press, 2009)

Morris, Rosemary, ed., *Church and People in Byzantium* (Birmingham: Centre for Byzantine, Ottoman and Modern Greek Studies, 1990)

Morrisson, C., and Sodini, J.-P., 'The sixth-century economy', in Laiou, ed., *The Economic History of Byzantium, From the Seventh through the Fifteenth Century* I, 171–219

Mullett, Margaret, and Scott, Roger, eds., *Byzantium and the Classical Tradition* (Birmingham: Centre for Byzantine Studies, University of Birmingham, 1981)

Murphy, Cullen, *Are we Rome? The End of an Empire and the Fate of America* (Boston: Houghton Mifflin Co., 2007)

Nelson, J., 'Symbols in context: rulers' inauguration rituals in Byzantium and the west in the early middle ages', in Baker, ed., *The Orthodox Churches and the West*, 97–118

Norton, Peter, *Episcopal Elections, 250–600. Hierarchy and Popular Will in Late Antiquity* (Oxford: Oxford University Press, 2007)

Noth, A., and Conrad, L.I., *The Early Islamic Historical Tradition: A Source-Critical Study* (Princeton: Darwin Press, 1999)

O'Donnell, James J., *Cassiodorus* (Berkeley: University of California Press, 1979)

—— *The Ruin of the Roman Empire* (London: Profile, 2009)

O'Flynn, J.M., *Generalissimos of the Western Roman Empire* (Edmonton, Alberta: University of Alberta Press, 1983)

Olster, David M., *Roman Defeat, Christian Response and the Literary Construction of the Jew* (Philadelphia: University of Pennsylvania Press, 1994)

O'Meara, D.J., *Platonopolis: Platonic Political Philosophy in Late Antiquity* (Oxford: Oxford University Press, 2003)

Osborne, Robin, and Tanner, Jeremy, eds., *Art's Agency and Art History* (Oxford: Blackwell, 2007)

Pagels, Elaine, *Adam, Eve and the Serpent* (London: Weidenfeld and Nicolson, 1988)

Palmer, Andrew, *The Seventh-Century in the West-Syrian Chronicles*, Translated Texts for Historians 15 (Liverpool: Liverpool University Press, 1993)

Panella, C., 'Le merci: produzioni, itinerari e destini', in Giardina, ed., *Società romana e impero tardoantico* III, 431–59

—— 'Gli scambi nel Mediterraneo Occidentale dal IV al VII secolo dal punto di vista di alcune "merci"', in *Hommes et richesses dans l'empire byzantin* I, 129–41

Papaconstantinou, Arietta, *Le culte des saints en Egypte: des Byzantins aux Abbassides* (Paris: CNRS Editions, 2001)

—— '"What remains behind": Hellenism and Romanitas in Christian Egypt after the Arab conquest', in Cotton, Hoyland, Price, and Wasserstein, eds., *From Hellenism to Islam*, 447–66

—— *Languages and Literature of Early Christianity: Coptic* (Paris: Lavoisier, 2009)

Papaconstantinou, Arietta, ed., *The Multilingual Experience in Egypt, from the Ptolemies to the Abbasids* (Farnham: Ashgate, 2010)

Papaconstantinou, Arietta, and Talbot, Alice-Mary, eds., *Becoming Byzantine. Children and Childhood in Byzantium* (Washington, DC: Dumbarton Oaks, 2009)

Parker, S. Thomas, *Romans and Saracens. A History of the Arabian Frontier* (Winona Lake, Indiana: American Schools of Oriental Research, 1986)

—— *The Roman Frontier in Central Jordan: Interim Report on the Limes Arabicus Project 1980–1985* (Oxford, BAR, 1987)

Patlagean, Evelyne, *Pauvreté économique et pauvreté sociale à Byzance, IVe–VIIe siècles* (Paris: Mouton, 1977)

Patrich, J., *Sabas, Leader of Palestinian Monasticism: A Comparative Study in Eastern Monasticism, Fourth to Seventh Centuries* (Washington, DC: Dumbarton Oaks, 1995)

Patrich, J., ed., *The Sabaite Heritage in the Orthodox Church from the Fifth Century to the Present* (Leuven: Peeters, 2001)

Pazdernik, C., 'The trembling of Cain: religious power and institutional culture in Justinianic oath-making', in Cain and Lenski, eds., *The Power of Religion in Late Antiquity*, 143–54

Peltomaa, Leena Mari, *The Image of the Virgin in the Akathistos Hymn* (Leiden: Brill, 2001)

Pentcheva, Bissera V., *Icons and Power. The Mother of God in Byzantium* (University Park, Pa: University of Pennsylvania Press, 2006)

Perczel, I., 'Pseudo-Dionysius and Palestinian Origenism', in Patrich, ed., *The Sabaite Heritage in the Orthodox Church from the Fifth Century to the Present*, 261–82

Piccirillo, M., *The Mosaics of Jordan*, ed. Patricia M. Bikai and Thomas A. Dailey (Amman, Jordan: American Center of Oriental Research, 1992)

Piganiol, André, *L'Empire chrétien (325–395)* (Paris: Presses universitaires de France, 1947)

Pirenne, Henri, *Mahomet et Charlemagne* (Paris: Félix Alcan, 1937)

Pohl, Walter, ed., *Kingdoms of the Empire. The Integration of Barbarians in Late Antiquity* (Leiden: Brill, 1997)

Pohl, Walter, with Reimitz, Helmut, eds., *Strategies of Distinction. The Construction of the Ethnic Communities, 300–800* (Leiden, Brill, 1998)

Potter, D., *The Roman Empire at Bay AD 180–395* (London: Routledge, 2004)

—— *Rome in the Ancient World. Romulus to Justinian* (London: Thames and Hudson, 2009)

Potter, T., *The Changing Landscape of South Etruria* (London: Elek, 1979)

Potts, David, *The Arabian Gulf in Antiquity* II (Oxford: Clarendon Press, 1990)

Poulter, A.G., *Nicopolis ad Istrum: A Roman, Late Roman and early Byzantine City* (London: Society for the Promotion of Roman Studies, 1995)

Poulter, A.G., ed., *The Transition to Late Antiquity on the Danube and Beyond* (Oxford: Oxford University Press for the British Academy, 2007)

Price, Richard M., *A History of the Monks of Syria by Theodoret of Cyrrhus* (Kalamazoo: Cistercian Publications, 1985)

—— *Lives of the Monks of Palestine by Cyril of Scythopolis* (Kalamazoo: Cistercian Publications, 1991)

—— 'Marian piety and the Nestorian controversy', in Swanson, ed., *The Church and Mary*, 31–38

—— 'The council of Chalcedon (451): a narrative', in Price and Whitby, eds., *Chalcedon in Context*, 70–91

—— *The Acts of Constantinople 553, with related texts from the Three Chapters Controversy*, translated with an introduction and notes, Translated Texts for Historians 51, 2 vols. (Liverpool: Liverpool University Press, 2009)

Price, Richard, and Gaddis, Michael, *The Acts of the Council of Chalcedon*, translated and with an introduction, Translated Texts for Historians 45, 3 vols. (Liverpool: Liverpool University Press, 2005)

Price, Richard, and Whitby, Mary, eds., *Chalcedon in Context. Church Councils 400–700* (Oxford: Oxford University Press, 2008)

Price, Simon, and Thonemann, Peter, *The Birth of Classical Europe. A History from Troy to Augustine* (London: Allen Lane, 2010)

Pringle, D., *The Defence of Byzantine Africa, from Justinian to the Arab Conquest. An Account of the Military History and Archaeology of the African Provinces in the Sixth and Seventh Centuries*, 2 vols. (Oxford: BAR, 1981, 2001)

—— 'Two fortified sites in Byzantine Africa: Aïn Djelloula and Henchir Sguidan', *Antiquité tardive* 10 (2002), 269–90

Raby, Julian, and Johns, Jeremy, eds., *Bayt al-Maqdis*, 2 vols. (Oxford: Oxford University Press, 1992, 1999)

Rajak, Tessa, *Translation and Survival. The Greek Bible of the Ancient Jewish Diaspora* (Oxford: Oxford University Press, 2009)

Rance, Philip, 'Battle', in Sabin, van Wees and Whitby, eds., *The Cambridge History of Greek and Roman Warfare* II, 347–48

Rapp, Claudia, *Holy Bishops in Late Antiquity. The Nature of Christian Leadership in an Age of Transition* (Berkeley: University of California Press, 2005)

—— 'Literary culture under Justinian', in Maas, ed., *Companion to the Age of Justinian*, 376–97

Rebillard, É., *The Care of the Dead in Late Antiquity*, Eng. trans. (Ithaca, NY: Cornell University Press, 2009)

Rebillard, É., and Sotinel, C., eds., *Les frontières du profane dans l'Antiquité tardive* (Rome: École française de Rome, 2010)

Reinink, Gerrit J., and Stolte, Bernard H., eds., *The Reign of Heraclius. Crisis and Confrontation 9610–641)* (Leuven: Peeters, 2002)

Reynolds, G.S., ed., *The Qur'an in its Historical Context* (London: Routledge, 2008)

Rich, John, ed., *The City in Late Antiquity* (London: Routledge, 1992)

Ringrose, Kathryn, *The Perfect Servant. Eunuchs and the Social Construction of Gender in Byzantium* (Chicago, Ill; University of Chicago Press, 2003)

Roberts, Michael, *Biblical Epic and Rhetorical Paraphrase in Late Antiquity* (Liverpool: F. Cairns, 1985)

—— *The Jeweled Style. Poetry and Poetics in Late Antiquity* (Ithaca, NY: Cornell University Press, 1989)

Rogers, G.M., *The Sacred Identity of Ephesos* (London: Routledge, 1991)

Romeny, Bas ter Haar, ed., *Jacob of Edessa and the Syriac Culture of his Day* (Leiden: Brill, 2008)

Rosenblum, M., *Luxorius. A Latin Poet among the Vandals* (New York: Columbia University Press, 1961)

Rostovzeff, M.I., *Social and Economic History of the Roman Empire*, 2nd ed. revised by P.M. Fraser (Oxford: Oxford University Press, 1957)

Rotman, Y., *Byzantine Slavery and the Mediterranean World*, Eng. trans. (Cambridge, Mass.: Harvard University Press, 2009)

Roueché, C.M., 'Acclamations in the later Roman empire: new evidence from Aphrodisias', *Journal of Roman Studies* 74 (1984), 181–99

—— *Aphrodisias in Late Antiquity* (London: Society for the Promotion of Roman Studies, 1989)

—— *Performers and Partisans at Aphrodisias in the Roman and Late Roman Periods* (London: Society for the Promotion of Roman Studies, 1992)

—— 'The functions of the Roman governor in Late Antiquity: some observations', *Antiquité tardive* 5 (1998), 31–6

—— 'Provincial governors and their titulature in the sixth century', ibid., 83–9

Roueché, C.M., ed., *De aedificiis. Le texte de Procope et les réalités*, *Antiquité tardive* 8 (2001), 7–180

Rousseau, Philip, *Pachomius*, (Berkeley: University of California Press, 1985)

Rousseau, Philip, and Papoutsakis, Manolis, eds., *Transformations of Late Antiquity. Essays for Peter Brown* (Aldershot, 2009)

Rousselle, Aline, *Porneia: On Desire and the Body in Antiquity*, Eng. trans. (Oxford: Blackwell, 1988)

Rubin, Milka, 'Arabization versus Islamization in the Palestinian Melkite community during the early Muslim period', in Kofsky and Stroumsa, eds., *Sharing the Sacred. Religious Contacts and Conflicts in the Holy Land*, 149–62

Ruffini, G., *Social Networks in Byzantine Egypt* (Cambridge: Cambridge University Press, 2008)

Rüpke, J., 'Early Christianity out of, and in, context', *Journal of Roman Studies* 99 (2009), 182–93

Russell, Norman, trans., *The Lives of the Desert Fathers. The Historia Monachorum in Aegypto* (Kalamazoo, Mich.: Cistercian Publications, 1980)

Russell, K.W., 'The earthquake chronology of Palestine and northwest Arabia from the 2nd through the mid-8th century AD', *Bull. American Schools of Oriental Research* 260 (1985), 37–60

Rutgers, L., *The Jews in Late Ancient Rome. Evidence of Cultural Interaction in the Roman Diaspora* (Leiden; Brill, 1995)

Sabin, Philip, van Wees, Hans, and Whitby, Michael, eds., *The Cambridge History of Greek and Roman Warfare* II: *Rome from the Late Republic to the Late Empire* (Cambridge: Cambridge University Press, 2007)

Sandwell, I., and Huskinson, J., eds., *Culture and Society in Later Roman Antioch* (Oxford: Oxbow, 2004)

Saradi, Helen, *The Byzantine City in the Sixth Century: Literary Images and Historical Reality* (Athens: Society of Messenian Archaeological Studies, 2006)

—— 'Towns and cities', in Jeffreys, with Haldon and Cormack, eds., *The Oxford Handbook of Byzantine Studies*, 317–27

Sarris, Peter, *Economy and Society in the Age of Justinian* (Cambridge: Cambridge University Press, 2006)

Sarris, P., Dal Santo, M., and Booth, P., *An Age of Saints? Power, Conflict and Dissent in Early Medieval Christianity* (Leiden: Brill, 2011)

Sartre, M., *Trois études sur l'Arabie romaine et byzantine*, Coll. Latomus 178 (Brussels: Revue d'études latines, 1982)

Sawyer, P.H., and Wood, I.N., eds., *Early Medieval Kingship* (Leeds: University of Leeds, 1977)

Scheidel, W., ed., *Debating Roman Demography* (Leiden: Brill, 2001)

Scheidel, Walter, ed., *Rome and China. Comparative Perspectives on Ancient World Empires* (Oxford: Oxford University Press, 2009)

Scheidel, Walter, and Friesen, Steven J., 'The size of the economy and the distribution of income in the Roman empire', *Journal of Roman Studies* 99 (2009), 61–91

Scheidel, W., Morris, I, Saller, R., eds., *The Cambridge Economic History of the Graeco-Roman World* (Cambridge: Cambridge University Press, 2007)

Schick, Robert, *The Christian Communities of Palestine from Byzantine to Islamic Rule. A Historical and Archaeological Study* (Princeton: Darwin Press, 1995)

Scott, Roger, 'Malalas, the *Secret History* and Justinian's propaganda', *Dumbarton Oaks Papers* 39 (1985), 99–109

—— 'Justinian's coinage, the Easter reforms and the date of the *Secret History*', *Byzantine and Modern Greek Studies* 11 (1987) 215–21

Schwartz, Seth, *Imperialism and Jewish Society 200 BCE to 640 CE* (Princeton: Princeton University Press, 2005)

Ševčenko, I., and Ševčenko, N.P., *The Life of St. Nicholas of Sion* (Brookline, Mass.: Hellenic College Press, 1984)

Shahid, I., *Rome and the Arabs. A Prolegomenon to the Study of Byzantium and the Arabs* (Washington, DC: Dumbarton Oaks, 1984)

—— *Rome and the Arabs in the Fifth Century* (Washington, DC: Dumbarton Oaks, 1989)

—— *Rome and the Arabs in the Sixth Century*, 2 vols. (Washington, DC: Dumbarton Oaks, 1995, 2002)

Shanzer, Danuta, and Wood, Ian N., *Avitus of Vienne: Letters and Selected Prose*, Translated Texts for Historians 38 (Liverpool: Liverpool University Press, 2002)

Shaw, Brent D., 'Latin funerary epigraphy and family life in the later Roman empire', *Historia* 33 (1984), 457–97

—— 'The family in late antiquity: the experience of Augustine', *Past and Present* 115 (1987), 3–51

—— 'War and violence', in Bowersock, Brown and Grabar, eds., *Late Antiquity*, 130–69

—— *Rulers, Nomads and Christians in Roman North Africa* (Aldershot: Variorum, 1995)

—— 'African Christianity: disputes, definitions and "Donatists"', in Shaw, *Rulers, Nomads and Christians in Roman North Africa*, XI

—— 'Challenging Braudel: a new vision of the Mediterranean', *Journal of Roman Archaeology* 14 (2001), 419–53

—— 'After Rome. Transformations of the early Mediterranean world', *New Left Review* 51 (May/June 2008), 89–114

Shepard, J., and Franklin, S., eds., *Byzantine Diplomacy* (Aldershot: Ashgate, 1992)

Sirks, A.J.B., *Food for Rome. The Legal Structure of the Transportation and Processing of Supplies for the Imperial Distributions in Rome and Constantinople* (Amsterdam: Gieben, 1991)

—— 'The colonate in Justinian's reign', *Journal of Roman Studies* 98 (2008), 120–43

Sizgorich, Thomas, *Violence and Belief in Late Antiquity. Militant Devotion in Christianity and Islam* (Philadelphia: University of Pennsylvania Press, 2009)

Smith, A., ed., *The Philosopher and Society in Late Antiquity* (Swansea: Classical Press of Wales, 2005)

Smith, Lesley M., ed., *The Making of Britain I: The Dark Ages* (Basingstoke: Macmillan, 1984)

Smith, R.R.R., 'Late Roman philosopher portraits from Aphrodisias', *Journal of Roman Studies* 80 (1990), 127–55

Smith, R.R.R., and Erim, Kenan T., eds., *Aphrodisias Papers* 2 (Ann Arbor, Michigan: Dept of Classical Studies, University of Michigan, 1991)

Smith, R.R.R., with Sheila Dillon et al., *Roman Portrait Statuary at Aphrodisias* (Mainz am Rhein: Verlag Philipp von Zabern, 2006)

Smith, Rowland, *Julian's Gods: Religion and Philosophy in the Thought and Action of Julian the Apostate* (London: Routledge, 1995)

Sodini, J.-P., 'The transformation of cities in late antiquity within the provinces of Macedonia and Epirus', in Poulter, ed., *The Transition to Late Antiquity*, 311–36

Sorabji, Richard, *Time, Creation and the Continuum: Theories in Antiquity and the Early Middle Ages*, (London: Variorum, 1983)

Sorabji, Richard, ed., *Philoponus and the Rejection of Aristotelian Science* (London: Duckworth, 1987)

—— *Aristotle Transformed. The Ancient Commentators and their Influence* (London: Duckworth, 1990)

Sotinel, C., 'Emperors and popes in the sixth century: the western view', in Maas, ed., *The Cambridge Companion to the Age of Justinian*, 267–90

Spieser, J.-M., 'L'évolution de la ville byzantine de l'époque paléo-chrétienne à l'iconoclasme', in *Hommes et richesses* I, 97–106

Stathakapoulos, Dionysios Ch., *Famine and Pestilence in the Late Roman and Early Byzantine Empire. A Systematic Survey of Subsistence Crises and Epidemics* (Aldershot: Ashgate, 2004)

—— 'Population, demography and disease', in Jeffreys, with Haldon and Cormack, eds., *The Oxford Handbook of Byzantine Studies*, 309–16

Stancliffe, Clare, *St. Martin and his Hagiographer. History and Miracle in Sulpicius Severus* (Oxford: Clarendon Press, 1983)

Stark, Rodney, *The Rise of Christianity. A Sociologist Reconsiders History* (Princeton: Princeton University Press, 1996)

Starr, C.G., *The Roman Empire, 27 BC to AD 476: A Study in Survival* (Oxford: 1982)

Sterk, Andrea, *Renouncing the World yet Leading the Church: the Monk-Bishop in Late Antiquity* (Cambridge, Mass.: Harvard University Press, 2005)

Stevens, S.T., Kalinowski, A.V., and van der Leest, H., *Bir Ftouha. A Pilgrimage Complex at Carthage*, Journal of Roman Archaeology supplement 59 (Providence, RI: Journal of Roman Archaeology, 2005)

Stevenson, J., ed., *A New Eusebius. Documents Illustrating the History of the Church to AD 337*, rev. W.H.C. Frend (London: SPCK, 1987)

—— *Creeds, Councils and Controversies. Documents Illustrating the History of the Church, AD 337–461*, rev. W.H.C. Frend (London: SPCK, 1989)

Swanson, R., ed., *The Church and Mary* (Woodbridge: Boydell and Brewer, 2004)

Synesius, *Essays and Hymns*, trans. A. Fitzgerald, 2 vols. (London: Oxford University Press, 1930)

Tardieu, M., 'Sabiens coraniques et "Sabiens" de Harran', *Journal Asiatique* 274 (1986), 1–44

Tate, G., *Les campagnes de la Syrie du Nord du IIe au VII siècle: un exemple d'expansion démographique et économique à la fin de l'antiquité* (Paris: P. Geuthner, 1992)

Tchalenko, G., *Villages antiques de la Syrie du nord*, I–III (Paris: P. Geuthner, 1953–58)

Testa, Rita Lizzi, 'The late antique bishop: image and reality', in Rousseau, *A Companion to Late Antiquity*, 523–38

—— '*Augures et pontifices*: public sacral law in late antique Rome (fourth–fifth centuries AD)', in Cain and Lenski, eds., *The Power of Religion in Late Antiquity*, 251–78

Thomson, R.W., and Howard-Johnston, James, with the assistance of Greenwood, Tim, *The Armenian History attributed to Sebeos* I–II, Translated Texts for Historians 31 (Liverpool: Liverpool University Press, 1999)

Thompson, E.A., *Romans and Barbarians. The Decline of the Western Empire* (Madison: University of Wisconsin Press: 1982)

Tougher, Shaun, *Julian the Apostate*, Debates and Documents in Ancient History (Edinburgh: Edinburgh University Press, 2007)

Tougher, Shaun, ed., *Eunuchs in Antiquity and Beyond* (London: Duckworth, 2002)

Treadgold, Warren, *Byzantium and its Army, 284–1081* (Stanford: Stanford University Press, 1995)

—— *The Early Byzantine Historians* (Basingstoke: Palgrave Macmillan, 2007)

Trombley, F.W., *Hellenic Religion and Christianization, c. 370–529,* 2 vols. (Leiden, 1993–94)

—— 'Religious transition in sixth-century Syria', *Byzantinische Forschungen* 20 (1994), 153–95

—— 'The operational methods of the late Roman army in the Persian war of 572–591', in Lewin and Pellegrini, eds., *The Late Roman Army in the Near East*, 321–56

Tsafrir, Y., 'Procopius and the Nea church in Jerusalem', *Ant. Tard.* 8 (2000), 149–64

Tsafrir, Y., et al., *Excavations at Rehovot-in-the-Negev* I, Qedem 25 (Jerusalem: Institute of Archaeology, Hebrew University, 1988)

Tsafrir, Y., and Foerster, G., 'Urbanism at Scythopolis-Bet Shean in the fourth to seventh centuries', *Dumbarton Oaks Papers* 51 (1997), 85–146

Urbainczyk, Theresa, *Theodoret of Cyrrhus. The Bishop and the Holy Man* (Ann Arbor: University of Michigan Press, 2002)

Urbano, A., 'Donation, dedication and *Damnatio memoriae*: the Catholic reconciliation of Ravenna and the church of Sant' Apollinare Nuovo', *Journal of Early Christian Studies* 13 (2005), 71–110

Van Dam, R., *Leadership and Community in Late Antique Gaul* (Berkeley: University of California Press, 1985)

—— *The Roman Revolution of Constantine* (Cambridge: Cambridge University Press, 2007)

Vanderspoel, John, 'From empire to kingdoms in the late antique west', in Rousseau, ed., *A Companion to Late Antiquity*, 427–40

Vanhaverbeke, H., Martens, F., and Waelkens, M., 'Another view on late antiquity: Sagalassos (SW Anatolia), its suburbium and its countryside in late antiquity', in Poulter, ed., *The Transition to Late Antiquity on the Danube and Beyond*, 611–48

Vann, Robert L., 'Byzantine street construction at Caesarea Maritima', in Hohlfelder, ed., *City, Town and Countryside,* 167–70

Van Rompay, L., 'Society and community in the Christian East', in Maas, ed., *The Cambridge Companion to the Age of Justinian*, 239–66

Vassilaki, Maria, ed., *Mother of God. Representations of the Virgin in Byzantine Art* (Milan: Skira, 2000)

—— ed., *Images of the Mother of God. Perceptions of the Theotokos in Byzantium* (Aldershot: Ashgate, 2004)

Vikan, G., *Byzantine Pilgrimage Art* (Washington DC: Dumbarton Oaks, 1982)

Vööbus, A., *A History of Asceticism in the Syrian Orient,* 3 vols. (Louvain: CSCO, 1958–88)

Walker, Joel Thomas, *The Legend of Mar Qardagh. Narrative and Christian Heroism in Late Antique Iraq* (Berkeley: University of California Press, 2006)

Wallace-Hadrill, A., ed., *Patronage in Ancient Society* (London: Routledge, 1989)

Walmsley, Alan, *Early Islamic Syria. An Archaeological Assessment* (London: Duckworth, 2007)

Ward, J.H., 'The Notitia Dignitatum', *Latomus* 33 (1974), 397–434

Ward, Benedicta, *Harlots of the Desert* (Oxford: Mowbray, 1987)

Ward-Perkins, Bryan, *The Fall of Rome and the End of Civilization* (Oxford: Oxford University Press, 2005)

—— 'Specialisation, trade and prosperity. An overview of the economy of the late antique eastern Mediterranean', in Kingsley and Decker, eds., *Economy and Exchange in the Eastern Mediterranean,* 167–78

—— 'Jones and the Late Roman economy', in Gwynn, ed., *A.H.M. Jones and the Later Roman Empire*, 193–212

Watson, Alaric, *Aurelian and the Third Century* (London: Routledge, 1999)

Watts, Edward, 'Justinian, Malalas and the end of Athenian philosophical teaching in AD 529', *Journal of Roman Studies* 94 (2004), 168–82

—— *City and School in Late Antique Athens and Alexandria* (Berkeley: University of California Press, 2006)

—— *Riot in Alexandria. Tradition and Group Dynamics in Late Antique Pagan and Christian Communities* (Berkeley: University of California Press, 2010)

—— 'The murder of Hypatia: acceptable or unacceptable violence?', in Drake, ed., *Violence in Late Antiquity*, 333–42

Weiss, Z., with contributions from E. Netzer et al., *The Sepphoris Synagogue. Deciphering an Ancient Message through its Archaeological and Socio-Historical Contexts* (Jerusalem: Israel Exploration Society and Institute of Archaeology, Hebrew University of Jerusalem, 2005)

—— 'Artistic trends and contact between Jews and "others" in late antique Sepphoris: recent research', in Gwynn and Bangert, eds., *Religious Diversity in Late Antiquity*, 167–88

Westberg, D., *Celebrating with Words: Studies in the Rhetorical Works of the Gaza School* (Uppsala, 2010)

Whitby, Mary, 'The occasion of Paul the Silentiary's *Ekphrasis* of S. Sophia', *Classical Quarterly* 35 (1985), 215–28

—— 'Defender of the Cross: George of Pisidia on the Emperor Heraclius and his deputies', in Mary Whitby, ed., *The Propaganda of Power*, 247–73

—— 'George of Pisidia's presentation of the Emperor Heraclius and his campaigns: variety and development', in Reinink and Stolte, eds., *The Reign of Heraclius*, 157–73

Whitby, Mary, ed., *The Propaganda of Power: The Role of Panegyric in Late Antiquity* (Leiden: Brill, 1998)

Whitby, Michael, 'Procopius' description of Martyropolis' (*De Aedificiis* 3.2.10–14)', *Byzantino-slavica* 45 (1984), 177–82

—— 'Procopius and the development of Roman defences in upper Mesopotamia', in Freeman and Kennedy, eds., *The Defence of the Roman and Byzantine East I*, 717–35

—— 'Procopius's description of Dara (*Buildings* 2.1–3)', in ibid., 737–83

—— *The Emperor Maurice and his Historian: Theophylact Simocatta on Persian and Balkan Warfare* (Oxford: Clarendon Press, 1988)

—— 'Recruitment in Roman armies from Justinian to Heraclius (ca. 565–615)', in Averil Cameron, ed., *States, Resources and Armies*, 61–124

—— *The Ecclesiastical History of Evagrius Scholasticus*, Translated Texts for Historians 33 (Liverpool: Liverpool University Press, 2000)

—— 'Factions, bishops, violence and urban decline' in Krause and Witschel, eds., *Die Stadt in der Spätantike*, 441–61

Whitby, Michael and Mary, *The History of Theophylact Simocatta*, trans. with introd. and notes (Oxford: Clarendon Press, 1986)

—— *Chronicon Paschale, 284–628 AD*, trans. with introduction and notes, Translated Texts for Historians (Liverpool: Liverpool University Press, 1989)

Whittaker, C.R., 'Late Roman trade and traders', in Garnsey, Hopkins and Whittaker, eds., *Trade in the Ancient Economy*, 163–81

—— 'Circe's pigs: from slavery to serfdom in the later Roman world', *Slavery and Abolition* 8 (1987), 87–122

—— *Frontiers of the Roman Empire. A Social and Economic Study* (Baltimore: Johns Hopkins University Press, 1994)

Whittow, M., 'Ruling the late Roman and early Byzantine city: a continuous history', *Past and Present* 129 (1990), 3–29

—— 'Rome and the Jafnids: writing the history of a 6th-century tribal dynasty', in Humphrey, ed., *The Roman and Byzantine Near East 2*, 207–24

—— 'Nicopolis ad Istrum: backward and Balkan?', in Poulter, ed., *Transition to Late Antiquity*, 375–89

Wickham, Christopher, *Early Medieval Italy: Central Power and Local Society, 400–1000* (London: Macmillan, 1981)

—— 'The other transition: from the ancient world to feudalism', *Past and Present* 103 (1984), 3–36

—— 'Marx, Sherlock Holmes and late Roman commerce', *Journal of Roman Studies* 78 (1988), 190–3

Wickham, Chris, ed., *Marxist History-Writing for the Twenty-First Century* (Oxford: Oxford University Press for the British Academy, 2007)

Wilkinson, T.J.W., *Town and Country in S. E. Anatolia .I. Settlement and Land Use at Kurban Höyük* (Chicago, Ill.: Oriental Institute of the University of Chicago, 1990)

Winkelmann, Friedhelm, *Der monenergetisch-monotheletische Streit*, Berliner byzantinische Studien 6 (Frankfurt am Main: Peter Lang, 2001)

Wolfram, H., *History of the Goths*, Eng. trans. (Berkeley: University of California Press, 1988)

Wolska-Conus, W., *La topographie chrétienne de Cosmas Indicopleustes* (Paris: Presses universitaires de France, 1962)

Wood, Diana, ed. *The Church and the Arts*, Studies in Church History 28 (Oxford: Blackwell, 1992)

Wood, Ian, 'Kings, kingdoms and consent', in Sawyer and Wood, eds., *Early Medieval Kingship*, 6–29

—— 'The end of Roman Britain: continental evidence and parallels', in Lapidge and Dumville, eds., *Gildas: New Approaches*, 1–25

—— 'The fall of the western empire and the end of Roman Britain', *Britannia* 18 (1987), 251–62

—— *The Merovingian Kingdoms 450–751* (London: Longman, 1994)

—— *The Missionary Life. Saints and the Evangelisation of Europe, 400–1050* (Harlow: Longman, 2001)

Wood, Philip, *'We have no King but Christ'. Christian Political Thought in Greater Syria on the Eve of the Arab Conquest (c. 400–585)* (Oxford: Oxford University Press, 2010)

Woods, David, 'Late antique historiography: a brief history of time', in Rousseau, ed. *A Companion to Late Antiquity*, 357–75

Woolf, Greg, 'World-systems analysis and the Roman empire', *Journal of Roman Archaeology* 3 (1990), 44–58

Wozniak, Frank E., 'The Justinianic fortification of Interior Illyricum', in Hohlfelder, ed., *City, Town and Countryside in the Byzantine Era*, 199–209

Zanini, E., *Le Italie byzantine. Territorio, insediamenti ed economia nella provincia bizantina d'Italia (VI-VIII secolo)* (Bari: Edipuglia, 1998)

Zuckerman, C., *Du village à l'empire: autour du register fiscal d'Aphrodito, 525–526* (Paris: Association des amis du Centre d'histoire et civilisation de Byzance, 2004)

# INDEX

293